Explaining Labour's Landslip

**Robert Worcester,
Roger Mortimore
and Paul Baines**

POLITICO'S

First published in 2005

Politico's Publishing, an imprint of

Methuen Publishing Limited

11-12 Buckingham Gate

London

SW1E 6LB

10 9 8 7 6 5 4 3 2 1

Printed and bound in Great Britain by St Edmundsbury Press

Bury St Edmunds, Suffolk

ISBN 1 84275 146 8

Contents

Acknowledgements

Data in tables 57-63 on pp 181-5 is included by kind permission of Dominic Wring and David Deacon, Communication Research Centre, Loughborough University.

Figure 37 on p 199 is copyright by the Conservative Party, and is reproduced by kind permission.

Figure 38 on p 200 is copyright by the Liberal Democrats, and is reproduced by kind permission.

Figure 26 on p 151, and Figures 39 and 40 on p 202, are reproduced with kind permission from the Labour Party.

Foreword

Rereading the Forewords to *Explaining Labour's Landslip's* two predecessors, *Explaining Labour's Landslide* (analysing the 1997 election), and *Explaining Labour's Second Landslide* (2001) has been a nostalgic recall of the history of my involvement in now ten British General Elections.

From being a "quiet American", threatened with the chop if it was revealed that an American pollster was doing the private polling for the Prime Minister, Harold Wilson, in the 1970 election, to Britain's "best known" pollster (according to Populus) over thirty-five years has been a wonderful observation post for a political scientist/political junkie who revels in the excitement of general elections. General elections anywhere in fact, whether in America (I spent 7 hours and 10 minutes straight on ITN's American election night coverage of the 2004 American Presidential election), Britain or Trinidad & Tobago.

The 2004 and 2000 American elections were great fun, especially last year with James Mates, whom I first met in the final week of the 1984 American Presidential election in New York. As a raw trainee, he was assigned to me as my "gofer" when I joined the ITN team led by the Editor David Nicholas. ITN's coverage was fronted by Alastair Burnet, the amazingly effective journalist (Editor of the *Economist* when I first met him) and television presenter.

And fun too in 2000, when BBC Radio joined Radios 4 & 5 and Peter Allen and I co-presented from Washington, and I led off ITN's and Sky's coverage before starting on the BBC Radio broadcast. I'd known Peter some 20 years before when he and I were frequently on London Broadcasting (LBC) together in its early days.

Indeed, I cut my media teeth on LBC in its first few months of life more than 30 years ago, when one night in November 1973 there were four by-elections and John Selwyn Gummer (Conservative), Reg Prentice (Labour), John Pardoe (Liberal) and I were on air from 10:30 p.m. until 4:30 a.m. the next morning to wait out the three recounts in Berwick-Upon-Tweed, and from that night on I was never anxious about appearing on radio or television again.

British elections weren't just spectator sport for me in the way American elections became after I moved to Britain in 1969. From 1970 each election day brought with it the anxiety of "getting it wrong", and although my poll for the Labour Party on the Tuesday before election day had the Tories ahead, we and all the others certainly did "get it wrong" in 1992.

Still, if one person in 200 in that election who voted for the Conservatives had voted for the second party in their constituency it would have been a hung Parliament and we'd have been heroes instead of bums, getting it "horribly wrong" as every BBC commentator seemed programmed to characterise it. Of course it didn't help when the BBC's exit poll seared the Director General John Birt, and he laid down the edict that polls weren't to be trusted ever again and codified it in his draconian and infamous Producer's Guideline on opinion polls.

As I said in the first Foreword, these now three books have precedents in the "Green" and "Red" books produced by the MORI teams which followed each general election from February 1974, and all of which were lodged in the ESRC Archives and which still await the critical eye of an aspiring scholar after a PhD thesis topic. Accompanying the books are many of the tabulations and the findings of the post-election "Candidates & Agents" surveys MORI carried out for the National Agents of the Labour Party from 1974 to 1987.

Another precedent to these three *Explaining Labour's Landslide/Landslip* (ELL) books is the series I initiated in 1979, edited books following seminars on the political communications of each election from 1979, first at the University of Newcastle, then Essex and now taken over as the EPOP conference. Various co-Editors have collaborated in the series, the first myself and Martin Harrop, then Ivor Crewe and Brian Gosschalk, more recently John Bartle and now also Simon Atkinson and Roger Mortimore.

But all these follow and expand on the long-running Nuffield *British General Election* books, authored and edited by Dr David Butler and co-authors going back 17 elections to 1945, and for the past 9 elections co-authored by Butler and Dennis Kavanagh. Certainly our "Green Books" and "Red Books" following each election informed the Butler series starting with the two 1974 general elections.

What purpose do these books serve? Like the BBC, we aim to educate, to inform, and to entertain. They are not intended to either replace or refute academic tomes which are based largely on the ESRC-funded British Election Study surveys. They are meant to be more entertaining, more telling the story using objective and systematic survey data, and putting on the public record what we have learned from our polls and others', ours carried out for some ten media/other clients, all following the election model introduced for Labour's private polling in the mid seventies and documented both in *British Public Opinion*[1], which I authored in 1991, and expanded on in these three *ELL* books after Blair's three election victories in 1997[2], 2001[3] and now 2005.

While general election books are written by political journalists every time providing an interesting overview, and the academics turn out their detailed analyses, often years later, our work aims to provide a comprehensive insight into the political psyche – the mindset and psychology – of the general public; it draws principally on the detailed MORI data which employs the model of the British voter explained in the text, and also from data from our competitor colleagues in the polling industry, backed up where possible with consideration of appropriate academic studies, something that the academics tend not to reciprocate. With citizens' opinions, attitudes and values measured systematically and statistically, rather than stereotypically and sloppily – as some political commentators do – our text provides a definitive insight into how the British people voted (or many not) in this general election.

I wish to pay tribute to the founder of Politico's, Iain Dale, whose initiative and grit added book publishing to his book selling and cut sharply into the more traditional publishers, by publishing books of political interest for the political chattering class solidly, cheaply, and quickly. This latest book's copy deadline is 27 August, its publication due during the Labour Party Conference, just one month later. Well done Iain for starting it and Methuen for continuing it.

Page 321 of *Explaining Labour's Second Landslide* said "We look forward to 5 May 2005…", forecasting four years ago the precise date of the 2005 general election. We did slightly less well forecasting the title of this book;

---

[1] Robert M Worcester, *British Public Opinion: A Guide to the History and Methodology of Political Opinion Polling* (Oxford: Basil Blackwell, 1991).
[2] Robert Worcester and Roger Mortimore, *Explaining Labour's Landslide* (London: Politico's Publishing, 1999).
[3] Robert Worcester and Roger Mortimore, *Explaining Labour's Second Landslide* (London: Politico's Publishing, 2001).

then we asked the political chattering class in Britain and British politics watchers abroad to "Watch out for the third book in the series, to be published, by Politico's, in the Autumn of 2005. Its title? *Explaining Labour's Third Landslide.*" We got that one wrong. The (new) publishers, Methuen, suggested an alternative title; I snapped another one back: *Explaining Labour's Landslip,* which they readily accepted.

As I said in the introduction to the 2001 book, there are many myths which arise from general elections, some deliberately planted and others arising out of commonly assumed "fact", which sound and consistent research proves "just ain't so", but the myths feed upon themselves, are repeated endlessly by pundits and commentators, and are believed by those whose own prejudices support them. True in this election as well.

One was how women had fallen out of love with Labour generally and Tony Blair specifically. In fact, in this election Labour had a 6% greater lead among women than among men; by contrast, in 1974 the Conservatives enjoyed a 12% greater lead among women.

In our last book we did our best to lay to rest the "biggest myth", that polls can be expected to do better than the laws of sampling and the reality of politics will let them. Not only do the "poll pickers", the academics and pundits who can always find something to pick at, but even market researchers who should know better, like a recent letter in *Research* from a market researcher who should know better, suggesting the pollsters shouldn't take too much comfort from this election's result, but do as good, i.e. virtually perfectly, next time as well! We'll try, but don't hold your breath.

In 2001, NOP's exit poll for the BBC forecast a 157-seat overall majority for Blair's Labour government while MORI's exit poll for ITV's election night programme predicted 175, so with a majority of 167, the two exit polls neatly bracketed the actual result within ten seats. And NOP's forecast for the Tory result was 177 and MORI 154, while the result for the Conservatives was 166, again astonishingly close. So much for Central Office's "shy Tories" theory, and we said so at the time.

This time the BBC and ITN decided to put all their eggs in one basket, so NOP and MORI were invited to conduct a joint exercise, and their academic team from our data forecast a majority of 66 – the exact result on the night. We will never get it that close again (except perhaps by luck, as polling is 95% skill and determination to get it right and 5% luck; if you're not lucky, it's not a good business to be in)[4].

Another myth is that this election was the most boring election ever, a boring repetition of editors' instructions to their reporters and feature writers to do a vox pop and prove their belief that this is the most boring election ever. In the past ten elections I've read, heard, seen articles and broadcasts, in mid-election if not before, describe this (whichever) election as the most boring ever. Well, it "just ain't so". In 1973, in anticipation of the 1974 election, we asked the British public how interested they were in politics. Sixty per cent said they were "very" or "fairly" interested. This figure has stayed statistically constant at elections ever since. Further, more people this time said they were interested in the election than four years earlier.

And then there is the silly averaging of all the polls of a polling company during general elections, which then "proves" that that polling company accurately "forecast" the outcome of the election, or not. Panel studies over the years since we began doing them in the 1974 elections have provided the proof, calling back on the same persons, that between 15% (1987) and 34% (2001) of electors have "churned" during the campaign period, either changing their mind about whether to vote or not, or to vote for one party or another, or both. The election this year saw even more churning than ever before. Stability in polling figures is usually an artefact of the methodology of the polling company, such as in the so-called rolling polls, interviewing over three or more days and aggregating the results, thus reporting a rolling average over the interviewing period.

Part of the blame for widespread misunderstanding of what the polls are reporting is in the sloppy coverage by political writers who should know better, and politicians who either don't or won't understand that polls are snapshots at a point in time, and not crystal balls, tea leaves or Ouija boards which foretell the future.

I treasure the memory of an hour-long session one Monday evening with Prime Minister James Callaghan in his Political Advisor Tom McNally's office at Number 10. That evening there were two indications of his failure

---

[4] Robert M Worcester, "Political opinion polling – 95 percent expertise and 5 percent luck", *Journal of the Royal Statistical Society Series A 159*, 5-20.

to understand, unlike Harold Wilson, what I was doing for him, and why. At one point he questioned a poll finding saying "But you told us we were going to lose at Grimsby" (Austin Mitchell's by-election), failing to understand that the poll was done before the government had called the by-election or the candidate had been selected. What Austin later told me was that, when selected, the poll provided the information which enabled him to come from behind to win.

The other Callaghan anecdote was that after poring over data with the Prime Minister for an hour I went home to supper, and watched *World in Action* which featured a live interview with the Prime Minister. Asked about a current poll finding showing Labour behind the Tories, he said "Well, I read them out of interest, but I don't pay a lot of attention to them." Later in the interview he was asked about the threat of the Scottish Nationalists which Mr Callaghan dismissed, saying "Why, everybody knows that only 20% of Scots are in favour of separatism."

Following this election, I was startled to hear a government minister report that "only 45% of young people voted". Surprised, I murmured to him after his speech that his figure was too high, that only 37% of 18-24 year olds had voted, according to our figures. A few days later I had an invitation to see him in his office in the House, and when I went along, was shown a draft summary table from the British Election Study, 1964-2005, which shows that the percentage of non-voters in British General Elections, by 18-24 year olds was 55%, and therefore by reduction 45% voted. The table also had the "All" figure as well, 29% non-voters, and therefore assumed that 71% voted in 2005, when we know from the turnout figures that 61% voted, an error of 10 percentage points. The table reads that, in 2001, 29% didn't vote, therefore 71% voted; the official turnout figure was 59%, 12 points overstated.

The table is marked "provisional – very much a best estimate based on early data returns". I'd hope so too, but worry that this can hardly be the case for 2001 and earlier, when none of the figures tally with official turnouts, going back to 1964.

More worrying is the use of pseudopolls (so described by Splichal, in Nancarrow *et al* [5]) - which I call "Voodoo polls" or when done over the

---

[5] C Nancarrow, M Evans and J Pallister, "Polls apart! Political, research and ethical lessons from UK pressure groups' use of opinion polls", *International Journal of Nonprofit & Voluntary Sector Marketing*, Vol 8, no 2 (2003), 181-193.

telephone "Phone(y) Polls" – "rigged" by the Countryside Alliance, which they describe as a pro-hunt lobby group. Nancarrow *et al* allege that pro-hunt organisations have directed supporters to email or other self-selecting polls in an effort to "swamp" others' replies by "piling in". Both the *Daily Mirror* and the *East Anglian Daily Times* have publicly complained about this type of intervention by the CA. According to Nancarrow *et al*, CA has also directed its supporters by email to the YouGov internet panel of respondents, urging their 40,000 supporters who receive these emails to "pile in".

While this book has been put together by the three authors, it is based on work done by a whole host of contributors, including the nearly forty thousand solid citizens who took time to respond to our questions when we called round or telephoned them asking them to take part in a survey of their opinions, or surveyed them in our exit poll. We thank them for their generosity in taking part, and thus in the words of one member of a panel some years ago when asked if she would be willing to be re-interviewed the following week responded, "Oh yes, it makes me feel so important; I feel I'm talking to the Prime Minister". In a way, she was, and they were.

And then there are the scores of MORI interviewers who armed with their computers and CAPI or CATI software call on or telephone citizens across the country in all weathers and sometimes at some risk, mostly loving their jobs so they tell us, and playing their part in the general election.

And the field supervisors and deputy supervisors and field controllers right up to the field director, all of whom are the solid foundation of the findings of each poll that appears on in the newspaper, is commented on in radio and television programmes, are downloaded from the MORI website, analysed by the political parties' analysts who fight for early sight of each poll's results, write them up and report them to party leaders and their advisors at their 7:30 am meetings.

But the raw data wouldn't be meaningful without the data entry and analysis teams at MORI who gather the interview results and produce, under the tightest possible timing, the hundreds of pages that our immediate analysis team are awaiting to scan, distil, chart, interpret and report to our clients, brief the political editors and frequently "do the inside piece" for the next day's paper.

Thanks are due to literally hundreds of MORI colleagues in the offices and in the field, too many to thank individually, but mention must be made of the leaders of MORI's Omnibus teams, Martin Kane, Stephan Vernhes and Sara Grant-Vest, the Field Director and Controllers, Area Managers and Deputies and all the field force, MORI Telephone Surveys team, Joe Stead, Paul Gardiner, Alex Priest and the telephone supervisors and their interviewers; MORI Data Services people led by my colleague of more than 25 years Kevin Wilks who has never let me down yet despite unreasonable demands in most every election over all those years, Chris Phillips who handled most of our data processing this time round, and of course the MORI Political Team.

As well as the three of us, directly involved and therefore members of the "Election 2005 Team" were Brian Gosschalk, CEO and a former head of Political Research, Mike Everett, MD, Ben Page, Head of MORI Social Research Institute under which MORI Political Research, now headed by Mark Gill, operates, and Simon Braunholtz, head of MORI Scotland and formerly head of the Political Unit, Simon Atkinson, also a former Political Unit head and this time responsible for the ITV/BBC Exit Poll assisted by among many others Alastair Townend, Chief Statistician Andrew Zelin and his team, Julia Clark, Gideon Skinner, Tom Huskinson, Patrick Fraser, Naomi Pollard, Graham Keilloh, Kully Kaur-Ballagan, Colin Wilby and most importantly my PA Kerry Colville who working all hours kept both my diary and me straight, Dave Evans, king of our web site www.mori.com, Systems colleagues Scott Phillips, Tim Attale and Melanie Reid, Graphics Team Leader Catherine Scully who was essential in helping us put the book together, Paul Ilett and the marketing team helping organise our media appearances, and our sterling receptionists Paula O'Callaghan, Jenny Palmer and Salli Barnard.

Of course there are the other 400 or so colleagues at MORI who watched as we swept through the building frantically pulling together our work for all our media clients meeting their deadlines while also interrupted to go down to the ISDN booth in the basement, to Millbank, Broadcasting House, White City and Gray's Inn Road, and also interrupted internal meetings to take over 200 calls from the media, and not just British but American, *Time* & *Newsweek*, *New York Times*, *Washington Post*, *Business Week*, *Wall Street Journal* and the television networks and of course C-Span; Canadians: Canadian Broadcasting (CBC) and *Toronto Globe & Mail*; Australian, Irish and Estonian, Brazilian and Spanish television,

Argentinean, Czech radio, HVG Hungarian press, SVT Swedish Television, German and French press, Hokkaido Press in Japan, various BBC local radio stations especially including Oxford, Independent radio including KMFM and CTR in Maidstone, Kent, especially Sheena Hastings of the *Yorkshire Post*, and all the others whose questions we fielded, data we provided, interviews (over 100) we gave, and time we spent in dealing with the demands of the media.

Dr Paul Baines, Principal Lecturer in Marketing, Middlesex University, with whom I have collaborated on several articles in scholarly journals and co-presented at several academic conferences and seminars, has taken a sabbatical with us during the run up to and during the 2005 general election, and has moved from academe to the white heat of election polling and been a tremendous ally. We were pleased to have him join us in the preparation of this book, and his involvement in our election work.

Dr Roger Mortimore has of course been the co-author of these three books now, none of which would have been possible without his determination and expertise. His excellent mind, deep understanding of the political scene, encyclopaedic knowledge and phenomenal memory have been devoted to "getting it right", and he has worked assiduously and effectively over these past months to ensure the integrity of the numbers and the fluidity of the text. I owe him a deep debt of gratitude for both enabling the work to be done on time and burnishing the prose that we offer.

Last but no means least, our clients, without whom none of this would have been possible, *Financial Times* Editor Andrew Gowers, UK News Editor Ed Crooks, Sarah Neville and the UK News team including Jim Packard, Emma Jacobs, daughter of the late Eric Jacobs my much-missed co-author of two books, the Subs, and Political Editor James Blitz, Ben Hall and Cathy Newman; *Observer* Editor Roger Alton and Deputy Editor Paul Webster, Barbara Gunnell, Gaby Hinsliff, Kamal Ahmed, and their terrific graphics team, Michael Agar and Cath Lavell, and also Frank Kane, Business Editor of the *Observer*; the *Sun's* Editor Rebekah Wade, her redoubtable Political Editor Trevor Kavanagh and his able deputy George Pascoe-Watson; Veronica Wadley, David Taylor and Joe Murphy on the *Standard*, Neil Buckley and Paul Gilfeather on the *Sunday Mirror*; Catherine Pepinster, Editor of *The Tablet*; Michael Saunders at Citigroup; and the Exit Poll teams at ITV and BBC and their academic advisors. We'd also wish to pay tribute to the Electoral Commission, to Sam Younger and Ben

Marshall especially, for commissioning thoughtful and usefully insightful research that informs us all.

And thanks to the ePolitix team led by Craig Hoy and Richard Parsons who were under terrific pressure and who gave me the opportunity to say what I thought about the election each and every day (save for a brief weekend in the US in the middle when Paul, Bobby Duffy and other colleagues filed the 600-1,200 word 'blog) seven days a week throughout the election, and to Sarah Southerton and Sally Dawson, who I've worked with month in and month out on ePolitix's *Parliamentary Monitor* monthly magazine and on the occasional piece for its sister weekly in term time, the *House Magazine*.

Finally, it only remains to say that despite our efforts to get it right, when Methuen produces the first copy we will no doubt each spot a typo or error which despite it being in its 26th draft, slipped through, and *mea culpa*, no one is to blame but ourselves! We do hope you enjoy the read.

Sir Robert Worcester

London, August 2005

Introduction

Labour's third election victory in eight years delivered a convincing majority of seats on the lowest share of the vote ever secured by a winning party in a modern British election. In terms of actual votes, Labour slipped by a further 1.1 million from its already reduced 2001 total. Tony Blair now has a majority three times the size of John Major's in 1992 based on only two-thirds of Major's endorsement at the ballot box. It was ultimately a negative election, voters choosing the least disliked of the alternatives. The polls suggest that while only a minority voted for Tony Blair, a comfortable majority preferred his re-election to the alternative of a Tory government led by Michael Howard.

All three leaders were left licking their wounds after the 2005 British general election: Tony Blair by a massive loss of public support, to the Liberal Democrats and the minor parties if not to the Tories, and the loss of many supportive Blairites on the Labour benches; Michael Howard by not even managing to elect as many MPs as Michael Foot in 1983; Charles Kennedy by failing to meet the Liberal Democrats' minimum expectations of raising their 52 MPs at the last election to 70, much less taking 20 seats from each of the two other main parties as whispered around Westminster in the final week of the election.

On election night, Roy Hattersley and Ken Clarke led a bi-partisan attack on the exit polls, Hatters losing it on ITN and Ken rubbishing the exit poll on the BBC, both dismissing the exit poll seat projection of a 66-seat majority for Labour, saying that "exit polls are always wrong". The exit poll was right (for the third election in succession); they were wrong (little point trying to count how often that has happened). And the telephone and internet polls in the morning papers came as close as is humanly possible to the actual result as well.

This book is about the British General Election held on 5 May 2005, and what opinion polls told us during the four years between that day's result and the previous British General Election, which we wrote about in *Explaining Labour's Second Landslide*. We have not written it to crow about how well we (and our colleagues in other polling organisations) did in predicting the result of the election. Contrary to the apparent beliefs of some politicians, the most important and powerful people in a democracy

1

are the citizens, but it is only when an election allows them to become voters that they get the chance to exercise that power. An election is an effective but brutal and not very eloquent means of expressing people's opinions; opinion polls measure opinions more sensitively. And this book puts those findings on record, we hope before too many myths about what the voters thought and intended in 2005 have a chance to become too entrenched.

Table 1: General Elections 2001 and 2005: Results Compared

	SEATS (n)			SHARE OF VOTE (% – GB only)			VOTES (millions – GB only)		
	2001	2005	Ch.	2001	2005	Ch.	2001	2005	Ch.
Conservative	166	198	+32	32.7	33.2	+0.5	8.36	8.78	+0.41
Labour	413	356	-57	42.0	36.2	-5.9	10.72	9.57	-1.15
Liberal Democrat	52	62	+10	18.8	22.6	+3.8	4.81	5.99	+1.18
Scottish National Party	5	6	+1	1.8	1.6	-0.3	0.46	0.41	-0.05
Plaid Cymru	4	3	-1	0.8	0.7	-0.1	0.20	0.17	-0.02
UK Independence Party	0	0	0	1.5	2.3	+0.8	0.39	0.62	+0.23
Others	19	21	+2	2.4	3.4	+1.0	0.61	0.90	+0.29
TOTAL	659	646	-13	100.0	100.0	0.0	25.56	26.44	+0.88
Turnout (%)							59.1	61.3	+2.2
Majority	167	66	-101	9.3	3.0	-6.3			
Swing						-3.1			

The Speaker is counted as Labour in both 2001 and 2005
The number of seats in Scotland was reduced by 13 between 2001 and 2005 as a result of boundary changes

The 1997 and 2001 "New" Labour triumphs at the ballot box were based on a more diverse coalition of support than those of earlier Labour governments – with little difference in voting by gender and less sharply defined by age or class than earlier elections – and these characteristics remain mostly true of the Labour vote in 2005.

When Harold Wilson narrowly won his last election in October 1974, Labour took 40% of the total vote, but just 19% of the "middle class" vote[6], meaning that only an eighth of his support came from outside the "working class"; by contrast, in 2005 Blair's middle class support was 30%

---

[6] "Middle class" as defined by market researchers, that is social grades A, B and C1. In the 1970s this was defined by the occupation of the Head of the Household; today it depends on the household's Chief Income Earner, but is otherwise comparable. See pp 219-23 for a detailed discussion of the classification of social class and its implications.

of a much expanded middle class, which, allowing for turnout, made up nearly half of the whole Labour vote.

Similarly, the virtual elimination of the "gender gap", which at most earlier elections delivered a much stronger Conservative vote among women than among men, was one widely-noticed feature of the first two Blair victories. In the months before the 2005 election, however, there was a widespread myth that women had been disproportionately "turned off" Tony Blair because of Iraq. In fact the opposite was true, both before the election (as was pointed out a year before[7]) and in the eventual vote[8]. Indeed, the 2005 election was unprecedented: a higher proportion of women than of men voted Labour, and a lower proportion voted Conservative, probably for the first time since women got the vote.[9]

Iraq played much less prominently as an issue at the election than many expected – it ranked 14th out of 16 issues, selected by only 18% of the public as being "very important in helping you decide which party to vote for", though it featured more among LibDems and was certainly a factor in their increased vote share. More fundamentally, though, Iraq acted as an "image-issue" rather than an "issue-issue" – it damaged Tony Blair's personal standing, and the public's trust both in him and in his government, thus having its effect on a much wider front. Labour's plummeting lead as the best party on healthcare and education, and the Tories' re-establishment of a lead on law and order, all owed more than a little to the general damage to confidence in the New Labour "brand".

Turnout was barely improved even after much effort by the government, political parties, Electoral Commission and the media, up from 59% in 2001 to 61%; with the single exception of the 2001 election, the 2005 turnout was lower by 10% of the electorate than in any other general election since the advent of the universal franchise in 1928. That, too, most likely owes more than a little to disillusionment with the political classes which the Iraq issue helped to strengthen.

---

[7] Robert M Worcester, "A Majority Of Over 100 With The Women's Vote? Or, No Overall Majority?", *Parliamentary Monitor*, April 2004; Roger Mortimore, Paul Baines and Tom Huskinson, "Women's Political Opinions 2001-5", paper presented at the Political Studies Association Conference, University of Leeds, April 2005.

[8] See Table 76 on p 216.

[9] See Figure 43 on p 226.

Over the 17 elections since the war the average turnout has been just under 75%. The last time turnout was higher than this was in the close-fought contest of 1992, when the result was so close that it came within a half-a-percent swing of a hung parliament. That election was followed by a sharp drop in 1997, but then turnout fell off the cliff in 2001. In this election, the recovery was minimal.

Furthermore, while turnout rose slightly among most groups, it fell further among the young, from 39% in 2001 to just 37% of 18-24 year olds getting to the polls this time. The fall was biggest among young men, pulling their turnout down towards that of young women, and the fall was probably greatest among those who would otherwise have voted Labour.

While there was a further decline in the turnout of young people, the "grey power" vote went up, further accentuating the voting weight of older people. People aged 55+, while 35% of the eligible voters (up 2% since the 2001 election), had a 75% turnout, and so represented 42% of voters in 2005.

This election was a foregone conclusion. The date was forecast on page 321 of our 2001 book, published in October 2001. The outcome, while not a third Labour landslide, was nonetheless a Labour victory of a magnitude undreamed of by Harold Wilson in his later years, by James Callaghan, Michael Foot certainly or Neil Kinnock. It delivered to Tony Blair for another four or even five years his "elective dictatorship", which is in the hand of any Prime Minister with an overall majority in the House of Commons of over a score of Members of Parliament, and he had over 60.

It was another step up for the Liberal Democrats but still not the breakthrough they prayed for. They added just ten seats, which on a bad day in the Commons could just about leave them holding a balance of power if enough Labour Members ignored their party whip. But there aren't that many "rebels" on the Labour benches who have given up all hope of preferment to office or the favours whips use to keep their flock in line. The "project", hoped for in the run-up to the 1997 election should New Labour have been elected with a thin majority, giving power-sharing to the Liberal Democrats or even the promise of a referendum on proportional representation or participation in the government, was never in prospect.

And for the Tories, another disaster. After William Hague's precipitate resignation the day after the 2001 election, the Party elected Iain Duncan

Smith to lead them, mostly because he wasn't Ken Clarke and was the best of a bad bunch, so they thought at the time. They had supported Hague's decision to oppose European expansion and thus be more in tune with the Eurosceptic electorate. In this they had thought they were following the will of the people as shown in the opinion polls and would be rewarded at the 2001 election, while expressing in their speeches and articles their disdain for Blair's "pandering" to public opinion. Instead, after four years of hard slog, Hague's efforts were rewarded by the addition of a single additional Tory Member elected in 2001.

This was a sad misreading of the polls. Either the Central Office backroom boys didn't or couldn't read the polls, or failed to understand what they were being told. Sure enough, the public were Eurosceptic, but Europe wasn't then a salient issue to many voters, and of those who were concerned about Europe the vast majority had already made up their minds for whom to vote. The lesson taught them by the voters in June 2001 was ignored in November 2001 when they voted in Duncan Smith as their leader, for many of the same reasons they had chosen Hague.

It took nearly two years of "flat-lining" to wake them up to the fact that they were potentially sleep-walking into a third Labour landslide. When they did jettison the hopeless Iain Duncan Smith and replace him with Michael Howard, one former Conservative Cabinet Minister was enthusiastic: "This party has finally got what it needs, a headmaster, instead of head boys".

The political system lost the 2005 British General Election. Many newspapers' leaders have been written about political apathy, especially among the young. Many "talking heads" have opined sagely on television and radio panels, unwatched and unheard by the people they are discussing – who are nevertheless not too apathetic to talk about issues that concern them, or to join pressure groups, or to speak out in protest about elections which see the same men in grey suits, speaking in politicians' speak, about issues that are non-controversial rather than distinguishing, approving advertisements and party election broadcasts which fail to differentiate between the parties and give evidence of the "clear blue water" which separates them, and give reason for choosing one party over another.

The parties do more polling, more focus groups, more analysis now than ever before, yet seem to listen to their findings less. People are not slow to give clear messages in such forums of what political parties and the media must do to capture the interest of non-voters, and suggest the means by which they can be brought back into the system. Much research was done by the media, especially the BBC, by the Electoral Commission, and by the parties themselves. These findings were presented, debated at seminars of the political actors and academics alike, occupied acres of newspaper comment and hours of broadcasting time, and still the party managers and spin doctors insisted on control, control and control, providing the media with strict constraints on their access to senior politicians, carefully controlling who was provided as the audience, who was allowed to appear. (One example: the Conservatives refused to provide an alternative spokesperson to appear on the *Today* Programme to discuss constitutional issues, and would not allow their otherwise-willing shadow spokesman John Redwood to speak on his own portfolio's subject matter.)

By their actions, the party managers seem to have put their mandate, "win the election", ahead of the democratic good of enabling the electorate to understand the parties' policies, look critically at their candidates, and understand their philosophies. They have replaced straightforward debate with smoke and mirrors, controlled audiences, scripted sound bites and video clips, to the point that many people, especially among the young, were so turned off by the spin and flannel that they voted with their feet, or perhaps their backsides, and didn't bother to engage. They were concluding that engagement was not something of interest either to the politicians or to the system, introduced over the years and fine-tuned by the control exercised by Peter Mandelson during the '92 – '97 years when gradually he gained approval of his introduction of the idea of "image" (i.e. perceptions not reality) being the key factor to win elections, and by concentrating on spin having short-term benefits and doing long-term damage.

And yet, although the modern spin doctors have misunderstood and misused it, this is an essential truth about elections. They *are*, in a sense, entirely about "image", not reality. Most voters will never meet the party leaders to judge their qualities personally. They will never study the philosophical foundations of the parties' ideologies, to set Marx against Mill or Hayek against Burke, to understand why they are socialists or conservatives or liberals. They will never be trained economists or professional educationalists or military experts to weigh up the detailed merits of the alternative policies a government could pursue – after all, it is because we need professional politicians to do this for us while we get on with our own jobs that we tolerate a chunk of our taxes going to pay them a living. For that matter, most voters will recognise few of the competing front-benchers apart from the leaders and a couple of high-profile ministers, and their knowledge of the party manifestos on any subject that doesn't directly concern them is likely to be limited to the bullet-point summary in their morning paper.

So how do rational voters choose how to vote? They have an "image" of the parties, and their leaders, and of their policy programmes, the summary of their own beliefs and perceptions. What else could they have, since they have no way of obtaining direct knowledge of the "reality"? As we shall see, understanding these "images" has been at the core of MORI's political polling for as long as we have been doing it; and the most recent British Election Study, the academic exploration of voting behaviour[10], has now settled on the same process (which they call "valence", but which in essence is this same idea of voters using their impressions of the parties and leaders as cues to their judgment of which choice will suit them best) as the main driving force behind voting behaviour in Britain.

But it is crucial to understand that there is nothing superficial or trivial about these "images". They are part of the same process by which rational people make decisions about almost anything. At the core of political image, be it of party or leader, is the notion of trust in all its forms. If voters trust a leader, they will be more likely to believe him when he explains his motives; if they trust a minister they will perhaps trust his judgment on a policy decision that they do not feel qualified to make for themselves; if they trust a party they will tend to assume that its stance is the right one and that of its opponents wrong, unless they know differently.

And because the voters are not stupid, the "spin" approach of short-term solutions, relying if not on outright lies then on deliberate obfuscation and misrepresentation, is eventually doomed. The short-term fix destroys the long-term trust which the parties and their leaders ultimately rely on. The public may be forced to make do with their perceptions, since they have no access to the reality, but they are perfectly capable of catching someone trying to manipulate those perceptions.

---

10 Harold D Clarke, David Sanders, Marianne C Stewart and Paul Whiteley, *Political Choice in Britain* (Oxford: Oxford University Press, 2004).

As Abe Lincoln is supposed to have said, you can fool all of the people some of the time, and some of the people all of the time, but you can't fool all of the people all of the time. And that was before the advent of the modern mass media, which delight in pointing out who is trying to fool who.

1. Interpreting Public Opinion

Views and How People Hold Them

In discussing our theories of public opinion, we are aware that for readers of *Explaining Labour's Landslide*[11] and *Explaining Labour's Second Landslide*[12] we are partly going over old ground. However, we would ask them to allow us to repeat ourselves, especially as this discussion of familiar concepts will be illustrated with new data which is the first step to understanding the outcome of the 2005 election.

There are at least three distinct purposes for which public opinion surveys during general elections (broadly described as "opinion polls") may be conducted.

1. To inform media news reporting and analysis during the campaign, which in turn informs, educates and sometimes entertains the electorate and protects them from being lied to by the politicians;

2. As marketing research by the parties and candidates, to assist their strategic and tactical conduct of the campaign;

3. To collect data for subsequent study enabling the result of the election and the course of public opinion during it to be analysed and better understood, by political pundits, commentators, political scientists and political analysts.

When we are conducting political opinion polls, our essential purpose is to measure the public's views and discover how these relate to their voting behaviour as systematically and objectively as we possibly can. There is no desire or incentive to sway public opinion or to bend it in one direction or another. We are judged by commentators and politicians alike on our accuracy, and judged harshly – as witnessed in 1992, when in literally hundred of articles and broadcasts we were judged to have "got it horribly wrong", even though (as noted above), if one person in 200 who voted

---

[11] Robert Worcester and Roger Mortimore, *Explaining Labour's Landslide* (London: Politico's Publishing, 1999).
[12] Robert Worcester and Roger Mortimore, *Explaining Labour's Second Landslide* (London: Politico's Publishing, 2001), pp 6-12.

Tory had voted for the second party in their constituency, it would have been a hung parliament as all the polls suggested.

We can measure five things with the tools of our trade: we can measure people's behaviour, what they do; we can measure their knowledge, what they know or think they know; and we can measure their views, and views can be broken down into three levels.

The first level is people's **opinions**, the "ripples on the surface of the public consciousness", easily blown about by the political winds and the media. These are lightly held, not held with conviction, not really thought about or discussed with family and friends, nor usually affecting them or their family.

Below the surface are **attitudes**, things which people have thought about, care about, have discussed with their families and friends and which frequently impact on themselves and their families. Attitudes are more strongly held and they are not easily blown about. You must have persuasion, you must have argument, and most importantly impart information that is new to the voter – and if this comes from someone they respect and will listen to, it will be more likely to convince people to change their minds.

Deeper still are the deep tides of the public's view which we call **values** (things like belief in God, the death penalty, euthanasia and, for 25% of the British public, animal welfare, which explains a great deal about banning fox hunting and the transport of live veal calves). Other people's values focus on the environment, global warming and the like. Whatever it is that people feel deeply about, their values change little, if at all, after the age of about 25.

An analogy I find most useful in thinking about electoral change involves iron filings and magnets. If you can imagine, say, 2,000 iron filings scattered on a large sheet of paper, each iron bit representing a respondent in an opinion poll and each of them representing c. 20,000 electors, and underneath the paper, four magnets, each using the media to swing about in an effort to 'glue' their support fast to them while attracting the other parties' supporters to be pulled away, yet not allowing their supporters to be captured by the strength of pull of the competing magnets. To maximise a party's support it must protect its own 'crop' of filings while attracting electors from the others.

A Model of Voter Behaviour

Ideally, well-designed polling will have a coherent idea behind it which provides a model that can guide what is to be measured, how, and why. In the case of polling for the media, the purpose may conceivably be mere curiosity, the investigation of a news story that stands in its own right without any wider implications, but more often – and certainly if the polling is for a political party or for post-election study – it should have a practical purpose in revealing the mechanism of voting decisions or the underlying attitudes that drive those decisions. It may concentrate on attitudes to particular issues or events; it may aim at discovering not only how many hold a particular view, but who they are; it may be concerned with why those views are held, or whether (and how) they might be changed.

MORI's polling, today mostly for the media although with its possible analytical usefulness (and value to this book) kept firmly in mind, is based on a model of voter decision-making developed in the early 1970s as a basis for the Labour Party's private polls, directed by Worcester between 1970 and 1989. As we discuss the model and the theory behind it, we shall consider the data that the research uncovered during the 2005 election, and see how this throws light on the reasons for Tony Blair's victory, and the relevance of many other factors to that outcome.

Worcester began to develop the "Political Triangle" model after the defeat of Harold Wilson in 1970, having been provided funds and remit to do so in July 1972. One of the first tasks he undertook was to develop a model of the decision-making process of the British voter, which would underpin the rest of the polling programme[13].

Finalised in the period running up to the February 1974 election, it drew both on American polling experience and on Butler and Stokes' analysis which was published in 1969[14]. The model gave strategic direction to the private polls – especially important given the Labour Party management

---

[13] The development of the model is described in more detail in Robert M Worcester, *British Public Opinion: A Guide to the History and Methodology of Political Opinion Polling* (Oxford: Basil Blackwell, 1991), pp 49-50, and also discussed in Robert Worcester & Roger Mortimore, *Explaining Labour's Landslide* (London: Politico's Publishing, 1999), pp 43-8.

[14] David Butler and Donald Stokes, *Political Change in Britain: Forces Shaping Electoral Change* (London: Macmillan, 1969).

11

structure in those days, when individual members of the National Executive Committee (and their pet academic advisors) with particular axes to grind would urge a myriad of individual questions which would contribute little to a coherent investigation of the tasks facing the party.

Since 1989, when MORI ceased to conduct Labour's private polls, we have continued to use (and build on) the same model as the backbone of our public polling programme for the media, but it has also demonstrated its continued usefulness for private polling when adapted for MORI's work in the successful 2002 re-election campaign of the Hon Patrick Manning, Prime Minister of Trinidad & Tobago[15].

An essential concept is that voting decisions are not driven by "facts", but by voters' perceptions of the facts. This can be a very different thing. But in the words of the First Century slave philosopher Epictetus: "Perceptions are truth, because people believe them".

The model began with the individual elector, and the forces impinging on his or her decision-making processes, determining whether or not the elector will turn out to vote and, if so, which party he or she will vote for. It took account of demographic and family factors, other considerations, issues, direct party and indirect media pressures, and local factors as well.

A later development was to incorporate values, not so much as an extra dimension but as a deeper understanding of how the other factors were viewed and the rock upon which they rested. In fact, overall, "values" count for most, as between half and three-quarters of voters still have their minds made up before any election is called, though this was apparently less true in 2005 than at previous recent elections[16].

---

[15] In an earlier campaign in December 2001, before British researchers were brought in, the polling had been carried out by an American polling firm using techniques and questions which tended to focus on the personality of the leaders, better suited to a presidential system. MORI introduced the "political triangle" model of campaign research (which Prime Minister Manning had seen in Britain at a Foreign Office seminar he had attended in 2000) into the country for this campaign, which saw a three-seat swing at the election, and the 18-18 deadlock was broken, with the PNM the victors with a 21-to-15 seat majority.

[16] The proportion of those respondents with a voting intention in MORI's first election campaign poll who said they had "definitely decided to vote for" the party rather than there being "a chance you may change your mind before you vote" ranged from 63% in 2001 to 73% in 1987, but fell to 57% in 2005. See Figure 7 on p 55.

12

Indeed, not only do most people who will in fact cast votes in a general election know long in advance for whom they will vote, but that vote will usually be for the same party they voted for in the last election, and for whom they will vote in the next one – at least if they support Labour or the Conservatives. (Liberal voters in Britain traditionally have been different, being an "opt-out" vote for those who are dissatisfied with their traditional party but can't bring themselves to vote for the opposition[17].)

Table 2: The Political Triangle, 1987-2005

Q (To all giving a voting intention) I want you to think about what it is that most attracted you to the ... party. Some people are attracted mainly by the policies of the party, some by the leaders of the party and some because they identify with the party as a whole. If you had a total of ten points to allocate according to how important each of these was to you, how many points would you allocate to the leaders of the party you intend voting for, how many to its policies, and how many to the party as a whole? Please bear in mind that the total of all your points should add up to ten.
(Mean scores out of ten are converted into percentages)

	1987 %	1992 %	1997 %	2001 %	7-11 Apr 2005 %	21-25 Apr 2005 %
Policies of the party	44	47	41	42	47	45
Leaders of the party	35	33	34	32	30	31
Party as a whole	21	20	23	24	21	24

Source: MORI
Base: c. 800/1,600 adults in each survey aged 18+ and naming a party

But the central structure of the model, key to understanding the decision-making process of those voters who might "float", is the "Political Triangle", the three interacting aspects of overwhelming importance by which voters choose between competing governments in Britain: their attitudes to the **parties** themselves, their **leaders** (as candidates for the premiership) and their perceived consonance and dissonance with the parties' policies to deal with the **issues** facing the country. A vital role of a party's private pollster in the run-up to and during elections is to identify the salience of the factors, people's perceptions and most importantly the misconceptions, and especially to identify the "swing" voters who will determine not only the outcome but the margin of winning and losing the

---

17 H Himmelweit, P Humphreys, M Jaeger and M Katz, *How Voters Decide* (London: Academic Press, 1981).

election, and the means by which their voting intentions might be "swung". We estimate these 'swing voters' at c. 4% of the electorate, the 20% of the electorate in 20% of the constituencies.

The first question is naturally to establish the relative importance of the three elements, which will change over time with circumstances.

The initial model in the 1970s assumed an equilateral triangle, representing equal weights between the three attitudinal constructs. Then the Falklands War showed how an event could pull the triangle out of its shape for the 1983 general election campaign, when "leader image", the choice between Margaret Thatcher and Michael Foot, became more of a decisive factor than the other two sides of the triangle, party image and issues.

Figure 1: The Political Triangle©, 2005

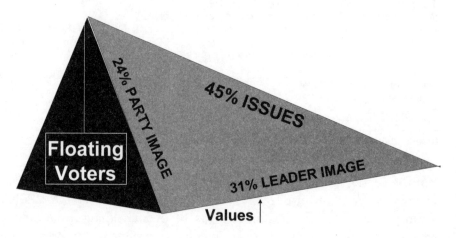

Source: MORI/*Financial Times*
Base: 862 GB residents aged 18+ and naming a party, 21-25 April 2005

Worcester made measuring the relative importance of the three factors an essential part of the research programme. This was achieved in the first instance by asking respondents themselves to judge between the three factors, as shown in Table 2.

In the 2005 election campaign, voters continued to perceive issues as more important than leader image and party image, with policies perceived as around twice as important as party image. This we can represent visually, including the fourth (values) dimension, as a tetrahedron, with the floating voters inside it attracted to differing degrees by the various factors (Figure 1).When the triangle is analysed by voting intention, differences between parties and the average voter are not statistically significant. LibDems rate policies as marginally more important than Labour voters (by 5%), contributing about 45% towards how they decide how to vote, and about as equally important as the Conservative voters, between 1997 and 2005 with little significant change in that period. Broadly, voters of all persuasions rate parties (at around 24%) and leaders (at about 32%) about equally over the same period, although leaders are clearly rated as more important than parties.

Table 3: The Political Triangle by Voting Intention, 1997-2005

Q   I want you to think about what it is that most attracted you to the ... party. Some people are attracted mainly by the policies of the party, some by the leaders of the party and some because they identify with the party as a whole. If you had a total of ten points to allocate according to how important each of these was to you, how many points would you allocate to the leaders of the party you intend voting for, how many to its policies, and how many to the party as a whole? Please bear in mind that the total of all your points should add up to ten.
(Mean scores out of ten are converted into percentages)

	All %	Con %	Lab %	LibDem %
25-28 April 1997				
Leaders	34	36	36	33
Policies	41	42	38	43
Parties	23	22	25	23
29 May 2001				
Leaders	32	29	34	32
Policies	42	44	39	44
Parties	24	25	23	23
21-25 April 2005				
Leaders	31	30	33	29
Policies	45	47	42	48
Parties	24	23	26	23

Source: MORI
Base: c. 800/1,600 adults in each survey aged 18+ and naming a party

15

How has the triangle itself changed? Over the period since Labour entered office after the 1997 landslide we find a relative decline in the importance of leaders and the relative increase in importance of policies, perhaps a triumph of substance over style, which is common to supporters of all three parties.

Despite these minor differences, the pattern is clear and has been throughout this Labour government from 1997 until present. The British public's principal reason for voting for a particular party, they think, is because of its policies, then its leader's image and finally the party's image. (Nevertheless, it must be understood that scoring the various factors on this basis is a relatively crude device, limited not only by respondents' own abilities to analyse their motives but perhaps also by reluctance to admit them.[18])

Table 4: Relative Importance of Influences on Vote

Q From this card, how important, if at all, would you say the things I am going to read out will be in helping you decide how to vote in the general election?

	Very important		Very or fairly important	
	2001	2005	2001	2005
	%	%	%	%
The parties' policies on national issues	58	54	88	86
The parties' policies on issues that affect your local area	52	45	84	83
The values that each party stands for	51	45	82	82
The parties' leaders	46	23	79	66
The quality of your local candidates	38	29	72	69

Source: MORI/*Financial Times*
Base: c. 2,000 GB residents aged 18+ in each survey

---

[18] For a deeper understanding of how factors are inter-related and of voters' true (sometimes unconscious) motivations, sophisticated multivariate statistical analysis is preferable. Because of the cost of such an exercise, the academic British Election Study, funded by the taxpayer through the ESRC, is the only published dataset on which this sort of analysis is possible. The making of that dataset quickly and widely available via the Internet, a relatively recent development, is to be heartily applauded.

In 2001 we experimented with a different question on the same theme[19], and the results were sufficiently interesting to repeat the exercise in 2005. This added the question of local as opposed to national issues and of local candidates, and also expressed the party element as "the values that each party stands for" rather than "identify[ing] with the party as a whole"; the new formulation found more of the public willing to admit the importance of party, pushing it ahead of the party leaders as a consideration. As Table 4 shows, by the 2005 election the perceived importance of the party leaders had receded a great deal further.

Only half as many people in 2005 thought that the parties' leaders were "very important" in determining their decision as had done so in 2001, a marked change and much the highest drop. So much for the notion that British elections are increasingly "presidential"; the party strategists and the media editors may be trying to push it in that direction, but the voters won't play ball.

The 2005 election seems to indicate that not only Blair but the party leaders more generally have finally fallen out of favour with the British public. We would argue that this is not likely to be the death of personality politics just yet, but perhaps a readjustment of voter interest towards political parties' policies on national issues, how those national issues affected the local area, and the values for which they are perceived to stand.

Most Important Issues

Issues or policies seem to be, in the voters' estimation at least, the most potent driving force in the 2005 triangle, so let us consider them first.

The questions that MORI has used for many years to explore the dynamics of the political triangle fall conveniently into two halves, those covering issues and those explicitly covering image (leader and party, which though different in detail are examined using similar techniques). In measuring issues, the aim is first to identify those issues of most relevance

---

[19] The results and the use that can be made of them to understand voting behaviour are discussed in Paul R Baines, Robert M Worcester, David Jarrett and Roger Mortimore, "Market Segmentation and Product Differentiation in Political Campaigns: A Technical Feature Perspective", *Journal of Marketing Management*, Vol 19, no 1-2 (February 2003), 225-250.

– not necessarily those that the electorate thinks are most important, but those which will have most effect on the votes of those who turn out – and then to discover the parties' standing on each.

MORI has tracked the overall salience of issues on a monthly basis (with occasional brief gaps) since 1979[20], asking 'What would you say is the most important issue facing Britain today?' and 'What do you see as other important issues facing Britain today?'. The interviewers do not prompt respondents with a list, but the answers are taken down on a code-frame (a pre-determined list of categories which the interviewer but not the respondent sees[21]) on the questionnaire. In our view it is important for these to be unprompted, as events affecting public opinion are often unsuspected in advance. (One polling agency was caught out some years ago by having a "prompt list" from which their respondents were asked to choose their most important issues, and as that list didn't include strikes were caught out when a major strike became – in our poll and Gallup's – the single most important issue by some margin.)

This question does a sterling job in tracking the nation's concerns and (thanks to the length of the trend data available) putting them into their historical context. But to influence people's votes, an issue needs more than mere top-of-the-mind prominence, as measured by the important issues question. An issue may be of high public concern and yet, because it does not adequately distinguish between the parties or because the public see the distinction as not relevant to the choice of government, play little direct part in voting behaviour. This was true of Europe in the 2001 election, and as we shall see, the issue of Iraq (and Europe) was in this position in 2005.

Four fences must be jumped for issues to bite:

1. **Salience**: If people don't care about an issue, one party or another's argument is not going to sway that voter to move allegiance; and they must care enough for it to over-ride the other considerations of party loyalty or trust in individuals.

---

[20] The monthly results are freely available at http://www.mori.com/polls/trends/issues.shtml.
[21] Answers not fitting the existing categories can be recorded verbatim, and these "other" responses are regularly reviewed to ensure there is no need to revise the pre-coded list. New categories have been regularly added to the list in MORI's monthly polls over the years.

2. **Discrimination**: If people don't discern differences between the parties on the issues they care about, then they are not going to be able to use the issue to choose between them.

3. **Ability**: If people don't think the party that has the best policy on the issue they care about has the ability (power) to do something about it if elected, they won't be moved; and

4. **Will**: If people don't think the party that has the best policy on the issue they care about has the will to something about it, they won't be moved either.

If all these aren't working, it won't move a potential supporter to float away from one party and vote for another on the day. The issues that can jump these four hurdles for the most voters are the ones that count.

The question we use to determine the electoral impact of issues asks:

"Q. What are the issues that are very important to deciding how you will vote at the general election?".

Those who rate each issue as 'very important' are then asked which party has the best policy on that issue:

"Q. Do you think that the Conservatives, Labour, the Liberal Democrats or some other party has the best policy on …?".

When MORI asked the British public which issues were most important in deciding which party to vote for in 2005, the results were as shown in Table 5.

Health care was the single issue named by most of the public as being very important in helping them decide how to vote, as was also the case in 1997 and 2001. Two-thirds of adults, and 73% of those who were absolutely certain that they would vote, picked health care from the list as one of the issues very important to them. Women were significantly more likely than men (74% compared to 60%) to say that health care was very important in deciding their vote, but it was nevertheless the most important single issue for men as well as women.

Tellingly, though, health care was only slightly less important as an election issue to voters in Scotland (61%), where the devolution arrangements meant that the outcome of the general election should be able to have no effect on health care. This may be as much a "knee-jerk" feeling that the issue *ought* to be important as any rational consideration of how much of a role it really plays in choosing between the parties.

Table 5: The Issue Agenda

Q   Looking ahead to the next General Election, which, if any, of these issues do you think will be very important to you in helping you decide which party to vote for?

	1997	2001	2005	Change 2001-5
	%	%	%	%
Health care	68	73	67	-6
Education	61	62	61	-1
Law and order	51	50	56	+6
Pensions	39	40	49	+9
Taxation	33	37	42	+5
Asylum*	n/a	27	37	+10
Managing the economy	30	31	35	+4
Protecting the natural environment	20	26	28	+2
Housing	22	21	27	+6
Public transport	18	31	26	-5
Unemployment	49	30	25	-5
Defence	12	11	19	+8
Europe	22	26	19	-7
Iraq	n/a	n/a	18	
Animal welfare	10	11	14	+3
Constitution/Devolution	7	8	8	0
Northern Ireland	12	7	n/a	
Trade Unions	9	6	n/a	
Other	2	3	2	
Don't know	2	3	4	

Source: MORI
Base: c. 2,000 GB adults 18+ each survey
*Asked as "Asylum seekers/immigration in 2001"

Nevertheless, health care was picked as important by fewer respondents in 2005 than in 2001. By contrast, education was perceived about as important as it had been, law and order more so.

The results clearly show the importance of the issues of pensions, taxation, and asylum even at the beginning of the election campaign. Whilst pensions had surfaced as an issue in the previous general election, when two in five rated it as an issue that was very important in deciding how they voted, by 2005 the number of people stating this had increased to almost half. Taxation had also increased in salience, from 37% of people citing is as an issue to 42% between 2001 and 2005.

Asylum was another issue that had increased in importance (whereas just over a quarter rated it as an important issue in 2001, this had increased to more than a third by 2005), as had, marginally, managing the economy, seen in 2001 as important in determining their vote by 31% of people, up to 35% in 2005. Economic management was nevertheless only in seventh place – however, as we shall see (p 105-6), the public's rating of its importance may understate its real significance as a determinant of voting.

Two issues which had been in the top eight in 2001, public transport and unemployment, slipped back in importance in 2005, as did Europe, cited as an important issue by one in four in 2001 but chosen by only one in five in 2005. Unlike unemployment or transport, Europe had been a major campaign theme of one of the parties (the Conservatives) in 2001, and for that matter in 1997.

It is important to understand how entirely the issues agenda is a national one, transcending regional, gender, age and other differences. There are considerable variations in emphasis, of course, but more or less the same list of issues covers the main concerns of almost all electors; there are few if any issues of overwhelming concern to one large group and of no interest to another. Nor are there many issues on which the basic aim is not universally accepted even when there are differences on the best solution to achieve it. The few entirely divisive issues tend to be of real concern to only a small fraction of the electorate – in 2005 these included (despite the assumption of many commentators and politicians to the contrary) Iraq, the ban on fox-hunting and (at last recognised by even the Tories as peripheral, and barely mentioned) Europe. There is nothing to match the controversial impact of, for example, abortion in American elections.

Some surprise may be caused by the low ranking of Iraq – for all the media concentration on it, to say nothing of the prominence being given to it both by the Liberal Democrats and George Galloway's Respect, just one adult in six said it was important in how they would vote, ranking it in irrelevance with Europe and Defence and not far ahead of animal welfare. But this is easily understood in conjunction with the four hurdles mentioned earlier – even for those voters to whom Iraq was highly salient, for many it will not have helped them discriminate between the parties (since if they were choosing between Conservatives and Labour, the parties' policies were not far apart and both had supported the war, and a vote for the Liberal Democrats would not resolve the issue since the LibDems were not likely to get into a position in which they had the ability to do anything about it). In any case, the issue was to some extent in the past – it was the original decision to invade on which feelings ran highest, however much resentment was stoked by the continuing human cost of the post-invasion occupation. Iraq's impact was, therefore, primarily an indirect one, having a profound effect on wider views of Tony Blair and of the Labour Party; it was an "image issue" rather than an "issue issue".

Of course, even the comparatively small percentage of the public saying Iraq was an important issue would make a huge electoral impact were they all to change their vote in the same direction in response to it. The impact of many issues is diluted because those who might be influenced by them would in any case vote for the party in whose direction it pushed them. Europe, for example, failed the Conservatives as an election-winning issue in 2001 because the vast majority of those who were most strongly attracted by the party's Eurosceptic promises were Tories already. Labour, similarly, stood to lose few votes through implementing the ban on fox-hunting, as no more than a tiny fraction of hunt supporters would have voted Labour even had the issue never been raised. (It is estimated that over eight in ten people on the Countryside March in London said they were Tory voters and the majority were regular readers of the *Daily Mail*.)

Iraq, potentially, was more potent. One poll which tried to measure this more directly, by YouGov for the *Daily Telegraph* on 26-28 April[22], found that one in eight (13%) of the public agreed "I probably would have voted Labour but because we went to war in Iraq I will vote for another party or not at all", with two-thirds of those defectors (so they said) swinging to the LibDems and the remainder to the Conservatives – voters that were potentially critical in the marginal seats campaigns of both opposition parties. We should be wary of taking these figures literally: 13% of the electorate amounts to five-and-three-quarter million potential votes. Yet

---

[22] YouGov General Election Survey 7, conducted for the *Daily Telegraph* and published 29 April. YouGov re-interviewed 2,070 members of an Internet panel on 26-28 April 2005. Details available at www.yougov.com.

Labour's vote fell less than one-and-a-quarter million from 2001. If this was really true, then had Blair not invaded Iraq there would have been roughly a 5% swing *to* Labour and an overall majority comfortably over 200! We are probably safe in assuming that plenty of those voters or non-voters who rationalised their opposition to Labour as being mainly or entirely driven by Iraq would have found some other cause for discontent if the Iraq war had never happened.

Best Parties on Key Issues

Clearly, if issues are important in deciding how people vote, then it is in political parties' interests to design a policy package which appeals to these voters by being seen to have the best policies on issues important to the most people. Figures 2 and 3 provide an indication of which parties were perceived to have the best policies on each issue by those who thought the issue was important (others don't even jump the first hurdle).

Labour's policies on health care, the most salient issue, were more popular than those of the other two major parties. Among the whole electorate, 34% said they thought Labour had the best policies on the issue, 22% the Conservatives and 9% the Liberal Democrats. However, more than a third either said they didn't know or that none of the parties has the best policies. As Figure 2 shows, Labour's lead among the two-thirds of potential voters who thought the issue important was much the same, 36% to 22%; even among this group a quarter felt they didn't know whose policies were best, and a further 6% picked none of the parties.

A separate survey[23] found that Tony Blair also had a personal lead of 46% to 31% over Michael Howard as being more trusted to deal with schools and hospitals. Middle class respondents (ABC1s) gave Blair as great a lead over Howard as did Labour's more natural constituency in the working class (C2DEs), but the young (18-34) favoured Blair over Howard by two-to-one while those aged 65 and over were almost evenly split.

---

[23] Fieldwork 18-19 April for the *Sun* – see Appendix 2, survey 39, for details.

Figure 2: Best Party on Issues (1)

Q At this General Election, which, if any, of these issues do you think will be very important to you in helping you decide which party to vote for?
Q Thinking of those issues you think are important please tell me if you think that the Conservatives, Labour, Liberal Democrats or some other party has the best policy on each.

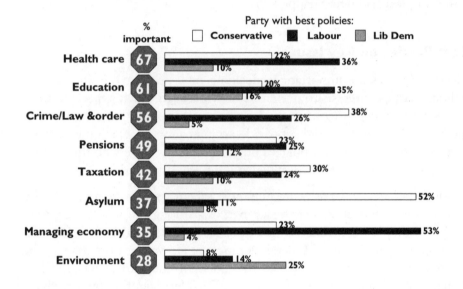

Source: MORI/*Evening Standard*
Base: Those choosing each issue as very important in total sample of 1,973 GB residents aged 18+, 7-11 April 2005

Nevertheless, Labour's lead on healthcare has fallen away sharply in the past decade. In July 1995, 61% of those who thought health care was very important to their vote said Labour had the best policies, and only 8% picked the Tories. In April 1997, just before Labour was elected into government, they led by 51% to 13% on the issue; in February 2001, in the final weeks of their first term, they still led the Conservatives by 44% to 13%, but their lead of 35 points at the 2001 election was more than halved to a still-sufficient but decidedly emaciated 14 points in 2005. This no doubt reflects the public's feeling that after eight years in office Labour has failed to deliver on its promises to improve the NHS – though, as we shall see, Labour may have painted itself into a corner on this issue, raising expectations that it cannot meet because the public will not judge it fairly.

Table 6: Best Party on Key Issues – Labour's Diminishing Advantage

Q At this General Election, which, if any, of these issues do you think will be very important to you in helping you decide which party to vote for?
Q Thinking of those issues you think are important please tell me if you think that the Conservatives, Labour, Liberal Democrats or some other party has the best policy on each.

| | "Very important in helping you decide which party to vote for" | Labour lead over Conservative as party with best policy *among all naming issue as important* | | | |
	7-11 Apr 2005 %	8 Apr 1997	10-14 May 2001	7-11 Apr 2005	Swing 2001-5
Health care	67	+38	+35	+14	-10.5
Education	61	+23	+34	+15	-9.5
Law and order	56	-2	+2	-12	-7.0
Pensions	49	+25	+30	+2	-14.0
Taxation	42	-15	-3	-6	-1.5
Asylum*	37	n/a	-22	-41	-9.5
Managing the economy	35	-22	+34	+30	-2.0
Protecting the natural environment†	28	-1	+7	+6	-0.5
Housing	27	+37	+29	+20	-4.5
Public transport	26	+37	+21	+21	0.0
Unemployment	25	+38	+53	+31	-11.0
Europe	19	-19	-16	-11	-2.5
Defence	19	-30	-20	-14	-3.0
Iraq†	18	n/a	n/a	-9	-
Animal welfare	14	+13	+6	+15	+4.5
Constitution/devolution	8	-21	+2	-14	-8.0

Source: MORI
*Asked as "asylum seekers/immigration" in 2001
†Labour lead over Conservative is given, although Liberal Democrat policies were more popular than either

Health is also an issue where the public tend to feel they understand what the parties are promising. Three in five of the public (62%) feel they are at least "fairly well informed" about the major parties' policies on health care, more than say so about the other major election issues (see Table 64 on p 187), though only 9% feel "very well informed". Interestingly, Conservative voters are less likely to feel well informed about party policies on this issue (63%) than Labour or Liberal Democrats (both 71%), even though Tories are more likely to come from groups who generally have a higher-than-average confidence in how well informed they are.

Education and law and order are the only other issues which more than half the public pick as very important. Labour continues to lead on education policy – the second most important issue – but has also suffered a declining lead on best policy for education (down 19%) since 2001.

The only top three issue on which the Conservatives led this time was crime – perhaps Labour's weakest point at this election, on which they declined from a 2-point lead in 2001 to a 12-point deficit in 2005, a movement of 14 points (or a 7% swing). Labour's lead on pensions dropped twice as fast, from 30% in 2001 to only 2% in 2005, a 14 point swing. On taxation, though, one of the issues by which the Tories set most store, they could not achieve a statistically significant increase on their narrow 2001 lead. The stalemate, born of voters' refusals to believe the promises of either party, remains.

By contrast, the Tories had a whopping great lead on immigration and asylum at 41%, a lead almost doubled since May 2001 among those characterising the issue as an important one for them in determining how they would vote.

So, the Tories enjoyed a lead on only two of the top eight issues in the 2005 election. Of the second tier of eight less important issues, all chosen by around one in four people or fewer, the Conservatives led on three (Europe, Defence and Constitution/Devolution). What Figures 2 and 3 demonstrate clearly is that on 'softer' issues like health care and education, Labour was perceived as by far the best party. The Conservatives did dominate 'harder' issues like law and order, taxation and asylum. The only issue on which Labour increased its lead among those thinking the issue important was on animal welfare, following the long-delayed Labour promise to ban fox hunting with dogs.

Across the issues, the Liberal Democrats led only on Iraq, on which their support easily outstripped the combined Conservative and Labour total, probably because of their consistent opposition to the government on this issue, and the environment.

Figure 3: Best Party on Issues (2)

Q At this General Election, which, if any, of these issues do you think will be very important to you in helping you decide which party to vote for?

Q Thinking of those issues you think are important please tell me if you think that the Conservatives, Labour, Liberal Democrats or some other party has the best policy on each.

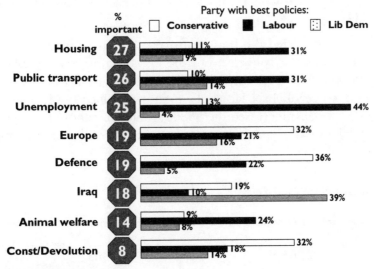

Source: MORI/*Evening Standard*
Base: Those choosing each issue as very important in total sample of 1,973 GB residents aged 18+, 7-11 April 2005

Comparing the public's list of important issues with the parties' campaigning priorities suggests one factor in the opposition's failure to dislodge Labour. The Conservatives were not tackling the issues on which most British people were making their minds on how to vote in this election (health care, education and law and order); instead, they were concentrating on issues where they knew they had a lead and hoped to convert more people to their views; a fatal strategy for the Conservatives in 2001 which was set to be repeated. The Liberal Democrats' early emphasis on education was better aimed, but again their switch to Iraq later in the campaign moved them away from most voters' main concerns.

Leader Image

Leader image is apparently more influential at the moment than party image, though less so than at previous elections. Emphasis on the character of the leaders is sometimes attacked as a symptom of an increasingly "presidential" system, yet the powers of a Prime Minister are such that voters are naturally concerned that a party leader aspiring to that post should be up to the job.

One might have expected the Iraq controversy to have strengthened that element rather than the converse; but the loss of confidence in Blair by many people who had previously taken his personal qualities as a reason to vote for him, while Michael Howard's ratings remained poor, may have diminished rather than increased the public's ability to choose between the two main parties on the basis of their leaders, and possibly to decide not to vote at all.

Figure 4: Best Prime Minister?

Q Who do you think would make the most capable Prime Minister – Mr Blair, Mr Howard or Mr Kennedy?

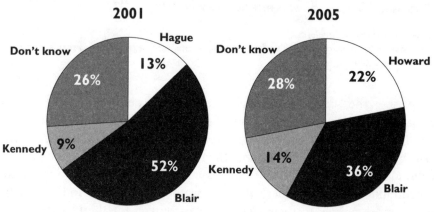

Source: MORI/*Financial Times*
Base: 1,001 GB residents aged 18+, 1-3 April 2005

The simplest poll measurement of leaders is their satisfaction rating, but this can be misleading as a predictor of vote choice since each rating is measured in isolation – increasing dissatisfaction with Tony Blair does not necessarily imply a public becoming increasingly reconciled to the idea of Michael Howard as Prime Minister. It is possible to be dissatisfied with both of them (and many of the public were). Better, and often used over the years, is the head-to-head measure – which leader would make the best (or better) Prime Minister?

Our poll in 2005 found Tony Blair's commanding majority of four years before evaporated, but still as many of the public picked him as picked Michael Howard and Charles Kennedy put together.

Table 7: Leader Image, April 2005

Q Here is a list of things both favourable and unfavourable that have been said about various politicians. I would like you to pick out all those statements that you feel fit [Mr Blair/Howard/Kennedy].

Attributes	Blair %	Howard %	Kennedy %
A capable leader	34	18	18
Understands the problems facing Britain	25	21	21
Has got a lot of personality	25	6	13
Understands world problems	24	12	11
Good in a crisis	19	5	2
Patriotic	16	22	12
Down-to-earth	15	7	31
More honest than most politicians	10	9	31
Has sound judgement	9	9	10
Average positive	*19.7*	*12.1*	*16.6*
Out of touch with ordinary people	36	30	7
Tends to talk down to people	27	22	2
Too inflexible	20	12	4
Rather narrow minded	15	22	6
Rather inexperienced	3	10	35
Average negative	*20.2*	*19.2*	*10.8*
No opinion	11	21	23
Net index (positive minus negative)	*-0.5*	*-7.1*	*5.8*

Source: MORI/*Financial Times*
Base: 1,106 GB residents aged 18+, 21-25 April 2005

However, to gain a full understanding of the leaders' strengths and weaknesses we take a more elaborate measurement. We present respondents with a written list of descriptions or attributes which might be applied to a politician, and ask them to select from it as few or as many as they feel fit each of the leaders. The list includes 14 descriptions, which were originally chosen in the 1970s following qualitative work (focus groups, long before Mandelson and Gould appeared on the scene) to discover which descriptions had most effect on the overall impression. Nine of the descriptions are broadly positive ones and five negative, although there is no particular magic to that ratio; the most important consideration is to encapsulate each concept – whether positive or negative – in the most natural way for our respondents, and in the way which seems to have most resonance in the overall judgment of a leader when the voting decision comes to be made. A similar process, also using nine positive and five negative descriptions, measures party image in the same way.

The validity of the image analysis is to a great extent dependent on the relevance and completeness of the attributes tested, which consequently need to be tested every now and then. A MORI survey in May 2001 (reported in detail in *Explaining Labour's Second Landslide*[24]) asked respondents how important they considered each quality to be in a leader. The findings seemed to confirm that all the attributes being used remain relevant and appropriate, but there was also a clear ranking: understanding the problems facing Britain, being capable and being good in a crisis were seen as important most widely, while having a lot of personality, not being too inflexible and not being inexperienced counted for something with fewer people.

Table 7 shows the results of the leader image test during the 2005 election[25], ranking the descriptions in descending order of the proportion of the public who feel they fit Tony Blair.

Mr Blair is still seen as a "capable leader", although he is also seen by 36% of the public as "out of touch with ordinary people" – a figure 6% higher than that of Michael Howard. More people think he "understands the problems facing Britain" than Howard, and he is regarded by twice as many people as Howard is as someone who "understands world problems". Also, four times as many people think that Mr Blair has "got a lot of personality"; however, this was the least important attribute to

---

[24] Robert Worcester and Roger Mortimore, *Explaining Labour's Second Landslide* (London: Politico's Publishing, 2001), Table 12, p 23.
[25] See Appendix 2, survey 40, for details.

voters when they were asked to assess their importance in 2001. Charles Kennedy easily outscores both as "down-to-earth" and "more honest than most politicians".

Table 8: Leader Image – Tony Blair in 2001 and 2005

Q Here is a list of things both favourable and unfavourable that have been said about various politicians. I would like you to pick out all those statements that you feel fit Mr Blair.

Attributes	April 2001 %	April 2005 %	Difference %
A capable leader	33	34	+1
Understands the problems facing Britain	25	25	0
Has got a lot of personality	24	25	+1
Understands world problems	22	24	+2
Good in a crisis	15	19	+4
Patriotic	15	16	+1
Down-to-earth	18	15	-3
More honest than most politicians	17	10	-7
Has sound judgement	13	9	-4
Average positive	*20.2*	*19.7*	*-0.6*
Out of touch with ordinary people	36	36	0
Tends to talk down to people	25	27	+2
Too inflexible	16	20	+4
Rather narrow minded	15	15	0
Rather inexperienced	11	3	-8
Average negative	*20.6*	*20.2*	*-0.4*
Net index (positive minus negative)	*-0.4*	*-0.5*	*-0.2*

Source: MORI/*Financial Times*/*The Times*
Base: c. 1,000 GB residents aged 18+ in each survey

Table 8 compares Tony Blair's image in 2001 and 2005. These figures are essential to understanding the impact of the Iraq issue on British politics and on the general election. *In almost every respect, Tony Blair's image was the same in 2005 as in 2001.* The public's opposition to his handling of the War on Terror and Iraq issue has not shaken the belief of those who think he is "good in a crisis" – indeed, the number increased. Nor is he thought to understand world problems less than he did four years, despite pursuing an unpopular foreign policy, and his unpopularity has not been translated into more voters thinking he is "out of touch with ordinary people". Only on the description "more honest than most politicians" (and to a lesser extent, just statistically significant, on "has sound judgment") has there been real deterioration in his image. We are surely safe in attributing this change to the Iraq issue: the damage to his image, therefore, came neither because he was seen as making a misjudgement in his policy nor because he was seen as defying public opinion, but because he was thought to have been dishonest in the way he pursued it. We examine this element, and other aspects of declining trust in Mr Blair and in the government, in the next chapter.

Table 9: Leader Image – Hague (2001) and Howard (2005)

Q   Here is a list of things both favourable and unfavourable that have been said about various politicians. I would like you to pick out all those statements that you feel fit Mr Hague/Mr Howard.

Attributes	William Hague April 2001 %	Michael Howard April 2005 %	Difference %
Patriotic	21	22	+1
Understands the problems facing Britain	17	21	+4
A capable leader	12	18	+6
Understands world problems	10	12	+2
More honest than most politicians	11	9	-2
Has sound judgement	5	9	+4
Down-to-earth	12	7	-5
Has got a lot of personality	5	6	+1
Good in a crisis	6	5	-1
Average positive	*11.0*	*12.1*	*+1.1*
Out of touch with ordinary people	28	30	+2
Tends to talk down to people	23	22	-1
Rather narrow minded	24	22	-2
Too inflexible	13	12	-1
Rather inexperienced	33	10	-23
Average negative	*24.2*	*19.2*	*-5.0*
Net index (positive minus negative)	*-13.2*	*-7.1*	*+6.1*

Source: MORI/*Financial Times/The Times*
Base: c. 1,000 GB residents aged 18+ in each survey

Table 9 shows how the public perceive Michael Howard, and the difference in this perception since 2001, although the leader at that time was William Hague. It shows that whilst Howard is not seen as "inexperienced" – as Hague was – he is nevertheless seen as "out of touch", but also as "patriotic", which would normally be considered positive but might have pejorative overtones in this context for a 'Little Britain' approach to politics. Howard is regarded as a slightly better leader than Hague was and as slightly better on "understanding the problems facing Britain".

More generally, though there is remarkably little significant difference in these statistics compared with those of 2001, when Hague was party leader, indicating how Howard has made relatively little progress in changing the British public's perceptions of the Conservative Party leader. That two leaders who are so different should have such similar public images suggests that much of the public's perception of them is based on stereotypes and assumptions, perception, even misconception, rather than real knowledge. This is a measure of the failure of Howard and his political guru to correct perceived flaws in his political persona, although on average the Tory Leader's image profile changed (compared with Hague's) more than the others', much of the change is accounted for by his not being as 'inexperienced' as Hague, and given the unpopularity of the Major Cabinet, it may be a mistake to include being experienced as a positive attribute.

Table 10: Leader Image – Charles Kennedy in 2001 and 2005

Q Here is a list of things both favourable and unfavourable that have been said about various politicians. I would like you to pick out all those statements that you feel fit Mr Kennedy.

Attributes	April 2001 %	April 2005 %	Difference %
Down-to-earth	18	31	+13
More honest than most politicians	20	31	+11
Understands the problems facing Britain	13	21	+8
A capable leader	15	18	+3
Has got a lot of personality	8	13	+5
Patriotic	7	12	+5
Understands world problems	8	11	+3
Has sound judgement	10	10	0
Good in a crisis	3	2	-1
Average positive	*11.3*	*16.6*	*+5.2*
Rather inexperienced	25	35	+10
Out of touch with ordinary people	6	7	+1
Rather narrow minded	5	6	+1
Too inflexible	3	4	+1
Tends to talk down to people	3	2	-1
Average negative	*8.4*	*10.8*	*+2.4*
Net index (positive minus negative)	*+2.9*	*+5.8*	*+2.8*

Source: MORI/*Financial Times/The Times*
Base: c. 1,000 GB residents aged 18+ in each survey

By contrast, Charles Kennedy has substantially changed public perception of himself as being "more honest than most politicians" and "down to earth" (Table 10) although paradoxically, having served another four years as party leader compared with 2001, he is more widely seen than before as "rather inexperienced", by one in three members (35%) of the general public; in fact none of the figures has fallen significantly, and the overall increase simply reflects his being better known now than he was when he fought his first election as leader. The average increase in the positive descriptions, though, is more than that in the negative, and he remains alone among the three leaders in having an overall positive net image index.

Perceptual Mapping: Illustrating and Interpreting Image Data

The image question bank produces a complex data set which at first glance is somewhat indigestible, and its interpretation is no trivial matter. Comparison between the different leaders is not entirely straightforward, as more respondents will have opinions of well-known leaders such as the incumbent Prime Minister than of lesser-known figures. How much should lower numbers of respondents assigning positive descriptions to the Leader of the Opposition be attributed to his obscurity and how much to his poor image?

For similar reasons, it can be difficult to make straightforward comparisons between different sub-groups (fewer of the young will have opinions than will middle-aged or older voters), or over time (the leaders are much higher profile figures at election times, and their ratings on all attributes, positive and negative, will tend to rise as polling day approaches). Fortunately, there is a statistical technique, correspondence analysis[26], which addresses precisely these difficulties and reduces this complex data set to an easily comprehensible and accessible visual format, a "perceptual map".

---

[26] For an explanation of the statistical theories underlying correspondence analysis and the technicalities of how to carry it out and interpret the results, see Joseph F Hair jr., Ralph E Anderson, Ronald L Tatham and William C Black, *Multivariate Data Analysis with Readings,* 4th edition (Englewood Cliffs, NJ: Prentice-Hall, 1995), p 516-27 and Brian S Everitt and Graham Dunn, *Applied Multivariate Data Analysis,* 2nd edition (London: Arnold, 2001), p 74-91.

Conceptually, a perceptual map is a diagram of "image space" based on differences between perceptions of, in this case, the party leaders. It produces a picture of *relative* image – how the leaders are viewed by comparison with each other, and to which leader particular attributes are most strongly seen as applying or not applying. Because it compensates for the differing strengths of image of the leaders, and for differences in the applicability of various descriptions, it finds the most distinctive features even of a very weak image, and assigns even rarely chosen descriptions to those leaders that they are most nearly seen as fitting.

Figure 5: Leader Image, April 2005

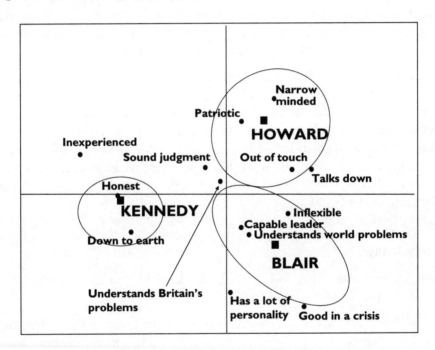

Source: MORI/*Financial Times*
Base: 2,256 GB residents aged 18+, 21-25 April 2005.

Figure 5 shows the perceptual map of leader image, arising from the matrix of data in Table 7. Ellipses have been added round each of the leaders to aid visual comparison. Broadly speaking, the map can be read on the basis that the nearer an attribute is plotted to a leader, the more strongly it is seen as applying to him (relative to the others)[27].

The perceptual map shows how the main distinction between the leaders in the public mind, expressed by the left-right dimension (the x-axis), is the difference between Kennedy and the other two leaders. It is perhaps telling that the two descriptions most closely associated with "Kennedyness" are that he is "more honest than most politicians" and "down-to-earth": he is seen as distinctive from other political figures, less remote and more like the man in the street. It is not simply a positive/negative distinction, for some positives such as "good in a crisis" and "understands world problems" are in Blair's territory, not Kennedy's. But it is Kennedy who is Everyman, most easily identified with by the ordinary voter. Sadly for him, it is probably the perceived impossibility of his reaching Number 10 that allows him to be set apart in this way.

And the other two? Tony Blair used to walk on water, if you remember. Not now. Sure, he's seen as "capable" and "understands world problems", and is the only one of the three in the least "good in a crisis", but "understands Britain's problems" is drifting away, and drifting towards Blair is trouble, spelled "inflexible" and "talks down to people". Is Blair beginning to look more and more like Mrs Thatcher in trousers? For it is these attributes which were most strongly attributed by the British electorate to the Iron Lady.

Party Image

Party image is measured with a similar bank of 14 descriptions which the public are asked to fit to the parties. (Table 11.)

It says much about the real standing of the Conservative Party that they could be beaten in an election by Labour, even when the three most widespread perceptions of the Labour Party were negative. But even more of the general public regard the Conservative Party as willing to "promise

---

[27] Strictly, this is a simplification. To read the perceptual map precisely, a line should be drawn from the attribute's position through the origin, and a perpendicular dropped to that line from the position of each of the three leaders: the attribute applies more strongly the nearer the intersection of that perpendicular with the original line is to the attribute itself. But in practice simple proximity tends to provide broadly the same interpretation.

anything to win votes" – nearly half of them, 45%, said so – indicating the public's view that they are unprincipled. They are seen just as much as Labour as being "out of touch with ordinary people" and "divided". They are now however seen by slightly more people than in 2001 to "understand the problems facing Britain" (up 4%).

Table II: Party Image, April 2005

Q Read through the list slowly keeping the ... Party in mind. Every time you come to a statement that fits your ideas or impressions of the ...Party just tell me the letter next to it. You may pick as many or as few as you like. You don't have to be certain, just pick the letters next to the statements you feel fit the ... Party.

Attributes	Labour %	Cons-ervative %	Liberal Democrat %
Understands the problems facing Britain	26	22	22
Represents all classes	23	9	29
Has a good team of leaders	23	8	7
Concerned about the people in real need in Britain	20	14	30
Has sensible policies	18	17	27
Professional in its approach	17	15	13
Looks after the interests of people like us	16	11	16
Moderate	16	12	31
Keeps its promises	6	3	7
Average positive	*18.3*	*12.3*	*20.2*
Will promise anything to win votes	40	45	19
Too dominated by its leader	37	16	6
Out of touch with ordinary people	27	32	8
Divided	22	23	5
Extreme	6	14	2
Average negative	*26.4*	*26.0*	*8.0*
No opinion	9	14	23
Net index (positive minus negative)	*-8.1*	*-13.7*	*12.2*

Source: MORI/*Financial Times*
Base: 1,106 GB residents aged 18+, 21-25 April 2005

The Liberal Democrats were perceived as representing all classes by nearly three in ten people (29%), the highest for all three parties, as moderate (30%), as having sensible policies (27%), and as "concerned about the people in real need in Britain" (30%), up 11% since 2001 on this perception. It would seem that for the LibDems those members of the public that do have an opinion have positive associations, but there are obviously either too few people aware of the LibDems at all, or prepared to treat them as an alternative to the major parties, for their proportion of the votes to make much impact on Election Day.

Table 12: Party Image – The Labour Party in 2001 and 2005

Q Read through the list slowly keeping the Labour Party in mind. Every time you come to a statement that fits your ideas or impressions of the Labour Party just tell me the letter next to it. You may pick as many or as few as you like. You don't have to be certain, just pick the letters next to the statements you feel fit the Labour Party.

	April 2001 %	April 2005 %	Difference %
Understands the problems facing Britain	28	26	-2
Represents all classes	24	23	-1
Has a good team of leaders	25	23	-2
Concerned about the people in real need in Britain	21	20	-1
Has sensible policies	27	18	-9
Professional in its approach	19	17	-2
Looks after the interests of people like us	21	16	-5
Moderate	20	16	-4
Keeps its promises	9	6	-3
Average positive	*21.6*	*18.3*	*-3.2*
Will promise anything to win votes	35	40	+5
Too dominated by its leader	26	37	+11
Out of touch with ordinary people	24	27	+3
Divided	11	22	+11
Extreme	3	6	+3
Average negative	*19.8*	*26.4*	*+6.6*
Net index (positive minus negative)	*+1.8*	*-8.1*	*-9.8*

Source: MORI/*Financial Times/The Times*
Base: c. 1,000 GB residents aged 18+ in each survey

Table 12 provides an insight into the public's changing perceptions of the Labour Party – there were clearly significant shifts. The number applying positive descriptions to Labour fell in every case between 2001 and 2005, the number applying negative descriptions rose. An overall slightly positive image index has been replaced by a clearly negative one. Labour were seen by two in five as willing to "promise anything to win votes", and a similar number of people (37%) thought that Labour was "too dominated by its leader", Tony Blair, a perception that had substantially increased over four years. Moreover, one in five (22%) thought that the party was divided, twice as many as said so in 2001. Of course, these two statistics are inter-related: the public felt that Blair and Brown were feuding over party leadership in the third Labour term and in many cases that it was time for Tony Blair to step down.

Table 13: Party Image – The Conservative Party in 2001 and 2005

Q Read through the list slowly keeping the Conservative Party in mind. Every time you come to a statement that fits your ideas or impressions of the Conservative Party just tell me the letter next to it. You may pick as many or as few as you like. You don't have to be certain, just pick the letters next to the statements you feel fit the Conservative Party.

	April 2001 %	April 2005 %	Difference %
Understands the problems facing Britain	18	22	+4
Has sensible policies	15	17	+2
Professional in its approach	13	15	+2
Concerned about the people in real need in Britain	9	14	+5
Moderate	12	12	0
Looks after the interests of people like us	11	11	0
Represents all classes	8	9	+1
Has a good team of leaders	7	8	+1
Keeps its promises	5	3	-2
Average positive	*10.9*	*12.3*	*+1.4*
Will promise anything to win votes	46	45	-1
Out of touch with ordinary people	36	32	-4
Divided	30	23	-7
Too dominated by its leader	13	16	+3
Extreme	12	14	+2
Average negative	*27.4*	*26.0*	*-1.4*
Net index (positive minus negative)	*-16.5*	*-13.7*	*+2.8*

Source: MORI/*Financial Times*/*The Times*
Base: c. 1,000 GB residents aged 18+ in each survey

The Conservatives' party image improved marginally between 2001 and 2005, the biggest change being the fall in the number believing the party to be "divided", but still on average the negative descriptions were picked twice as often as the positive ones.

The Liberal Democrats saw dramatic improvements in the number of electors believing that they were "Concerned about the people in real need in Britain" and that the party "Represents all classes". Consequently, when the correspondence analysis technique is applied to the public's perceptions of the parties so that we can compare all three parties in the perceptual map (Figure 6), the most positively perceived party amongst the general public is the LibDems.

Table 14: Party Image – The Liberal Democrats in 2001 and 2005

Q Read through the list slowly keeping the Liberal Democrats in mind. Every time you come to a statement that fits your ideas or impressions of the Liberal Democrats just tell me the letter next to it. You may pick as many or as few as you like. You don't have to be certain, just pick the letters next to the statements you feel fit the Liberal Democrats.

	April 2001	April 2005	Difference
	%	%	%
Moderate	25	31	+6
Concerned about the people in real need in Britain	19	30	+11
Represents all classes	21	29	+8
Has sensible policies	27	27	0
Understands the problems facing Britain	22	22	0
Looks after the interests of people like us	11	16	+5
Professional in its approach	14	13	-1
Has a good team of leaders	8	7	-1
Keeps its promises	6	7	+1
Average positive	*17.0*	*20.2*	*+3.2*
Will promise anything to win votes	16	19	+3
Out of touch with ordinary people	9	8	-1
Too dominated by its leader	4	6	+2
Divided	6	5	-1
Extreme	2	2	0
Average negative	*7.4*	*8.0*	*+0.6*
Net index (positive minus negative)	*9.6*	*12.2*	*+2.6*

Source: MORI/*Financial Times/The Times*
Base: c. 1,000 GB residents aged 18+ in each survey

Nevertheless, despite these positive associations, they did not win the election. The question remains why one of the best perceived parties still trails in third place come Election Day. The answer is of course that the pattern and distribution of votes in the first past the post system are weighted against them, and probably also because voters feel safer voting for the Devil they know, rather than the Saint they do not.

The perceptual map of party image also shows just how difficult the Tory party has it these days – and indeed has had for a very long time. Its strongest characteristics are that it is seen as "will promise anything to win votes" and "out of touch with ordinary people", and while the Liberal Democrats are seen as "moderate", as having "sensible policies" and as "keeping their promises", they also have the useful attribute – captured from Labour since 2001 – of being "concerned about people in real need".

Figure 6: Party Image, April 2005

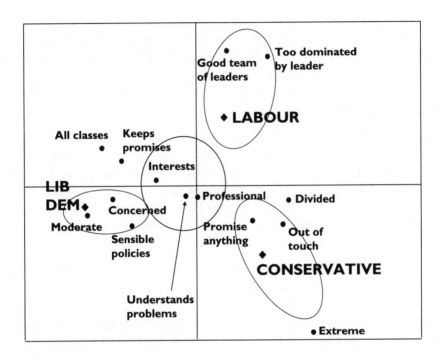

Source: MORI/*Financial Times*
Base: 2,256 GB residents aged 18+, 21-25 April 2005.

Labour is vividly seen as being "too dominated by its leader", which the map shows is about as far from the LibDems and Tories as it can be, but also that it "has a good team of leaders". Up for grabs by any of the three parties at the moment is a key attribute that Labour had locked in solid in 2001 but now floats in between all three parties, "looks after the interests of people like us", as well as "understands the problems facing Britain" and being "professional".

Political Values

As already mentioned, the fourth element in the Political Triangle model, which turns the triangle into a tetrahedron, is political "values".

There is little to be gained arguing with a voter's values.

41

In the past, perhaps, support for a particular party was widespread on a value level rather than as merely an attitude. This is probably no longer the case for many people. But the 2005 election offers a good example of how other values can be brought into play. The opposition of a section of the public to the government's policy on Iraq, and British involvement in the invasion there, was clearly enough for some voters to over-ride a lifetime's loyalties or to render other issues, and which party had the best policies to deal with them, irrelevant.

Values may give a direct or an indirect steer to the voter. In the simplest case, it may be an unchanging value that an individual will always, under any circumstances, vote for the candidate of a particular party. But if the position is more complex – a commitment to pacifism for example, or opposition to abortion – then the voter has still to translate that value into a voting prompt, and the image of the leaders or parties may play its part in the voter's judgment of how to vote best to live up to his or her values.

These can be difficult to measure, and even more difficult to relate to party choice. In the USA, much valuable use is made of the "Michigan question", asking voters which party they identify with rather than which they vote for, but use of the same measure here has never been so successful, as British voters do not seem to make the same distinction between vote and identity[28].

This is partly, perhaps, because with very many fewer partisan elections in which to vote, British voters have not had to consider the possibility of "ticket-splitting" as a matter of course, or needed a concept of long-term identity in the face of frequent switches of votes between parties. It is also hampered by British politics traditionally lacking the concept of an "independent" in the American sense of a voter who admits loyalty to no party and judges the candidates in each case on their merits, which may

---

[28] The question has had much academic discussion, and there is by no means universal agreement that the measure is a failure in Britain, though it can hardly be denied it is problematical. The measure is discussed in relation to modern academic theories of voting behaviour in the latest volume of analysis of the British Election Study, Harold D Clarke, David Sanders, Marianne C Stewart and Paul Whiteley, *Political Choice in Britain* (Oxford: Oxford University Press, 2004). For a practical investigation of how respondents understand and answer the question, and the implications of this, see John Bartle, "Improving the Measurement of Party Identification in Britain" in Justin Fisher, Philip Cowley, David Denver and Andrew Russell (eds), *British Elections and Parties Review*, Volume 9 (London: Frank Cass, 1999).

owe something to the ideological distinctions between American parties being traditionally rather less clear-cut than those in Britain. The decline of the historical level of party loyalty, though, makes this a likelier position for the modern British voter, though one which popular terminology has no name for. Perhaps "partisan disassociation"?

During the early 1970s in trying to understand the typology of Labour's support, considerable multivariate analysis was done, especially differentiating what we now describe as "Old" and "New" Labour supporters, which the research clearly showed came from different demographic and attitudinal stances. To characterise these simply, Worcester invented a simple segmentation which he called the "Political Pie", described with a pie chart back in the mid 1970s. In 2001 and again in 2005 we used this question, adapted to the times, which seemed to make sense to our respondents, as when asked to chose between the categorisations, there were almost no "don't knows".

We asked the sample to describe their political views on a scale allowing them to choose between two wings of any of the major parties, dividing Labour into "New Labour" and "Old Labour", Conservatives into "Thatcherites" and "One Nation Tories", and the Liberal Democrats into their constituent parts, Liberals and Social Democrats.

The question was not designed to divorce identity from voting intention – very few of the sample said they identified with a faction of one party yet were intending to vote for a different party, though there were a few who either identified with a party but were apparently unsure whether to vote at all, or knew how they intended to vote while accepting none of the offered identities. Nevertheless, most of the voting public could readily identify with one of the options we offered them.

At the 2001 election, Labour was polling at 41%, very close to their final result, and we found that nearly three out of four identified with "New Labour"; the Tories split roughly half and half between Thatcherites and One Nation Tories, and just how weak the party was going into the election is demonstrated by the fact that just 20% of the public chose to be characterised by one designation or the other, most of the rest of their support instead opting into the "don't know" category. The Liberals by two to one were the majority share of the LibDems' supporters.

Table 15: The Political Pie

Q   Which one of these definitions, if any, comes closest to your political views?

	June 2001 %	August 2003 %	January 2005 %	29 April -1 May 2005 %
Old Labour	12	15	16	12
New Labour	29	17	19	23
Labour	**41**	**32**	**35**	**35**
One Nation Tory	11	10	6	7
Thatcherite Tory	9	12	11	9
Tory	**20**	**22**	**17**	**16**
Liberal	12	15	12	16
Social Democratic	7	7	6	6
Liberal/Social Democrat	**19**	**22**	**18**	**22**
Nationalist	1	1	3	3
Other	5	3	2	2
None of these	6	13	15	9
Don't know	8	7	9	11

Source: MORI
Base: c. 1,000 GB residents aged 18+ each survey

It is striking how much changed during the period between 2001 and the 2005 election. Support for New Labour slipped dramatically from 29% to 17%, cut nearly in half, while Old Labour identifiers only rose 3 points.

Michael Howard ("Thatcherite") replaced another "Thatcherite" in Iain Duncan Smith in November 2003 to the dismay of the "One Nation" Tories. Tories generally, though, were even thinner on the ground than in 2001, just 16%, with the Thatcherites now marginally the bigger group. As many now think of themselves as "Liberals" as identify with either Tory faction. (Perhaps they took to heart the ludicrous request of a party spokesman that the media should stop calling the Conservatives "Tories"?)[29]

It is interesting to see how well these general descriptions translate into voting intentions. Four-fifths (81%) of the Thatcherites said they intended to vote Conservative, with only a tiny sliver intending to defect to Labour (1%) or the Liberal Democrats (2%), perhaps out of protest or personal antipathy to Howard. Only three in five of the "One Nation Tories" said

---

[29] Tom Happold, "Please stop calling us Tories, say Tories", *Guardian*, 31 March 2005.

they intended to vote Conservative, but again very few had decided to switch to either of the other two major parties, feeling unrepresented anywhere.

"New Labour" was the second most loyal group, though less tied to their party than the Thatcherites, 73% intending to vote Labour but 8% preferring the Liberal Democrats, and 2% the Conservatives. Less loyally, only 56% of "Old Labour" planned to vote for Tony Blair, while 15% of the group had opted instead for Charles Kennedy and his party, partly perhaps over Iraq.

The Liberal Democrat coalition, though, was much more diverse. While 56% of "Liberals" said they would vote LibDem, 9% chose instead each of the other two major parties, and the Social Democrats split 38% LibDem, 14% Labour and 12% Conservative, while a third supported none of the three parties, much the highest proportion among the six mainstream descriptions.

Even more intriguing, though, were the reports of these groups as to how they had voted in 2001: the "Liberals" were equally likely to have voted Liberal Democrat (27%) or Labour (28%), and Labour was much the biggest party among the Social Democrats (34% to 19% for the LibDems and 10% for the Tories). Labour's strength also dropped off among those describing themselves as "Old Labour" (71% said they had voted for the party in 2001, compared to 56% who were intending to do so again), but nevertheless a substantial part of the vote that defected from Labour seems to have been people who thought of themselves as Liberal or Social Democrat rather than Labour – though we are not able to measure, unfortunately, how they would have described themselves in 2001 and whether the voting intention caused the description rather than vice-versa.

One in six of those intending to vote Conservative said that none of the definitions fitted or they didn't know which was closest; only 8% of Labour supporters and 9% of Liberal Democrats were in the same boat. Were this the USA, we would probably conclude that the Tories had best appealed to the "independent" uncommitted voters; but in fact it is clear that the number identifying themselves as "Tories" of either wing is far below even the core Conservative support, and the non-identifiers far from being independents are in many cases lifelong Conservative voters.

45

It seems that the Conservatives to a much greater extent than the other parties may have weakened or splintered their ideological identity so that even their loyal supporters no longer know where they stand; but it is possible also that it signals the emergence of a distinctly-defined third faction – "modernisers", "libertarians" or whatever – who admit to being neither "One Nation" nor "Thatcherite". This is something to explore in future surveys.

Political Marketing

An understanding of public opinion is essential to an understanding of the strategic conceptual planning of election campaigns. In the monthly tracking carried out by MORI for nearly thirty years, the proportion of the public who told us that they had presented their views to their local councillor or Member of Parliament rarely reached one in ten, yet which MP – much less local councillor – admits they are not in touch with the mood of their constituency? The reality is they do see hundreds if not thousands of their constituents, but for the most part, the same people over and over, especially between elections, missing the vast bulk of their constituents.

Polling however taps a true cross-section of the electorate, and while this is published and available nationally, few local constituency polls are ever done, not by the local media which could but does not, nor by constituency MPs, who during elections cannot under the financial constraints laid down in the Representation of the People Act. Thus there is a case for providing every MP access to a poll of his or her constituents before every general election, open for public inspection, paid for by the taxpayer, in the same way as every Parliamentary candidate is provided access to their constituents via the free postal delivery of their election address.

Many MPs try to augment their surgeries and post bags with DIY polls, usually unrepresentative catch-as-catch-can, self-selected, and poorly designed, sometimes on their web pages, sometimes questionnaires left in public places or inserted into newsletters.

There is no argument now that professionally conducted market research is a major part of the development of marketing strategy, using both qualitative and quantitative techniques, and for concept testing, tracking, and all of the tactical political marketing that follows on from the strategic political planning that precedes putting a political marketing plan into action.

(Long gone, except in the public pronouncements of the dinosaurs that "the only poll that counts is the poll on election day", is the honest belief of the likes of Norman Atkinson in February 1983, who said to me after my presentation to the National Executive Committee of the Labour

Party, "Why, twenty members of my general management committee and I can do a better job of assessing British public opinion than you can, Bob Worcester". Neil Kinnock, then just an NEC member and not leader, responded quickly "What do you need the other twenty guys for, Norman?", which took the steam out of the moment as every one laughed. I must confess, I did take some satisfaction when a few years later his general management committee deselected him for Bernie Grant.)

The Evolution of Modern Campaigning in Britain

The political triangle model, as outlined so far, provides information useful to the media or perhaps to the academic community, clues as to what happened in the election and why. But for the parties' private polling we would need to go a step further, since the primary purpose of private polling should not simply be to diagnose the existing political position but to understand it and how to improve it.

Private polling and its use – or to take a slightly wider view, the whole process known as political marketing – has become somewhat controversial in recent years. Naïve commentators sometimes still assume that it was an innovation of Tony Blair. Of course it was not. In particular, it is only since 1997 that the media seem to have noticed the existence of qualitative research – focus groups – and now all private polling, whatever its methodology or purpose, is routinely dismissed by its opponents as "focus groups", as if no more need be said to prove its worthlessness. But party polling and its use in election campaigning is of course much older.

The use in elections of what we would now call market segmentation – the discipline of designing market appeals to specific groups of customers – dates back at least to the early 1930s when it was used by the Labour Party under the name of "stratified electioneering"[30]. While the tactic is now almost universal, it has often been seen to be undemocratic to target specific groups and leave out other sectional interests.

The first more recognisably modern campaign was probably that which followed the Conservative Party's appointment of the advertising agency,

---

[30] See Dominic Wring, *The Politics of Marketing the Labour Party* (Basingstoke: Palgrave Macmillan, 2005).

Colman, Prentis & Varley, to guide their 1959 election campaign. Harold Macmillan's director of communications at Central Office was the ad man, Geoffrey Tucker. He brought together advertising people, film makers, market researchers (NOP) and campaign strategists to carry off the prize of a third term with the slogan "You've never had it so good". Labour's reaction was to "condemn the Conservatives for introducing something into our political life which is alien to our British democracy"[31].

Labour struggled to catch up. First under Gaitskell and then after his death in 1962 under Harold Wilson, the party employed pollsters and sought the advice of advertising and PR sympathisers (the so-called "Three Wise Men", David Kingsley, Dennis Lyons and Peter Davis), to craft themes and design campaigns with which to win power, which in 1964 they did, then solidifying their slender majority at a second election in 1966, winning by a sufficient margin to carry them through to their surprise defeat in June 1970. It was these same "Three Wise Men" who recruited Worcester to conduct polls for the Labour Party which he did for 19 years.

Barry Day, speechwriter to Ted Heath in 1970, helped explain how the Conservatives organised their marketing programme at the same period:

> "The programme was controlled by a tightly knit little group of professional communicators. The group was composed of four key elements that were fundamental to its eventual success and which, I suspect, are key to any comparable operation. There was the *Political* representative...who acted as the 'client' and who could and did say an immediate yes or no with the full authority... There was the *Party* representative...He could deliver the party 'machine'. Focus of the group was the *Director of Publicity*... temporarily a party employee but essentially a professional secondment from the world of advertising and marketing. Finally the *specialists* from the fields of advertising and film making." [32]

The next phase began after Labour's defeat in 1979, and it took a decade for the Labour Party to catch up (and eventually surpass) the Tories in

---

[31] Dennis Kavanagh in David Butler and Austin Ranney (eds), *Electioneering: A Comparative Study of Continuity and Change* (Oxford: Clarendon Press, 1992).
[32] Barry Day, "The Politics of Communication, or The Communication of Politics" in Robert M Worcester and Martin Harrop (eds), *Political Communications: The General Election Campaign of 1979* (London: George Allen & Unwin, 1982), pp 5-6.

employing the techniques and expertise of modern campaigning. They mainly learned from the Americans, both by watching American campaign techniques and by visiting the US during the election period and talking with their American counterparts. Ron Hayward, then General Secretary of the Labour Party, visited the US during the 1976 Democratic National Convention, visiting the Democratic National Committee while in Washington to learn what he could about their approach to campaigning. Later, after their massive defeat in 1983, Labour's then Director of Communications, Peter Mandelson, and his polling advisor, Philip Gould, visited Washington to see the experts. Bob Squier, political guru and filmmaker to many Democratic candidates, described their visit to his office thus: "[they] brought with them a large valise filled with sponges and sponged up every idea he could present to them, off the walls, the ceiling and the floor, for several hours"[33].

Mandelson and Gould were tireless in their efforts to move the Party from its 1983 amateur effort into modern campaigning mode for the 1987 election, and they understood well how to use focus groups. (Labour had used them in 1972, to good effect, but then Harold Wilson was a master of political marketing. Mandelson's predecessor at Labour Party headquarters, Percy Clarke, was another matter, on one occasion dismissing a proposal to undertake such qualitative research as "offering nothing I can't pick up at the local Labour Club on a Friday night"[34]. As well as Philip Gould, out doing focus groups nightly, they brought in qualitative advertising researchers (one who worked at Saatchi & Saatchi, the Tories' agency, by day, and as a volunteer Labour Party focus-group moderator every night, delivering her crisp and informative memorandum report in time for the 7:30 a.m. meeting of the advisory team, before their presentation to the 8 a.m. Campaign Strategy Committee meeting in the office of the General Secretary of the Party). They employed quantitative research in profusion, daily tracking polls (first introduced in the February 1974 election), panel baselines and recalls (begun in 1972), "fast feedback" from the interviewers as to the mood on the ground as they assessed it (also February 1974), and used the results of multivariate techniques to advise their political marketing, both strategy and tactics.

---

[33] Comment made by Squier to Worcester in telephone conversation immediately after the Mandelson/Gould visit.

[34] Private comment made to Worcester.

When Labour narrowly lost the 1992 general election campaign, John Smith's election to the leadership temporarily checked the advance of Mandelson and Gould and their marketers, but after his death in 1994 and the subsequent election of arch-moderniser Tony Blair, the Peter and Philip marketing show was back in business, in time for the pendulum swing of the dying days of the John Major Government to deliver to Labour its greatest landslide in the General Election of 1997.

If private polling were concerned purely with ad-testing and campaign planning, pointing a party at the best way to put across honestly the policies they had already chosen, probably even its most virulent opponents would see nothing threatening in it. But two developments which are part of this second phase of development are more controversial – use of research not merely to discover how best to put across a policy ("message development") but to guide the policy development process itself, and targeting or segmentation, the concentration on key sections of the electorate while ignoring those whose votes seem less important. With these two developments we leave the sphere of pure research and arguably move towards "government by opinion poll" – a development which we would view with as much dismay as anyone else.

The key distinction is between what marketing theorists would call product-oriented and market-oriented strategies – in simple terms, in the former case a company knows what it wants to sell and tries to find somebody to buy it, while in the latter it identifies its likely buyers first and then designs the product to best fit their demands. Translated into political terms, it is the difference between on the one hand a party that determines its policy programme without reference to the voters, then designs its election campaign so as to promote to each section of the electorate those parts of its programme that will most appeal to them, and on the other hand a party that first identifies the electors whose votes it most wants to win and is prepared to design not merely its campaigning but the details of its policy programme to maximise its appeal to them.

Of course, the division is not clear cut – most parties do an element of both. Unquestionably the latter strategy is generally considered to be politically unprincipled ("an insidious reversal of the political process, turning leaders into followers", as Norman Lamont described the use of

51

focus groups to guide party policy in a post-election newspaper article[35]), yet one doubts if any modern party ever really designs a manifesto without an eye to how it will play in Peoria.

There is, though, a further possible development: political commentators are arguing that the conflation of policy and message is occurring in practice within political parties *per se* – where the message is the policy – representing a sea-change towards a new deleterious form of government[36].

But whatever the shape of the grand design, and however deeply the spin-doctors have their fingers in the pie, the essential task of the political marketers is to identify the key voters and what approach should be used to woo them. And in this nothing has fundamentally changed since MORI started working for Harold Wilson, or for that matter since the "Tadpoles" and "Tapers" were working for Disraeli's fictional statesmen; nor will it change unless Britain abandons the "first-past-the-post" electoral sysem. The only people who matter politically are those who might change their votes, and only then if they vote in constituencies that might change their party; the rest of the electorate might reasonably feel neglected, but from the point of view of a party needing to maximise the electoral impact of its limited resources, they are wasted effort.

Targeting the Marginal Seats

MORI's work for the media has tended to concentrate on polling a nationally representative sample, giving a picture of the views of the electorate as a whole that is valuable for the news reporting of the campaign (the exit poll, being aimed at predicting the number of seats won, is mainly an exception). In private polling, however, it may be more useful to concentrate the same research on key sub-groups of the electorate, such as "floating voters" in marginal constituencies, whose decisions will in practice decide the outcome of the election.

The geographical unit of importance to the UK election strategist is the marginal constituency. Marginality has traditionally been defined in Britain

---

[35] Norman Lamont, "Focus groups? I thought we elected politicians to make big decisions", *Daily Telegraph*, 5 July 2005.
[36] See Bernard Ingham, *The Wages of Spin* (London: John Murray and Sons, 2003).

as a seat where a first-placed party has an electoral majority over the second placed party (as a proportion of the votes cast within the constituency at the last election) of 10% and below, although it has always been a concept incorporating an elastic and subjective element. Almost all the opinion polls published during the election concentrate on the national picture, but that might be very misleading in terms of the number of seats that the parties win. Pundits were persistently telling the public in this election campaign, often without a hint of any caveat, that the Tories needed to get a swing of more than 10% to win. But that was not true – what they needed was a swing that big *in their marginal seats*.

Political parties tend to focus their relatively scarce resources[37] on those seats that they feel that they are more likely to win from the opposition. Identification of target constituencies is one of the most important aspects of an election campaign, regarded as a crucial exercise by all parties and the first phase of a more sophisticated "segmentation". These may simply be the most marginal, or may take into account other factors.

In 2005, for example, the Liberal Democrats targeted constituencies with high concentrations of Muslim or student voters, to whom they believed they had a particular appeal, even though many of these would normally be regarded as "safe" Labour seats. The number of seats targeted will depend on the resources available and how well the party believes it will do, though the risk of over-confidence or of unwillingness to admit to realistic limits may dissipate the party's efforts damagingly. In 2005, for example, the Conservative Party's focus on more than 164 seats[38] was certainly over-ambitious and diverted attention from more realistic targets.

Within marginal constituencies, parties target the floating voters. Most people still vote (if they vote at all) out of lifelong party loyalty, and generally only about one in five electors in any constituency are "floaters". In marketing terms, they can be regarded as potential customers with little or no brand loyalty and perhaps not in the market at all. Targeting these

---

[37] Those resources are even scarcer after the Political Parties, Elections and Referendums Act 2000, which sets strict limits on national spending. Figures for 2005 are not yet available, but in 2001 the major parties spent less than half what they had done before the Act in 1997. The legal spending limit for parties in 2005, covering the whole 12 months up to the election, was a little under £23 million.

[38] Michael A Ashcroft, *Smell The Coffee: A Wake-up Call for the Conservative Party* (London: CGI Europe, 2005).

potential voters constitutes the second phase of the voter segmentation exercise.

Further, of the 628 constituencies being contested in Great Britain at the 2005 general election, only 126 (one in five) had had a majority less than 10% at the previous election, the traditional definition of a "marginal" seat. So only around 4% of the electorate, 1.75 million adults, are floating voters in marginal constituencies, and many of them may not vote: they determine not only who wins, but the size of the majority – whether Mrs Thatcher's 143-seat majority in 1983 or Tony Blair's 179 in 1997. These are the natural prey of the marketing men.

Floating Voters and Volatility

The degree to which voters have not made up their minds who they are intending to vote for is known as *electoral volatility*. It indicates to us how uncertain the result of an election might be, since there could be a significant swing to one way or another come Election Day itself. Since elections are actually decided by relatively small proportions of the electorate, an understanding of volatility is important to the political strategist.

In the 2004 American Presidential Election, if 60,000 voters in Ohio had voted for the Democratic challenger instead of for the Republican President, Bush would not have been re-elected. Similarly, in the 1992 British General Election, if one person in two hundred in a small number of marginal constituencies had voted Labour or LibDem instead of Conservative, the result would have been a hung parliament, rather than a narrow Conservative 21-seat majority.

Figure 7 provides an indication of the volatility at the beginning and end of the campaigns for each of the last five elections. The volatile proportion of the electorate typically varies between a quarter and a third of those who have a voting intention at the start of the campaign; to these we could add the professed "don't knows", usually a further 10% to 15%, but we suspect that the old adage "don't knows don't vote" still largely holds true.

In 2005, there appeared to be a higher degree of volatility than is typical in British elections. At the beginning of the campaign the number saying they might change their minds was higher than we have ever previously found it; as the campaign went on, volatility had dropped a little, from two-fifths saying they might still change their mind who to vote for down to around a third; but this still represented a high proportion of the electorate. By the time of our final poll, more than a quarter were still uncertain what they would do; at the same point in 1987, only 11% had said the same.

Figure 7: Electoral Volatility since 1987

Q (To all giving a voting intention) Have you definitely decided to vote for the... party or is there a chance you may change your mind before you vote?

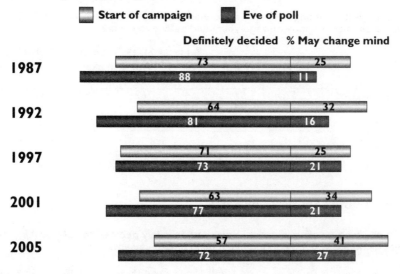

☐ **Start of campaign**   ■ **Eve of poll**

Definitely decided   % May change mind

	Start of campaign	Eve of poll
1987	73 / 25	88 / 11
1992	64 / 32	81 / 16
1997	71 / 25	73 / 21
2001	63 / 34	77 / 21
2005	57 / 41	72 / 27

Source: MORI
Base: c. 750/1,500 GB residents aged 18+ giving a voting intention in each survey

Naturally the number of people who have made up their minds tends to rise during the campaign. (After all, that is what the campaign is for.) Table 16 tracks the making up of minds during the 2005 election – a process which clearly accelerated in the last couple of days before the election, again as we would expect, and implying that no events beyond the imminence of the poll itself had any particular galvanizing effect on this occasion.

Table 17 provides an indication of who were undecided, broken down by party. The LibDem vote was relatively "soft", since half of the party's supporters indicated at the start of the campaign that they might change their mind and vote for another party, and a third were still saying so in the eve-of-poll survey. Labour support was also relatively soft, starting at two in five wavering and falling to just over a quarter. Even for the Conservatives, a third of their support had not made up their mind at the start of the campaign, and almost a quarter said the same with only a couple of days to go.

Table 16: Electoral Volatility, 2005

Q (To all giving a voting intention) Have you definitely decided to vote for the... party or is there a chance you may change your mind before you vote?

	1-3 Apr %	7-9 Apr %	7-11 Apr %	21-25 Apr %	28-29 Apr %	29 Apr - 1 May %	3-4 May %
Definitely decided	57	57	64	62	66	63	72*
May change mind	41	42	32	35	34	36	27
Don't know	2	1	4	3	*	1	1

Source: MORI
Base: c. 750/1,500 GB residents aged 18+ giving a voting intention in each survey
*In final poll, "definitely decided" includes those who said they had already voted by post

Table 17: Vote "Softness" by Party

Q (To all giving a voting intention) Have you definitely decided to vote for the... party or is there a chance you may change your mind before you vote?

"May change mind"	All %	Con %	Lab %	LD %
1-3 April 2005	41	33	40	50
3-4 May 2005	27	23	28	32

Source: MORI
Base: c. 750/1,500 GB residents aged 18+ giving a voting intention in each survey

There was little difference in the proportion of "floating voters" between marginal and safe seats. In our survey of 21-25 April[39], they made up 34% of those giving a voting intention in Conservative or Labour held marginals, 37% in Labour safe seats and Liberal Democrat held seats and

---

[39] The last for which we can reliably make the analysis, as there is always a proportion of respondents in telephone surveys who fail to give us an accurate postcode, meaning we cannot determine in which constituency they live.

31% in Conservative safe seats. (For the most part this simply reflects the fact that the Conservative vote was least soft – the stronger the Tories' 2001 performance in a constituency the more Conservative voters it could be expected to contain and therefore the fewer floating voters.) There is some indication that the floating vote may have been particularly high in Labour-held seats where the Liberal Democrats were the challengers, which would be perfectly reasonable, but the sample size is too small to regard the conclusion as reliable.

It follows from these figures that the pool of key voters, floating and in marginal constituencies, may have been somewhat bigger than is usually the case in British elections – as many as three-and-a-half million at the start of the campaign.

Tactical Voters

One of the biggest uncertainties in the marginal seats was – as it usually is – how many supporters of the third party in each constituency would vote tactically rather than for their preferred party. There had been considerable speculation about "tactical unwind"[40] – the theory that LibDems who voted tactically for Labour in 2001 would be less prepared to do so this time, because of Iraq, which could have handed a number of Labour marginal seats to the Tories.

Tactical voters are an extra complication for the political strategist. They are not floating voters in the normal sense – their primary party loyalties may be as solid as a rock – and they cannot be treated as such. Yet their votes are vital and they must be wooed somehow. If the natural appeal to the floating voters and that to the tactical voters are at odds, there may be a problem.

ICM published two pairs of polls in marginal seats, for Channel 4 and the *News of the World* on 7-10 and 12-14 April (see Table 113 on p 326 for details), which provided a more detailed look in terms of voting intention in the key seats than is possible from the relatively small number of interviews in marginals which would be included in a typical national poll,

---

[40] See David Smith and Peter Kellner, "Tories fail to exploit doubts about Labour", *Sunday Times*, 1 May 2005; Ferdinand Mount, "Labour's biggest opponent this time is the Won't Vote Party", *Daily Telegraph*, 13 April 2005.

which does not by its nature focus on marginal seats. They did, indeed, find Liberal Democrat share up in the Labour-Conservative marginals. In other words, Labour was in danger of losing seats to the Tories not because of a Tory increase in vote, but because Liberal Democrat votes would reduce its majority or chances of winning a majority in a target seat.

But there was a puzzle. In Conservative-Liberal Democrat marginals – which are many fewer in number – the Conservative vote was also down but surprisingly the Labour vote was up, suggesting that the tactical vote had also broken down there, or that substantial numbers of voters make up their minds to vote tactically very late in the campaign. For what it was worth, ICM's findings were also broadly in line with the breakdown from our polls, though they were not designed to allow a reliable separate measure of voting intention in marginal seats to be taken, and could not be treated as more than indicative.

What seemed to be happening was that in 2001, the third party's vote in these marginal seats had been squeezed, and the voters who voted tactically four years ago had still not made up their mind to do so at this time of the campaign. At least the LibDems had to hope that was the case. Nobody suggested any plausible reason why Labour supporters might be any less willing than in 2001 to vote LibDem to keep out the Tories.

Early in the campaign, we attempted to measure tactical voting more directly[41]. We found that already one in eight of those who had a voting intention (12%) said that they would vote to keep out another party and not vote for the party that most represented their views, which is more than the 10% who said the same in the final week in 2001. Certainly we would expect the number of tactical voters to rise by the end of the campaign: anybody who lived in a constituency where the LibDems believed that they had a chance would have been deluged with literature pointing out the tactical situation.

If tactical voting was already higher than in 2001, how could a tactical unwind appear to be happening in the Conservative-Liberal Democrat marginals? The answer must be that much of the early swing to the Liberal Democrats from parties with "little chance of winning in this constituency" was in the Labour-held seats, in most of which the Liberal

---

[41] Fieldwork 7-11 April for the *Evening Standard*; see Appendix 2, survey 36, for details.

Democrat chance of winning was fairly slim as well (though in the event, of course, there were a few spectacular gains there). But where they needed the votes most, in the much higher number of seats where they were in a close contest with the Tories, they were left like Alice having to run hard just to stand still, late into the campaign, needing to recapture the tactical votes of Labour supporters that had already been theirs in 2001, before they could worry about detaching further voters from the Tories who might need to be fished with a quite different bait.

Figure 8: Tactical Voting

Q Which of the following comes closest to your reasons for intending to vote for the ... party?

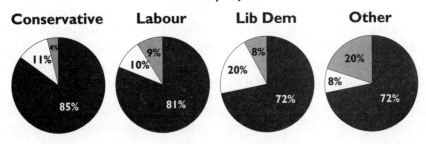

- ■ **It is the party that most represents your views**
- ☐ **The party you support has little chance of winning in this constituency so you vote for ... party to try to keep another party out**
- ▨ **Don't know**

Source: MORI/*Evening Standard*
Base: 1,549 GB residents aged 18+, naming a party, 7-11 April 2005

Voter Segmentation

The next stage of party strategy may be segmentation, the identification of particular types of voters to be targeted by tailoring the campaign to appeal to their particular needs or desires. This is not the simplistic process that is usually portrayed. At every election, pundits either announce a new group of voters that are being targeted this time around or they re-state the increased importance of an old group, often without any polling evidence to support their claims. In 1997, the supposed target was "Worcester

59

woman" (no relation!) – a relatively young woman juggling family and kids and living in middle England. That election also threw up "Mondeo man" – a similar group to "Worcester woman" in many ways but male! The Tories in 2001 talked about "Pebbledash People", married white-collar couples aged 35-50 living in suburban semi-detached, often pebble-dashed, houses.

This is not real segmentation that any practical party strategist would take seriously, though it may sometimes be useful raising the morale of the "troops" with an easy-to-understand objective, and makes what editors think is good copy in a "boring" election (and to them, every election is "boring"). Really, such groupings are trite and relatively unhelpful to the political parties. In fact, their only contribution to any political debate is to highlight the "horserace" – who's ahead of who – between the parties.

Nevertheless, political parties *do* target not only specific marginal seats but specific voter groups through particular policy appeals, especially those voters that are undecided on how to vote, both through indirect marketing methods (e.g. press relations) and through direct marketing methods (e.g. direct mail or telephone canvassing). The catchy media-friendly tags like "pebbledash people" are often misleading simplifications of far more sophisticated research that segments the electorate in useful ways and indicates the best way to appeal for each segment's votes.

We consider in more detail the targeting and segmentation strategies used by the parties in 2005 in Chapter 3, together with other elements of the campaign.

2. The 2001-2005 Parliament

Tony Blair's Second Term: Overview

Even those who find it hard to understand how (or why?) Tony Blair succeeded in being re-elected cannot suggest it was a surprise. Labour led consistently in the voting intention polls almost throughout the Parliament, and neither Iain Duncan Smith, the Leader of the Opposition from 2001 to 2003, nor his successor Michael Howard, ever looked an opponent preferred by the public. Yet Blair had a far from easy ride.

Satisfaction with the government and Prime Minister first soared to heights unheard of in a second term in the wake of Tony Blair's handling of the British response to the September 11 attacks, but then plummeted as he stood firm with President Bush and joined in the American invasion of Iraq and its increasingly embarrassing aftermath. This was reflected in poor results in local and European elections, and in dramatic LibDem gains of safe Labour seats in the Brent East and Leicester South by-elections. But then by-elections, much less local and European elections, are poor predictors of the outcome of general elections.

At Westminster, his first-term Foreign Secretary the late Robin Cook, who had been effectively demoted to Leader of the House, resigned over Iraq and from the back-benches formed a focus for internal dissent. (It can have been lost on few alert observers that it was the resignation of her former Foreign Secretary from the Leadership of the House, into which he had similarly been sidelined, that brought down Margaret Thatcher.)

The international situation rather overshadowed domestic events, but in many ways they were little more propitious. Public service reform and improvement, flagship policies of the 2001 manifesto, were unconvincing to the public whatever the government's claims of objective achievement. As trust in the government began to crumble in the face of accusations of lying and "spin", the government lost a valued Secretary of State, effectively forced to resign by the fallout from an argument between spin doctors. As the Parliament drew to a close, Blair also lost his Home Secretary to an unlikely sex scandal at, of all places, the *Spectator*.

Table 18: Events During the Parliament up to the Invasion of Iraq

Date	Event
2001	
7 June	Labour government re-elected with majority of 167.
16 July	More than 100 Labour MPs vote against the government over attempt to oust Gwyneth Dunwoody and Donald Anderson from Select Committee Chairmanships.
11 September	Terrorist attacks on the World Trade Center and the Pentagon kill c.3,000.
13 September	Iain Duncan Smith elected Conservative leader.
7 October	US-led coalition including British forces begins missile attacks on Afghanistan.
19 October	Coalition ground forces invade Afghanistan.
12 November	Northern Alliance forces enter Kabul.
17 November	Taliban surrender Kandahar, their last major stronghold.
2002	
1 January	Euro notes and coins go into circulation (though not in Britain).
3 February	Labour Spring Conference: Blair describes opponents of his public service policies as wreckers, angering trade union leaders.
30 March	Death of the Queen Mother, aged 101.
2 May	Local elections – Labour losses. Monkey mascot elected Mayor of Hartlepool.
28 May	Stephen Byers resigns, mainly over allegations that he misled MPs over the departure of spin-doctors Jo Moore and Martin Sixsmith.
1-4 June	Golden Jubilee Weekend.
22 September	Countryside March: around 400,000 protest in London.
24 September	Government publishes intelligence "dossier" on Iraqi Weapons of Mass Destruction.
8 November	UN Security Council passes Resolution 1441, giving Iraq "a final opportunity to comply with its disarmament obligations". Weapons inspectors allowed to return to Iraq five days later.
2003	
16 February	London protest march against invading Iraq, biggest in British history – estimates of numbers vary from 750,000 to 2 million.
10 March	Jacques Chirac declares France will veto any new UN resolution which would automatically lead to war in Iraq.
17 March	Former Foreign Secretary Robin Cook resigns from government in protest at impending invasion of Iraq.
18 March	Commons debate on Iraq War – 139 Labour MPs vote against.
20 March	War in Iraq begins with bombing of Baghdad.

Figure 9 charts the voting intention fortunes of the parties through the Parliament. It will be seen that the polling trend runs only from the Autumn of 2002, and therein lies a tale, one essential to understanding the political background to the 2005 general election.

Table 19: Events From the Invasion of Iraq to the End of 2004

Date	Event
2003	
9 April	Baghdad falls to US-led forces.
1 May	Labour loses seats in local elections, but retains first place in Scottish Parliament and Welsh Assembly.
12 May	Clare Short resigns over Iraq.
29 May	On BBC Radio 4, Andrew Gilligan alleges the government's dossier on Iraqi WMD was "sexed up" to improve the case for war.
9 June	Gordon Brown announces that the "five tests" have not been met and Britain will therefore not join the Euro.
9 July	David Kelly named as Gilligan's source by MOD.
18 July	David Kelly commits suicide.
18 September	Brent East by-election – LibDem gain from Labour.
29 October	Iain Duncan Smith ousted as Conservative leader by 90-75 no confidence vote of his MPs.
6 November	Michael Howard elected unopposed as Conservative leader.
14 December	Saddam Hussein captured by US forces.
2004	
27 January	Government wins top-up fees debate in biggest Labour rebellion of Parliament.
28 January	Hutton Report published: government exonerated, BBC blamed.
2 February	Ken Livingstone ratified as Labour candidate for Mayor of London.
4 February	Blair says he was unaware the 45-minute claim over Iraqi WMD referred only to battlefield weapons when he urged MPs to vote for war.
20 April	Blair pledges referendum on EU constitution.
6 May	Blair meets Colonel Gadaffi in Libya to proclaim co-operation against Al-Qaeda.
10 June	European and local elections – Labour losses.
30 June	Handover of power in Iraq from occupying forces to new Iraqi government.
14 July	Butler Report into intelligence on Iraqi WMD finds intelligence was unreliable but government was not to blame.
15 July	By-elections: Labour holds Birmingham Hodge Hill despite huge swing but LibDems gain Leicester South.
15 December	David Blunkett resigns as Home Secretary over allegations of having "fast-tracked" a visa for his lover's nanny.

From late 2002, MORI changed the methodology of its "headline" poll figure – since then we have reported as the primary indicator of the political climate the voting intentions only of those members of the public who say they would be absolutely certain to vote in an immediate general election[42]. For the previous third of a century of MORI's existence, our

---

[42] See Appendix 1, pp 300-1, for a discussion of the methodology.

headline figure was calculated in the traditional way, reporting the responses of all those who gave a voting intention; we have continued also to report the traditional measure, the results from which over 2001-2005 are shown in Figure 10.

Figure 9: Voting Intentions, 2001-5 ("Absolutely Certain to Vote")

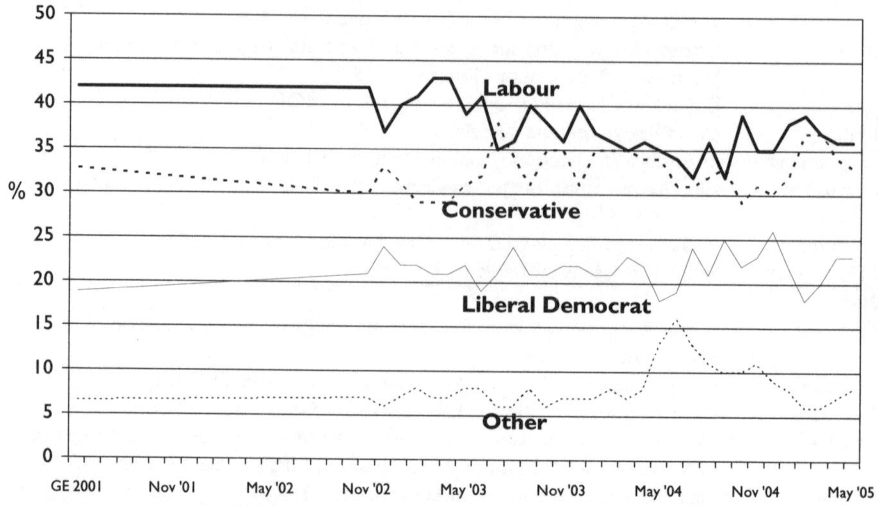

Source: MORI Political Monitor
Base: c. 2,000 GB residents aged 18+ each monthly survey
(MORI did not measure certainty of voting in its monthly polls before November 2002)

Comparing the two graphs it will immediately be seen that taking only the views of those certain to vote significantly and consistently reduces Labour's share of the vote and their lead over the Conservatives. For much of the history of polling in Britain, it has been possible to ignore turnout – most people voted, most of those who did not gave no voting intention to the pollsters, and filtering responses by certainty of voting would probably have made little difference to the poll figures. Since the 2001 election however, when turnout fell to 59%, it has been making a very substantial difference.

This is not just a polling issue, though, but a political one. Labour supporters are consistently and substantially less sure that they will vote than Conservatives and Liberal Democrats; furthermore, the effects are progressive so that at intermediate stages between a low turnout and a full

64

turnout Labour's projected lead grows as the projected turnout rises. Our polling at the last couple of elections, also, made it clear that the difference is not only a theoretical one but does indeed translate into a lower turnout by Labour supporters when it comes to the point. So turnout will have a real and significant political effect on the election outcome, and becomes a major consideration in the parties' approach to a general election.

Figure 10: Voting Intentions, 2001-5 (Based on All Naming A Party)

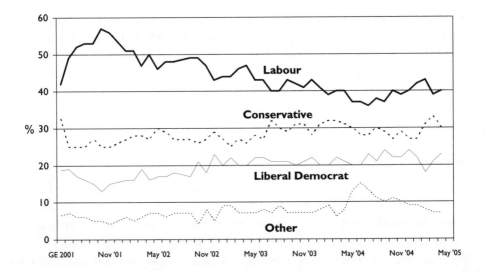

Source: MORI Political Monitor
Base: c. 2,000 GB residents aged 18+ each monthly survey

If Labour will suffer from a low turnout then the party will naturally consider what it can do to get the turnout up. Promoting higher turnout is in any case a laudable aim, good for democracy and difficult for the Conservatives to criticise publicly. But the importance of turnout to Labour's fortunes may not be entirely unconnected with the enthusiasm with which they have embraced the search for methods of promoting voting, and is at any rate an essential strategic and tactical factor in the translation of the political situation into an electoral scenario.

Domestically, the key themes of the 2001-5 Parliament were much those we predicted four years ago. In *Explaining Labour's Second Landslide*, written shortly after the 2001 election, we concluded with a brief survey of "The Second Term", devoting a short chapter to each of the factors we saw as likely to contribute to its success or failure[43]: the challenge to deliver on its election promises, of which the most important to the public was the need to improve public services; safe handling of the question of joining the Euro (that is, not calling a referendum on the issue unless the government could win it, while not causing a political crisis by failing to call it); and the continuing failure of the Conservatives to find either a convincing leader or a purpose. All played their part.

We did not mention, since it could be taken as read, that all this was subject to the tyranny of what Harold Macmillan described, in his much over-quoted phrase, as "events, dear boy, events". Big events shape public opinion; public opinion shapes the political scene. Four months before the invasion of the Falklands, Mrs Thatcher was the least popular prime minister in polling history. John Major was little known when he became Prime Minister in November 1990, just before the Gulf War; his rating rose faster than anyone before; conversely, after "Black Wednesday", his rating fell even faster.

In Tony Blair's second term, the unpredictable "events" would overshadow all the other factors. The terrorist attacks on America on 11 September 2001, and what followed from them – British involvement in the invasions of Afghanistan and Iraq, and continuing controversies over the latter including the Hutton and Butler enquiries – will surely be seen by posterity as the most important events in that four-year period of British politics, eclipsing the government's limited success in improving the public's satisfaction with public services, failure to join the Euro or the continuing tragicomedy of the Conservative Party leadership.

It is instructive that one has to pause and remember to include Afghanistan in the litany of events, for it gains barely a whisper of mention today. Would British politics have been entirely different if there had been no Iraq invasion, or if Britain had refused to take part? Or would the vitriol of Blair's opponents have hung instead on the Afghan venture and the continued failure to find Bin Laden rather than the missing Iraqi Weapons of Mass Destruction? The answer is by no means obvious.

---

[43] Robert Worcester and Roger Mortimore, *Explaining Labour's Second Landslide* (London: Politico's Publishing, 2001), pp 305-320.

Yet for all the sound and the fury, it is vital not to overestimate the direct significance of Iraq to the election. As we shall see, 9/11 briefly bolstered support for Blair as a competent crisis leader, before it was weakened both for standing "shoulder-to-shoulder" with President Bush, who had already been vituperatively caricatured in the British press since his controversial election a year before, and then for more concrete support for the "war on terror" and the Afghan invasion.

By the 2005 election, though, Iraq ranked just 14th in the list of issues cited by voters as very important to their decision at the start of the campaign[44], selected by only 18% of adults. But its effect on the wider standing of the government and Prime Minister was more insidious and more far-reaching.

For, as we have already suggested, the vital factor in an election is "image", the perceptions by which the public judge the parties and their leaders, and it was by tarnishing (and for many voters entirely destroying) Tony Blair's image that the Iraq War and its surrounding circumstances had most effect in the election.

As was predicted in *Parliamentary Monitor* a year in advance:

> "My own view is that Iraq will not have too much of a direct effect on the outcome of the election. However the decline of trust in the PM will – which was caused partly, but by no means entirely, by the failure to find any weapons of mass destruction in Iraq, for cosying up too close to the American President whose unpopularity in this country is both deep and wide, and for his too evident loyalty to unpopular colleagues who have let him (and themselves) down by their behaviour, and for setting himself up for a fall in appearing to the electorate to promise public service delivery when he hasn't been able to carry out his promises." [45]

The character critiques of Blair's first term included "cronyism" (the establishment of which in the vocabulary of political rhetoric may be William Hague's one lasting achievement). But probably the most corrosive factor acting to destroy trust in the Prime Minister and government was the widening awareness of the government's use of

---

[44] Fieldwork 7-11 April for the *Evening Standard*; see Appendix 2, survey 36, for details.
[45] Robert Worcester, "Vox Pop: One Year To Go", *Parliamentary Monitor*, May 2004, p 8-9.

"spin". Often this could be characterised as simple lying. Perhaps the most telling example, though, involved only media manipulation but with an indefensible degree of cynicism, the infamous comment of a ministerial special adviser, Jo Moore, that September 11 would be "a good day to bury bad news".

As is the way with such "scandals", the problem quickly escalated as the media berated the absence of rolling heads. It worsened when the BBC-reporter-turned-government-press-officer, Martin Sixsmith, was apparently sacked by the simple expedient of announcing without consulting him that he had resigned. By setting the word of the familiar Sixsmith against the generally-faceless bureaucracy of government, a classic own goal was scored and most of the public were in little doubt that the government had blatantly lied; as Martin Bell demonstrated at the polls in 1997, a known and respected BBC face will win the battle for public trust against a politician every time. (Well, almost every time – Andrew Gilligan didn't quite get the same benefit of the doubt from the public.) In this case, it cost Stephen Byers his place in the Cabinet.

It is highly ironic that probably the most controversial decision released in the wake of the September 11 attacks was Gavyn Davies' appointment as BBC chairman (cronyism again, as it was portrayed at the time)[46], since the culmination of the spin cycle was the BBC's confrontation with the government which ended in the resignation both of Davies and of his Director-General, Greg Dyke.

The influence of all these factors is evident as we take an overview of the government's fortunes as charted by the main polling indicators – voting intention and the satisfaction ratings of the government and the Prime Minister. Satisfaction fell much more sharply than Labour's vote share; voting is a zero-sum game and the Tory alternative was not popular either. Yet perhaps what is almost more striking than the government's loss of support is that there is no clear turning point in the trends, only a general decline to a trough of "mid-term blues" followed by a partial recovery in a pattern familiar from the history of the Thatcher governments.

---

[46] As noted at the time by the BBC: http://news.bbc.co.uk/1/hi/uk_politics/1588323.stm, accessed 6 July 2005.

For much of his first term as Prime Minister, Tony Blair and his government enjoyed persistently high opinion poll ratings – indeed, unprecedentedly so. This applied not only to a sustained lead in voting intentions, which may have been as dependent on the disarray of the Opposition as on the administration's own showing, but on the more intractable ratings of satisfaction with the Government and with Tony Blair himself. This had all the characteristics of the "honeymoon" period that other governments have enjoyed in the past, but was more marked and considerably more prolonged.

Figure 11: Satisfaction with Blair and His Government 1997-2005

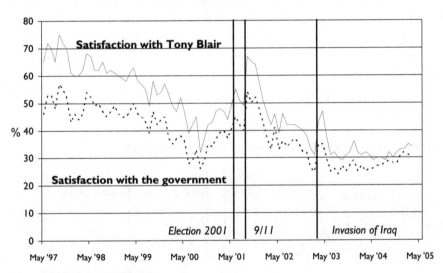

Source: MORI Political Monitor
Base: c. 1,000 GB residents aged 18+ in each monthly survey
(c. 2,000 until February 1998)

That honeymoon period did not last long into the second term, however. Indeed, as the graph of the satisfaction ratings shows, the decline had set in by mid 1999, from which point the overall trend was downwards. Taking a 50% satisfaction rating for Mr Blair himself as a somewhat arbitrary boundary, we see that he dipped below this line in only one monthly poll between his election and February 2000; from May 2000 onwards the trend was to remain below that line, with only two brief peaks above it – one after the 2001 election as the culmination of several months' sustained improvement in ratings, the other a much sharper but fleeting leap in ratings following the September 11 terrorist attacks and widespread satisfaction with Blair's handling of the situation that created.

The pattern from 2001, disregarding the 9/11 and Iraq invasion peaks, is a progressive decline until it bottoms out with Blair's satisfaction score steady at around 30%.

It is revealing, though, to compare Tony Blair's satisfaction ratings with those of Margaret Thatcher in her second term. Superimposing Thatcher's monthly satisfaction ratings onto Blair's (Figure 12) it can be seen that there was not a single point in his first three years in office where Blair's ratings did not surpass Thatcher's – dramatically so at the height of his honeymoon. Yet they reached the election at the end of their first term with similar scores, and the trend of the ratings in the first three years of their second terms seems similar if we disregard the huge upward blip caused by September 11, Blair's ratings being mostly below Thatcher's at the height of the Iraq controversy but stabilising to a very similar level with a year to go to the election.

Figure 12: Comparing Satisfaction with Blair and Thatcher

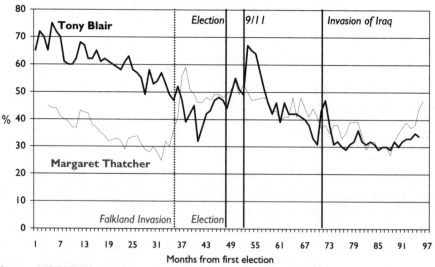

Source: MORI Political Monitor
Base: c. 1,000/2,000 GB residents aged 18+ in each monthly survey

Unlike Thatcher, though, Blair failed to achieve a substantial improvement in the election run-up. Blair's final pre-election rating, 34% satisfied, was worse than that of any previous Prime Minister who had avoided defeat.

This was, plainly, more than routine "mid-term blues", and probably because the government's image was being driven more by its foreign adventures and their consequences than by the domestic agenda. Re-election in these circumstances was by no means routine.

Events: 9/11 and What Followed

Immediately following the terrorist attacks on the twin towers in New York and on the Pentagon on 11 September 2001, Tony Blair made it clear that Britain would back the USA in its response, and also that he considered Britain to be just as much under threat from – and indeed just as much under attack by – the enemies of the West as was the USA. In our first poll of public reactions, three days after the attacks[47], 83% of the public said they were "very" or "fairly" worried that something similar could happen in the UK. And by more than two to one, people in this immediate snapshot of British public opinion thought that the world was less safe at that moment than during the Gulf War, Vietnam or the Cold War.

The impact on British public opinion was a considerable and lasting one. A month after 9/11, more than three people in four believed that the world "has changed forever" as a result of the attacks, only one in five disagreeing. One hypothesis was that this would fade with time but a year later virtually the same figures were found, and in August 2003, just a month short of two years after, the findings were still almost identical[48].

Table 20: The World Has Changed

Q Please tell me whether you agree or disagree: "September 11th has changed the world forever".

	9 Oct 2001 %	5-8 Sep 2002 %	8-17 Aug 2003 %
Agree	77	77	78
Disagree	19	21	19
Don't know	3	2	3

Source: MORI
Base: c. 500-1,000 GB adults 18+ in each survey

Nothing surpassed the way the British generally and certainly the British establishment reacted to the events of September 11, the playing of the Star Spangled Banner at the Palace, the Prime Minister's "Shoulder to Shoulder" speech, the Queen and Royal Family in the congregation at St

---

[47] Fieldwork 14 September 2001 for the *News of the World* – see Appendix 2, survey 6, for details.
[48] See Appendix 2, surveys 8, 19 and 26..

Paul's Cathedral for the Memorial Service. Thousands of mourners left flowers in front of the American Embassy in London in an outpouring of solidarity, and some 50,000 British subjects and others signed the book of condolence for the dead and injured.

Figure 13: Support for Bush and Blair in Britain

Q Do you approve or disapprove of the way George W. Bush is handling the American response to the terrorist attacks on 11th September?
Q Do you approve or disapprove of the way Tony Blair is handling the British response to the terrorist attacks on 11th September?

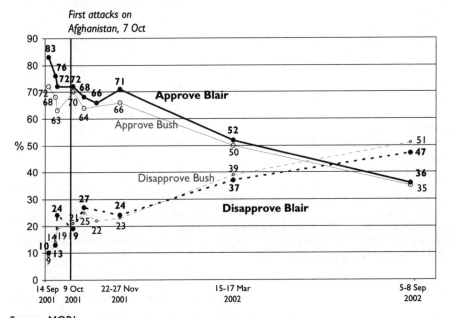

Source: MORI
Base: c. 500-1,000 GB residents aged 18+ each survey

Initial levels of approval for the actions of President Bush and Prime Minister Blair were very high (if not as high as the remarkable ratings found in the US, which held at over 90%), but fell some ten points in the first fortnight before settling around a steady mid-sixties approval figure for Blair, a couple of percentage points lower for Bush. (See Figure 13.) But by March 2002, there had been a sharp drop, and disapproval was ahead of approval by September.

73

Table 21: Trust in Institutions, 2001-2

Q I would like to ask you a question about how much trust you have in certain institutions. For each of the following please tell me if you tend to trust it or tend not to trust it.

		Apr-May 2001		Oct-Nov 2001		Mar-Apr 2002	
		Tend to trust	Tend not to trust	Tend to trust	Tend not to trust	Tend to trust	Tend not to trust
The army	%	72	14	82	11	77	15
Television	%	57	37	71	25	58	35
The police	%	66	29	65	29	67	28
Radio	%	58	31	65	24	59	31
Charitable or voluntary organisations	%	66	20	63	24	63	24
The United Nations	%	51	28	59	24	55	28
Justice/the British legal system	%	49	41	53	39	46	45
The British parliament	%	34	54	47	43	37	50
The Civil Service	%	45	37	45	40	48	37
The British government	%	31	58	43	49	33	56
Trade unions	%	37	41	41	44	39	43
The religious institutions	%	n/a	n/a	38	47	38	44
Non-Governmental Organisations	%	35	30	31	39	30	34
Big companies	%	28	57	22	65	25	61
The press	%	15	77	20	75	20	74
Political parties	%	15	74	16	76	15	74

Source: Eurobarometer 55, 56, 57 (European Commission)
Base: 1,347 UK adults, 17 April-11 May 2001; 1,312 UK adults, 22 October-19 November 2001; 1,311 UK adults, 30 March-24 April 2002.

One effect of the attack on the West and its values seems to have been a surge in affection for its democratic institutions among the public, detected by the European Commission's Eurobarometer surveys, a surge which however had melted away again by the following spring. (Table 21.) Trust in the government rose by 12 percentage points between Spring and Autumn 2001, and trust in Parliament by 13 points; trust in the media also rose, though more sharply in the case of television than of radio or the press. But the Spring 2002 survey found the ratings close to their earlier levels, where they have mostly remained in subsequent surveys.

Tellingly, though, there was no boost in trust for political parties. Whatever the affection for individuals or institutions, the parties remained distrusted; as we shall see, the public tend to see parties as part of the problem, not of the solution.

Afghanistan

From the outset, there was not only support for American action and for the actions of George W Bush, but for the commitment of British troops to assist in the conflict. In the first MORI poll after the attacks, taken on 14 September[49], three people in four supported military action against the groups or nations responsible for the attacks. Asked another way, nearly seven in ten, 69%, said they supported Britain and the United States taking military action against countries that assist or shelter terrorists.

But even at this early stage there were reservations: "if that meant getting into a war", support for military action fell to 55%, and if "innocent civilians in other countries might be hurt or killed", support fell further, to 43%, with 46% opposed. There were some politically-related variations, which look more significant in retrospect than they seemed at the time. Only a bare majority, 53%, of Liberal Democrats supported the use of troops, compared with 67% of Conservative supporters and 72% of Labour supporters. How much this was because the base of LibDem support was pacifist or isolationist by nature, and how much because even at this stage they were less susceptible to persuasion by Tony Blair, is an intriguing speculation.

More importantly, though, significantly fewer women than men said they approved of the way President Bush was handling the American response to the attack, and between 6% and 11% fewer women than men in different polls approved of the way Tony Blair was handling the British response. Also, significantly fewer women were supportive of British troops being involved in military action alongside American forces: 57%, compared with 74% of men. This gender distinction in attitudes to the situation and the best response to it was to persist through the invasions of Afghanistan and Iraq, and was still present in retrospective assessments of the government's record on the issue by the time of the election.

---

[49] See Appendix 2, survey 6, for details

MORI's tracking polls found support for the war holding up above two-thirds through to the end of November, after the fall of Kabul on the 12th of that month (see Figure 14). Immediately following the beginning of the bombing in Afghanistan in early October, 71% of the British said they believed that Britain was right to join America in the military strikes. And two thirds, 66%, said they believed the approach of George W Bush and Tony Blair to the crisis was helping to make the world a safer place.

Figure 14: Support for Using British Troops After 9/11

Q (Before the War started) And if the United States were to take military action against those responsible for the attacks, would you support or oppose British troops being involved in this action?
Q (After the War started) Now that the US has taken military action, do you support or oppose British troops being involved in this action?

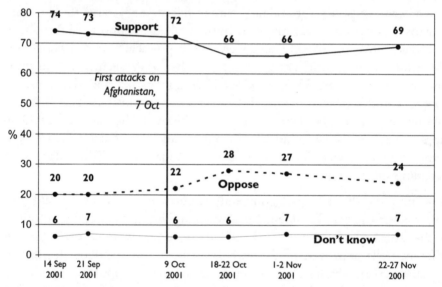

Source: MORI
Base: c. 500-1,000 GB residents aged 18+ (See Appendix 2 for details)

But the united front was beginning to crack by the end of the first six months. In March 2002, 52% still approved of Tony Blair's handling of the British response but 39% disagreed; a similar number, 40%, mostly the same people, thought "the British government is too supportive of the American government on these international issues"[50].

The Anglo-American "Special Relationship"

Yet the strong public support for Blair's initial reaction seemed to fly in the face of a widespread "anti-Americanism" and, especially, contempt for President Bush, which later burgeoned into very solid opposition to the war in Iraq.

This, though, is to simplify the position to the point of misunderstanding it. Britain is not "anti-American". Nor, for that matter, is Europe. The American people, and many aspects of US culture, are welcome and popular. Nevertheless, the United States of America has a PR problem. In its world political role, it is far less popular, and that has undoubtedly worsened with the Presidency of George W Bush – in part, at least, something that can be blamed on the dangerously ludicrous caricature of the President put forward by the British media. President Bush is not a psychopathic half-wit as many of the columnists and cartoonists would have use believe.

Table 22: The British Public's Liking of Americans

Q Please tell me whether you agree or disagree: "I like Americans as people".

	1986 %	1991 %	25-27 Oct 2002 %
Agree	69	66	81
Disagree	18	16	11
Don't know	13	18	8

Source: MORI
Base: c. 1,000 GB residents aged 18+ in each survey

Over the past thirty years I've tried to keep an eye on anti-Americanism, both as an American citizen enjoying British hospitality for so many years, and for the past dozen years as Chairman of the Pilgrims Society, the organisation dedicated to the furtherance of Anglo-American good

---

[50] Fieldwork 15-17 March 2002, for *Time* magazine – see Appendix 2, survey 12, for details.

fellowship. (Indeed, in 2004 I was granted dual citizenship, now possible for American citizens; asking the Minister at the American Embassy if they had any objection to my becoming a dual citizen, his response was to say "I can't think of anyone more suitable".)

So why then was I surprised, as has been every audience with which I've shared the finding, that the percentage of those who say "I like Americans as people" has risen, not fallen, since the time of the famous Reagan-Thatcher "love-in" in the 1980s? It must be because of all the anti-American newspaper articles and statements by self-appointed spokesmen and women who sound off in the media about British public opinion. In fact the British like Americans as people, and this affection seems to have been fostered rather than shaken by the traumatic events of recent years.

Table 23: Favourability Towards Countries and Organisations

Q Now I am going to read out the countries and institutions again, and this time I would like you to tell me how favourable or unfavourable your overall opinion or impression of each is. Take into account any of the things which you think are important. Remember that it is your overall opinion or impression that we are interested in.

	China %	EU %	Russia %	UK %	US %	UN %
Very favourable	I	5	I	25	8	9
Mainly favourable	16	31	16	55	43	41
Neither	50	35	51	10	25	32
Mainly unfavourable	18	16	18	7	15	10
Very unfavourable	4	5	3	I	6	2
No opinion	12	9	11	I	3	7
Favourable	17	36	17	80	51	50
Unfavourable	22	21	21	8	21	12
Net	-5	+15	-4	+72	+30	+38

Source: MORI/Expert Group
Base: 2,058 GB residents aged 15+, 23-27 January 2003

Nor is their country a problem as such. A MORI survey for the Expert Group, conducted at the end of January 2003 during the build-up to the invasion of Iraq, found that half the public took a generally favourable view of the United States, three times as many as had a favourable view of China or Russia. One in five had an unfavourable impression. (Table 23.)

However, twice as many said they distrusted the USA "on matters of world security", and indeed 15% distrusted the USA on such matters "completely". International organisations – the United Nations and even the normally despised European Union – collected much lower distrust scores. (Table 24.)

Again, we find there was a significant difference between men's and women's opinions of the USA. Distrust of the USA on world security issues was at a similar level among women (42%) and men (43%), but trust among women was lower (31%, against 39% among men), with the remaining women having no opinion either way.

Table 24: Trust in Countries and International Organisations

Q Now I am going to read out the countries and institutions again, along with some world leaders, and this time I would like you to tell me the extent to which you trust or distrust each on matters of world security?

	China %	EU %	Russia %	UK %	US %	UN %
Trust completely	*	4	1	15	4	9
Trust somewhat	10	34	15	51	31	45
Neither trust nor distrust	38	32	39	15	20	27
Distrust somewhat	30	17	28	14	28	11
Distrust completely	11	5	8	3	15	3
No opinion	11	8	9	2	3	6
Trust	10	38	16	66	35	54
Distrust	41	22	36	17	43	14
Net	-31	+16	-20	+49	-8	+40

Source: MORI/Expert Group
Base: 2,058 GB residents aged 15+, 23-27 January 2003

But distrust of the USA on world security paled beside distrust of its President on the same subject: only 18% of Britons trusted George W Bush on this, and 64% distrusted him; 34% distrusted him completely. Tony Blair's ratings were a little better (39% trusted him, 43% distrusted him), but his net score was still negative. Again, there was a significant difference between the sexes, women being less likely to trust Mr Bush than men, though more likely to have no opinion rather than to distrust him. But this fed through into more women than men distrusting Tony

Blair as well as fewer trusting him; net trust in Mr Blair was 0 among men but -8 among women.

Table 25: British Distrust of Blair, Bush and Putin

Q Now I am going to read out the countries and institutions again, along with some world leaders, and this time I would like you to tell me the extent to which you trust or distrust each on matters of world security?

	Vladimir Putin %	Tony Blair %	George W Bush %
Trust completely	I	7	2
Trust somewhat	20	32	16
Neither trust nor distrust	38	17	15
Distrust somewhat	19	27	30
Distrust completely	6	16	34
No opinion	17	2	3
Trust	21	39	18
Distrust	25	43	64
Net	-4	-4	-46

Source: MORI/Expert Group
Base: 2,058 British 15+, 23-27 January 2003

It was the alliance with President Bush, above all else, that bolstered opponents of British involvement in Iraq in their opinions. Again, this must not be misread as a wider rejection of the American political system or the "special relationship"; on the contrary, the British public accepts that their country's links with the USA are important to them. Regularly updating a survey first carried out by Gallup in 1969 (Table 26), we found that the perceived importance of America waned during the early 1990s, but has been steadily increasing again in the last few years until it returned to its 1969 level in 2003. Europe is still most likely to be seen as important, as has been the case since the 1980s, but a third see America as more important, while the Commonwealth has slipped in importance to less than half its 1969 level.

And when we asked about Britain's "most reliable ally" in April 2003 with the invasion of Iraq in full swing, the USA was the only game in town, with three people in four saying it was the US; the next strongest contender was Australia, with just 4%. Over half, 55%, said that France was our least reliable ally. (Well, no change there in more than a millennium!)

Table 26: Europe, the Commonwealth and America

Q Which of these – Europe, the Commonwealth or America – is the most important to Britain?

	1969 %	1984 %	1986 %	1989 %	1991 %	1993 %	1996 %	2002 %	2003 %
Europe	21	39	39	50	52	57	45	50	42
Commonwealth	34	25	26	21	22	18	22	19	16
America	34	26	29	19	19	15	22	29	34
Don't know	11	10	6	10	7	10	11	2	8

Source: MORI, except 1969 (Gallup)

But most people in the rest of Europe think America is full of warmongers. Across the EU (including the 10 new member states which joined in 2004), only 22% of the public believe the US plays a positive role regarding peace in the world, and 39% that it plays a positive role regarding the fight against terrorism[51]; this latter figure steadily worsened from Autumn 2002 to Autumn 2004. In Britain the figures are higher, 32% and 55% respectively, but still only a third of Britons see the USA as a force for peace. In such circumstances, Blair's decision to join the Americans in the invasion of Iraq would inevitably raise suspicion about his motives.

Iraq

The invasion of Iraq was, immediately before it began on 20 March 2003, possibly the least popular war with the British public of any in which British troops have joined since opinion polls were invented. The previous month, opponents of military action in Iraq had staged a protest march in London which according to some reports drew two million participants, much the biggest mass demonstration in British political history.

---

[51] European Commission Standard Eurobarometer 62, Autumn 2004. A total of c. 26,000 adults across the EU were interviewed by TNS Opinion & Social on 2 October-8 November 2004. British fieldwork was conducted by TNS UK, who interviewed 1,310 UK adults face-to-face, in home, on 5 October-8 November 2004. Details at http://europa.eu.int/comm/public_opinion/index_en.htm.

Tony Blair's answer to the challenge posed by the march and by the opposition which extended to his own back-benches and even to corners of his Cabinet table, was, in effect, to ask the public and his colleagues to trust his judgment rather than their own. Back in 1997, they might have done; but by this stage the public's trust in the Prime Minister was much less unquestioning. By the third week of January, just 26% approved of the way Mr Blair was handling the current situation with Iraq. Satisfaction with the way Mr Blair was doing his job as Prime Minister fell from 33% at the end of January, already the second-worst rating of his premiership, to a new low of 31% a week after the march.

Yet he was clearly winning over some support on the issue even at this stage: approval of his handling of Iraq was up to 36% by the end of February, though it dipped slightly again in the next fortnight as the prospect of war drew nearer.

Table 27: Support for War in Iraq Under Different Scenarios

Q Would you support or oppose British troops joining any American-led military action against Iraq in each of the following circumstances?

		Support	Oppose	Don't know
The UN inspectors find proof that Iraq is trying to hide weapons of mass destruction, and the UN security council votes in favour of military action	%	74	17	7
The UN inspectors find proof that Iraq is trying to hide weapons of mass destruction, but the UN security council does not vote in favour of military action	%	48	37	15
The UN inspectors do not find proof that Iraq is trying to hide weapons of mass destruction, but the UN security council votes in favour of military action	%	46	41	12
The UN inspectors do not find proof that Iraq is trying to hide weapons of mass destruction, and the UN security council does not vote in favour of military action	%	26	63	11

Source: MORI
Base: 968 GB residents aged 18+, 14-16 March 2003

Furthermore, the public were prepared in principle to support a war, in certain circumstances: in September 2002, 71% of people in Britain

82

supported British troops joining any American-led military action against Iraq with UN approval, and on 14-16 March 2003, a week before the invasion, three-quarters of the public told us that they would support British involvement if there were to be proof that Iraq was hiding Weapons of Mass Destruction (WMD) and the Security Council were to vote in favour of action.

However, just 26% of the public said that they approved of British involvement without a "smoking gun" and a second UN vote, while 63% disapproved. They got neither smoking gun nor UN vote. After heroic efforts to arm-twist delegates on the Security Council to support a British resolution giving United Nations approval to the use of military force, which failed in the face of the French threat of a veto no matter what the outcome of the vote, and after the failure of the inspectors to find any WMD, Blair and Bush sent the bombers and the troops in anyway.

But even so, at that point the general tendency was to blame the French for their obstructionism rather than to condemn Blair's belligerence. On March 18, an internet poll by YouGov found that two-thirds of the British public said they believed that President Chirac was wrong to say the France would veto any UN resolution that triggered the use of force if Saddam Hussein failed to disarm, and only 2% blamed Tony Blair for the failure of the members of the Security Council to work together to deal with the Iraq crisis, while 50% blamed Chirac, 35% President Bush, and 12% said they did not know. In the same sounding, and shortly before the vote in the House of Commons, 52% said that, if they were an MP, they would vote to support the Government while 42% said they would vote against it[52]. Other polls indicated that most of the public would be happy to see "regime change" in Baghdad, even if they didn't think British troops should be used to achieve it.

No sooner had the first shots been fired than public opinion started to swing in favour of the war and kept on going[53]. Within a couple of days the polls were finding solid majorities in favour where previously they had

---

[52] Peter Kellner, "Iraq – the public and the war: a report on You Gov opinion surveys before, during and after the conflict," www.yougov.com, accessed 1 September 2003.

[53] See Paul R Baines. and Robert M Worcester, "When the British Tommy Went To War, Public Opinion Followed", *Journal of Public Affairs*, Vol 5 (2005), 4-19, for a more detailed discussion of how public opinion changed, and why, during this time.

found solid majorities against, a movement which even reports of civilian casualties, "friendly-fire" incidents and later widespread looting and lawlessness apparently did nothing to check: our poll on 28-30 March, with British troops in Basra and the Americans advancing on Baghdad, found 56% saying they supported "Britain taking part in the military action against Iraq", while 38% remained opposed. The scale of the change of opinions made it one of the most dramatic turnarounds that MORI has ever measured: an effective 27% swing in two weeks.

The direction of the shift, if not perhaps its scale, was predictable. Previous conflicts have shown a consistent pattern that public support increases once the action begins, although the case of Iraq was unusual in that there was such a solid majority against involvement before the war started.

Table 28: Approval of Blair's Handling of Iraq

Q Do you approve or disapprove of the way the Prime Minister, Tony Blair, is handling the current situation with Iraq?

	Sep 2002 %	Oct 2002 %	17-20 Jan 2003 %	Feb- Mar 2003 %	14-16 Mar 2003 %	28-31 Mar 2003 %	25-27 Jul 2003 %
Approve	40	35	26	36	30	47	32
Disapprove	49	47	62	53	54	44	55
Don't know	11	18	13	12	16	9	13
Net approve	-9	-12	-36	-17	-24	3	-23

Source: MORI
Base: c. 1,000 GB residents aged 18+ each survey

The swing in favour of Blair personally, approving of his handling of the situation, is perhaps more relevant to the subsequent political impact than attitudes to the invasion as such. This was considerably smaller, though still an impressive transformation to achieve in a fortnight – a 13.5% swing.

Who was it who (temporarily in many cases) changed their minds?

Throughout the run-up to the war, the most clear-cut demographic pattern was that women were much more hostile to the war; by the final weekend before the invasion, men were almost twice as likely as women to approve of Mr Blair's handling of the situation. That "gender gap" was maintained, with very similar swings among men and women (not a statistically significant difference) once the war began. (Table 29.)

Table 29: Who Swung to Blair?

Q Do you approve or disapprove of the way the Prime Minister, Tony Blair, is handling the current situation with Iraq?

	14-16 March		28-31 March		Change		
	App	Dis	App	Dis	App	Dis	Swing
	%	%	%	%	±%	±%	%
All	30	54	47	44	+17	-10	13.5
Male	40	47	55	37	+15	-10	12.5
Female	21	62	38	50	+17	-12	14.5
16-24	30	56	48	42	+18	-14	16.0
25-34	24	59	52	39	+28	-20	24.0
35-44	30	59	47	44	+17	-15	16.0
45-54	31	52	51	41	+20	-11	15.5
55+	34	50	40	47	+6	-3	4.5
AB	36	51	45	46	+9	-5	7.0
C1	28	55	46	46	+18	-9	13.5
C2	33	54	50	41	+17	-13	15.0
DE	25	57	46	41	+21	-16	18.5
North	31	55	46	44	+15	-11	13.0
Midlands	28	55	50	41	+22	-14	18.0
South	33	53	48	40	+15	-13	14.0
London	28	54	36	55	+8	1	3.5
Conservative	33	57	52	42	+19	-15	17.0
Labour	46	42	60	32	+14	-10	12.0
LibDems	15	72	26	66	+11	-6	8.5

Source: MORI
Base: c. 1,000 GB residents aged 18+ in each survey

An ICM poll for the BBC in February 2003[54] threw light on the nature of the gender difference in attitudes: men's and women's opinions were similar in their assessment of the current situation but very distinct in their decisions on the appropriate response to it.

The ICM poll found men and women in agreement on the threat posed by Iraq: 34% of men and 33% of women thought the British and American

---

[54] ICM interviewed 1,006 adults aged 18+ by telephone on 10-11 February 2003, on behalf of the BBC. Details available at www.icmresearch.co.uk.

governments had proved their case that Saddam Hussein had weapons of mass destruction. And 56% of men and 57% of women believed there were links between Saddam Hussein's regime and Al Qaeda and associated terror groups. They were also equally unlikely to agree that war in Iraq would deter other countries from developing WMDs (32% of men and 31% of women agreed).

But then comes the important difference: men were more likely than women to feel that this situation justified an attack on Iraq so long as the UN backed it. One contributory factor to this, presumably, was that 65% of men and only 44% of women thought at that point that such a war would succeed in removing Saddam Hussein from power. Women were also much more sceptical of Mr Blair's motives, saying by 48% to 41% that he "acts as the foreign minister of the US and does anything that Bush wants him to do" rather than that "he does what he believes to be right for Britain"; men, by contrast, gave Mr Blair the benefit of the doubt by 51% to 38%.

Whereas the attitudes of men and women changed to a broadly similar degree when the war started, the picture is very different when we look at attitudes by age. Before the war, there was no clear pattern, and most age groups seemed to think in broadly the same way[55]. But there was a dramatic difference in the way that opinions changed once the invasion had begun. Those aged under 55 swung very sharply in Mr Blair's favour, 15% or more, and gave the Prime Minister a clear lead in approval among each of the four age groups. In sharp contrast, the 55-and-overs swung only 4.5%; from being the most pro-Blair group pre-war they became the least pro-Blair, with disapprovers outnumbering approvers by 47% to 40%.

A similar difference is evident in the class breakdown – ABs swung much less than other classes, although the result was that the opinions of all classes ended up fairly similar, whereas before ABs were substantially more supportive of Mr Blair than the rest of the country. This is perhaps not so surprising – ABs are more interested in politics and more likely to read quality newspapers than other classes, and may consequently be more

---

[55] In the mid-March poll the 25-34 year olds were somewhat less approving of Mr Blair than other age groups, but this was not a pattern that had been consistently present in earlier polls, and may have been only a statistical blip or the result of some specific short-term cause.

likely to have already considered the issues in depth and thought through their attitudes before the war started; those who had paid less attention until British troops invaded Iraq would naturally have less entrenched opinions at that point and therefore be the ones most prone to change their minds. A similar explanation may be behind the age differences, though generational factors and memories of previous wars may also have played their part in shaping opinions in that case.

By the time the war started, then, there was a very definite gender difference in attitudes which may have depended more on questions of practical interpretation than on any divide in principles, but otherwise a fairly consistent pattern of an even split of opinions, the balance narrowly tipped in favour of the Prime Minister, across all classes, all age groups except the oldest and all regions except London (which with its substantial Muslim population and cosmopolitan influences would naturally be expected to be less supportive of the venture).

Arguably this lack of a sectional focus for opposition may have saved Blair from worse electoral consequences; on the other hand it may have simply made the issue more dangerous, as a universal and untargeted appeal could shake the foundations of Labour support across the board.

It is worth noting how sharp the distinction already was between Liberal Democrats and supporters of the other two parties, even before the war began. Charles Kennedy's opponents have accused him of both inconsistency and opportunism in his use of Iraq as an issue to build LibDem support, but it would be a mistake to suppose that opponents of the war only began to flock to his banner in its aftermath; indeed, as we have seen, the divide was there even as early as the attack on Afghanistan. Assuming this was not simply a product of distrust of Tony Blair (and there seems no reason why that should have been stronger among Liberal Democrats than Tories, all other things being equal) it suggests an ideologically distinctive base to Liberal Democrat support that they have – perhaps unjustly – been suspected of largely lacking in the past.

Incidentally, the supposition from previous wars that the shift in opinion would occur at the moment the shooting started, when British troops were suddenly in peril and when it would be unpatriotic not to support them, may have been mistaken. Research conducted at Bournemouth University, comparing tracking poll data with the daily headlines in the newspapers, has concluded that the shift took place *before* the first shots were fired, at the moment the media began to treat the issue as a confrontation between Blair and his opponents, domestic and international; but also that the shift in emphasis of the headlines may be as much a reflection of the public mood as its cause[56].

This might imply that public opinion moves in such circumstances not because of any impending threat to British troops, as is often supposed, but from the acceptance of a *fait accompli* and judging an existing as opposed to a hypothetical situation. This makes perfect sense. A public which would genuinely rather not have gone to war was prepared to make the best of it when presented with a *fait accompli*, especially as the practical aim of regime change was one of which most of them approved.

Perhaps the most surprising factor in the Iraq War was that it was Tony Blair who took Britain into it, in the teeth of public opposition. Prior to the war, the Prime Minister was widely thought to be a "focus groupie" and a slave to polling evidence, hesitant to go against the will of the majority of the British public in his quest for a second and, now a third, Labour landslide. But no doubt he knew that history shows a successful war can turn round public opinion, counting on his ability to argue successfully for British participation in the war.

Public opinion in previous wars has been supportive of the government – until things started going wrong. In World War Two, Gallup tracked the falling confidence in Neville Chamberlain: in November 1939, two months into the war, they found a remarkable 68% level of approval of his performance as Prime Minister; but in the following months his poll ratings fell sharply, by January 1940 to 56% and by 9-10 May 1940 to 32%, which contributed to his resignation and Churchill becoming Prime Minister at the head of an all-party coalition. By July 1940, after Dunkirk in May and in the midst of the Battle of Britain, Churchill received an 88% approval rating, with only 7% of the British public disapproving of his performance, still a record today[57].

---

[56] Barry Richards, "The national press and opinion shift", paper presented at EPOP Conference, Cardiff University, September 2003.
[57] John Lukacs, *Five Days in London: May 1940*, (New Haven and London: Yale University Press, 2001).

In more recent times, Margaret Thatcher apparently benefited hugely from the "Falklands Factor". Her satisfaction rating of 25% in December 1981 had made her then the least popular Prime Minister since polling began. But after the Argentine invasion of the Falkland Islands, as the war to recover them progressed, Mrs Thatcher's ratings rose, to 41% in April three weeks after the invasion, to 56% in May, and peaked at 59% in June after British troops regained control of the islands[58]. Although her ratings subsequently slipped back a little, they remained high enough for a landslide general election victory in June 1983.

However, in contrast to the situation over Iraq, the public had supported the attempt to recapture the Falklands from the beginning. In MORI surveys for *The Economist* and the BBC's *Panorama* programme, 83% initially (April 14) believed that Britain was right to send the naval taskforce to the Falkland Islands, steady a week later at 85%, and again 3-5 May at 85%.

In any case, the political effect of the Falklands Factor is usually overstated: both Mrs Thatcher's ratings and the Tories' voting intention rating had begun to climb a couple of months before the Argentinians invaded the Falklands, driven probably by perceived economic improvement; while the enhancement of her image for competent leadership cannot have harmed Tory chances in 1983, it is by no means clear that they would not have won almost as easily even had the Falklands War never occurred.

John Major also seemed to benefit from leading the country at the time of the first Gulf War, when he had only just entered Downing Street and was little known to the British public (despite having served as both Foreign Secretary and as Chancellor of the Exchequer). Standing tall together with the present President Bush's father, and achieving the successful recovery of Kuwait and the humiliation of Saddam Hussein, his satisfaction ratings rose from an initial 37% satisfied (though with 41% don't knows) to 63% satisfied by the third week of February. He too won the subsequent general election.

---

[58] Simon Jenkins and Robert M Worcester, "Britain Rallies Around the Prime Minister", *Public Opinion Magazine*, June-July 1982, pp 53-55.

Tony Blair might reasonably have taken from history the message that a good war can do wonders for the rating of a British Prime Minister. But he might also have remembered that such boosts in popularity can be fleeting – for example, in John Major's case, by August 1994 his satisfaction rating had set a new record low, of 17%; and Churchill lost the general election held even before the victory he had engineered was complete.

Furthermore, viewed in purely domestic political terms, Blair had a problem Thatcher in the Falklands did not, and one which perhaps no Prime Minister has faced in prosecuting a war since the ex-appeaser Chamberlain in 1939 – it was his own past supporters, not his opponents, who were most opposed to the policy, and to President Bush, already a hate figure with the left. The issue clearly had the potential to undermine New Labour's coalition of support completely.

Once Baghdad had fallen, commentators were quick to note the degree to which support for the war was higher than it had been before the invasion started, and interpreted this as a "Baghdad Bounce". But this was always overplayed. Blair's ratings after Baghdad fell were no higher than they had been before the whole venture began to be mooted (47% satisfied with his performance as PM in April 2003 compared to 46% the previous June); and they were a degree lower than those that Mrs Thatcher achieved after the Falklands War (59% satisfied in June 1982); "Baghdad Bounce" was never going to be Mr Blair's Falklands Factor.

And, of course, as the euphoria wore off and more questions began to be asked about the genesis of the war, it quickly became once more a major liability rather than any sort of asset.

Gilligan, Kelly ... and Hutton

The reaction against the government and collapse in support for the invasion was not an immediate one. As late as July more recalled having supported the War than had admitted doing so to pollsters at the time, and by five to four the public said they believed the commitment of British troops to invade Iraq was right. It was only to slide away, and very largely turn negative, following the suicide of the government weapons expert Dr David Kelly.

But even when things were going well, the political signs were ambiguous. At the height of the war Blair's personal ratings had benefited less from the shift in the public mood than had approval for the policy. Now, as Blair's integrity was questioned over how he had persuaded the Commons to vote for the war, the Prime Minister's personal support fell far more sharply than public support for the war.

On 25-27 July, just after Dr Kelly's suicide had been reported, we found only 32% still approving Blair's "handling of the current situation with Iraq", while 55% disapproved. Nevertheless, 50% still said they now believed "it was right for British troops to invade Iraq and take part in deposing the Saddam Hussein Government", and only 41% that it was wrong.

Yet oddly, perhaps, the Kelly affair and the Hutton Report that followed it seem to have failed to cement this personalisation of the issue. Superficially, the circumstances were conducive to it. The substantive issue, whether Blair's government had misled the Commons by misrepresenting intelligence from Iraq, touched directly on the Prime Minister's integrity. The immediate instance of investigation, too, touched on Blair's personal involvement. (One of the allegations surrounding the circumstances of Dr Kelly's suicide was that Blair had personally intervened in the normal Ministry of Defence internal investigation and disciplinary procedures following a leak, and that this directly contributed to the pressures on Dr Kelly that led him to take his life.)

Table 30: Trust and the Kelly Affair

Q In general would you describe each of the following as trustworthy or not?

		Trust-worthy	Not trust-worthy	Don't know	Net
The BBC	%	59	26	15	+33
Andrew Gilligan, the BBC journalist	%	32	30	38	+2
Tony Blair	%	41	49	10	-8
Geoff Hoon, the Defence Secretary	%	24	45	30	-21
Alastair Campbell, the Prime Minister's Director of Communications	%	14	60	26	-46

Source: MORI
Base: 982 adults aged 18+, 25-27 July 2003

Despite this, the public seem not to have pinned the blame on Blair personally, or at least not exclusively so. At the end of June 2003, Tony Blair's net trust score (that is those who would describe him as trustworthy minus those who would describe him as not trustworthy) stood at -22%. Yet after Kelly's death, with Blair's integrity apparently pitted against that of the normally trusted BBC, his trust rating rose, to a still damaging but less indefensible -8.

While many of the public were unconvinced whether they should trust the journalist at the centre of the controversy, Andrew Gilligan (32% thought he was trustworthy and 30% not, but 38% had no opinion), the Corporation as a whole had a much tighter grip on public trust. Three in five (59%) considered the BBC trustworthy, more than twice as many as the 26% who thought it was not. Geoff Hoon, already much pilloried for his conduct of the war and under fire again after Kelly's death as the minister with departmental responsibility, performed worse. But the real focus for public distrust, acting as a lightning conductor for his elected masters, was Tony Blair's right hand man and chief spin doctor, Alastair Campbell.

Table 31: Blame for David Kelly's Death

Q From what you know or have heard, who do you think bears a major responsibility for the death of the Government scientist, Dr Kelly, in July 2003?

	%
Dr Kelly himself	26
The media generally	24
Geoff Hoon (the Defence Secretary)	22
Tony Blair	22
Ministry of Defence/Civil Servants	21
Andrew Gilligan (reporter on the BBC Radio 4 Today Programme)	14
Alastair Campbell	13
BBC	9
Parliament	8
Other	2
None	1
Don't know	18

Source: MORI/*Financial Times*
Base: 952 GB residents aged 18+, 11-16 September 2003
(Asked with showcard of options)

Blair was not widely blamed for Kelly's death, nor did he face widespread demands for his resignation. (21% thinking the Prime Minister should resign at any given time is virtually a cold reading.)

Table 32: David Kelly's Death: Who Should Resign?

Q   Which, if any of the following do you think should resign as a result of the death of Dr Kelly?

	%
Geoff Hoon (the Defence Secretary)	33
Tony Blair	21
Alastair Campbell	17
Andrew Gilligan (reporter on the BBC Radio 4 Today Programme)	15
Greg Dyke (Director General of the BBC)	7
Richard Sambrook (Head of News and Current Affairs at the BBC)	4
Kevin Marsh (the Editor of the Today Programme on BBC Radio 4)	3
Other	1
None	19
Don't know	24

Source: MORI/*Financial Times*
Base: 952 GB residents aged 18+, 11-16 September 2003

This may explain why the actual publication of the Hutton Report, exonerating the government over Kelly's death and excoriating the BBC, had so little political relevance. The issue had already become one of "spin", rather than centring on Blair's personal involvement; this was perhaps in the long run more damaging to the credibility of the government, and in the short-term pushed Alastair Campbell into centre stage (from which he then jumped before anybody could seriously contemplate pushing him).

The belief that the Hutton Report was a "whitewash", rather than adding frustration to Blair's opponents by denying them ammunition, as would normally be the case in such circumstances, was in itself perfect ammunition, adding further contributory evidence to their thesis of government lies and obfuscation. Consequently, we can also see why Iraq became an "image issue" rather than an "issue issue". The evidence it gave the government's opponents of the untrustworthiness of the government went far wider than the specifics of the decision to invade, which was after all by the time of the election past history and not a decision that could be corrected by a change of government.

Figure 15: War in Iraq

Q Which, if any, of the following statements comes closest to your own view about the war in Iraq?

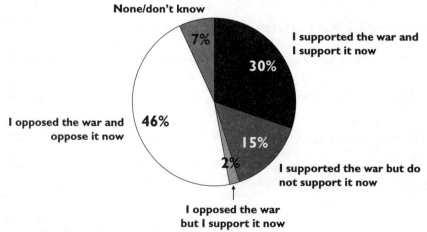

None/don't know

7%

I supported the war and
I support it now

30%

I opposed the war and
oppose it now

46%

15%

2%

I supported the war but do
not support it now

I opposed the war
but I support it now

Source: MORI/*Observer/Sunday Mirror*
Base: 1,007 GB residents aged 18+, 28-29 April 2005

It is instructive to consider the public's view of the invasion of Iraq by the time the election came round. Often in such circumstances we might expect to see a complete denial of past changes of opinion, the public unwilling to admit (whether only to us, or also to themselves) that they once held the position they now oppose. Yet recall of opinions on Iraq was relatively realistic, especially if we discount the brief surge in support at the immediate moment of invasion. 45% of the public admit they supported the war once, a third having now changed their minds. If they were called to judge Tony Blair purely on his policy judgment on this crucial issue, he might count on an almost even split.

But of course that is not the question. Trustworthiness, not competence, is the yardstick by which he had to be judged, and the fatal impression of spin at work casts doubt on all that is within its sphere. For a government accused of elevating spin over substance it was the ultimate yet inevitable irony – the spin had become more damaging than the substance and was rising up to kick its progenitors in the teeth.

The Personal Factor: Blair, the Voters and Trust

Tony Blair's satisfaction ratings coming into the 2005 general election were lower than those of any previous Prime Minister who has succeeded in being re-elected: 34% were satisfied with Blair in the final pre-campaign poll at the end of March; that was up from a low of 29% in August 2004. As we have already seen, satisfaction with Mrs Thatcher touched 27% in August 1986, the year before her third victory – but her ratings had recovered to 47% satisfied by the last pre-campaign poll. Blair's 35% final rating was only marginally better than John Major's 32% before the 1997 election. (In fact, astonishingly, the previous lowest-ever pre-election satisfaction rating for a re-elected Prime Minister was Blair's own, 44% in 2001.[59])

Figure 16: How the Public Felt Let Down

Q Which of the phrases I am going to read out best describes your trust in Tony Blair?

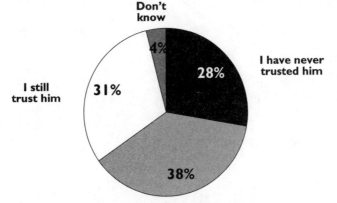

Source: MORI/*Financial Times*
Base: 1,002 GB residents aged 16+, 20-22 June 2003

---

[59] This is judging by the MORI figures since 1979 and the Gallup figures before that, as recorded in Anthony King and Robert J Wybrow, *British Political Opinion 1937-2000: The Gallup Polls* (London: Politico's Publishing, 2001), pp 183-198.

It is clear that one element in these low ratings is a collapse in the public's trust in Tony Blair personally. In late July 1997, the hopes the country had of its new leader were high. Labour won by a landslide on 1 May 1997. Psephologists and pundits alike put down the popularity of Tony Blair as the principal factor in Labour's victory. People were prepared to take him at his own valuation as "a pretty straight sort of guy". By the middle of his second term, this was no longer the case; while it is true that Michael Howard fared little if at all better, Blair had lost a major element in his appeal.

Table 33: Public Trust in Tony Blair and Conservative Leaders

Q And in general would you describe each of the following politicians as trustworthy or not?

	Oct 2000 %	Jun 2003 %	Nov 2003 %	Feb 2004 %	Jan 2005 %	Apr 2005 %
Tony Blair						
Trustworthy	46	36	35	32	32	32
Not trustworthy	49	58	58	60	57	61
Don't know	5	6	7	9	12	7
Net	**-3**	**-22**	**-23**	**-28**	**-25**	**-29**
William Hague						
Trustworthy	41					
Not trustworthy	49					
Don't know	10					
Net	**-8**					
Iain Duncan Smith						
Trustworthy		48				
Not trustworthy		36				
Don't know		16				
Net		**+12**				
Michael Howard						
Trustworthy			37	38	28	36
Not trustworthy			35	40	47	52
Don't know			28	22	26	12
Net			**+2**	**-2**	**-19**	**-16**

Source: MORI
Base: c. 1,000 GB residents aged 16+/18+ in each survey

This lack of trust was certainly compounded by the feeling of many of the public that they had trusted Blair once and been let down. As we shall see, distrust of politicians in general is almost taken for granted by the public, yet they had made an exception in Blair's case; six years later they did not. In a MORI survey[60] in June 2003, fewer than a third of the public said they "still trust" Tony Blair, while nearly four people in ten said that they "used to trust him before the beginning of the year", but "don't trust him now"; only 28% said they had never trusted him.

People in the working class and those living in council houses – Labour's natural constituency – were most likely to have lost faith in the Prime Minister.

Of course, the present government is not the first in recent history to be distrusted. In 1983, just after Mrs Thatcher's 143-seat majority victory, fewer than one person in six (16%) said they thought they could trust Government Ministers to tell the truth. In 1993, following John Major's slightly unexpected 21-seat majority in the 1992 General Election, only one person in nine (11%) said they could trust his Government's Ministers not to tell porkies.

The main focus of distrust for the Major government was the accusation of "sleaze", which was rather an all-purpose insult encompassing a number of aspects of disreputable behaviour by ministers and Conservative MPs. But even at the time it was plain that the public, far from seeing this as a specific problem of a specific government, took for granted that all politicians were the same and that Labour in office could not be expected to behave any better. Polls even before Labour's first re-election showed more than half the public believing that the Blair government was, indeed, as sleazy as the Major government had been; by February 2002 one in six thought Blair's government was worse. (See Table 34.)

Whereas attacks on the Major Government had particularly centred on the sexual misbehaviour of his MPs, justified by the ill-advised "Back to Basics" campaign and of natural delight to the tabloid press, the two elements on which the Blair government's trustworthiness has been particularly attacked are "cronyism" and the use of "spin"; the second of these has become much the more damaging, merging as it has into a wider accusation of persistent lying. The Iraq War controversy, in particular, has

---

[60] Fieldwork 20-22 June 2003 for the *Financial Times* – see Appendix 2, survey 25, for details.

given momentum to this as a personal accusation against Blair as well as a wider distrust of the government as a whole.

Table 34: Who is the Sleaziest?

Q The previous Conservative Government under John Major was accused of sleaze. Do you think the current Labour Government is more or less sleazy than the previous Conservative Government, or is there no difference between the two?

	25-26 Jan 2001 %	15 May 2001 %	21-26 Feb 2002 %
More sleazy	12	10	18
Less sleazy	30	27	22
No difference between the two Governments	54	56	54
Neither is/was sleazy	1	1	1
Don't know	2	6	4

Source: MORI
Base: c. 1,000 GB residents aged 16+/18+ (See Appendix 2, surveys 2, 3 and 11)

Issues of government trust run deeper than short-term factors and disillusionment with the present regime. The government was never likely to win its run-in with the BBC, not because of the facts of the case but because no modern government ever would. (And, notwithstanding the forced departures of the BBC's Chairman of Governors and Director-General while Tony Blair survived to win an election, the BBC has to be accounted the winner in terms of which side the majority of the public believed.) Government – not just this government but every government – has a problem: when they say something, very few people believe them.

Yet we have consistently found that even when the public distrusts or is dissatisfied with a broad class of people or institutions, it can make dramatic exceptions in favour of individuals, especially those it feels it knows well. People who say they distrust "MPs in general" or "most MPs" will often simultaneously say they trust their own local Member. Indeed, even now 61% of the public feel Charles Kennedy is trustworthy and 52% say the same of Gordon Brown. Tony Blair, at the start of his premiership, was a similar exception and it was crucial to his electoral appeal. In our leader image survey in October 1997, 36% of the public selected "more honest than most politicians" as a description fitting Tony Blair (a rating much better than it might sound, as this is not a yes-no question but involves selection of appropriate descriptions from a list, tending to elicit only the most strongly-held impressions); by April 2005, only 10% were applying that description to Mr Blair.

How much does "trust" matter? Critics sometimes suggest that it is too vague a concept, overused in polling and not capturing the crucial elements in voter motivation. But this is a complete misunderstanding and again brings us to the importance of image. "Trust", however vague the concept may seem, is clearly one of the key elements in the way people express to themselves (as well as to pollsters) their impression of people or institutions, and one which is an important driver of the decisions they make regarding them. Trust in a brand-name may lead them to try a new product that bears it; trust in a critic may lead them to watch a show or eat at a restaurant he or she endorses; and trust in a politician will play a major part in deciding whether they vote for him or his party. In this sense "trust" can be a much wider concept than belief that he or she will tell the truth.

Even when "trust" is confined to an impression of truthfulness, its consequences are highly practical. As we shall see when we turn to the public's assessment of the government's record on delivering improvements in public services, its hope of recognised achievement foundered on the public's disbelief of its factual claims.

We can see, too, how the more diverse elements of existing mistrust in government in general made the present government vulnerable to criticism of the War in Iraq and of the events which the Hutton Enquiry investigated. In July 2002, we carried out a national survey for the University of East Anglia[61] under a grant from the ESRC's Science and Society Programme. They'd asked us to look at public attitudes to science and scientists, and the information sources received by the public, and selected five topical issues to use as case studies: climate change, genetic testing, genetically modified food, radiation from mobile phone handsets, and radioactive waste, all topical, all affecting millions of citizens, and all controversial, with not all scientists in agreement as to the benefits and risks of adopting or dealing with each issue.

---

[61] The full findings are on our web site and that of the University of East Anglia, www.uea.ac.uk. For technical details see Appendix 2, survey 18.

99

On each issue, and on every test, the Government failed to persuade the British public that they can be trusted. we suspect this would be true of any government in power. In all, our colleagues at UEA asked us to examine 13 aspects of the way people feel about the Government in relation to these scientific issues: are they fair, do they change policies without good reason, do they distort facts, have the necessary skilled people to judge, share information, too influenced by industry, and so on; Table 35 shows four of the key items. The comparability of the responses across issues suggests that what we are measuring is confidence in the Government's trustworthiness, rather than reactions to each particular scientific issue.

Table 35: The Sceptical Citizenry

Q ...to what extent do you agree or disagree with the following statements?
  a. The government distorts facts in its favour regarding...
  b. The government is acting in the public interest with regard to...
  c. The government listens to what ordinary people think about...
  d. The government provides all relevant information about...to the public.

	a	b	c	d	Ave
Net scores (agree minus disagree)					
Regarding...	%	%	%	%	%
Climate change	+46	-20	-48	-55	-42
Genetic testing	+37	-9	-39	-58	-36
Genetically modified food	+44	-13	-40	-50	-37
Radiation from mobile phone handsets	+29	-17	-32	-50	-32
Radioactive waste	+50	-18	-43	-60	-43
Average	+41	-15	-40	-55	-38

Source: MORI/UEA
Base: c. 300 GB residents aged 15+ for each question, 6-31 July 2002

Does the public, then, expect the government to:

1. **Distort the facts?** On average, half the public believed that "the government distorts facts in its favour" on these issues, and only about one person in nine had confidence they did not, with from a third to nearly half the public unable to give us a guess.

2. **Act in the public interest?** More gave the Government the benefit of the doubt, but still it was only about one person in four, although nearly a third, 32%, said they thought that the Government was

acting in the public interest over the issue of genetic testing. Four in ten however were sceptical, if not cynical.

3. **Listen to public opinion?** No way. The best the Government could do was on mobile phones, where only (sic) 47% disagreed, and a pitiful 15% felt that "the government listens to what people think", and by the way 22% believed the government listened to concerns raised by the public.

4. **Come clean?** Come on. One person in ten was the best the government could do on this one, with around two-thirds still laughing at the idea.

Apply those four measures to the David Kelly enquiry and the wider issue of the genesis of the War in Iraq, and it's not hard to see why the government had a credibility problem. But any other government these days would probably get exactly the same reaction. It is also of course, quite apart from the electoral impact, a major obstacle to the government in its task of running the country.

Labour Gets the TB-GBs

One natural reaction to falling trust in the Prime Minister, and the suspicion that he might become an electoral liability, is to speculate about and perhaps promote a leadership challenge. In the last two years before the election this was fuelled by the supposed bad blood between the Prime Minister and the Chancellor of the Exchequer, Blair's alleged going back on an agreement to stand down in Brown's favour, and the feud between their parliamentary supporters. Whatever the truth of it, it was always likely to be irrelevant to the election since, however deep the hatred neither man could dislodge the other. Protected by party leadership rules that make a challenge to a sitting Prime Minister a practical impossibility, Blair could never be dislodged from Number 10 like Margaret Thatcher was – he could stay until he chose in his own good time to retire, provided of course that he won the general election.

But Brown was made almost equally secure in Number 11 by his strong performance in presiding over the economy, arguably Labour's strongest card in its bid for a third term; perhaps a rasher leader might have dismissed or reshuffled him anyway, but Tony Blair has always been politically cautious.

Traditionally, economic competence has been seen as one of Labour's weaknesses, an issue on which the Conservatives persistently have a better image and can often swing general elections.

Not any more. In terms of the relative image of the parties, Labour moved ahead of the Tories in the late 1990s as the party with the best policy on managing the economy – whereas the Tories had previously had a clear lead, at the 1997 election the two were neck-and-neck, and Gordon Brown's stewardship of the Exchequer gave Labour a clear lead by 2001.

The record (in terms of the public's perceptions, at any rate) is sound. In 2003, 78% of the public said they were satisfied with their standard of living, 63% described the present state of the economy as "good" rather than "poor" and 54% predicted the same for the economy in five years' time[62]. More were satisfied than dissatisfied with Gordon Brown's performance as Chancellor after the 2004 budget, better poll figures than

[62] Fieldwork on 10-15 April 2003, for the *Financial Times*. See Appendix 2, survey 24.

any of his predecessors in the last 20 years if slightly disappointing by his own standards.

Figure 17: Gordon Brown and His Budgets

Q Can you tell me whether you are satisfied or dissatisfied with the way Gordon Brown is doing his job as Chancellor of the Exchequer?
Q Do you think the Budget proposals are a good thing or a bad thing
(a) for you personally? (b) for the country as a whole?

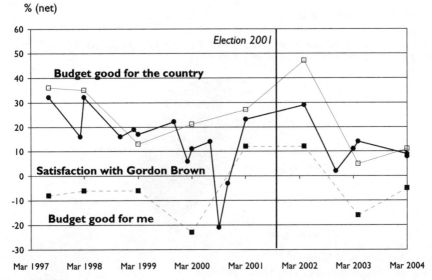

Source: MORI
Base: c. 800-1,000 GB residents aged 15+

On taxation, too, things swung Labour's way, although their lead on that issue has always been narrower since 1997 and the Tories briefly in 2000 clawed their way back to parity.

All did not go entirely smoothly for Labour, it is true. By September 2003, the Labour lead on managing the economy had slipped to only 11 points (down from 26 as recently as February 2002), and on taxation the Tories were level again. In the latter case, this may well be another consequence of growing scepticism over delivery: tolerance of taxation policies is naturally to some extent dependent on the belief that the tax revenue is being usefully employed. But Labour is more trusted on that issue than the Tories, notwithstanding the opposition's successful campaign on the issue

103

("You paid the taxes, so where are the nurses?") during the 2001 general election.

Gordon Brown has so far managed to convince the public that his budgets are, on the whole, good for the country, even though generally people have felt they are bad for them personally: in 2004, 45% said they thought the budget would be good for the country while only 34% thought it would be bad[63].

Figure 18: Value For Money?

Q Do you think a Labour or a Conservative Government would be most effective in getting good value for the public money it spends?

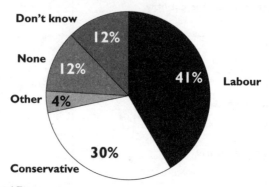

Source: MORI/*Financial Times*
Base: 1,005 GB residents aged 18+, 15-18 April 2005

Of course, Labour's slipping lead on managing the economy looked ominous, but by the time of the election the position had been almost entirely recovered. It may be, too, that fewer of those who accept that the economy is in a healthy state are prepared to give the government credit for it than was the case a couple of years ago: certainly, those who disagree that "In the long term, this government's policies will improve the state of Britain's economy" outnumbered those who agreed steadily for two years before Brown was able to return the situation to an even keel shortly before the election.

---

[63] Fieldwork on 19-23 March 2004; see Appendix 2, survey 29, for details.

Another factor, but perhaps a misleading one, is that the salience of economic issues has receded, seeming to make them of far less electoral moment. Judging by the important issues question, economic issues seem to be far less important than in the past. When Iraq or race relations are not on top of the heap, it is public services – the NHS, education, crime – that leap to the public mind, not unemployment, inflation, the economy generally or even tax, as once they might have.

Figure 19: Expectations for the Economy

Q On balance, do you agree or disagree that "In the long term, this Government's policies will improve the state of Britain's economy"?

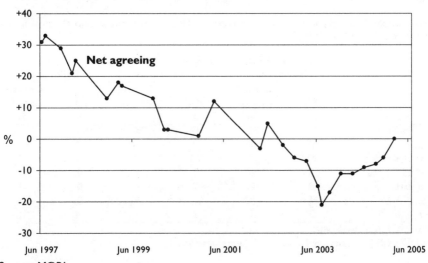

Source: MORI
Base: c. 1,000 GB residents aged 18+

It was different in the early 1990s. In March 1990, prices and inflation were seen as the second most important issue facing the country (26%), and the economy in general mentioned by 24% (fourth highest mention). In the last MORI Political Monitor before the 2005 election[64], only one in eight (12%) said the economy and just 2% mentioned prices/inflation. Voters, it seems, worry more about which party can get the country out of

---

[64] Fieldwork conducted 17-22 March; see Appendix 2, survey 33 for details.

an economic mess than they do about which is least likely to create such a mess in the first place.

Yet, what makes this significant is that comparison of the public's faith in the government's economic policies with their voting intentions shows a very clear relationship. Of those who said in February 2005[65] they would vote Labour if there were a general election tomorrow, 74% agreed that "In the long term, this government's policies will improve the state of Britain's economy", and only 15% disagreed; of Conservative voters, on the other hand, 72% disagreed and only 21% agreed.

Table 36: Voting Intention Impact of Gordon Brown as Leader

Q   How would you vote if there were a General Election tomorrow and Gordon Brown was leader of the Labour Party?

	Actual voting intention		If Gordon Brown were leader		Difference	
	All	Certain to vote	All	Certain to vote	All	Certain to vote
	%	%	%	%	%	%
Conservative	29	31	27	30	-2	-1
Labour	43	40	45	45	+2	+5
Liberal Democrats	21	21	20	19	-1	-2
SNP/Plaid Cymru	3	3	3	3	0	0
Green Party	2	2	2	1	0	-1
UKIP	1	*	1	*	0	0
Other	2	3	3	2	+1	-1

Source: MORI/*Financial Times*
Base: 1,976 GB residents aged 18+, 11-16 September 2003

Brown's position is bolstered further by his public standing – more popular than Blair, more trusted and more likely to be considered the most capable Prime Minister. When the public were asked in September 2003 how they would vote if Brown rather than Blair were leader (Table 36), Labour's share of the "certain" votes rose 5 points under Brown – what is more, Labour's share was as high among those certain to vote as among the whole public. It looked as if Brown might even be able to solve Labour's turnout problem. Certainly, the Conservatives were stupid to launch, and wise to drop like a hot potato, their apparent plan to campaign

---

[65] Fieldwork conducted 25-28 February 2005, see Appendix 2, survey 32, for details.

on a slogan of "Vote Blair, get Brown", and it was clever of Labour to respond to the short-lived Tory initiative with a "Get Two for the Price of One" response.

Yet this, of course, is mostly based on a very superficial understanding of his abilities, character and politics – he may be everything the voters think he is, but has so far kept his counsel in public that they should hardly be confident of it. The idea that he would be the champion of Old Labour, an incorrigible Eurosceptic or an anti-American opponent of the "War on Terror" who would immediately pull British troops out of Iraq, all of which some of his backers seem to believe, is almost certainly nonsense.

A Brown pitch-forked into the leadership say three weeks before an election might possibly indeed achieve such a transformation purely on a honeymoon effect; but given a long enough period in Number 10 for the public to start judging him on his own record and personality, it could easily be a different story. He might do far worse than this poll suggests. He might even do better. But at the moment the public don't know him remotely well enough to predict their own voting behaviour.

Five Tests Worth Failing

Perhaps one minor political benefit the government received from the concentration on Iraq was the diversion of attention from its failure to call a referendum on entering the Euro; and Blair certainly had Brown to thank for enabling him to avoid a major political embarrassment.

Table 37: European Single Currency – Voting in a Referendum

Q If there were a referendum now on whether Britain should be part of a Single European Currency, how would you vote?
Q If the Government were to strongly urge that Britain should be part of a single European currency, how would you vote?

		Referendum now			If government were to urge		
		In favour	Against	Don't know	In favour	Against	Don't know
June 2001	%	25	55	20	30	53	17
Aug-Sep 2001	%	25	57	17	29	55	16
October 2001	%	26	57	17	31	53	15
January 2002	%	33	51	15	39	47	14
Feb-Mar 2002	%	30	55	14	35	51	15
May 2002	%	31	53	16	36	50	14
July 2002	%	31	55	14	35	52	13
September 2002	%	29	56	15	35	52	13
November 2002	%	31	55	15	35	51	14
January 2003	%	31	57	11	34	56	11
Mar-Apr 2003	%	30	56	13	34	52	13
May 2003	%	29	58	12	33	54	13
June 2003	%	27	59	14	32	55	12
September 2003	%	24	61	15	28	59	13
February 2004	%	28	60	12	31	57	11
June 2004	%	26	61	12	29	59	11
Oct-Nov 2004	%	24	62	13	27	60	13
February 2005	%	26	57	16	30	55	15

Source: MORI Financial Services/Citigroup
Base: c. 2,000 GB residents aged 16+ on each survey

At one point Europe seemed the issue closest to Tony Blair's heart and the single currency his best chance of "securing a place in history". But the public have never shared his enthusiasm for the European project. Throughout the Parliament, polls showed opponents of the Euro outnumbering its supporters by two-to-one.

Some optimists believed that support for the Euro would build of its own accord once the currency was up and running successfully on the continent and British visitors had had a chance to use it and appreciate its convenience. Fat chance! The introduction of the single European Currency and coinage on 1 January 2002 came and went. But British opposition remained stubbornly solid, even before it became clear from polls on the continent that the public in some countries of the Euro-zone were beginning to repent of their bargain.

Of course, the polls in advance do not take into account any changes of opinion that might be achieved during the campaign, and EU supporters well remember the 22% swing in six months under Harold Wilson's government before the 1975 referendum on staying in the Common Market. But, as our regular polls for Citigroup (Table 37) have demonstrated, only a small proportion of the public have such faith in the government (even with Gordon Brown as Chancellor) that they admit they would take its advice and be swayed in the Euro's favour if so urged. On average over the last four years, the increase in the "yes" strength has been only just over 4% of the public.

Naturally, a full-scale political campaign preceding a referendum would hope to make more impact than this. We have developed a separate survey question on support for the Euro that measures not only the size of the "pro" and "anti" camps but how certain they are that they will not change their minds; this consistently finds between two in five and a half of all adults open to persuasion, saying "I am generally in favour of British entry into the Single European Currency, but I could be persuaded to vote against it if I thought it was in Britain's economic interests to do so", or "I am generally opposed to British entry into the Single European Currency, but I could be persuaded to vote for it if I thought it was in Britain's economic interests to do so". In July 2004, for example, more than half of those who have a view said they might be persuaded to change their minds, equally split between those "generally in favour" of joining the Euro (26% of the public) and those "generally opposed" (24%). So there is potential scope for a swing.

It might be noted that the overall balance of views is less hostile when elicited by the four-way question than by the simpler for-against method: the July 2004 survey found 36% saying they were in favour of Britain participating in the single currency, whereas using the simpler question the

109

highest number in favour at any time during the Parliament was 33%, and the survey nearest in time to July 2004 found just 26%. This may indicate that some of those who would not vote to join the single currency "now" nevertheless support it in principle when the time is ripe.

Figure 20: British Support for Joining the Euro

Q Which of the following best describes your own view of British participation in the single currency?

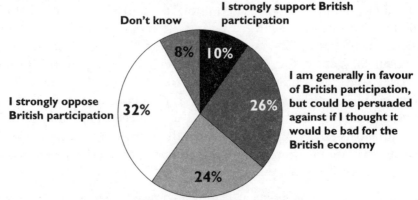

Source: MORI/Foreign Policy Centre
Base: 1,063 GB residents aged 15+, 22-27 July 2004

But even on this less daunting set of figures, opponents of the single currency outnumber its supporters by a wide margin, and three times as many are strongly against joining as are strongly in favour, a big hurdle to overcome in a referendum where differential turnout might be as much a factor as the overall balance of opinions.

Nor, as some have feared (or hoped), could the referendum be rigged by manipulating the wording. We consistently and continually hear from politicians: "What matters is how you ask the question (and so forth) in a referendum". They are wrong. Of course, as pollsters we are always alive to the sometimes dramatic effects on our results that changes in question wording can have. In February 2005, when the wording of the question to

110

be used in the proposed European constitution referendum was released, "Should the United Kingdom approve the treaty establishing a constitution for the European Union?", ICM used it in a poll and got results widely divergent from those produced by the carefully-crafted neutral opinion poll questions at the same period[66].

But opinion polls are not the same as referendums. Polls are top of mind; referendums are not. Polls are ongoing; here today, gone tomorrow. They are not binding. When an interviewer on behalf of a polling organisation asks your opinions, your attitudes or your values, your behaviour or your knowledge, it is not binding. You do not feel an obligation to think carefully and thoroughly about what it is that is being asked. It is relatively unimportant; it is not something you have thought about necessarily, you are just courteous enough to answer the questions. The media will not have covered the question matter in advance, for the most part, and the wording is vital – if it is biased or seems to point you in some direction, you may be swayed. (More than half a century's experience has taught pollsters, for example, always to explicitly point out the alternatives. We would always – unless carrying out a deliberate experiment, as ICM were – end a straight question like the referendum wording with "... or not?". Having not done so may explain the entire apparent discrepancy in the findings of the ICM referendum wording poll.)

Referendums on the other hand are considered. At the end of a three- or four-week campaign people know what is at issue, and the people who cast their vote have thought something about it. It is not sprung on them, nor is it a surprise to them that elicits an instant response. It is on a certain day; you know when it is. If you intend to vote, you're ready for it. It is morally binding because the electorate has been asked by their elected government to help them decide on an issue – normally, in this country, of sovereignty.

A referendum is by definition nationally important and because of that, it is the subject of media focus, and frankly the wording is very unimportant. Because of the wording of the Italian constitution, when they had a referendum on abortion in 1981, you had to "Vote 'No' to say 'Yes'". And

---

[66] ICM interviewed random samples of 522 and 506 adults aged 18+ on 2-3 February 2005, on behalf of Vote No. Data were weighted to the profile of all adults. Using the referendum question, 39% said the UK should approve the treaty; using ICM's standard "referendum tomorrow" question, 26% said they would vote "yes".

so that was the slogan of the people who were for keeping abortion legal, and everybody knew exactly what was at issue and how they were voting. That is not so in an opinion poll.

True, there might in theory be a substantial advantage for the government in its power to dictate the *timing* of a referendum. But that pre-supposes that there is some point in time when the government could win, and that has simply never been the case with the Euro – nor, we can see in retrospect, was it ever likely that it would be. Much is made of the volatility of public opinion on such matters, but with little significant movement in the public's hostility to the Euro over many years now, it is difficult to see how the europhiles can garner enough support to chance a vote on the Euro in the foreseeable future.

More threatening, perhaps, is the government's power to keep on asking the question until they get an answer that they like; but even that loses much of its sting if the answer is clearly going to be the same time after time. There was no time during the 2001-5 Parliament when Blair could have called a referendum on the Euro without the virtual certainty of failure and humiliation.

Calling and losing a referendum would certainly have been politically disastrous. To do so would destroy his credibility and that of his Government in the same way that the events of 16 September 1992 destroyed the Conservative Government of John Major and that of his Chancellor Norman Lamont when the pound fell out of the ERM. Why would Prime Minister Blair risk it? What's in it for him?

There is no pressure on the Prime Minister to do anything about the Euro. Fortunately for the government, the "five tests" which Blair had declared must be met before he would call a referendum left plenty of room for political manoeuvre. (It helped that the public understood little about them. In a MORI poll for the *News of the World* back in June 2000, we found only 8% who could name even one of the five tests and not a single respondent who could name them all.)

So, few can have been very surprised when Gordon Brown announced in June 2003 that the Euro had failed to meet the five economic tests. A potential political booby trap had been safely circumvented.

Delivery

But all the foregoing considerations are, in a sense, distractions. The government was not primarily re-elected in 2001 to fight terrorists, or to join the Euro. What about the day job?

The public values, and fears for, its services. Though issues such as Iraq today or unemployment in the 1980s may be forced onto the public's agenda by circumstances, public services consistently score highly among the public's concerns – in particular, the National Health Service. When asked what were the most important issues facing the country, the NHS was the most frequently named single issue in all but six monthly surveys in the first five years of the present Labour government. Labour, of course, has enhanced the importance of its performance on public services by making them the basis of central pledges in both its 1997 and 2001 election campaigns.

But for the intrusion of international events, then, we might have expected Labour's delivery on its public services pledges to have been the central fact in the public's judgment of the government's record and in the voters' decision on whether to allow Tony Blair a third term; and even allowing for Iraq, it was a significant factor in the election. Perceptions of service delivery have tended to be closely related to voting intention throughout the Parliament.

It is not enough, of course, for the government simply to fulfil their pledges to their own satisfaction. Delivery is a subjective concept, and it is the voters' verdicts, not those of the politicians nor those of neutral experts, which matter. Not only are the public harsh judges, but they imbue their judgments with a degree of inbuilt pessimism and scepticism, so that they consistently tend to assume that the overall national picture is worse than their own personal experience or local services would suggest. Probably partly as a result of this, and partly because of a general distrust of government claims and official statistics, few of the government's claims about successful improvement of services are believed by most of the public: they feel the government has not delivered, and they are less optimistic than they were in 2001 that it will eventually do so, though Labour clawed back some ground before the election.

113

What Does "Delivery" Really Mean?

It is simply not enough for a government to improve services, or to pursue any other policy successfully, in the knowledge that the public will recognise the success; if that success is not communicated to the voters, it will have no political pay-off.

The public will only be moved by their own perceptions of what the government has done, which may or may not be accurate. Image, not substance, again. Unfortunately for governments, people are not naturally inclined to believe that things are getting better: we frequently find a sort of "nostalgia" effect in polling (in many different subjects, not just political ones): the public's tendency, all other things being equal, is to consider that things have got worse. (This is even true when their own levels of satisfaction, as measured by contemporary polls, are higher than in the past).

Delivery as a political end means delivery to the satisfaction of the voter or consumer, not achieving some more objective level of performance. Lord Saatchi expressed the fundamental relationship in marketing as "Satisfaction equals Performance minus Expectation"[67]; we would go further, as this insight omits a crucial factor – more accurately, satisfaction equals *perceived* performance minus expectations.

Further, achieving politically-effective "delivery" is specifically concerned with meeting the expectations that the government raised in the people that voted for it – in New Labour's case over improvement of standards in public services. Taking these two points together, we can state a general principle (which is intended not as a comment on New Labour, but on the subjective nature of any electoral judgment):

> **"Delivery" is not keeping your promises; it is convincing the public that you have kept your promises.**

This is more complex than it might appear, since it depends not only on the public's perception of the government's performance but on their understanding of what promise was made in the first place: if the public

---

[67] Which he specifically formulated as "Saatchi's Law" in a speech to the Conservative Party Conference in October 2004.

comes to believe that what was promised coincides with what in fact has been achieved, then they will believe the promise has been kept.

This might seem merely an invitation to the cynicism of politicians and their spin doctors. But in fact they are far more likely to be victims than perpetrators of this "false delivery syndrome", for few spin doctors are half as good at deluding the public as the public are at deluding themselves. If there is a discrepancy between the promise as made and the promise as understood by the voters at the following election, this may well be because the voters themselves chose not to interpret the promise as the politician who made it intended.

What matters is not what you promise, but what the public understands by those promises, and what expectations they arouse

and, as a corollary of this

A government may not have full control over what it is held to have promised.

This clearly poses a potential problem for governments. Even realistic promises may create unrealistic expectations; and worse, the public may move the goalposts.

This may mean that almost any reforming government is fighting a losing battle. No matter how specific the details of New Labour's policy pledges on, say, the NHS, if the public simply interprets it as meaning "a Labour government will improve the NHS sufficiently to meet with my approval", can it hope to do it? Clearly not if the standards necessary to secure public approval are unattainable.

So an election-winning prescription might be

Underpromise and over deliver [68]

---

[68] This is precisely the opposite of the natural scheme of things – parties, especially opposition parties aspiring to governmental power, tend to over-promise and under-deliver. See Paul R Baines, Ross Brennan and John Egan, "'Market' Classification and Political Campaigning: Some Strategic Implications", *Journal of Political Marketing*, Vol 2, no 2 (2003), 47-66.

The Local-General Paradox

The limited ability of a government to control the setting of its own appraisal targets is currently being further exacerbated by the way the public judges the government's performance. "Joined-up government" has come to be an over-used catchphrase of recent years, but the government might just as well complain that they are not faced with a "joined-up public": the public seems unprepared to translate satisfaction with personal experience or local provision of services into a satisfaction with the national performance – there is significantly higher satisfaction at local than at national level even though it might seem as if the national position can be no more than the aggregate of all the local ones. The public judge standards of public services not, apparently, by their own experiences, but by a general impression derived from many sources which paints a much gloomier picture. Contrary to received wisdom, the grass always seems greener on our own side of the fence.

It is a problem of which the government is well aware. Tony Blair explained it to Labour's Spring Conference in March 2004[69]:

> "There is much scratching of the head in political circles over this apparent paradox: People who feel personally optimistic in Britain; but collectively pessimistic. They say their own health care in the NHS is good; but the NHS in general is bad. Their schools are good; but education is bad. They are safer; but the country is less safe. Their future is bright; but the nation's is dark."

The Prime Minister may well have been specifically referring to a MORI survey for the Department of Health conducted between November 2003 and February 2004. This found that while 67% of the public agreed that "My local NHS is providing me with a good service", only 48% would admit that "The NHS is providing a good service nationally". This translated to 59% of the sample saying they were "satisfied" with the NHS, and yet only 30% agreeing that "The government has the right policies for the NHS". This is clearly a problem for the government.

---

[69] Tony Blair, Speech to Labour's Spring Conference, Manchester, 13 March 2004

Surveys consistently find this dichotomy of opinions in other public services as well, as comparison of Table 38 with Table 39 (taken from the same survey) will show.

Table 38: Satisfaction with Public Services Nationally

Q I am going to read out a list of public services. From what you know or have heard, please tell me how satisfied or dissatisfied you are with the way each service is provided for Britain as a whole?

		Satisfied	Dissat-isfied	Neither/don't know	Net
Primary schools	%	60	11	28	+49
Secondary schools	%	48	21	31	+27
Bus services	%	48	28	24	+20
Train services	%	32	43	25	-11
Police	%	57	32	12	+25
GPs	%	70	21	9	+49
NHS hospitals	%	57	30	12	+27

Source: MORI/Cabinet Office
Base: 1,000 GB residents aged 18+, 26-29 March 2004

Table 39: Satisfaction with Public Services Locally

Q I am going to read out a list of public services. From what you know or have heard, please tell me how satisfied or dissatisfied you are with the way each service is provided in your local area?

		Satisfied	Dissat-isfied	Neither/don't know	Net
Primary schools	%	65	8	26	+57
Secondary schools	%	55	17	27	+38
Bus services	%	52	27	20	+25
Train services	%	43	30	27	+13
Police	%	59	30	12	+29
GPs	%	78	17	5	+61
NHS hospitals	%	65	24	11	+41

Source: MORI/Cabinet Office
Base: 1,000 GB residents aged 18+, 26-29 March 2004

This is not unique to the problems of national government. In MORI's work for local government, for example, we consistently find a picture of very high satisfaction with individual services: user satisfaction ratings of more than 90% are common for libraries and secondary schools, and very few authorities record less than 80% satisfied with their refuse collection.

117

Yet satisfaction with the way a council is running the area typically stands at 55% to 65%.

Nor is this disjunction confined to perceptions of public service delivery. The public are consistently more satisfied with the performance of their own MP than with MPs as a whole; they are more optimistic about the financial prospects for their own household in the near future than for the economy as a whole. This mode of thinking seems to be built into the way public opinion is formed at the moment; but it gives New Labour a real problem in convincing the public that it is delivering improvements in public services.

Scepticism About the Government's Claims

Nor are they helped by a lack of any public confidence in Official Statistics[70]. Even if services are improving, the message, it seems, will not spread itself: the government has not succeeded in convincing the public that it is delivering.

In Table 40, a survey for the Cabinet Office in March 2004 testing public acceptance of a series of "positive delivery facts" is shown. All but the four italicised items are statements that the government claimed as true at the time of the survey and for which "objective performance data of delivery exists"; the remaining four are negative. It will be seen that four of the seven most widely believed statements were the negative ones, and that two – that violent crime is rising and that asylum applications are higher than five years ago – were thought to be true by four-fifths of the public. Only six of the "delivery facts" were believed by more than they were disbelieved by, whereas fifteen were more disbelieved than believed. Subsequent surveys by ICM in May-June and September 2004, also for the Cabinet Office and using a slightly different list of statements[71], found some increase in acceptance, but still only 8 of 25 were believed to be true by the majority of respondents.

---

[70] As recognised in the report by the Statistics Commission, "Legislation To Build Trust In Statistics" (May 2004), which concluded that "the level of public trust [in statistics] is currently lower than is desirable in a modern democratic state in which so much of policy and operational decision-making rests on an evidence base largely composed of statistics".

[71] Details at www.icmresearch.co.uk.

But not only does the public fail to accept that delivery on promises about public services has already occurred, but they have proved reluctant to believe that it will be achieved any time in the near future. Each quarter during the last Parliament, MORI's Social Research Institute looked at the public's predictions of the Government's delivery on the key issues facing the country. The Delivery Index measures expectations for public services generally as well as on five key public service areas – education, the NHS, public transport, policing, and the environment.

Table 40: Public Perceptions of Delivery, 2004

Q I am now going to read out a number of statements about how Britain's public services have changed over the last few years. For each one, I would like you to tell me whether you think it is true or false.

	True %	False %	Don't know %
Violent crime is rising	83	13	3
Asylum applications are higher now than 5 years ago	80	14	6
The number of students going to university is the highest ever	71	21	9
Truancy levels are the highest ever	68	22	10
Breast cancer treatment is now the fastest ever	62	23	16
Road improvements to tackle congestion are under way	61	35	4
Average waiting times for NHS surgery have increased	58	36	6
Exam results in schools are now the best ever	55	36	9
Fewer people die from cancer and heart disease	53	40	6
More money is being invested in public transport	49	44	8
Patients have more choice about their treatment and care	46	46	8
Old trains are being replaced with new ones	45	47	9
Police numbers are the highest ever	43	47	10
Getting a GP appointment is quicker	39	56	5
There is faster access to treatment in NHS hospitals	36	57	7
Fewer people are killed or seriously injured on the roads	35	58	8
There are smaller class sizes in primary and secondary schools	31	57	13
Asylum applications have fallen dramatically in the last 12 months	28	63	9
There are thousands more doctors and nurses working in the NHS	27	65	9
There are free nursery places for all 4 year olds	27	52	21
There are more train services	27	59	14
Burglary has been cut by 40%	26	65	9
More people are using buses	26	67	8
There are stricter penalties for persistent offenders	24	70	6
There are thousands more teachers	22	69	9
Crime is falling	20	76	4

Source: MORI/Cabinet Office
Base: 1,000 GB residents aged 18+, 26-29 March 2004

Labour was re-elected in 2001 with the public placing a great deal of faith in its capabilities – a majority of the public (far more than actually voted Labour, in fact) believed that in the long term the government's policies would improve public services. But this optimism quickly faded. By March 2002, the majority were predicting the opposite, and continued to do right up to the eve of the election; only in the post-election measure (13-15 May 2005) do we see the government almost breaking even, and perhaps indicating that a widening of belief in its abilities may have been one factor contributing to its re-election.

Table 41: Expectations for Public Services

Q On balance, do you agree or disagree with the statement that "in the long term, this government's policies will improve the state of Britain's public services"?

		Agree	Disagree	Net agree
21-26 June 2001	%	54	32	+22
18-24 October 2001	%	45	42	+3
29 November 2001	%	46	40	+6
15-17 March 2002	%	36	54	-18
24-26 May 2002	%	38	50	-12
5-8 September 2002	%	38	52	-14
13-16 December 2002	%	35	52	-17
28-31 March 2003	%	36	50	-14
20-22 June 2003	%	31	59	-28
7-8 July 2003	%	28	62	-34
19-21 September 2003	%	31	57	-26
12-14 December 2003	%	30	57	-27
19-23 March 2004	%	37	55	-18
18-20 June 2004	%	39	52	-13
17-20 September 2004	%	35	54	-19
26-30 November 2004	%	36	54	-18
25-27 February 2005	%	39	52	-13
13-15 May 2005	%	43	45	-2

Source: MORI Delivery Index (now the Deloitte/MORI Index)
Base: c. 1,000 GB residents aged 18+

Figure 21 charts expectations for the five individual service areas – will they get better, stay the same or get worse over the next few years? The net scores (the percentage expecting the service to improve minus the percentage expecting it to get worse) show the public has been consistently more optimistic about the future of education than the other four, with the plurality usually predicting improvement. Net scores on the quality of the environment have always been among the worst, and this has been much clearer in the last couple of years.

But politically more interesting are the public's most cherished service, the NHS, and public transport. Both hit a trough in mid 2003 when the number of pessimists about their future substantially outnumbered the optimists, partly no doubt because the public felt the government was being distracted by the war in Iraq. However, both figures subsequently rose sharply in the last few months before the election, as the government began to get its message across.

Figure 21: MORI Delivery Index

Q Thinking about ... over the next few years, do you expect it to get better or worse?

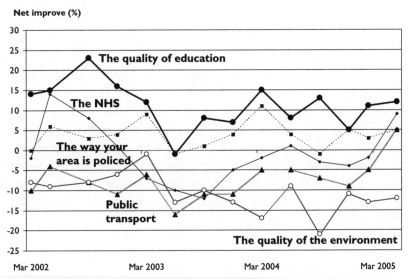

Source: MORI Delivery Index (now the Deloitte/MORI Index)
Base: c. 600-1,000 GB residents aged 16+ each survey

Relating Delivery and Voting Intention

There is a clear relationship between faith in the government's ability to deliver and voting intention. In February 2005, MORI's final pre-election Delivery Index, we found 39% of the public agreeing that "In the long term, this government's policies will improve the state of Britain's public services" and 52% disagreeing. Those who agreed split two-to-one in Labour's favour in their voting intentions (56% said they would vote Labour at a general election and 27% for other parties, with 17% don't knows, won't votes or won't says). Those who disagreed, on the other hand, intended to vote nearly three-to-one against Labour (35% Conservative, 20% Liberal Democrat and 9% for minor parties, only 13% Labour; 23% had declared no voting intention). Labour voters also took a net optimistic view on all five of the individual policy areas (ranging from +6 on the environment to +41 on education), while both Tories and Liberal Democrats took a pessimistic view in every case.

Of course, we can't say in which direction this relationship operates: it might just as well be that those people who generally trust and have faith in the government – and are therefore most likely to vote Labour – are for that reason likely to believe in the government's capabilities in public services, as vice-versa. If the former, it would be pointless for the government to concentrate on delivery as a passport to electoral success, since that would put the cart before the horse. However, the fact that Liberal Democrat strength is not highly correlated with the delivery question (15% among those who agree, 20% among those who disagree) implies perhaps that public services are a driver of faith in the government rather than vice-versa, since one would otherwise expect that those who demonstrated their general lack of trust in Labour by defecting to the LibDems would be disproportionately sceptical of government claims for its public service policies as well. But whichever is true, it seems plain that perceptions of the government's public service policies are closely tied up with Labour voting.

Public Service Policies

So much for the overview. What views does the public have of the specific public services policies that the government has adopted or should adopt?

The general image of public services seems to be that they are worthy and often important, and staffed by dedicated public servants who struggle against poor management, bureaucracy and above all inadequate funding. In September 2001, two-thirds of the public considered them "under-funded" and two in five "bureaucratic". Just as revealing are the descriptions at the bottom of the list: only one in twenty thought of public services as "open", and almost as few "honest" or (perhaps worst of all) "good value for money". What is worse, the image deteriorated significantly between 1998 and 2001.

Table 42: Perceptions of Public Services

Q. These are some words that people have used to describe public services (like schools or hospitals). Please read through the list, and read out the letters that you think apply.

	1998 %	2001 %	Change %
Under-funded	69	68	-1
Friendly	37	20	-17
Bureaucratic	34	41	+7
Hardworking	34	30	-4
Keen to help	31	17	-14
Efficient	23	11	-12
Faceless	22	21	-1
Infuriating	20	23	+3
Unresponsive	18	17	-1
Unaccountable	18	18	0
Good value for money	15	8	-7
Honest	14	7	-7
Open	9	5	-4

Source: MORI/Cabinet Office/New Local Government Network
Base: c. 5,000 GB residents aged 16+ (1998); c. 2,000 GB residents aged 15+ (2001)

Table 43: Tax and Spend

Q People have different views about whether it is more important to reduce taxes or keep up government spending. How about you? Which of these statements comes closest to your own view?

	25-28 April 1997 %	2-3 Nov 2000 %	7-9 Apr 2005 %
Taxes being cut, even if it means some reduction in government services, such as health, education and welfare	7	12	15
Things should be left as they are	14	20	23
Government services such as health, education and welfare should be extended, even if it means some increases in taxes	76	61	56
Don't know	3	7	6

Source: MORI
Base: c. 1,000 GB residents aged 18+ on each survey

The public's preferred solution to the perceived ills of the public services, is, therefore, greatly increased funding, and indeed the majority often express themselves willing to pay higher taxes to achieve this. (Table 43.) Even though the most recent survey in our series, during the 2005 election, shows a continuing decline in the number calling for increased spending since the days immediately before Blair was first elected, those who say they would prefer public service improvements even at the cost of higher taxes remain a majority of the electorate.

A MORI survey in 2002 found a very clearly defined priority for public spending increases, with expansion of public services programmes supported by the overwhelming majority, but most preferring to keep steady or even cut spending on defence and foreign aid[72].

Figure 22: The Public's Spending Priorities

Q I am going to read out a list of government programs. For each, tell me whether you feel it should be expanded, cut back or kept about the same.

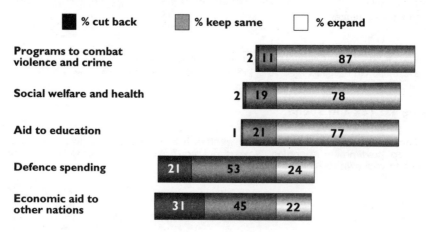

Source: MORI/German Marshall Fund of the US/CCFR
Base: 1,000 GB residents 18+, 5-30 June 2002

---

[72] Fieldwork on 5-30 June 2002 for the German Marshall Fund of the United States and the Chicago Council on Foreign Relations; see Appendix 2, survey 16, for details.

But bearing in mind that "good value for money" perception, taxpayers will expect to see tangible improvements for their investment. The government may be right to be wary of tax rises to fund public services, however much the taxpaying public claims to want them.

Furthermore, the means of funding adopted must be sensitive to public opinion. In November 2001, ICM found[73] that 54% of the public said they would be willing to pay more in income tax to "fund the recovery of the National Health Service", but 82% thought that "the government should consider options other than raising income tax to improve the NHS". A MORI poll in 2000 which explicitly set out possible options found funding from the national lottery was the most popular means of raising NHS funding, with diversion of funds from other areas of government expenditure also favoured by considerably more than increased taxation, which was only favoured by just over a quarter of the public[74]. Again this raises the suspicion that voters will resent feeling the cost of public service investment in their pockets – unless they are very sure that the pain is worthwhile (which, as we have seen, may be a big ask with an instinctively sceptical public).

Widening Choice

One key strategy in the government's attempt to maximise public satisfaction with services has been the aim to introduce more freedom of choice for service users or customers, and policy-makers and practitioners have concentrated a lot of time and effort into determining how greater choice might look on the ground. However, this is an area where the professionals are ahead of the public in their thinking, particularly in the detail. While there has been some research into public attitudes to choice, the results are not always consistent. Nevertheless, some broad conclusions about the public mood seem clear.

Choice is attractive. It is associated with incentive, better customer service, and giving power back to the citizen. People especially expect to have a

---

[73] ICM interviewed 545 adults aged 18+ on 29 November 2001 for the *News of the World*. Full details at www.icmresearch.co.uk.
[74] Fieldwork 22-27 June 2000 for the British Medical Association; see Appendix 2, survey 1, for details.

choice in the different ways they can access services (e.g. face to face, telephone, email). However, some of this desire for choice may reflect a deeper desire to feel listened to.

People don't think they have much choice at the moment. They also say that if they had they would take advantage of it, for example to get a choice of hospital if it would mean a quicker operation.

However, choice is not the top priority for public services. This is summed up in the view, "If it's a monopoly and it's good, I don't need any choice". Typically, when asked, people want to see more staff and resources, and better outcomes, rather than more choice – which is seen as "icing on the cake".

Nor are people sure how choice will improve standards across the board for all. Instead, choice is seen as a zero-sum game – I win, you lose – in which one person may benefit by getting their personal preference, but only at the expense of someone else getting a worse option. If this is not the reality of the government's choice policy – and clearly it is not intended to be – the message needs to be communicated much better.

Table 44: Anticipated Effects of Subsidising Private Sector Services

Q Do you think that giving people a government subsidy to use private hospitals will make the NHS better, worse or make no difference at all?
Q Do you think that giving people a government subsidy to use private hospitals would make the quality of healthcare available to you better, worse or make no difference at all?
Q Do you think that giving people a government subsidy to use private schools will make schools better, worse or make no difference at all?*

| | Private hospitals | | | Private schools | |
| | The NHS | | Available to you | Schools | |
	2-4 July 2004	21-25 April 2005	21-25 April 2005	2-4 July 2004*	21-25 April 2005
	%	%	%	%	%
Better	21	27	34	12	18
Worse	31	31	22	36	32
No difference	41	36	40	46	41
Don't know	6	6	4	6	9

Source: MORI
*Asked as "...make the state schools better..." in 2004.

Table 44 demonstrates this fear in the case of two public services, health and education, over the specific possibility of increasing choice by subsidising the cost of private services. In both cases, more expected the effect on public services to be negative rather than positive – even though in the case of the NHS far fewer expected that they would suffer themselves.

When people start to think about choice in more detail, they begin to see potential problems. In particular, they are concerned about the creation of sink schools or ghetto areas for public services while good schools and hospitals suffer from over-subscribing (perhaps a natural follow-on from their conception of choice as a zero-sum game), about being offered "bogus" choice rather than a real choice, and about the information-rich benefiting over the information-poor. Worse, there are worries about choice getting in the way of swift action in the case of an emergency.

Consequently, information, and the role of professionals, is crucial. Very few of the public feel confident that they can make a correct choice unaided; most would want advice and information to help them in their decision – particularly pensioners, people from working class backgrounds, and black and minority ethnic users. The views of professionals are central to the debate, as doctors and teachers rather than politicians or bureaucrats will be those people trust most to help them make their choices. However, we know that they have their own concerns about the impact of more choice in public services, particularly around increased bureaucracy, the danger of creating a two-tier system, and patients with higher (unrealistic?) expectations making ill-informed choices.

Choice, therefore, may be a viable policy but it is also a risky one – certainly no guaranteed vote-spinner in the short term.

The Private Finance Initiative (PFI)

Intimately tied up with questions of choice is the government's reliance on the Private Finance Initiative as one avenue for improving public services. Although the left has set its face against this policy, the public is by no means so clear in its rejection of it; if PFI can produce a perceived improvement in public services, it is unlikely to be unpopular.

127

The question of the acceptability to the public of PFI, or any other manifestation of private sector involvement in public services, needs to be considered in the context of the effectiveness of the expedient in bringing about recognisable improvement, or the public's belief that it will. Delivery is much more important to the public than process. Thus, a September 2001 MORI survey which asked respondents to pick the definitions which were closest to what they meant by "public services" found the most frequently selected definitions were that they should be "available for everybody to use" (40%) and that the service should be "important for the whole community" (38%). A quarter (25%) felt it to be a defining characteristic that the service should be paid for through taxes, yet only 4% felt it crucial it should be "free at the point of use". More importantly, only 22% defined public services as being managed by central or local government and 10% that the staff should be employed by central or local government; and, furthermore, only 12% specified that the service should be non-profit making. This clearly suggests an open field for greater private sector involvement, or even total provision of a public service by the commercial sector, provided the service was provided well and made universally available.

Yet this is not to say that, all things being equal, the public would not prefer public services to be provided by the public sector. In an August 2001 survey, 64% of the public said that their view was that schools, 64% hospitals, 57% trains, 46% "public sector utilities like water and gas" and 43% pensions should be "entirely" or "mostly" provided by public sector companies[75].

Probably this attitude feeds at least partly on a fear that partial privatisation will be a precursor of diminished and eventually disappearing services. But this view, also, is a minority one.

Qualitative research has found that, while there tends to be agreement among the public that the public sector is inefficient by comparison with the private sector, this is subject to two qualifications. First, inefficiency is not only confined to the public sector – participants believe that some private sector organisations are just as inefficient (regular readers of *Private Eye* will immediately think of some of that organ's bugbears among the

---

[75] Fieldwork on 23-28 August 2001, for *The Times* - see Appendix 2, survey 5, for details.

companies providing contracted-out services to local and central government), while others believe that inefficiency is a function of size rather than any public-private divide.

Second, many do not consider inefficiency to be always a crucial consideration; irrespective of efficiency, people often trust the public sector more because the service is accountable to the public, whereas the private sector is governed by the needs of shareholders. Because of this, there remains strong support for the public sector ethos. Participants already perceive there to be a lack of clear responsibility in terms of the subcontracting of basic council services and this impacts negatively on support for wider relations between the public and private sectors. Indeed, the public appear more accepting of some public-private partnerships if the public sector retains overall management, and hence accountability, of the service.

Again, the government's policy is by no means necessarily a vote-loser, but it needs careful handling.

The Conservative Leadership

Meanwhile, like an old silent film played on a modern projector, the Tory leadership saga continued its jerky progress at an even-faster-than-natural rate. If it is a silent movie, it probably features the Keystone Kops. William Hague had been the first Conservative leader since Alec Douglas-Home never to win a general election; his successor, Iain Duncan Smith ("IDS"), became the first since Austen Chamberlain to be ousted by his own MPs before he even had a chance to fight one[76].

William Hague had been an unsuccessful leader, and probably the wrong leader at that time, yet it was perfectly reasonable to consider him leadership material. The election of "IDS", by contrast, was an aberration of the type few but the current Conservative Party could have achieved; yet his choice was the entirely predictable outcome of the misguided electoral system as it operated in the circumstances following William Hague's precipitate resignation.

The key to understanding it, as to much else that is wrong with the Conservative Party, is that for more than a decade Conservatives have been unable to conceal the fact that they hate each other far more than they hate their political opponents or what they stand for.

Table 45: Conservative Party Leadership Election, 2001

	First round	Second round	Third round	Members' ballot
Kenneth Clarke	36	39	59	100,864
Iain Duncan Smith	39	42	54	155,933
Michael Portillo	49	50	53	Excluded
Michael Ancram	21	17	Excluded	
David Davis	21	18	Withdrew	

The electoral system introduced under William Hague provided that the Conservative MPs would select two candidates, who would then be put to a postal vote of the paid-up membership. This not only created a risk that

---

[76] Neville Chamberlain, who also never led the party in a general election, remained Conservative leader after Churchill's appointment as Prime Minister in May 1940, and resigned the leadership only through ill health five months later, only weeks before he died.

a leader might be elected who could not command the confidence of the majority of the party's MPs (which, after all, is also possible with Labour's electoral college), but that the professional politicians were excluded entirely from voting in the final stage of the decision – the point at which, for the first time, there was a clear choice to which their experience and knowledge of the qualities required by a leader might be applied.

Nobody can have doubted that the membership, euro-sceptic almost to the last blue-rinse and twin-set, would vote for almost any other candidate in preference to Kenneth Clarke – a tragedy for the party in that he was in every other way eminently suitable for the job, both much the best-known and liked of the candidates among the wider public (for which read floating voters). Nevertheless, had Clarke's opponent in the final round been Michael Portillo, the outcome would have been less predictable, as Portillo equally faced a band of implacable opponents among the membership who would not have voted for a "moderniser". But the key to the situation was that the pro-European and modernising factions were not at opposite ends of the party's ideological spectrum; the cleavages were cross-cutting. This produced a situation tailor-made for a third candidate to slip through the middle by satisfying the opponents of both – had the euro-sceptics found a less unlikely standard-bearer than IDS his victory would probably have been even easier, though his very anonymity may have been an asset in the short-term since it meant he had no personal baggage with the party at large.

As it was, Duncan Smith only just squeezed over the line in the final MPs' ballot, but the amazement that he had done so was misplaced – too much of Portillo's earlier support was really a "stop Clarke" coalition to be entirely solid, and for that matter vice-versa.

Duncan Smith provided his own political epitaph: The "Quiet Man". He made too little impact in his two years as leader to justify his retaining the post, though it was surprising nevertheless when the Conservative MPs found the resolve to dismiss him, and utterly astonishing when they managed to choose his successor without a political bloodbath.

Under Duncan Smith, the Conservative voting intention share remained becalmed at or below its 2001 level of 33% until the final few months of his leadership when, with Labour suffering from the aftermath of the Iraq war, it improved dramatically. (In the first six months of 2003, the

Conservative share of those certain to vote averaged 30%; in the next four months it averaged 35%.)

However, because Labour's support had fallen since the election, with the Liberal Democrats increasing their share, Labour's lead over the Conservatives was consistently lower than it had been at the general election. Because the media tend to report the lead, not the share, many Conservative supporters had been lulled into the belief that their party was doing better. It was not.

Figure 23: Satisfaction with Conservative Leaders 1997-2005

Q Are you satisfied or dissatisfied with the way William Hague/Iain Duncan Smith/Michael Howard is doing his job as leader of the Conservative Party?

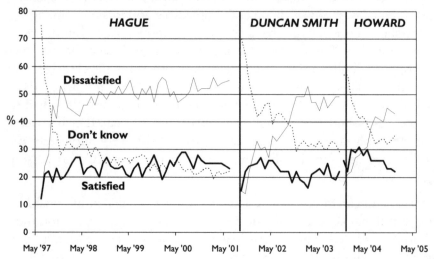

Source: MORI
Base: c. 1,000 GB residents aged 18+ every month

Perhaps the starkest evidence of his failure is to be found in the shift in approval of the job that Duncan Smith was doing as Leader of the Conservative Party. His ratings never reached a respectable level. The number of don't knows in his satisfaction ratings stayed too high for too long, but worse, as more of the public began to recognise him, his approval ratings deteriorated. As Table 46 shows, his don't know and disapproval ratings over time were almost mirror images. When he became

132

leader in September 2001, 15% of the public had said they were satisfied with the job he was doing and 15% said they were dissatisfied; the rest didn't know. Then month after month the news got worse and worse, until at his lowest point, in February 2003, the satisfaction metric reached just 16% and dissatisfaction rose to over half the public, 53%; even those intending to vote Tory gave him the thumbs down, 51% saying that they were dissatisfied with his performance. His final ratings, in October 2003, were a little better but still he had achieved only a 7-point increase in satisfaction since the start of his leadership (to 22%), but a 34 point increase in dissatisfaction (to 49%).

Table 46: Recognition of Iain Duncan Smith

Q Now, thinking about politics. Can you tell me the name of the leader of the Conservative Party?

	All %	Men %	Women %	18-34 %	35-54 %	55+ %
Iain Duncan Smith	62	71	54	50	65	72
Other	3	3	4	4	4	2
No/don't know	35	26	42	46	31	26

Source: MORI/*Financial Times*
Base: 1,002 GB residents aged 18+, 20-22 June 2003

The public didn't just not know what they thought of Iain Duncan Smith, for too many of them didn't know who he was at all. At the start of his leadership, the *Daily Mirror* commissioned a jokey poll that showed his picture was less well-recognised than that of Dolly the Sheep[77]. But by the time he had been leader for almost two years, the joke was wearing thin: halfway through the Parliament, less than two-thirds of the public could name the Conservative leader, far fewer women and young people; worse, only 72% of intending Tory supporters could recall his name.

This was not entirely Duncan Smith's fault, or even within his control. His election was announced two days after the 9/11 attacks on the United States, and the necessary political truce made it difficult to make an

---

[77] Fieldwork 23-28 August 2001 - see Appendix 2, survey 5, for details.. Shown pictures of six "figures currently in the public eye", 57% recognised Dolly the Sheep, 52% the Wimbledon champion Goran Ivanisevic and 51% Duncan Smith. A soap star and two reality TV contestants were less widely recognised.

immediate impact. But it never got any better. The Afghanistan and Iraq invasions led to more wasted months without a chance to establish himself as a credible opposition leader, unable to attack the government since he and his party have supported its most important and controversial policy. Whether history might have been different if IDS had been able to attack the government from day one is perhaps unlikely, but circumstances certainly dealt unkindly with him. The Brent East by-election, when the Liberal Democrats came from third to snatch a Labour seat, fighting on an anti-War platform, while the Conservative vote share fell, was almost certainly a factor in the thinking of many of the MPs who voted him out of the leadership.

Nevertheless, it is instructive to compare Duncan Smith's image as leader in September 2003 with that of Michael Howard 18 months later (Figure 5 on p 35). It could be said that his inexperience was manifest, and (as a former serving Army officer) his patriotism unquestioned.

Figure 24: Leader Image Late in the Duncan Smith Leadership

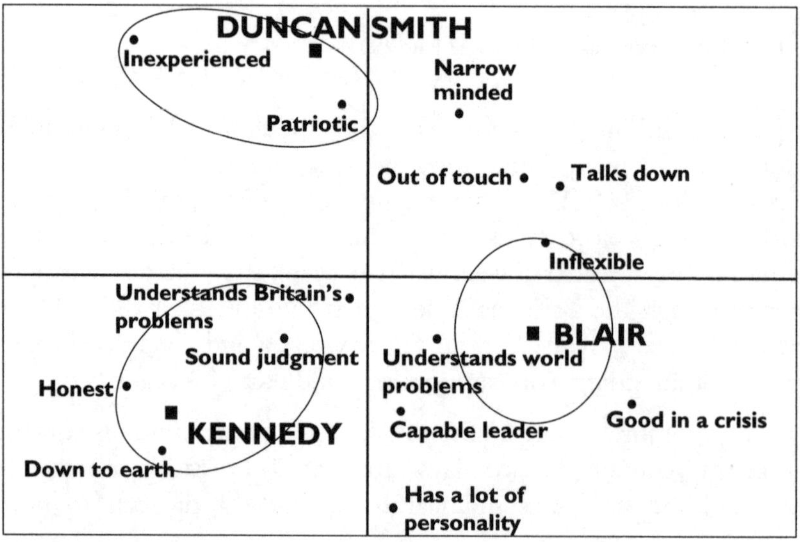

Source: MORI/*Financial Times*
Base: 952 GB residents aged 18+, 11-16 September 2003.

134

Iain Duncan Smith's colleagues came to the same conclusion about his weak image that the perceptual map clearly shows; whether they were right to believe that Michael Howard's image would be more of an asset, readers must judge for themselves.

Neither Howard nor any of his likely rivals had public profiles much higher than Duncan Smith's, as our poll for the *Financial Times* in September 2003 indicated (Table 47). How much blame for such a situation the leader must take is perhaps a matter of opinion, but it meant that when Duncan Smith was replaced his successor had the chance to start almost with a clean slate.

Table 47: The Invisible Shadow Cabinet

Q   Who, if any, of the following do you think are members of the Shadow Cabinet?

	%
Michael Ancram	26
Michael Howard	26
Theresa May	24
Ann Widdecombe	24
Kenneth Clarke	21
Oliver Letwin	19
John Redwood	15
Michael Heseltine	11
Charles Clarke	10
None	2
Don't know	38

Source: MORI/*Financial Times*
Base: 952 GB residents aged 18+, 11-16 September 2003

When Michael Howard was elected unopposed as the fourth leader of the Conservative Party in six years in November 2003, one news outlet remarked – laying it on a little thick – that it was the "culmination of a political re-birth for the Conservative Party"[78]. Nevertheless, the man described as having "something of the night about him" by his arch-enemy Ann Widdecombe did energise the Tories, attempting to purge the party of the Thatcher legacy and its crippling divisions over Europe.

He got off to a fine start, sorting out Central Office with a vengeance and not before time – briefly one got the impression that Central Office might

---

[78] See BBC News online at http://news.bbc.co.uk/1/hi/uk_politics/3224341.stm

135

be planning how to beat Blair at the polls instead of how to stab each other in the back. He cut the Shadow Cabinet to a manageable size, and took on his party's prima donnas just as the headmaster they needed should. The party in Parliament was not just united behind him, it was positively enthusing, and not just in the Commons, in the Lords as well.

Yet there were few tangible results. During 2004, the Conservatives only caught Labour in the voting intention polls on only a couple of occasions (in March and again in September – see Figure 9 on p 64). At all other times Labour was generally reasonably comfortably in the lead, and the brief exceptions owed more to the public loss of confidence in the government than any positive image of the Tories. In September, reported divisions between Gordon Brown and Tony Blair threw a dark cloud over the Labour Party conference and probably depressed the Labour vote as they became seen to be divided. During this time public dissatisfaction with the government was increasing, but the voters were not flocking to the Tory cause as a result.

Howard did however enjoy a honeymoon period from November 2003 to March 2004, when voters were less dissatisfied with him than they had been with Duncan Smith. Grass-roots morale clearly rose as well.

Yet despite a consistently positive reception from the media commentators, and despite Labour paying him the compliment of treating him seriously as an opponent, he was unable to persuade even a third of the public to express satisfaction with his leadership. Once, in May 2004, his approval rating as leader was (fractionally) higher than Tony Blair's – the first time any of the four Conservative leaders faced by Mr Blair achieved that in the ten years since he became Labour leader. But Howard fell a long way short of the figures he might hope to achieve were the public seriously to consider making him the next Prime Minister.

Tory MPs seem to have short memories. They talked about how wonderful Mr Howard was at the dispatch box, just as they lauded William Hague when he hit his stride in 1998. "He's getting the best of Blair in the House", they'd tell me then. "Take a video of Prime Minister's Question Time to a focus group and see what they'd say," I'd reply. "They'll tell me 'Why is he playing games? It's not the Oxford Union.'" It's not the Cambridge Union either.

Howard's 'don't knows' were to me surprisingly high. The first of the 1983 intake into the Cabinet, he's held high profile jobs both in Government and in Opposition, and his appearances both on radio and television are memorable, unlike his predecessor's. Perhaps that was the point – too many people remembered the negative highlights of his cabinet career (the Paxman question repeated twelve times in search of a straight answer, the record number of judicial reviews of his decisions during his time as Home Secretary), but they gave him the benefit of the doubt until he had proved himself one way or the other as leader. For once the caricatures of the cartoonists, raiding every available vampire cliché in reference to his Transylvanian ancestry, may have had the public laughing with him rather than at him, for all their intention to underline his rather sinister image. But the verdict, when it came, was negative again, the "don't knows" drifting to "dissatisfied" until they became a torrent.

Figure 25: Blair and Howard – "Like Him? Like His Policies?"

Q   Which of these statements comes closest to your views of Mr Blair/Mr Howard?

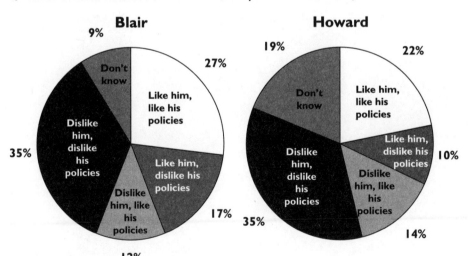

Source: MORI/*Financial Times*
Base: 1,005 GB residents aged 18+, 15-18 April 2005

The "like him, like his policies" question (Figure 25) sums up Howard's failure – and it must be remembered that at the time it was posed most commentators regarded Blair as a liability to Labour. Twice as many had

137

no opinion of Howard as of Blair – only to be expected – and the same proportion, a third, dismissed both man and manifesto in each case.

But overall, 44% said they liked Blair and only 32% liked Howard; Blair, for all the personal vilification of him in which the Tory campaign joined, was disliked by 47% of the public, Howard by 49%. In fact Howard's policies fared better than Blair's and better than Howard did. On this evidence it was Howard, not Blair, who was dragging down his party.

Once again the Tory leadership process had failed to throw up a winner. But perhaps they didn't have one they could have picked.

Go Back to Your Constituencies and Prepare For ...?

The Liberal Democrats came into the 2005 general election more hopeful than for many years. The Iraq war had given them two stunning by-election victories (at Brent East in 2003, on a 29% swing, and Leicester South with a 21.5% swing), and a near miss at Birmingham Hodge Hill (where a swing of 27.7% was not quite enough). Fortuitously, the constituencies where the vacancies had arisen could almost have been hand-picked for the purpose, and on the most optimistic assumptions such results could only be replicated in a handful of other seats in a general election. But the party's general standing in the polls was also high, consistently around 21% to 22% and occasionally higher, better than at any point mid-Parliament since the high tide of the SDP-Liberal Alliance in the early eighties. Add the five or six point boost that the Liberal Democrats invariably achieve during election campaigns, their supporters reasoned, and they could expect a swathe of seats to fall across the country. For instance, Simon Hughes told ePolitix (the political news website) a fortnight before polling day:

> "I don't know the number of seats we will win but I know that traditionally we've gained support during the election campaign because the broadcast media have to give us equal coverage. In the last two elections we went up six per cent in each campaign and in 1983 we went up 14%. We began this campaign at our best base ever of about 20% and all the opinion polls are showing a consistent move forward." [79]

But this theory was based on a misunderstanding, partly because of a technicality of poll methodology – which we pointed out at frequent intervals to little avail[80]. The voting intention polls in this parliament were not comparable to those from the previous half-century of polling.

Traditionally, pollsters have used "unprompted" voting intention polls between elections, not reminding respondents of the available options by listing the parties or candidates. Because many of those who eventually vote for the LibDems apparently forget about the party between elections,

---

[79] Simon Hughes, interview with epolitix.com, 21 April 2005 (accessed 5 July 2005).
[80] See for example Roger Mortimore, "The LibDems and the Polls: Go back to your constituencies and prepare for...?", *British Public Opinion* newsletter, Vol XXVI no 2 (2003), p 6.

this tends to mean that their ratings are low mid-Parliament and rise as elections approach, when the voters begin to consider their options, or indeed – briefly – after by-elections. In the 1997-2001 parliament, only ICM of the regular pollsters was using a prompted question, and their LibDem rating was consistently higher than MORI's or Gallup's. For the same reason, ICM found smaller LibDem gains during the election campaigns than the other pollsters – the "awareness factor" was already incorporated into their pre-election poll figures. But after 2001, there was a change: MORI (not without misgivings, since we feared the figures might be misunderstood and misreported, which indeed they were [81]) switched to using a prompted voting intention question, Gallup stopped polling, and almost all the newcomers also used prompted questions.

Table 48: Prompted and Unprompted Voting Intentions

	All giving a voting intention				Absolutely certain to vote			
	Con	Lab	LD	Oth	Con	Lab	LD	Oth
	%	%	%	%	%	%	%	%
All	33	41	21	5	37	36	21	6
Prompted	30	42	23	5	36	37	23	4
Unprompted	35	40	19	6	39	35	19	7
Difference	-5	2	4	-1	-3	2	4	-3

Source: MORI
Base: 959 GB residents aged 18+, 28 November-1 December 2003

It was clear that part, at least, of the higher-than-usual LibDem voting intention rating should be attributed to the change in polling methodology, rather than a real difference in the public mood. To check that this was indeed the case, MORI conducted an experiment in 2003, split-sampling a survey so that half the respondents were asked their voting intention in the "new" prompted form and the other half in the "old" traditional unprompted format. As Table 48 shows, our suspicions were fully confirmed: LibDem share was four points higher prompted than

---

[81] But, unfortunately, no more misreported and misunderstood than were the figures reported by the traditional method, which the media persisted in portraying as our prediction of the next election or, at best, our projection of what the result would have been if an election had been held on the day of the poll. We discussed the two measures, and our decision to switch to a "prompted" methodology, in more detail in *Explaining Labour's Second Landslide* (London: Politico's, 2001), pp 263-8.

unprompted (whether based on all expressing a voting intention or only on those absolutely certain to vote). In other words, the LibDems had already had their cake, or most of it, and any increase in support during the election run-in this time they would have to earn.

There were other discouraging signs for the LibDems. Charles Kennedy's personal ratings as leader were surprisingly poor, especially in light of his positive leader image. Perhaps the voters demanded gravitas rather than friendly blokeishness.

Positioning themselves, too, posed major problems, as highlighted by the intra-party argument over the "Orange Book"; disillusioned Labour voters, such as many of those to whom they successfully appealed in Brent and Leicester, were looking for a party on the left of New Labour, committed to some of the principles that they felt Tony Blair's party had abandoned. But this would hardly be attractive to wavering Conservative voters, whose capture has been the backbone of the party's gains in the previous two general elections and who were their best hope for sustainable gains, given that the Tories held 15 of the 19 seats where the LibDems were within 10% of victory and that the average Labour share in those seats was an already-well-squeezed 14%. Could the LibDems really convince Tories that they were a centre party while simultaneously persuading Old Labour grumblers that they were more of the left than the centre-left?

Table 49: LibDem Target Seats, 2005

In the Tories' ...	LibDems were second in	In Labour's...	LibDems were second in
10 most marginal seats	4	10 most marginal seats	1
20 most marginal seats	8	20 most marginal seats	2
30 most marginal seats	12	30 most marginal seats	4
40 most marginal seats	15	40 most marginal seats	5
50 most marginal seats	17	50 most marginal seats	6
60 most marginal seats	20	60 most marginal seats	7
70 most marginal seats	23	70 most marginal seats	7
80 most marginal seats	26	80 most marginal seats	7
90 most marginal seats	27	90 most marginal seats	7
100 most marginal seats	31	100 most marginal seats	7

Perhaps it ought to be impossible, but they seemed, at one point, to be achieving it. Revealing Populus polls for *The Times* at the time of the party conferences in September 2003 and 2004 showed while Labour and LibDem voters on average believed the LibDems to be marginally to the left of Labour, Tories tended to think that the LibDems were well to the right of Labour[82].

If Charles Kennedy could continue to pull off that trick, he would have been on to a good thing. But it was to become increasingly difficult the more the spotlight was on the Liberal Democrats.

---

[82] Populus interviewed representative samples of c. 1,000 GB residents by telephone on 11-14 September 2003 and 2-5 September 2004 on behalf of *The Times*. Details at www.populuslimited.com.

Local Elections 2001-4

General elections are not of course the only elections contested by the national parties. Every May or June brings a chance for the opposition to try its strength in the elections to local authorities, including now a number of directly-elected mayoralties, and the European Parliament elections and those to the Scottish Parliament and Welsh Assembly will normally also fall due once at least in a Parliament.

Pollsters are frequently berated by ill-informed pundits or party spokesmen on the make when a party performs much better at the local elections than its vote share in the monthly polls would seem to indicate. If the Tories have just achieved 37% of the vote at the local elections ("real votes in real ballot boxes"), they will argue, how can your polls putting the party at 30% possibly be right? The local elections during the 2001-5 Parliament could hardly offer a clearer answer. The regular polls try to measure how the public would vote in a general election, and there is now a big divide between local election voting and general election voting; doing well in the one is no guarantee of even a respectable performance in the other.

The story of the local elections in the 2001-5 Parliament was of continuous losses, and indeed humiliation, for Labour. (Table 50). In 2002 results included the election of independent mayors in supposed Labour strongholds – a football mascot in Peter Mandelson's Hartlepool, the controversial "Robocop" in Middlesbrough. In 2003, as Iraq was just beginning to register as being a political liability rather than an asset, they lost control in a jaw-dropping 28 councils, including Birmingham, Coventry and Bristol for the first time in a generation. In 2004, it was Leeds, Newcastle and Cardiff, and they fell to third place in the vote projected nationally, the only silver lining being the notional gain of London's mayor, achieved by the humiliating climb-down of effectively sacking their own candidate and readmitting Ken Livingstone to membership in strict breach of party rules.

Similarly, the Tories might seem rampant on the basis of their local results: 53 councils and more than a thousand council seats regained, and ahead in votes on all three occasions.

Why were these elections, and the other subsidiary elections, of so little use in telling us what would happen on 5 May 2005?

Table 50: Local Elections 2002-4 – On The Night Gains and Losses

	2002	2003	2004	Total 2002-4
Councils controlled (net change)				
Conservative	+9	+31	+13	+53
Labour	-7	-28	-8	-43
Liberal Democrat	+2	+5	-2	+5
Others	+2	-1	-3	-2
No overall control	-6	-7	0	-13
Council seats (net change)				
Conservative	+238	+568	+288	+1094
Labour	-334	-831	-464	-1629
Liberal Democrat	+37	+189	+123	+349
Others	-73	-70	-3	-146
Estimated national equivalent vote				
Conservative	34%	35%	37%	
Labour	33%	30%	26%	
Liberal Democrat	25%	27%	27%	
Others	7%	8%	10%	

Sources: House of Commons Library Research Papers 02/33, 03/44 and 04/49 (which includes national equivalent vote calculations by Colin Rallings & Michael Thrasher).
Table refers only to gains/losses in the annual local elections and makes no attempt to include by-elections or to correct for boundary changes

First, and most obviously, turnout is far lower at local than at general elections, less than two-thirds of even the current derisory general election turnout. That missing third are of course more likely to be Labour supporters than anything else (not only because Labour is strongest in the demographic groups least likely to vote, the young, the less well-off and the ethnic minorities, but because the natural unpopularity of government will ensure that when Labour is in power its opponents are more motivated to register a vote in protest than its adherents are to cast one in support). But, even were that not the case, you might expect the quarter of the population who usually vote at general elections but not local elections to be sufficiently different from those who always vote that the outcome would be at least a little different when they all get to the ballot boxes.

Second, there is little interest in local elections, as most people believe that they now have little power to do anything of real importance despite the fact that they care a great deal about many of the services local governments deliver.

Nor can we assume that people will vote the same way in local and in general elections. The days of rigid party loyalty when most of the public could be expected to vote for the same party at every opportunity through their lifetime are long gone. Certainly we know personally people who voted for three different parties in the 2004 London elections (when voters had five separate votes), and our on-the-day poll for ITN found that only 38% of the London electorate voted for the same party across the board.

The public have always been prepared to vote differently in local and parliamentary elections, and puzzle when the pundits go on about how this would be if it had been a general election. The electorate know how many beans makes five, and prove it with their votes; many take the opportunity to "send a message" to the party they expect to vote for at the general election. They know they are putting the wind up their political masters, and they are getting the taste for doing it whenever they can, be it in local elections, European elections, or by-elections.

10 June 2004, "Super Thursday" (one wonders whether the nickname was intentionally ironic) was the last and biggest of these three local election bonanzas, nearest in time to the general election and the only one after Michael Howard's accession to the Conservative leadership. If any elections would be a pointer to the general election, it surely should have been these. Everybody throughout the UK had at least one vote to choose their Member of the European Parliament; they had between two and four votes in many places in England and Wales voting both for their Euro MP and for their local council, and five (sic) votes in London: two preferences for Mayor, constituency and list votes for the Assembly, and their European vote.

Turnout across England and Wales was up an average of 9% from four years before, at 40% – principally, we would surmise, for four reasons: first, because there were three elections, not just one, to get people out; second, because in the four northernmost regions of England (32% of the electors) an all-postal vote with ballot papers delivered through every letter-box[83] achieved around a 44% turnout, and increased the turnout there by some 13% (but turnout was also up by some 4% in the 68% of

---

[83] In theory, at least – *The Times* was assiduous in reporting all the cases it could find where this had not worked in practice, and there was no shortage of them.

the country where polls were open with ballot boxes into which a paper ballot could be cast); third, because these elections were the now regular opportunity for protesting (rather than seriously electing a government); and fourth, because for most of the country the weather was good.

The party share represented by the local council results[84] were Conservatives 37%, Labour at 26% and the Liberal Democrats 27%: unarguably a humiliation for Labour, who lost 479 council seats, though less clearly an unmixed triumph for the Tories (in first place with control of 13 councils gained, but having made little progress in urban areas and with a vote share well short of what they would need to win a general election). For the Liberal Democrats, a mixed message – they gained council seats but made a net loss in councils controlled.

Labour's performance was almost as bad as that of John Major's government in 1995, when the Tory share fell to 25%, and was certainly a worse performance than has ever been recorded by a government that was subsequently re-elected. Labour spokesmen were quick to point out that their loss of seats was much less than in 2000 – more disingenuous spin, since the losses were effectively compared with the baseline of 2000, and were *on top of* the losses they sustained then. On the other hand, a fairer point was that in 2000 William Hague's party had achieved a projected 38% share, yet in the following year's general election added just a single MP to their then 164 seats in the Commons.

Indeed, translating those vote shares into seats, projected on uniform swing to a general election outcome – a statistical nonsense, "just a bit of fun" as Peter Snow would say – would have given the Tories 290 seats, Labour 253, and the Liberal Democrats 72 seats. So much for "beating Labour into third place"! The Tories would still be a sandwich short of a picnic: it would be a hung Parliament, and the Liberal Democrats with the balance of power would probably still keep a Labour Prime Minister in Downing Street.

But the consequences of the local elections must be counted not only in statistical tables and short-lived embarrassment for ministers facing

---

[84] These figures and those in the table are those calculated by Colin Rallings and Michael Thrasher, the local government election experts at the University of Plymouth (see House of Commons Library Research Paper 04/49), and differ slightly from the BBC figures available on the night, which inevitably were based only on a small sample of wards.

journalists, but in longer-lasting human terms. Labour's lost council seats meant that hundreds of Labour Party members, many senior and influential within their local parties, were councillors before one of these election nights and not after; others kept their seats but lost council leaderships, committee chairmanships or memberships and perhaps even their turn as mayor. Most if not all would be blaming Tony Blair and his government for their personal disasters. But these are the very men and women on whom the outcome of a general election may ultimately depend, the grass-roots membership who organise local campaigns, knock on doors and stuff leaflets through letterboxes. Would they work as hard for Labour in 2005 as they did in 1997 and 2001? Not likely.

Though perhaps impossible to measure, the morale of the "troops" on the ground can be a crucial factor in a general election, especially when the task is to turn grudging latent support into votes at the ballot box. Local campaigns do matter, as academic analysis has shown[85]. In both 1997 and 2001, Tory morale at local level was at rock bottom, and on each occasion in the marginal seats – where all parties naturally concentrated their campaigning efforts – they performed significantly worse than across the country as a whole. Michael Howard's elevation certainly revitalised Tory morale, and the local elections will have helped cement that improvement in many parts of the country; Labour morale at the same time must have plummeted. As we shall see, in 2005 it was the Tories who over-performed in the marginals, and the protection that Labour has received for years from the bias in the electoral system began to unwind; it would by no means fanciful to suppose that Labour's local election defeats were a significant factor in bringing this about.

---

[85] See David Denver, Gordon Hands and Iain MacAllister in "The Electoral Impact of Constituency Campaigning in Britain, 1992-2001, *Political Studies* Vol 52 no 2 (June 2004), 289-306.

UKIP If You Want To...

Meanwhile, in the European Parliament elections of June 2004, the message was simple – UKIP won.

Not literally, of course, but UKIP doubled its share compared with five years previously, and took 12 seats. Of the major parties, only the LibDems increased their share since 1999, and they scored well below their current "general election tomorrow" poll ratings, a very disappointing failure to capture the protest vote. Labour won their lowest share of the vote in any national election since 1918; yet while the Conservatives were comfortably ahead of them, it was *their* worst share of the national vote since 1832.

Table 51: British Elections to the European Parliament, 1999 & 2004

Party	1999 %	2004 %	Change	1999 Seats	2004 Seats	Change
Conservative	35.8	26.7	-9.1	36	27	-9
Labour	28.0	22.6	-5.4	29	19	-10
Liberal Democrats	12.7	14.9	+2.2	10	12	+2
Scottish National Party	2.7	1.4	-1.3	2	2	0
Plaid Cymru	1.9	1.0	-0.9	2	1	-1
Green Party	6.3	6.3	0	2	2	0
UKIP	7.0	16.1	+9.1	3	12	+9
Others	5.6	11.0	+5.4	0	0	0
Total	100	100		84	75	

The unenlightened might suppose that the election of British members to the European Parliament might reflect the voters' verdict on the competing programmes of the European Parliament parties, or at least depend on whether the voter was broadly pro- or anti-European. Not so, of course. The vast majority of the public know little about the European Parliament, and care less. European Parliament elections are almost invariably fought as a side-show of domestic politics – the parties campaign under their own names rather than of the European Parliament blocs with which they are aligned, and appeal to voters on domestic rather than Community issues.

It follows from this that many voters treat EP elections as second-order, and vote to express their opinions of national politics, just as they do in local government elections and parliamentary by-elections. What gives the European elections a different dimension from either of these is that it uses a proportional representation electoral system.

Up to the elections of 1994, British elections to the EP were conducted on a constituency basis, "first past the post", as elections to Parliament and local authorities still are. This meant that each MEP represented a comparatively small geographical area, and accepted responsibility for all its voters; but it also had the consequence that the winning party's lead was vastly exaggerated in seats, that smaller parties had no realistic chance of winning seats, and that a high proportion of voters had no local MEP from their chosen party. But in 1999 this familiar system was replaced by a party-list version of proportional representation, used in no other British elections. Now voting for a minor party is no longer a wasted vote that the major parties can ignore – it has the real potential to elect minor party MEPs and, since elections are a zero-sum game, to deprive the major parties of seats at the same time.

At the same time, the new electoral system may have worsened engagement between MEPs and voters (though it was never very effective), further encouraging gesture voting intended to "send a message" to Westminster rather than caring about the outcome as such. In 1991, under the old constituency system, a MORI survey found that just 7% of the public could name their MEP. (By way of comparison, in the same survey 51% could name their Member of Parliament.) Advocates of proportional representation suggested that the introduction of that system which led to each citizen being represented by between 3 and 11 MEPs instead of only one, would improve relationships between voters and MEPs and, by implication, would increase the proportion of the public who were at least aware who their MEPs were. But MORI focus group research for the Electoral Commission in 2003 found that virtually none of the participants could name any of their MEPs; while not constituting a reliable quantitative measure, the research seemed in line with a general impression that fewer, not more, voters are aware of who their representatives in the EP are than was the case a decade ago.

But Europe was not entirely absent as an issue in the European elections. Certainly the success of UKIP must be interpreted as the conscious expression of Euroscepticism. Not that there is any contradiction here – the hostility of the public to Europe, and the contrast with the

149

determinedly Europhile nature of the government, naturally made it one of the issues on which voters were most concerned to "send a message", and European elections offered a natural occasion on which to do so.

All of which goes to explain why the sudden rise of UKIP to 16% of the vote in the European elections did not necessarily herald their breakthrough at the general election – a reasonable fear for the Conservatives since undoubtedly it would be they who suffered most were such a vote to be repeated. Voters are not stupid, and know that at a general election they need to use their vote to make a choice between Blair and Howard for Number Ten: an ICM poll in the *Guardian* shortly after the European elections found only a quarter of those who supported UKIP in the local elections expected to stick with the party at the general election[86] (and in the event, of course, the party's vote amounted to only a third even of this). Of course, UKIP's success also had a good deal to do with the charismatic appeal of their best-known standard bearer, Robert Kilroy-Silk, before he left to form his own party, Veritas. (One of the authors played in a quiz league match at which another competitor confused this with Dignitas, the Swiss-based organisation that campaigns for the right to put the elderly out of their misery; judging by Kilroy-Silk's subsequent career, perhaps she should have been given the points.) But even had Kilroy-Silk stayed, it is unlikely that UKIP would have made much real impact on the general election – the Tories were going to lose regardless.

---

[86] ICM interviewed 1,009 adults aged 18+ by telephone on 11-13 June 2004 for the *Guardian*. Full details at icmresearch.co.uk.

3. The 2005 Election Campaign

The Long Campaign, January-April

Modern elections do not wait for the sound of the starter's gun – a Prime Minister's visit to Buckingham Palace to secure a dissolution – before the campaign gets underway. In a sense the campaign is continuous, running right through the parliament, but the turn of the year before an expected election forms a natural hiatus, and tends to be taken by parties and commentators alike as the election's real starting point.

Figure 26: Controversial Labour Attack Poster

Source: The Labour Party

Michael Howard began 2005 as he meant to go on, making statements in January on the issue that came to dominate their campaign whether they liked it or not, asylum. Labour's campaign got off to a shaky start with the election posters that they unveiled depicting Oliver Letwin, the Tory shadow chancellor and Michael Howard, the party leader, as flying pigs (see Figure 26). This created a furore in the media over whether or not this was anti-Semitic and a slur against both men, who have Jewish heritage. The advert, with the strap line "Britain is working hard, don't let the

Tories wreck it again", was reportedly the brainchild of Labour strategist-cum-sportswriter, Alastair Campbell, who was back in from the cold despite his resignation over the outcome of the Hutton Inquiry surrounding the death of Dr David Kelly.

Table 52: Pre-Election Timeline, 1 January-4 April 2005

Date	Event
24 January	Howard announces asylum plans including annual quotas and overseas claim processing.
28 January	Labour criticised for posters depicting Letwin and Howard as flying pigs.
6 February	Blair surpasses Harold Wilson to become Britain's longest serving Labour Prime Minister.
10 February	Prince Charles announces he will marry Camilla Parker Bowles on 8 April.
11 February	Blair outlines Labour's six election pledges at Labour conference in Gateshead.
18 February	Ban on fox-hunting in England and Wales comes into force.
21 February	Howard announces council taxes for OAPs would be halved, up to a maximum discount of £500 per annum. Institute of Fiscal Studies calculates cost would be £1.3bn.
2 March	Howard and Blair exchange blows in Prime Minister's Questions over high-profile case of pensioner, Margaret Dixon, whose NHS operations were cancelled several times.
4-6 March	LibDem Conference in Harrogate: Kennedy launches party election slogan "The Real Alternative".
11 March	Government Terrorism Bill passed after Lords insist on inserting a sunset clause.
14 March	Abortion issue raised in national press after interviews with party leaders published in *Cosmopolitan* and Howard reveals he would support a decrease in the legal time limit for termination of pregnancies from 24 to 20 weeks.
16 March	Budget: Brown provides one-off refund for OAPs on council tax and an increase in stamp duty threshold favouring first time buyers.
17 March	Labour poster claims that "The Tories will cut £35bn from public services". ITV News political editor Nick Robinson later forces Blair to concede that in fact the figure represents not a "cut" but simply a lower increase than Labour proposes.
22 March	Liberal Democrats launch ten "positive proposals" – similar to Labour's pledges – in their press advertising campaign.
25 March	Howard deselects Howard Flight after his comment to Conservative Way Forward supporters that the Conservative Party would cut spending more than they had announced if they got into power.
2 April	Pope John Paul II dies, delaying Election announcement (expected to have been 4 April).
4 April	Richard Mawrey QC, sitting as a judge in the election court, declares some 2004 local election results in Birmingham void.

Labour also launched a poster depicting Howard waving a watch to hypnotise the electorate, which protesting Tories interpreted as a "Fagin"-style character, famous from Charles Dickens' *Oliver Twist*, which also created a furore – perhaps more justifiably, as it was at the very least a direct personal attack.

The main political parties launched their election campaigns long before the formal announcement of the election date, putting out policy statements and election posters in an attempt to strike clear blows and make gains in political capital before the campaign proper. Changes to the anti-terrorism bill provided some media spectator sport, as the Lords insisted on changes to what many regarded as a "bad bill"; the government's implication that it would make an election issue of the Opposition's resistance to their original proposals came to nothing, probably wisely.

During these preliminary skirmishes, the parties made some attempts to target special interest groups, particularly women – with all party leaders interviewed for the "April" (sic) edition of *Cosmopolitan*, published on 14 March. Pensioners were courted with pledges from all parties on council tax. Students were particularly courted by the Liberal Democrats. New homeowners were initially courted by the Conservatives but also by Labour and the LibDems. And gay voters were also targeted, with all parties being interviewed by the gay magazine *Attitude* for their March issue.

The only controversy that carried through into the campaign proper, though, was the argument over the costing of the Tories' promises. Howard's sensitivity over his spending plans forced him into his third sacking within as many weeks of a candidate for apparent heterodoxy: Adrian Hilton had already been forced to stand down for calling the European Union a "papist plot" in the *Spectator*, as had Danny Kruger after his advocacy of "a period of creative destruction in the public services" was attacked by the left-wing press, notably Polly Toynbee in the *Guardian*.[87] Now the constituency association of a sitting front bench MP, Howard Flight, were ordered to deselect him after the leaking of remarks at a private meeting which suggested the party might plan bigger cuts than

---

[87] Polly Toynbee, "A mission to destroy", *Guardian*, 11 March 2005.

were promised in the manifesto. Again, of course, this was the triumph of image over substance – Central Office was too fearful of the party's programme being misrepresented or misunderstood to allow intelligent and (as far as we can tell) loyal but "off-message" candidates to stand. Whether the alternative image of a party of pliant yes-men banned from thinking for themselves is preferable in the long run (or even in the short run) must be questionable. Labour has, after all, on occasions come close to being a laughing stock for the same reason – their defector Brian Sedgemore characterised the bulk of Labour MPs as "clones" or "Stepford wives"[88]. It will hardly enhance the image of politics.

---

[88] Brian Sedgemore, "I urge everyone to give Blair a bloody nose at the election", *Independent*, 26 April 2005.

The Course of the Campaign

Events conspired to delay the announcement of the general election. Whilst it had been expected that the election would be called on 7 April, both Prince Charles' wedding to his long-time consort Camilla Parker Bowles (of which, judging by his statement, the Prime Minister appeared not to have been forewarned), and the death of Pope John Paul II, meant that Tony Blair formally announced the election on 5 April for 5 May, giving the parties a campaign period of only 30 days, and consigning contentious legislation such as the Gambling Bill and the ID Cards Bill – among others – to the business of the next parliament. The 30-day campaign was shorter than in either 1997 (when John Major deliberately chose a long campaign in the hope of clawing back some of Labour's lead) or than in 2001 (when the Foot and Mouth Disease outbreak threw out all calculations), but was a similar length to most other modern British elections.

All three parties launched their main manifestos and slogans in typical farcical style. Labour quickly changed their slogan from "Britain forward not back" to "If you value it, vote for it!"; the LibDems delayed their launch as Charles Kennedy tended his newborn son and recovering wife, and he seemed incapable of remembering his party's pledges on the economy; the Conservatives also changed their slogan from "Are you thinking what we're thinking?" to "Taking a stand on the issues that matter", with the party sledge-hammering away on the issue of asylum to no avail.

The Tories produced three main manifestos – one overall manifesto and two regional variants for Scotland and Wales, as well as a whole series of policy documents entitled "action on ..." targeted at specific policy areas (e.g. education, crime), older people, business generally and Londoners. By contrast, the Liberal Democrats not only had a main manifesto including one for Scotland and Wales but policy documents (what the media called mini-manifestos) both on a myriad of policy issues and aimed at numerous interest groups, including young people, old people, ethnic minorities, gays, families and Londoners among others. Labour produced one manifesto for all regions, policy documents on various issues (e.g. education, welfare reform) and for specially targeted groups, including young people, the elderly, women and families.

155

Table 53: Election Campaign Timeline, 5 April-5 May 2005

Date	Event
Tue 5 April	Blair announces the general election date as 5 May.
Wed 6 April	Paul Marsden, a former Labour MP who had defected to the LibDems and was not contesting the election, announced that he intended to rejoin the Labour Party.
Thu 7 April	Parliament prorogued. MG Rover put into administration.
Fri 8 April	Original date for Royal Wedding. Funeral of Pope John Paul II.
Sat 9 April	Prince Charles marries Camilla Parker Bowles in Windsor.
Sun 10 April	Conservatives launch campaign slogan "Are you thinking what we're thinking?".
Mon 11 April	Dissolution of Parliament. Howard launches Conservative manifesto.
Tue 12 April	Kennedy's wife gives birth to their son, Donald James: LibDems delay their manifesto launch. PwC (MG Rover administrators) announces that production at Longbridge would cease, with consequent mass redundancies.
Wed 13 April	Labour manifesto launch.
Thu 14 April	Kennedy launches LibDem manifesto with promises of a local income tax and free healthcare for pensioners.
Tue 19 April	Cardinal Joseph Ratzinger elected as Pope Benedict XVI.
Wed 20 April	*The Sun* decides to back Labour, urging its readers to give Tony Blair "one last chance", announcing its decision with quasi-papal smoke signals.
Fri 22 April	Blair attacks Conservative policy on Asylum.
Sat 23 April	Labour unveil new slogan, "If you value it, vote for it!", in a bid to frighten voters who are considering voting LibDem or Conservative.
Sun 24 April	World Poverty Day: all parties concentrate on global issues.
Mon 25 April	LibDems demand a public enquiry into Iraq, Conservatives launch their mini-business manifesto, Labour campaigns on the economy.
Tue 26 April	Brian Sedgemore, outgoing Labour MP, defects to the LibDems citing Iraq war. Conservatives unveil new campaign slogan, "Taking a Stand on the Issues that Matter".
Thu 28 April	Number 10 publishes the legal advice it received from the Attorney-General on the legality of the Iraq War. BBC *Question Time* Election Special aired at 8.30pm, hosted by David Dimbleby, draws in over 4m viewers.
Sun 1 May	Secret memo outlining Iraq War strategy leaked to media in a bid to damage Blair's trust with voters.
Mon 2 May	May Day bank holiday. British soldier Anthony Wakefield killed in Iraq – widow blames Blair.
Thu 5 May	Election Day.

Perhaps the nearest thing to tension in a mostly predictable campaign was the question of *The Sun* newspaper's allegiance – previously Tory-inclined in the 1992 campaign and infamous for its claim that John Major's Conservatives were victorious because "it was the *Sun* wot won it!"; it came out eventually and unsurprisingly for the Labour Party. Blowing red smoke from its chimney to signify its decision, in a manner reminiscent of that used by the Vatican to signal the election of the new pope two days earlier, the paper said it would give Blair the "benefit of the doubt" by continuing to support Labour having changed its colours from blue to red shortly before the 1997 British General Election that elected Blair in the first place.

After the brief distraction of World Poverty Day, with less than two weeks left before polling day, the LibDems turned the election campaign to their advantage with a press release highlighting the defection of arch-New Labour critic Brian Sedgemore to their party over Iraq. They gave a series of press conferences throughout the week on this issue, given further momentum after the news media obtained copies of the Attorney-General's Iraq war legal advice, in a bid to win marginals with a high anti-Iraq student vote.

The Conservatives made less headway — not least because they had supported the war at the time, and found it hard to make the argument that had they been in full possession of the facts — the intelligence assessment and the legal advice — that they might not have gone to war in the first place.

Labour countered both attempts to derail its leader and its relative poll lead with press conferences on continued investment in public services. Tony Blair and Gordon Brown — realising that Blair on his own was an electoral liability and that Brown held the public's trust on the economy/public services investment trump card — campaigned so hard together that they could have been a political version of Rod Hull and Emu, although who was puppet and who was puppeteer was not immediately obvious!

By now, the Conservatives' policy on immigration was attracting attention only for its controversial nature rather than for its content. NOP's poll for the *Independent* on 22-24 April[89] showed that 38% of all voters agreed and 37% disagreed with the statement that "the Conservatives are using immigration as an excuse to raise the issue of race". With only around a week to go before polling day, Howard's campaign for the Conservatives was starting to look a little more desperate as they unveiled a negative

---

[89] John Curtice, "Conservative policies on immigration are popular - but they simply aren't enough", *Independent*, 26 April 2005.

poster campaign with a slogan parodying Labour's: "If you value truth, vote for it".

In the last few days of the campaign, Howard focussed on the issue of trust and the Iraq war – despite a number of polls showing a decline in support for the Conservatives over the previous week – in a last ditch attempt to swing Labour-Conservative floating voters to his side. Labour sought to get out their vote – as higher turnout benefits their vote – and the Liberal Democrats focussed on presenting themselves as the "Real Opposition" to Labour at the Tories' expense – a strategy that appeared to be at least partly working as they dominated discussions about Iraq.

Table 54: Developing Importance of Issues During the Campaign

Q Which two or three of the following issues will be most important to you in deciding which party to support in the coming general election? (Please tick up to three).

	5 Apr %	9-10 Apr %	14 Apr %	18-19 Apr %	22-23 Apr %	25-26 Apr %	28 Apr %	2-3 May %	5 May %
Health	41	47	43	44	43	41	43	45	44
Immigration & Asylum	40	33	44	42	43	42	42	40	37
The economy	27	30	28	28	28	29	31	31	32
Crime	36	33	37	35	39	35	35	35	30
Education	20	26	21	22	21	22	23	23	28
Tax	30	31	29	27	30	29	27	28	26
Pensions	27	27	25	28	26	27	28	26	22
Family life & childcare	16	16	13	15	15	14	13	14	16
Iraq	9	7	8	8	7	10	11	12	16
Europe	13	9	11	11	10	11	10	10	12
The environment	13	15	10	12	12	12	12	12	11
Transport	8	8	6	6	6	7	6	6	5
Don't know	3	2	3	3	3	4	3	3	3

Source: YouGov/Sky News
Base: c. 1,000-1,700 GB members of internet panel each survey

On 28 April, Labour continued fielding questions from journalists about the illegality of the war in Iraq and the Attorney-General's legal advice. Whilst trust in Blair was seen by most pundits as likely to decline further, it is questionable how effective the opposition campaigning on the issue was.

The Populus poll published in *The Times* on 30 April[90] found that when the public were asked "Do you agree or disagree that 'The Conservatives calling Blair a liar makes me less likely to vote Labour?'", 12% of Labour voters agreed and 16% of Liberal Democrats, implying a likely fall in Liberal Democrat tactical voting for Labour in Labour/Conservative marginals which was subsequently borne out.

YouGov's tracking panels during the campaign show how generally steady the public's interest in different issues was during the campaign. By comparison with MORI's respondents, YouGov's panel gave education a much lower priority (perhaps because they were restricted to naming their three most important issues, rather than all that they considered important). Health and immigration/asylum remained neck-and-neck as most important until the last moment, when asylum fell away a little. The only substantial movement was the doubling in salience of Iraq in the last fortnight as the campaign concentrated on it, but even at its highest level it remained peripheral.

The Conservatives and the Liberal Democrats – along with bashing Blair over Iraq – focussed on education and health respectively, the two most important issues according to our poll at the start of the campaign, but in the case of the Tories at least too little too late.

---

[90] Populus interviewed 730 adults aged 18+ by telephone on 27-28 April 2005 for *The Times*. Full details available at www.populuslimited.com.

Issues Raised in the Campaign

Three issues were of sufficient prominence in the campaign to merit examination in more detail: asylum and immigration, on which the Tories focussed, Iraq, on which the Liberal Democrats in particular attacked the government, and the general question of economic competence and the credibility of the parties' various tax and spending plans, on which all parties attacked each other as usual.

Asylum and Immigration

One issue that has relentlessly increased in salience, especially since the 2001 election, is race relations/asylum/immigration. Whereas the percentage naming it as one of the most important issues facing the country was invariably in (low) single figures in 1997 and 1998, it is now consistently named as a concern by between a quarter and a third of the public in unprompted important issues polls, and it has risen to sixth place as an election issue.

Immigration and asylum are slightly unusual issues in that there is not universal agreement on the ends at which policy should aim. Nevertheless, the issue is less divisive than it might appear, since the vast majority of the public agree in wanting to minimise immigration and to tighten rules for admission of asylum seekers and enforcement of them. (That majority can even be found, albeit a little less strongly, among ethnic minorities in Britain: in a MORI survey for BBC Asian Network during the election, for example, three in five British Asians agreed that "There are too many immigrants in Britain"; Indians were more likely to "strongly agree" with this statement than other Asian groups.)

But because doubts will always remain how far opposition to immigration is driven by simple racism, and whether political campaigns on the issue are a deliberate appeal to latent racist attitudes, the liberal media will always ensure that raising immigration as an election issue is portrayed as more controversial than would be, for example, a concentration on crime or pensions. A party choosing to make it a central plank of their campaign as the Tories did (in their poster campaign as well as in their election press conference agenda) needs to take into account that the instinctive acceptability of their message to many voters may be offset by the tone of the coverage it will receive, even from sources that would otherwise be neutral or allow the party the benefit of the doubt.

The Conservative Party's focus on asylum, the fulcrum of their campaign strategy – as advocated by strategist-general, Lynton Crosby – was in all likelihood a tactical mistake in their campaign for this reason. Whilst it was the sixth most important issue in April 2005 at the beginning of the campaign (see Table 5 on p 20), the issue was one on which it was easy to portray the Conservatives as narrow-minded doing more general damage to their image.

Figure 27: Governmental Honesty about Immigration

Q   To what extent do you agree or disagree with the following statement?
"The Government is open and honest about the scale of immigration into Britain"

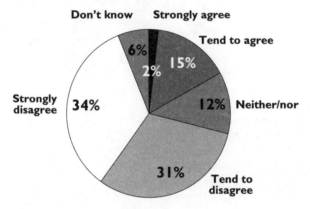

Source: MORI/*Evening Standard*
Base: 1,973 GB residents aged 18+, 7-11 April 2005

Nevertheless, discontent with government policy on the issue was overwhelming (Four-fifths of the public said the government had been "unsuccessful" in tacking illegal immigration, and 85% that it "could do more ... to ensure Britain is not seen as a soft touch for bogus asylum seekers or economic migrants", in an ICM poll in February 2004 for the *News of the World*[91], and during the election the Tories had a bigger lead

---

[91] ICM interviewed 1,001 adults aged 18+ by telephone on 4-5 February 2004 for the *News of the World*. Details at icmresearch.co.uk.

over Labour on asylum than on any other issue, 52% to 8% among those who named the issue as important. The Tories' rating had virtually doubled from the 28% who said they had the best policy in September 2004, suggesting success in their campaigning.

Figure 28: The British Public's Views on Immigration

Q Which one of these statements comes closest to your views on laws about immigration in Britain ?

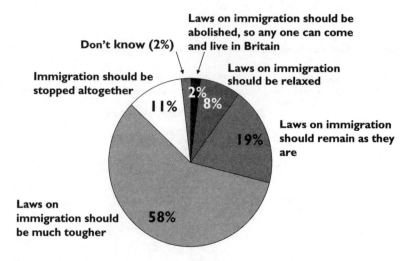

Source: MORI/*Observer*
Base: 1,004 GB residents aged 18+, 7-9 April 2005

The Tory lead was presumably fuelled by public distrust of the government's honesty on immigration: asked whether or not they agreed that the government was being open and honest about the scale of immigration, two-thirds of the public disagreed that it was (see Figure 27). Only one in six agreed. And the policy probably extended their appeal into groups where their influence would otherwise not reach. Lord Ashcroft's polling found that it played best with those least likely to vote Tory, amongst the DE social group[92]. The results, though, suggest it yielded little dividend in votes.

---

[92] Michael A Ashcroft, *Smell the coffee: a wake-up call for the Conservative Party* (London: CGI Europe, 2005).

The public now believe there is a serious problem in relation to immigration to Britain (see Figure 28). Seven in ten now feel that immigration should either be stopped altogether (11%), or that laws on immigration should be much tougher (58%); just one in five think they should remain as they are, and one in ten that laws on immigration should be relaxed or abolished.

It is important to understand how much the public's ignorance may be contributing to these attitudes. Surveys have consistently shown that most people greatly overestimate the proportion of ethnic minority people living in this country: in 2002, the national average estimate was over one in five (23%)[93], which compares to nearer one in twelve in reality (7%-8%).

But given the extent to which they distrust the government's honesty on the issue, they are unlikely to be quickly disabused of these misconceptions. Tony Blair's inability during the election (in an interview with Jeremy Paxman on *Newsnight* on 20 April) to estimate the number of failed asylum seekers in Britain became a pretext for his opponents to attack him, and cannot have helped defuse the issue in the long run.

It is clear though that one obstacle to the Tories' exploitation of the immigration issue was that it was the Tories that were doing it – another fatal example of image being more powerful than substance. An ICM survey in January found that while 82% of the public said they supported "the idea that immigration should be controlled more strictly", only 65% said they supported "Conservative policy to control immigration more strictly".[94]

It is not yet clear how fair the impression, which clearly came across from the media, that immigration was the Tories' main campaigning issue, really is. Since the election party spokesmen have blamed journalists for hijacking their press conferences, insisting on returning to the issue when the party was trying to move on, and research for the New Politics Network has shown that, at least in terms of literature, the assertion that the Tories concentrated on immigration/asylum is unfounded: "On the basis of this data, it seems fair to argue that the emphasis placed upon

---

[93] Fieldwork in April 2002 for the Commission for Racial Equality; see Appendix 2, survey 13, for details.
[94] ICM interviewed random samples of 528 and 484 adults aged 18+ by telephone on 11-13 February 2005, on behalf of *Newsnight*.

Conservative campaigning on immigration has been overstated. It featured in fewer leaflets than many other policy domains, was not universally negative and did not vary by marginality. On this last point, it indicates that the party took a principled stance on this issue rather than playing the 'race card' in tight electoral contests."[95]

Iraq

Whilst the Conservatives were effectively dogged by the asylum issue, which seemed to be having a more negative effect than positive by the end of the campaign, Labour was having an equally difficult time of it, with the Iraq issue and its handling of the intelligence it received and the basis for which it went to war in the first place. As we have seen, most of the public now opposed the war, though some 15% admitted they had changed their minds having once supported it. (See Figure 15 on p 94.)

Figure 29: Lies Over Iraq?

Q Thinking about the British government's decision to take part in the invasion of Iraq, which one of these do you personally think was true?

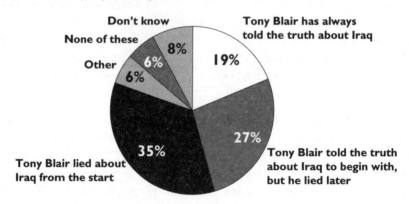

Source: MORI/*Financial Times*
Base: 1,009 GB residents aged 18+, 29 April-1 May 2005

[95] Justin Fisher, *General Election 2005 - A Voter's Eye View* (London: New Politics Network, 2005).

The election debate in the final few days centred on Lord Goldsmith, the Attorney-General and the legal advice he gave Blair on whether or not the Government had the legal authority to go to war against Iraq. The weekend before the election, five adults in six said the publication of the Attorney-General's advice had not changed the way they intended to vote, though 11% said it had. (On the other hand a fifth of these said they were going to vote Labour, as many as were going to vote Liberal Democrat.)

More damagingly, a third of the public thought Blair had persistently lied about Iraq, and another quarter said he had told the truth to start with, but lied later; the Conservative message that Blair was a liar was getting across.

But all this hoo-hah didn't seem to be having any effect on how much people trusted Tony Blair whatsoever. The public didn't trust him anyway it seems, and his trust rating did not decline from the lack of trust that was felt for him by the general public in January 2005, in a period when trust in Michael Howard by contrast increased slightly. (See Table 33 on p 96).

Economic Competence

As always, one focus of the campaign was the parties' attacks on each others' spending or saving plans and an attempt to establish confidence as the most competent party.

The issue of managing the economy was long regarded as a key indicator of voting performance. The Conservatives had dominated the issue since the late 1970s, but Britain's ejection from the Exchange Rate Mechanism – a European device for stabilising European currencies and a prelude to the Euro – caused John Major and his then chancellor Norman Lamont untold reputational damage to their perceived ability to manage the economy, and the Conservatives have not recovered their reputation since.

As we have already seen, Labour's commanding lead on the issue under Gordon Brown's stewardship ebbed during the 2001 Parliament but was re-established in time for the election, one of the few salient issues on which Labour was almost as well placed in 2005 as in 2001.

Labour was weaker, though, on tax and spending than on economic management. By the middle of the election campaign, almost half the

165

public felt the government had done a bad job handling taxation and public expenditure.

Furthermore, most of the public felt that if re-elected Labour would raise their taxes. But they still elected a Labour government, as they did in 1997 with an historic landslide when they thought Labour would increase taxes, and again in 2001 when they said Tony Blair had increased taxes and would do so again. Why? Because it's not just concern about the level of taxation that matters, but whether voters think the government is spending their money on their priorities and not wasting it – and whether the opposition would be any better.

Figure 30: The Government's Record on the Economy and Tax

Q   Since it was elected in May 1997, do you think the government has done a good job or a bad job at managing the economy/ handling taxation and public expenditure?

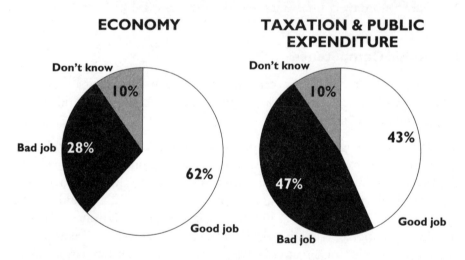

Source: MORI/*Financial Times*
Base: 1,005 GB residents aged 18+, 15-18 April 2005

One of Michael Howard's central claims was that a Conservative government would cut Labour's waste and get greater value for money for the taxpayer. Yet the public were not convinced. Two in five people (41%) said that a Labour government would be most effective at getting good value for the public money it spends – a third more than thought the Tories would be best.

In any case the Tories could make little capital over tax risers while the public expected them from both parties. True, four-fifths of the public believed that Labour would put taxes up post-election if they won, but two-thirds (67%) felt that the Conservative Party would do the same (see Figure 31).

Figure 31: Belief in Future Tax Rises

Q If a Labour/Conservative Government is elected after the next general election, do you think it will or will not increase tax?

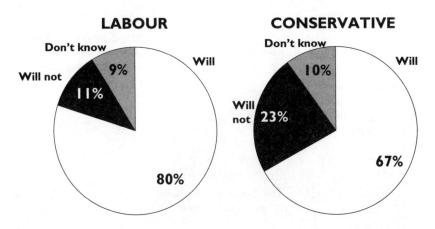

Source: MORI/*Financial Times*
Base: 1,005 GB residents aged 18+, 15-18 April 2005

The Conservatives' approach to taxation was to increase investment in public services, but by £35bn less than Labour intended – which Labour labelled as "cuts" early in the campaign and were lambasted for sharp practice by Nick Robinson and others in the media – and to cut tax by £4bn based on these "savings". This was not especially popular with the general public: only a quarter (26%) felt that they had got it "about right", though this may have owed a little to the tendency that policies identified as being Conservative were less well received than the same policies in the abstract. Nevertheless, in total 42% supported cutting taxes by £4bn or

167

more, slightly more than opposed the proposal. In other words, the British public were almost equally split on whether or not to cut taxes to this extent, bearing in mind its perceived relation to investment in public services. But, of course, their distrust of government to spend wisely would naturally lead many to assume that substantial tax cuts would be possible given greater efficiency without damaging public services – as, indeed, both major parties were arguing.

Figure 32: Perceptions of Conservative Taxation Policy

Q   As you may have heard, the Conservatives have set out how they would cut public spending to enable them to reduce taxation by £4 billion. Which one of the following statements, if any, comes closest to your own view?

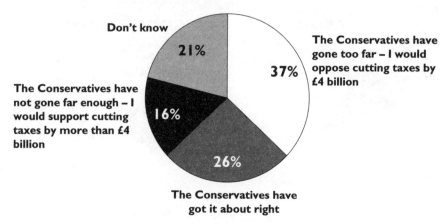

Source: MORI/*Financial Times*
Base: 1,106 GB residents aged 18+, 21-25 April 2005

Yet at the same time three-fifths of the public say they support using taxes "to narrow the gap between rich and poor"[96]. Even given that a substantial part of that 60% probably number themselves among the poor in that equation, it is an impressive finding if it can be taken at face value. But, since no major party was suggesting doing so, it is slightly irrelevant to the 2005 general election.

---

[96] Fieldwork conducted 7-9 April 2005 for the *Observer*, for details see Appendix 2, survey 35.

Party Strategy: Target Seats

It is perfectly possible that marginal seats might behave differently from the rest of the country; and, indeed, they did so in both 1997 and 2001, with Labour doing better there than in the safer seats. This might happen for two reasons: most of the parties' campaigning efforts are concentrated in the marginal seats, so voters there can get a very different experience of the election campaign and may accordingly behave differently; and it makes much more sense to vote tactically in marginal seats, where it might make a difference, than in safe seats where your second-choice party is no more likely to win than your first choice. Consequently it makes sense for the parties to identify target seats and concentrate their efforts there.

The Conservative Party's Target Seats Unit were aiming to convert more than 164 seats[97], making a total target floating voter population of around 1.1 million voters distributed in marginal seats nationwide, i.e. 3% of the 43 million total electorate.

Conversely, the Labour Party's resources were targeted, first, simply to hold onto 80 of their most vulnerable seats, principally against Conservative opposition. These seats included 62 seats won by Labour in 2001 by majorities of 10% or less from the Conservatives (where the Tories could therefore win with a 5% direct swing from Labour to the Conservatives). Nevertheless, the Conservatives faced an uphill struggle. With a solid majority of 167 in 2001, notionally reduced to around 156 after boundary changes and by-elections, the loss of 62 seats would still have given the Labour Party a working majority of around 32 seats. The Conservatives needed an even bigger swing in vote, more than 6% directly from Labour to Conservative, simply to win a hung parliament. Except for Blair's win in 1997, no such swing had been recorded at any election since the War. The task was Herculean.

Labour also targeted fifty opposition-held seats with majorities of up to around 9%, bringing their total number of constituencies targeted, including those that they were holding, up to 130. This was substantially less than the 164-plus target seats number for the Conservatives, and the Labour Party had more money to spend in attempting to win the votes in

---

[97] See Michael A Ashcroft, *Smell the coffee: a wake-up call for the Conservative Party* (London: CGI Europe, 2005).

169

these seats. Nevertheless, making gains was always going to prove to be an uphill struggle since the party was clearly weaker than in 2001, and they were far more likely to put most of their resources – including time spent campaigning by Labour leaders, mobilisation of regional agents and activists, money, and use of central telephone canvassing units – into the seats that they were defending.

The LibDems seem to have identified three distinct types of target seat – those they hoped to win from Labour (where, mostly, they needed big swings and relied especially on student and Muslim votes to deliver them), their more established battleground with the Tories (both defending recent gains and hoping to make further inroads), and within both these groups a much-leaked but never officially acknowledged sub-group of potential gains where the identity of the sitting MP provided extra motivation for success. This latter group of constituencies made up the so-called "decapitation" strategy, aimed at "taking out" opposition party leaders. If we count only marginals with a majority of 20% or under, the Liberal Democrats were targeting about ½m floating voters, out of an electorate of around 43 million, i.e. 1.1% of the electorate.

What issues did voters in marginal seats consider important to Britain? Figure 33, based on an analysis of 9,653 British adults aged 18+ from MORI Political Omnibus surveys conducted between September 2004 and March 2005, indicates the salience of issues in different categories of marginals in the six months up to the start of the election campaign. Note the relative unimportance, across all types of marginal seat, of issues such as Europe, the economy, pensions and taxation. They were simply not on the radar for voters in marginal seats, any more than they were anywhere else.

The key categories here are the seats Labour held over the Conservatives by majorities of less than 20% (labelled "Lab-C (0-10)" and "Lab-C (10-20)"). In the more marginal of these, the NHS was by a margin the most important issue while defence/foreign affairs (i.e. Iraq) was second. In the 10%-to-20% band, these two issues were less clearly ahead with race relations/immigration/asylum and crime/law and order almost as significant. This explains why the Conservatives campaigned on cleaning up hospitals and MRSA, and on immigration and asylum – no doubt their private polls told them of the significance of these issues. In fact, polls undertaken by Lord Ashcroft indicate that immigration was one of the

170

four most important issues in Conservative-Labour marginals when asked about the most important issues "affecting the country", cited by around 50% of voters, but its importance dropped considerably (to around 25%) when the voters were asked to state the four most important issues "affecting their family"[98].

Figure 33: Issues by Type of Marginal Seat

Q What would you say is the most important issue facing Britain today?
Q What do you see as other important issues facing today?
   (COMBINED FIGURES, CODED FROM UNPROMPTED ANSWERS)

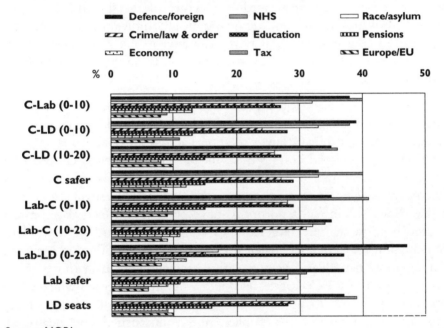

Source: MORI
Base: 9,653 GB residents aged 18+, September 2004 – April 2005

For Conservative-Liberal Democrat marginals (0-10%), the three leading issues were the NHS, Defence and Immigration. In Conservative-Labour

---

[98] See Michael A Aschcroft, *Smell the coffee: a wake-up call for the Conservative Party* (London: CGI Europe, 2005).

171

marginals, it was NHS, Defence and Race. In the Labour-Liberal Democrat marginals (0-20%), the key issues were Education (much higher here than elsewhere), Defence and the NHS. Interestingly, the LibDems had been campaigning to some extent on education, particularly higher education, mainly by targeting the student vote in constituencies like Cardiff Central and Cambridge, using their opposition to the Iraq war rather than their policy of opposition to the Government's top-up fees.

Neither at this stage, nor during the election campaign itself, were there any issues that were salient in marginal constituencies yet not salient nationally. Nor would we expect there to be. Constituencies are normally marginal because they are towards the centre of the spectrum not only politically but attitudinally and demographically. Individual constituencies or groups of constituencies may have distinctive problems or agendas, but the marginals as a whole will tend to be not too far in their concerns from those of the median voter.

This has consequences for the effects of targeting and segmentation. When this is a crude process, aimed at finding a single wide-ranging policy mix and communications strategy to appeal across the board to key voters, it will have to a broad compromise meeting the collective concerns of most of the electorate if it is to succeed. In such cases the apparently undemocratic tactic of considering the concerns of only a small segment of the electorate will in fact tend not to have pernicious effects. By contrast the much more closely targeted and fragmented tactic of a modern segmentation marketing campaign may end by concentrating on a myriad of much more parochial concerns or those which individually move only a very small part of the electorate, and may result in a campaign which while appealing sufficiently to a bare majority of voters in a small number of key seats leaves the rest of the public entirely unsatisfied and neglected. Disillusionment with the political system and falling turnout, especially among untargeted groups, would be a predictable consequence.

Of course in a representative democracy like that in operation in Britain "all votes are equal but some are more equal than others" as one wag stated in the *Economist* during the 1992 election campaign.

172

Party Strategy: Target Voters

Typically, British political parties use more sophisticated methods than newspapers give them credit for, and have now started using geo-demographic software packages which allow parties to identify geographic areas where there are more floating voters – those who might vote for another party than the one they voted for previously. The Conservatives are reputed to have funded the purchasing of the Republicans' "Voter Vault" software to help them in targeting their direct marketing appeals. This method reportedly worked particularly well in Putney where the Conservative candidate, Justine Greening, took the seat from Labour with a 6.5% swing.

It is worth wondering, however, how much the adoption of geo-demographics illustrates not the strength of the parties' resources but their weaknesses – half a century ago any well-organised constituency party in a marginal seat would have maintained a constantly updated marked electoral register based on their canvass returns, and would have had no need to resort to commercial software to predict where it could find floating voters. Computer-generated address labels may represent an advance in efficiency over the hand-written envelopes of the past, especially now the parties can no longer command the voluntary manpower needed to do the writing, but they lack the personal touch that voters value.

This election marked something of a departure from previous elections in the degree to which types of voters as well as constituencies were explicitly targeted during the campaign. There was a clearer attempt to demarcate specific groups of voters rather than specific policy propositions *per se* (e.g. pensions). Labour and the Liberal Democrats both produced a set of mini-manifestos for a variety of groups including women, families, and younger and older voters amongst others, whilst the Conservatives published only a mini-manifesto for the elderly.

Table 55 analyses the parties' appeal to the main demographic segments targeted in the 2005 British General Election by the three major parties – the young, the old, and women.

Finally, the political parties have woken up to the power of older voters. What on earth has taken them so long?

173

Table 55: Key Voter Segments 2005

Target Group (Proportion of the electorate)	Aged 18-24 (11%)	Aged 65+ (21%)	Women (52%)
Key Manifesto Commitments	**Labour** *Education and employment* 50% of young people entering higher education Increase number of apprenticeships to 300,000 Increase in per pupil school funding to £5,500 by 2007-2009 **Conservative** *Education* No university top-up fees Headteachers given power to expel disruptive students **LibDem** *Employment and education* Reform of the New Deal to encourage employment No tuition fees or top-up fees	**Labour** *Pensions and Health* Introducing the Pension Protection Fund and a pensions regulator Introduction of community-based tailor-made NHS services **Conservative** *Taxation and Pensions* 50% discount on council tax bills Basic state pension increased in line with earnings not prices **LibDem** *Pensions and Taxation* A Citizen's Pension scheme giving over-75s £100 more per month. Replacement of council tax with local income tax based on ability to pay	**Labour** *Crime and Employment* New measures to tackle domestic violence Establishment of Women and Work Commission **Conservative** *Health and Crime* Cleaner hospitals to deliver infection-free wards 5,000 extra police officers per year to tackle crime **LibDem** *Gender Equality* New mothers offered Maternity Income Guarantee Equal pensions for women
Best Party on...	Education = Lab Unemployment= Lab	Taxation = Con Pensions= Lab Health = Lab	Crime = Con Health = Lab Unemployment = Lab

Vote	2001 %	2005 %	Chg	2001 %	2005 %	Chg	2001 %	2005 %	Chg
Con	27	28	+1	40	41	+1	33	32	-1
Lab	41	38	-3	39	35	-4	42	38	-4
LDem	24	26	+2	17	18	+1	19	23	+4

Sources: Party Manifestos, MORI Election Aggregates 2001/5, MORI/*Evening Standard* Best Party on Key issues survey (7-11 April 2005)

This sector of our society was traditionally neglected by political strategists, until it was pointed out nearly a decade ago that "grey power" had four times the political punch that the youth vote did, because there were twice as many of them, and they were twice as likely to vote. In 2001, the Conservatives had a 1% lead among voters aged 65+, and 70% of them voted.

MORI's first poll of the campaign, on 7-9 April for the *Observer* and *Sunday Mirror*, had Labour nationally on 40%, the Conservatives on 33%, with the Liberal Democrats on 19%; only 61% were certain to vote. But if only old folks had the vote, it wouldn't be like that: looking only at those 55 and over, who are absolutely certain to vote, Labour had 35%, the Conservatives 42%, and the Liberal Democrats 16%, a Tory lead of 7%, and 77% of them were sure they would vote.

The low level of modern turnouts puts political power disproportionately in the hands of older voters. Over the 18 months up to the election, twice as many 55+s were saying they were certain to vote as 18-34 year olds. No wonder the political parties were trying to outdo the others in their promises to the grey voters in this election.

Yet the young were by no means entirely ignored either. Their low turnout disguises the importance to the parties of campaigning for their votes, since their very youth implies they may be more easily persuaded, magnifying the impact of a good campaign. Young voters are of course the least experienced, and through that lack of experience will normally be the least knowledgeable group, with the natural consequence that their political convictions may be less solidly anchored than those of their elders.

The LibDems targeted the young, but especially concentrated on students, particularly in constituencies where the student vote could make a difference. Students are slightly more important in deciding the outcomes of British general elections than they have been in the past. Until 1969, when the voting age was reduced from 21, very few students could vote all. At the 1970 election, students numbered roughly 450,000 in an electorate of around 38½ million (1.1%); now there are around 2 million in an electorate of 43 million (4.7%). The key question was whether or not students will turn up to vote. Turnout of the young to some extent depends on how meaningful they find the election. The key issue for 18-24 year old students between January 2004 and March 2005 when asked to name the most important issues facing Britain was defence/foreign affairs/international terrorism (named by 49%), but conversely more mature students, aged 25-34, regarded the NHS (48%) as the most important. The idea that students formed a cohesive target group for the Lib Dems was therefore arguable, since Labour was regarded by most voters generally as the best party on the NHS, but the Liberal Democrats led on Iraq.

It seems worthy of note that in all three segments Labour's share of the vote fell less than it did nationally; the Tories did no better than average among 18-24 year olds and 65+s, and worse among women. Labour's targeting, it seems, may have worked; that of the Tories was less effective.

Lord Ashcroft's private polls, at a reported cost of three-quarters of a million pounds, and published after the election in *Smell the Coffee: A Wake-up Call for the Conservative Party,* came to a damning verdict on the Tories' campaign[99]. He found that voters had a more negative view of the Conservative Party at the end of the general election campaign than they did at the beginning, with those voters who rejected the Tories associating the party with "the past, with policies for the privileged few and with lack of leadership".

This election marked a departure from previous elections in another way too. Although the post-war average turnout has been around 74%, the 2001 election recorded a significant drop in turnout to 59%, only three in five voters bothering to make their way to the ballot box or send in a postal vote. In fact, nearly five million people fewer voted in the 2001 election, or around one in eight people in the electorate as a whole. By 2005, such apathy looked set to continue, and political parties worked hard to identify not only floating voters but those more likely to vote, principally through their own face-to-face, and increasingly their central telephone unit, canvassing activity. Had any party succeeded in getting its vote out better than its opponents, there were major gains to be made. But an eventual 61% turnout indicates clearly enough that none did. (We consider the turnout problem in more depth in Chapter 5.)

---

[99] Michael A Ashcroft, *Smell the coffee: a wake-up call for the Conservative Party* (London: CGI Europe, 2005).

Targeting Women

There is considerable debate as to whether or not there is such a thing as the women's vote. Some commentators have concluded that there isn't[100] – and that men and women tend to vote more or less in the same way – and others that there is a women's vote[101] – and that the Iraq war has cost it some of these and Labour's policy on pensions was costing those of older women.

Figure 34: Gender and Late Voting Decisions

Q   When did you decide which party to vote for?

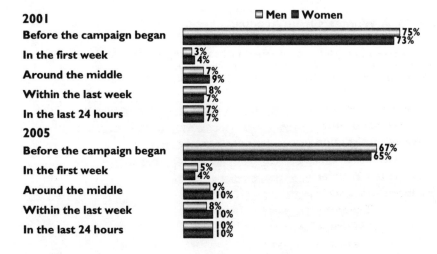

Source: MORI
Base: 1,349 GB residents aged 18+ who claimed to have voted, 14-19 June 2001; 1,399 GB residents aged 18+ who claimed to have voted, 5-10 May 2005

The Labour Party did make a concerted effort to target women who represent around 52% of the electorate and 52% of voters in 2005. For this strategy to make any sense, women must in some way be distinctively

---

[100] See Zoe Williams, "Is there any such thing as the women's vote?", *New Statesman*, 4 April 2005; Zoe Williams, "Sorry, Tony, you're just not on our wavelength", *Evening Standard*, 1 April 2005.
[101] See Rosemary Bennett, "Older women shun Labour", *The Times*, 24 March 2005; Michael White, "War cost women's votes, says PM", *Guardian*, 14 March 2005, Jackie Ashley, "Why all sorts of women fell out of love with New Labour", *Guardian*, 6 May 2004; Mary Ann Sieghart, "War and the women's vote", *The Times*, 7 May 2004.

different from men in their behaviour during an election, the factors that will affect their votes or the way in which they decide. Some researchers have argued that women make up their minds how to vote later than their male counterparts[102], although we found only very slight evidence for this assertion in our polls. Men were more likely to report that they had made up their minds before the campaign began, but there isn't much of a gender difference over the course of the campaign (see Figure 34). This was likely part of the reason why Blair pursued a so-called "Masochism strategy"; wandering around the country taking the flak for his stance on the Iraq war, and being seen to be united with Gordon Brown, to woo the woman voter.

Figure 35: A Women's Issue Agenda?

Q   What would you say is the most important issue facing Britain today?
Q   What do you see as other important issues facing today?
    (COMBINED FIGURES, CODED FROM UNPROMPTED ANSWERS)

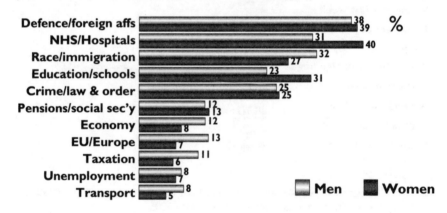

Source: MORI
Base: c 12,000 GB adults 18+, January-December 2004

---

[102] See B C Hayes and I McAllister, "Women, electoral volatility and political outcomes in Britain", *European Journal of Marketing*, Vol.35, no 9/10 (2001), 971-983.

178

Whilst women were a key Labour target, they do not seem to identify radically different issues from their male counterparts as Figure 35 demonstrates.

Women do place political issues in a slightly different order of priority, with more women regarding health and education as important than men, while they place less importance on the economy and tax. Does this represent a women's agenda? Using the unprompted question on "the most important issues facing Britain today", we found that the issues that were of most concern to women were in the order (*men's position of importance in brackets*): 1) NHS (*3rd*), 2) defence/terrorism (*1st*), 3) education (*5th*), 4) immigration (*2nd*), and 5) law and order (*4th*). Not much of a gender gap there since they both share the same top 5 "basket of issues". Nor did it make any difference if we concentrated only on the "single most important" issue – there are no overwhelming women's priorities that get lost under less relevant concerns by asking them to name more than one important issue.

Similarly, in the election issues questions, this time picking options from a list, men's and women's top five choices are the same (healthcare, education, law & order, pensions and taxation), although healthcare and education have a clearer lead among women than men.

However, women are more likely to answer "don't know" to pollsters' questions. Why is this? Perhaps because they feel that they do not want to commit themselves to an opinion which they do not hold strongly. On the other hand, men might well be prepared to commit themselves to such opinions. It does not seem to imply that they are more volatile, more easily persuaded to change their minds, which if true would justify the efforts being directed at them.

Over the years, as Table 56 shows, the average net change between elections in women's votes has been no more than that of men; over the period since 1974 women's votes have changed fractionally less, in fact, an average of 6.9% of the men's vote moving compared to 6.7% of the women's votes. While these are net figures, and may of course conceal greater switching under the surface but being cancelled out by other voters switching in the opposite direction, the clear implication is that all other things being equal one should not expect to a bigger net gain in votes from a campaign aimed at women than from a campaign aimed at men. It may

179

be, as the chauvinistic adage would have it, that it is woman's prerogative to change her mind, but it doesn't seem to be a prerogative that she exercises more than men.

The implication for the political marketers is that there appears to be no particular advantage in designing policies specifically targeted at women, at least not just for women of all ages, because they are not sufficiently distinct a target segment to warrant this.

Table 56: Net Election-to-Election Voting Volatility by Gender

	Oct 1974 %	1979 %	1983 %	1987 %	1992 %	1997 %	2001 %	2005 %
Men								
Share								
Con	32	43	42	43	41	31	32	34
Lab	43	40	30	32	37	45	42	34
Lib	18	13	25	23	18	17	18	22
Change								
Con		11	1	1	2	10	1	2
Lab		3	10	2	5	8	3	8
Lib		5	12	2	5	1	1	4
Net switches		9.5	11.5	2.5	6.0	9.5	2.5	7.0
Average 1974-2005								**6.9**
Women								
Share								
Con	39	47	46	43	44	32	33	32
Lab	38	35	26	32	34	44	42	38
Lib	20	15	27	23	18	18	19	23
Change								
Con		8	1	3	1	12	1	1
Lab		3	9	6	2	10	2	4
Lib		5	12	4	5	0	1	4
Net switches		8.0	11.0	6.5	4.0	11.0	2.0	4.5
Average 1974-2005								**6.7**

Source: MORI

Indeed, rather the reverse – all the issues that are important to high numbers of women are also important to high numbers of men, but there are some issues important to many men which strike far fewer chords with women – it is men's issues, not women's issues, which might theoretically be in danger of slipping off a single consensus agenda.

The Campaign in the Media

According to research conducted by Dominic Wring and David Deacon of the Communication Research Centre, Loughborough University[103] in work undertaken for the Electoral Commission, four in ten articles (39.5%) in the national media were concerned with the electoral process itself, rather than about specific issues or parties (see Table 57). In other words, the media covered the horserace – who's ahead of whom, issues about the campaigns and strategists (e.g. Lynton Crosby, Saatchi, Milburn, and Campbell), and discussions of the electoral system (see Table 58).

Table 57: The Issue Agenda in the Media

Top 10 Themes, 2005

	Theme	Prominence
I	Electoral Conduct	39.5%
2	Asylum/ Immigration	7.3%
3	Political Impropriety	6.7%
4	Crime	5.8%
5=	Iraq	5.7%
5=	Taxation	5.7%
7	Economy	4.5%
8	Education	3.7%
9	NHS	3.5%
10	Social Security	2.7%

Source: Dominic Wring and David Deacon, Communication Research Centre, Loughborough University
Notes: Up to three themes could be coded per item. To qualify as a theme, a subject must occupy at least 10 seconds of broadcast time or 2 full sentences of a printed news report.

The main issue covered by nearly 7% of all election stories in the national media was, of course, immigration and asylum, the issue on which the Conservative campaign rested, and targeted for its importance in Tory-Labour marginals as a salient issue by *de facto* Tory campaign chief, Lynton Crosby. A similar proportion of national media stories were coded by the

---

[103] The report covers the period 4 April to 27 April 2005 inclusive. The research is based on detailed coding and analysis of all election news in the week-day editions of the *Guardian, Independent, The Times, Financial Times, Daily Telegraph, Daily Mail, Daily Express, Daily Mirror, Sun* and *Daily Star*, the weekday editions of BBC1 Main Evening news, ITV Main Evening News, BBC2 Newsnight, C4 7pm News, and Sky Main Evening News.

181

Loughborough researchers as concerned with political impropriety, notably the revelations of electoral fraud in Birmingham Council elections in 2004 (being tried in court as the election got under way) and the implications for the use of postal votes in the general election. Crime, Iraq and taxation were each the subject of around 6% of stories in the national media.

Table 58: Sub-Themes Within the "Electoral Conduct" Theme

Sub-theme	Percent
Discussion of Campaigning Strategies	15.4%
Opinion Polls, Focus Groups, "Horse Race"	6.7%
Passing references to the chosen daily topic agendas of political parties	4.0%
Political tensions and infighting within Parties & defections	3.5%
Party Spin/ PR/ News Management	2.2%
All other themes in this category	7.7%
Total for category	39.5%

Source: Dominic Wring and David Deacon, Communication Research Centre, Loughborough University

The economy, the NHS and education as issues were relatively less covered, by fewer than one in twenty articles in the national media – an interesting finding considering that the NHS and education were the top two important issues in deciding how people would vote in the 2005 election (see Table 5 on p 20). In other words, the media were not covering those issues of importance to the public.

Table 59: Differing Issue Prominence During the Course of the Campaign

Average daily number of articles (all Media) dealing with Iraq and asylum/immigration, 2005

	Iraq	Asylum/immigration
Week 1	2.6	2.0
Week 2	0.8	11.6
Week 3	5.8	12.6
Week 4	24.7	3.0

Source: Dominic Wring and David Deacon, Communication Research Centre, Loughborough University
Notes: Due to time constraints, only the first three days of week 4 are available for this calculation. To facilitate comparison across the 4 weeks, we present here the daily average number of items (all media) that had Iraq or Asylum and/or Immigration as a prominent theme.

So what were they covering? It seems that, on balance, the media were responding to the agenda-setting initiatives of the Conservative Party, in terms of the coverage on asylum/immigration, and the Conservatives and particularly the Liberal Democrats, in terms of the coverage on Iraq. Table 62 indicates that stories on asylum/immigration had started to peter out by the final week, but stories on Iraq quadrupled from around 1 in 16 (5.8%), to around 1 in 4 stories (24.7%) in the national media.

Table 60: Good News/Bad News

Proportion of Themes coded on Iraq & Asylum/Immigration (all media) that were, respectively, "Good News", "Bad News" or "Mixed/ Descriptive" for each party

		Iraq–related %	Asylum/ Immigration %
Labour	Good News for..	3	2
	Bad News for..	57	33
	Mixed/ Descriptive..	32	10
Conservative	Good News for...	0	4
	Bad News for..	2	25
	Mixed/ Descriptive...	1	22
Lib Dem	Good News for...	2	0
	Bad News for...	2	0
	Mixed/ Descriptive...	1	1
Other parties	Good News for...	0	0
	Bad News for...	0	1
	Mixed/ Descriptive...	0	2

Source: Dominic Wring and David Deacon, Communication Research Centre, Loughborough University
A Theme was coded as "Mainly or Solely Bad News for..." where more than 50% of the article material that related to the coded theme was focused explicitly on the negative implications of the topic for a political party. The same rule applied for "Mainly or Solely Good News". The "Mixed implications for..." category was used where there was a broadly equitable distribution of positive and negative judgements discussed in the piece. The "Descriptive Only" category was used when a report simply provided information on a topic, but didn't report any political controversy regarding it (e.g. "Labour will be unveiling their plans for reform of....").

But whilst the opposition parties succeeded in setting the agenda, did they succeed in obtaining negative coverage for the Labour Party on those issues on which Labour were vulnerable? Table 60 indicates that in fact nearly 6 in 10 stories (57%) written on Iraq were "bad news for Labour", and 1 in 3 stories written on asylum/immigration were "bad news for Labour". Nevertheless, whilst 3 in 10 (32%) stories on Iraq were largely mixed/descriptive, 1 in 4 stories on asylum/immigration "were bad news for the Conservatives" – a figure nearly as high as that for Labour – indicating that the Conservative news management strategy backfired.

When it came to representing the parties in the press, it was the leaders of the political parties who occupied the limelight. Unsurprisingly, Tony Blair occupied the most time in both newspapers and on TV with 13% of the press time and 23% of the article space devoted to direct quotation. (See Table 61Table 61.) Michael Howard occupied a similar amount of TV time, 12%, (required under broadcast licenses and codes of conduct, and as part of the Representation of the People Act 1987) but, perhaps more surprisingly, he occupied a similar amount of press time (22%). Kennedy obtained a respectable amount of TV time (10%), but fared less well in the newspapers, where he obtained less than a quarter of the coverage (5%) garnered by the Conservatives and the Labour Party. Interestingly, whilst Gordon Brown secured much less time on TV than Kennedy, he did succeed in gaining more press space.

Table 61: "Look Who's Talking"

Amount of Direct Quotation allocated to Political Parties (Press and TV), 2005

	All TV		All Press	
	Seconds	*%*	*Words*	*%*
Tony Blair	2736	13	13254	23
Gordon Brown	245	1	3408	6
All other Labour	4866	22	13314	23
Michael Howard	2554	12	13043	22
All other Conservative	4121	19	8243	14
Charles Kennedy	2254	10	3124	5
All other Lib Dem	3313	15	2919	5
All other Parties	1573	7	1239	2

Source: Dominic Wring and David Deacon, Communication Research Centre, Loughborough University

Table 62 indicates that of those other politicians that were featured in the media generally, Alan Milburn, Labour campaign co-ordinator, and David Davis, Conservative Shadow Home Secretary, were the most prominent.

George Galloway, leader of the minor party Respect, got more coverage than any Liberal Democrat bar Charles Kennedy.

Table 62: Top 10 Most Featured Politicians (All Media), 2005

	Politician	Prominence
I	Tony Blair	15.9%
2	Michael Howard	11.5%
3	Charles Kennedy	6.3%
4	Gordon Brown	5.6%
5	David Davis	1.2%
6	Alan Milburn	1.0%
7=	John Prescott	0.9%
7=	Oliver Letwin	0.9%
7=	John Reid	0.9%
10=	George Galloway	0.8%
10=	Charles Clarke	0.8%

Source: Dominic Wring and David Deacon, Communication Research Centre, Loughborough University
Notes: Percentages are based on the total of all UK-based politicians coded.

Table 63: Attack and Defence: Stance of Party Actors in Coverage

	Labour	Conservative	LibDem
	%	%	%
Presenting policy	39	27	38
Defence	21	13	7
Attack	25	49	43
Mixed	15	11	12

Source: Dominic Wring and David Deacon, Communication Research Centre, Loughborough University
This variable assesses the stance of each actor identified in election news coverage – i.e. are they attacking others outside of the party, defending themselves from criticisms, or presenting their policies and positions? An adept politician will often seek to do several or all of these things in any given media appearance. When this occurred their main stance in the appearance was coded; where it was impossible to make a clear decision as to their main stance, the "mixed stance" value was used.

Table 63 outlines the stance that the parties took when appearing in the news. In the main, the LibDems and the Conservatives used the opportunity to attack the opposition (not necessarily just Labour but each other as well) in 43% and 49% of cases respectively. Labour, on the other hand, attacked the opposition in only one in four cases (25%), and tried to present their policies in four in ten cases (39%). The Conservatives presented their policies in only three in ten cases (27%), the lowest of the three parties, and an indictment of the poor quality of the policy platform of a party trying to come across as a government-in-waiting.

The Influence of the Media on the Voters

Political parties try to dominate the news agenda, through spin and sound bites, the media try to "get one over on them" – make them look stupid – and the voters try to make sense of it all!

Figure 36: Media, Party and Public Interactions

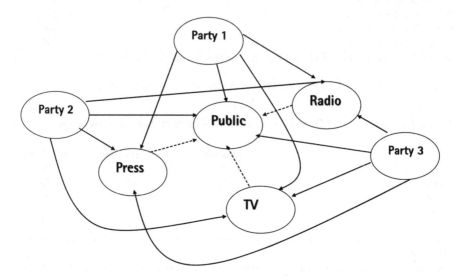

Figure 36 illustrates how complex this whole communication process can be, and the model assumes that the political parties themselves don't interact with one another, which we know that they do. For instance, political parties change their approach on how they present a particular policy in the media as they learn how the media portrays that particular policy for the other party when presenting their own policies. Over the last few years, the Labour Party has "test-marketed" a number of policy ideas through leaks to the press, to see how they are reported to the public. A good example was Blair's initiative to institute on-the-spot fines to yobs (the idea being that those caught committing minor offences would be

186

frog-marched to cash-points to pay off fixed penalty fines). The policy was eventually withdrawn as the government concluded that the public opposition was too great.

The problem for political parties is that the media do not always present their policies as parties would like them to be presented! In other words, the media are not uncritical (hence the dotted line between the media and the public). They present the policies as they see fit and with their own political bias and agenda. For this reason, a three-way "dialogue" begins between the actors within news outlets (i.e. press, radio and television), the politicians within the parties, and the public.

This interaction is a crucial element in the way the public builds up its "image" of the parties, the leaders and especially their policies. The parties' opportunities to communicate directly with the public are limited – for the most part they are dependent on the media portrayal of their message.

Consequently, political parties try to set the news agenda to ensure maximum coverage of their strongest issues.

Table 64: How Informed the Public Feel About Party Policies

Q I am going to read out a number of current issues, and for each one, I would like you to tell me how well informed you feel about the major parties' policies on each. Firstly, how well informed do you feel about the major parties' policies on …?

Issue		Very well	Fairly well	Not very well	Not at all	Don't know
Healthcare	%	9	53	26	7	4
Education	%	8	51	29	7	4
Crime, law and order	%	8	48	31	9	4
The management of the economy	%	7	44	34	10	5
Taxation	%	8	41	36	10	5
Iraq and foreign affairs	%	11	37	35	13	5
Asylum and immigration	%	6	33	41	15	4
Pensions	%	6	33	44	12	8
The European Union	%	6	32	43	14	6

Source: MORI/*Financial Times*
Base: 1,973 GB residents aged 18+, 7-11 April 2005

The media coverage of the campaign matters in particular because the public admit they do not know a great deal about the competing party policies on important issues, and the public is prepared to be informed

187

when an election comes around. At the beginning of the campaign[104], very few members of the public stated that they felt "very well informed" about the parties' policies on a number of key issues, as Table 64 shows.

It is worth noting that the public's perceptions of how well informed they were about party policies was not dependent on how important they considered the issue. True, the issues on which they felt best informed, healthcare, education and law & order, were the three they thought would be most important in deciding their vote; but their fourth most important issue, pensions, was one of those on which they felt least well informed, and they also expressed their ignorance about policies on asylum and immigration, another highly salient issue. No doubt this partly reflects the amount of attention the parties had paid to putting across their policies on each issue, but in the case of asylum probably also reflects a high degree of mistrust for the parties – making the distinction between knowing what the major parties were *saying* was their policy, and knowing what it really was.

For the parties to be able to put their message across to the voters, the voters must be prepared to trust what the parties are saying. It has become, of course, routine for the media to take as its role to be to challenge the parties, as well as to attempt to interpret what they are saying to the voters. But what if the voters don't trust the media either?

As already noted, trust in politicians to tell the truth is persistently low, challenged only by even more people distrusting journalists. More detailed research generally indicates that broadsheet journalists are distrusted by fewer people than tabloid journalists, and television is trusted by more people than newspapers of either type.

The public's distrust of the media is magnified by their perception that it is not merely a passive channel for information, but has real influence and even power. As Table 65 shows, the public feel the media have more impact on their everyday lives than political institutions or other types of business, and indeed MPs on the whole agree with them, though placing the influence of the media second to that of local councils, which clearly impact on MPs more than on the public.

---

[104] Fieldwork 7-11 April for the *Financial Times*; for details see survey 36 in Appendix 2.

Table 65: Influential Institutions – Views of the Public and MPs

Q   From this list, which two or three of the following do you believe has the most impact on people's everyday lives? You can select up to three options.

	General public %	MPs %	Difference %
Media	52	65	-13
Local councils	47	77	+30
Business	41	45	+4
Westminster Parliament	30	34	+4
Prime Minister	25	27	+2
Civil Service	22	25	+3
European Union	17	20	+3
The Cabinet	8	8	0
None	*	0	0
Don't know	6	0	-6

Source: MORI survey for *An Audit of Political Engagement* (London: Electoral Commission/Hansard Society, 2004)
Base: 1,976 UK residents aged 18+, 11-17 December 2003

Can the press really swing votes? *The Sun*'s "holy smoke" gimmick was a great piece of theatre in the best traditions of light-hearted Fleet Street marketing stunts, but it barely disguised the knowledge that few voters will vote Labour if they were not otherwise intending to do so simply because Rebekah Wade and Trevor Kavanagh (Editor and Political Editor, respectively, of *The Sun*) advise them to. But editorial decisions in selection of material, prominence of stories, perhaps even the angle of the reporting, can undoubtedly have some effect, because of the voters' reliance on the media to inform them about the parties' policies and the character of the leading players. But the effect of the admittedly partisan newspapers is restricted: they cannot effectively suppress or distort the news their readers receive, because virtually all also have access to broadcast news and current affairs coverage, and rely on it more as a news source.

The newspapers' direct influence is not only sectional, limited by the reach of their readership, but subordinate to that of the BBC, which by contrast is almost ubiquitous, and has generally been trusted by its audience (though this may have been shaken, temporarily at least, by the Iraq controversy). At the start of the election campaign, 64% of the public said they were regularly reading one or more of the London or Scottish dailies; 16% were reading the single title with the highest circulation, *The Sun*; but 78% said they regularly watched BBC1 as a "source of information you use

189

for news, current affairs and issues of the day"; widen the definition to include other BBC TV and radio channels and the news.bbc.co.uk website, and the figure reaches 89%. And the BBC's main terrestrial rival, ITV1, can claim 55% penetration on the same basis.[105]

Of course, the voting habits of newspaper readers tend to coincide with the preferences of their newspaper. But to interpret that as influence ignores two factors, based on the same basic fact – the British newspaper market is a competitive one that offers its customers plenty of choice. It is just as plausible that readers choose to read a newspaper that they agree with as that they come to their papers with an open mind and are manipulated by the wiles of Richard Littlejohn or Polly Toynbee.

That is the first factor, powerful on its own – we are fortunate in having a wide choice of newspapers in Britain to suit all tastes. (Even the politicophobe is catered for, by the *Daily Star*, which tends to put on readership sharply during elections by avoiding reporting them if at all possible.) But the second factor reinforces this: the primary function of editors and the aim of almost all newspaper owners (yes, even Rupert Murdoch) is to sell newspapers, as many as possible. If they insist on telling their readers what they do not want to hear, they will find they do not remain their readers for long. A politically crusading campaign may be morally satisfying but it can dent the circulation, as witness for example the *Daily Mirror*'s anti-Iraq-War campaigning. Most successful editors will be far more concerned to follow their readers than to lead them; the red smoke from the chimney at Fortress Wapping reflected above all not the Murdoch, or Wade, or Kavanagh, conviction that Blair deserved another chance, but an acknowledgement that this was what the majority of *Sun* readers wanted to be told, or would at least tolerate.

Nevertheless, it is interesting to look at changes in vote among readers of different newspapers.

Only three daily papers' readerships moved significantly to the Tories between 2001 and 2005 – the *Mail, Express* and *Sun*. This may reflect those papers' treatment of the immigration and asylum issues. (London's evening paper, the *Evening Standard,* is a special case as the swing here may simply

---

[105] Aggregate of data from MORI Omnibus surveys. MORI interviewed 4,229 adults aged 18+ in April 2005. See Appendix 2, surveys 36 and 40.

reflect a radical restructuring of the readership as the newspaper's character has changed in recent years to resemble far more than in the past its stablemate the *Daily Mail*.)

Table 66: Voting by Newspaper Readership, 2005

	Vote 2005						Change since '01		
	Con %	Lab %	LD %	Oth %	Lab Lead %	Turn-out	Con	Lab	LD
All	33	36	23	8	+3	61%	0	-6	+4
Daily Express	48	28	18	6	-20	69%	+5	-5	-1
Daily Mail	57	22	14	7	-35	69%	+2	-2	-3
Daily Mirror	11	67	17	5	55	63%	0	-4	+4
Daily Record	7	55	16	22	+48	59%	-1	-4	+6
Daily Telegraph	65	13	17	5	-53	77%	0	-3	+3
Financial Times	47	29	21	3	-18	65%	-1	-1	0
Guardian	7	43	41	9	+36	73%	+1	-9	+7
Independent	13	34	44	9	+21	76%	+1	-4	0
Daily Star	21	54	15	10	+33	46%	0	-2	-2
The Sun	33	45	12	10	+12	52%	+4	-7	+1
The Times	38	27	28	7	-11	71%	-2	-1	+2
Evening Standard	40	37	17	6	-3	60%	+11	-5	-4
Metro	29	40	20	11	+12	50%	+3	+4	-14
None	27	37	27	9	+10	55%	0	-8	+5

Source: MORI Final Election Aggregate Analysis
Base: 15,948 GB residents aged 18+, April-May 2005

Labour lost everywhere, but most sharply among *Guardian* readers, swinging to the LibDems presumably on the issue of Iraq in particular. But *Independent* readers, already the strongest supporters of the Liberal Democrats, moved no further towards them, the Labour defections benefiting the minor parties.

The interesting case, though, is that part of the public who read no paper regularly, and for whom any media effects must come mostly from the broadcasters. They swung slightly, but only slightly, more than average from Labour to the Liberal Democrats. The curious coincidence in the press at the moment is that the influences of the right and the left are so finely balanced that they almost entirely cancel each other out, so that the overall change among the whole public is the same as that among the non-reader – if you believe, as most of the public do, that the BBC and ITV are neutral and unbiased and therefore by implication cannot be influencing the views of their devotees at all.

In fact, television is probably far more influential, though its reach is so close to universal that research into its effects is hampered by the lack of an adequate control group. Certainly figures like Trevor McDonald (who a poll a couple of years ago identified as the most trusted figure on British TV) command a respect and public confidence that no print journalist can rival.

Table 67: British Public Trust in the Media 2001-4

Q I would like to ask you a question about how much trust you have in certain institutions. For each of the following institutions (press, radio and television), please tell me if you tend to trust it or tend not to trust it.

	Apr-May 2001 %	Oct-Nov 2001 %	Mar-Apr 2002 %	Mar-Apr 2003 %	Oct-Nov 2003 %	Feb-Mar 2004 %	Oct-Nov 2004 %
Television							
Tend to trust	57	71	58	58	54	54	43
Tend not to trust	37	25	35	35	38	37	51
Net	+20	+44	+23	+23	+16	+14	-8
Radio							
Tend to trust	58	65	59	62	60	59	64
Tend not to trust	31	24	31	27	31	29	27
Net	+27	+41	+28	+35	+29	+30	+37
The press							
Tend to trust	15	20	20	20	17	20	14
Tend not to trust	77	75	74	72	78	73	82
Net	-62	-55	-54	-52	-61	-53	-68

Source: European Commission Eurobarometer surveys
Base: c. 1,000 GB adults and 300 NI adults each survey

Yet even trust in television, and by implication its influence over the viewers, is apparently withering. The European Commission's Eurobarometer survey (a cross-national survey that includes an adequate sample size in the UK with the data separately reported) has asked, twice yearly for a number of years, about how much trust the public places in press, radio and television; the results are shown in Table 67. [106] Notably, eight people in ten distrust what they read in the papers; more than four times as many people in Britain trust the radio as trust the press.

Trust in the radio has been fairly steady over the last few years, and trust in the press has fluctuated within a narrow band, though the Autumn 2004 survey found it at its lowest. But trust in TV suddenly plummeted in the most recent survey. The reason does not seem obvious, nor unfortunately is data yet available from the Spring 2005 survey, which would indicate whether this was still the case at the time of the election. If so, we might have to readjust our usual assumptions that TV will be as influential as it has been in the past.

If even trust in television is now only a minority belief, then all the channels by which political parties and candidates can communicate with a mass audience are polluted – all that is left is personal contact, leaflets through the door (which may not be read) and telephone canvassing (which may be so resented as to be counter-productive). In practice, though, for all their distrust of the media the public use it as their principle source of information, and the content of the main TV news bulletins in particular is likely to be on of the most significant influences on floating voters.

In any case, the influence of the media does not necessarily depend on the audience believing what it sees or reads, let alone being prepared to be directly swayed by the editorial pronouncements of its newspaper of habit.

Newspapers undoubtedly have the power of agenda setting, and the broadcasters even more so, though they may make less deliberate use of it. This works on two levels. With their own readers or viewers, a medium's concentration on particular issues can affect the salience with which they are viewed, at least to the extent of whether they are "top-of-the-mind" or not.

MORI's monthly measurement of "important issues facing the country" with an unprompted question has proved effective in demonstrating the existence of this agenda-setting process in Britain: responses seem to be

---

[106] British fieldwork for the Eurobarometer surveys was conducted by INRA UK and Ulster Marketing Surveys in Spring 2001, by GfK Martin Hamblin Ltd and Ulster Marketing Surveys from Autumn 2001 to Spring 2004, and by TNS Opinion & Social in Autumn 2004.

strongly driven by the weight of media coverage of particular issues[107], as indeed has been generally found to be the case with the "most important problem" formulation in other countries[108]. We can offer a specific illustration from the first half of 2004. Over this six-month period there was a substantial rise in the number mentioning Europe or the EU, not surprising as coverage escalated in the run-up to the European elections; but more interestingly, there were very sharp differences in the changes in the answers given by readers of different newspapers between the first and second quarters of the year.

Although it would require detailed content analysis of the various newspapers over that period to confirm a link between newspapers' coverage and the distinctive opinion changes of their readers, there must be a least a strong presumption that in this case the perceived salience of the issue of Europe was being driven by the way the issue was handled in respondents' favourite newspapers.[109]

But a second agenda-setting effect, though less easy to measure quantitatively, is also well attested. The contents of the newspapers tend to drive the early morning broadcast media, notably the influential *Today* programme on BBC Radio 4, and during an election will also prime the questions of the journalists at the parties' morning press conferences. A single news story can set the tone for a whole day.

---

[107] See for example Colin Lacey and David Longman, *The Press As Public Educator: Cultures of Understanding, Cultures of Ignorance* (Luton: Luton University Press, 1997).

[108] The classic expositions of the phenomenon are Maxwell McCombs and Donald Shaw, "The agenda-setting function of mass media", *Public Opinion Quarterly*, Vol 36 (1972), 176-187, and more recently Maxwell McCombs, Donald Shaw and David Weaver, *Communication and democracy: Exploring the intellectual frontiers in agenda-setting theory* (Mahwah, NJ: Erlbaum, 1997).

[109] The detailed figures are given and the findings discussed in Mark Gill, Simon Atkinson and Roger Mortimore, *The Referendum Battle* (London: Foreign Policy Centre, 2004), pp 25-27.

The Impact of the Campaign

In each of the last seven elections, MORI have asked the public towards the end of the campaign or shortly after polling day what information they have received on the campaign from the various political parties and through the media. These surveys provide us with a picture of how effectively the parties are getting their case across to the electorate and how well the media are informing the electorate about their political choice.

Constituency Campaigning

The 2005 election brought about a renewed focus on constituency campaigning, with the public reporting an increased contact with canvassers – one in five said they were called on by representatives of one of the parties, up from 14% in 2001 but well below the highest level of 32% in 1987, an election which saw Labour undertake huge efforts to bring out its supporters in a bid to head off the SDP threat.

Our figures also show a steady increase in leafleting from 1979 until 1997 with around nine in ten people reporting having received a leaflet from one or more of the political parties in their constituency. In the 2001 election, a substantial drop was recorded, to around seven in ten people, perhaps as a result of the election being seen as a "foregone conclusion", though perhaps also because the leaflets that were delivered were ignored, forgotten or binned without being read. In 2005, this downtrend was reversed with nine in ten people reportedly receiving a leaflet – perhaps an indication that the political parties believed this was a more closely contested election this time around.

Telephone canvassing remains a marginal activity – literally – with only seven people in every hundred reporting having received a phone call, up only 2% on 2001. Political parties use telephone canvassing in key seats campaigns to bring out the vote in those parts of the country where they either have most chance of changing a seat's colour to their own advantage, or need to shore up their own vote to avoid it switching allegiance to another party. If 7% of the 43 million people that comprise the British electorate were contacted – around 3 million people – and since there are about a million marginal voters in the British electorate, it is likely

195

that a good proportion of those "undecided" or liable to switching were contacted during the campaign. Whether it made any difference or not is another matter.

Table 68: Campaign Penetration 1979-2005

Q. During the past few weeks have you...?

% saying "yes"	21-23 Apr 1979 %	2 Jun 1983 %	3-4 Jun 1987 %	1-3 Apr 1992 %	23-24 Apr 1997 %	24-30 May 2001 %	5-10 May 2005 %
...had any political leaflets put through your letterbox?	50	78	80	86	89	69	89
...seen any party election broadcasts on TV?	78	83	68	71	73	58	70
...seen any political advertisements on billboards?	35	45	43	55	70	50	62
...watched the leaders debate on TV?					36	43	46
...seen any political advertisements in newspapers?						37	48
...heard any party election broadcasts on the radio?	12	27	18	18	15	16	20
...been called on by a representative of any political party?	25	29	32	30	24	14	21
...received a letter signed by a party leader individually addressed to you?			8	13	20	12	28
...been telephoned by a representative of any political party?					7	5	7
...helped a political party in its campaign?			5	6	4	3	3
...visited a political party's website?						2	4
...used the internet to access information on candidates or parties?						2	7
...attended a political meeting addressed by a candidate?		2	2	1	2	1	2
...received a video through your letterbox from a political party?					27	1	3
...received an e-mail from a political party?						1	3

Source: MORI
Base: c. 1,000 GB residents aged 18+ in each survey
(Note that previous measures were taken during the final week of the election campaign)

Campaigning in the Media

A slightly greater proportion of people reported having seen the leaders' debates on TV in 2005 than in the last two elections, perhaps indicating a trend to a more American-style approach to election campaigning and broadcasting. It is important though to point out that the leader's debates in this country differ markedly from those of our Atlantic counterparts in that their leaders debate with each other directly rather than separately facing a pre-selected studio audience, moderated by David Dimbleby, as was the case in Britain. Nevertheless, despite this difference – arising allegedly because Blair refused to debate with the other leaders directly, though Charles Kennedy and Michael Howard had agreed – the programme drew a very respectably-sized audience of 4.1 million people for the BBC1 *Question Time* Election Special, airing Thursday 28 April at 8.30pm[110].

A bigger increase was observed with party election broadcasts (PEBs): seven in ten people reported having seen one or more of them compared with around six in ten in 2001, a drop from 1997 when seven in ten people had seen one.

The Tories also undertook a substantial cinema advertising campaign for the first time in many years[111] – the only party to do so this election – in a bid to woo the younger voter. Cinema is a potentially interesting medium since it is unregulated, unlike its television counterpart, although expensive. The advert was shown on 440 screens in around 80 cinemas, between Friday 15 April and election-day, Thursday 5 May. Nevertheless, it seems to have been singularly ineffective. In TNS' Cinemawatch research conducted for *Marketing* magazine during the period of the campaign, the Conservative cinema advertising campaign was not recalled in the top twenty advertisers at all, indicating that at most it was remembered by 6%. [112] Since cinema advertising is relatively expensive, and since it is predominantly targeted at the young, few of whom vote, it could be argued to have been money very badly spent indeed.

---

[110] http://news.bbc.co.uk/1/hi/uk_politics/vote_2005/frontpage/4497707.stm
[111] See Conservative Party website: http://www.conservatives.com/tile.do?def=news.story.page &obj_id=121755
[112] "Cinemawatch", *Marketing*, 25 May 2005.

197

Political advertisements in newspapers were seen by half the public in 2005 compared to two-fifths in 2001 – an increased recall displaying the increasing importance of this medium for election advertising in Britain. Conversely, party election broadcasts by radio were heard by one in five – up only 4% – and down from its peak of over a quarter in 1983.

The COI's radio advertisement for the Electoral Commission, designed as part of its remit to improve declining turnout, was remembered by one in ten people (10%) with Orange hitting top spot with a two in ten recall (21%)[113].

Poster Advertising

Three-fifths of the public saw political advertising on billboards at some time during the campaign, but in this case more detailed figures are available. *Marketing*, the news magazine for the marketing industry, has regular features each month analysing recall of advertisements placed in different marketing media entitled "Posterwatch", "Radiowatch", "Directwatch" and "Presswatch" as well as a weekly "Adwatch" section, outlining the results of the question: "Which of the following TV/radio/poster campaigns/direct mailings do you remember seeing recently?".

The posters tend to be used particularly to promote the parties' campaigning slogans. In the 2005 election, the public were subjected to such inspirational examples as the conspiratorial "Are You Thinking What We're Thinking?" – which the public weren't – and later "Taking A Stand On The Issues That Matter" – don't matter may have been more apt – from the Conservatives. "The Real Alternative" – wishful thinking – was the Liberal Democrats' slogan. Labour's was the grammatically incorrect "Britain Forward Not Back", and the obscure "If You Value It, Vote For It", which the public didn't (at least not Blair) but did anyway (vote for his party).

In the Posterwatch research, no political poster campaigns registered in any of the fortnightly top tens in 2005 up to the first half of March.

---

[113] "Radiowatch", *Marketing*, 11 May 2005. TNS interviewed a sample of c. 1,000 adults aged 18-64 on 26-28 April 2005.

However two-fifths of the public (39%) could recall seeing the Conservative Party's 48- and 96-sheet posters in the second half of March. Labour and Liberal Democrat posters were not in the top ten posters in either period, indicating unaided recall below 30%. The most recalled poster advert in the first half of the month was the Bridget Jones double-DVD advert pasted on buses, remembered by over seven people in ten (71%), while the Halifax ad was recalled in the back two weeks of March by nearly six in ten people (58%) – a stark reminder that politics battles for mind-space with every other product and service advertised, and usually loses. [114]

Figure 37: Conservative Campaign Poster

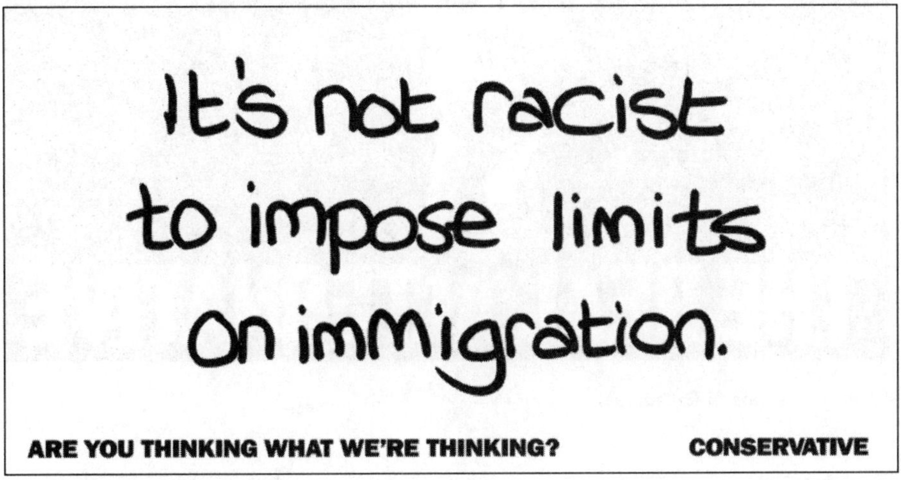

ARE YOU THINKING WHAT WE'RE THINKING?   CONSERVATIVE

Source: The Conservative Party

In April, 45% of respondents recalled the 48-sheet posters for the Conservative Party in the first two weeks of April, and 55% for the second two weeks of April, once more the highest rate of recall for any of the parties that month.[115]

---

[114] "Posterwatch", *Marketing*, 20 April 2005. NOP World interviewed samples of c. 1,000 British adults by telephone on 11-13 March 2005 and on 1-3 April 2005.
[115] "Posterwatch", *Marketing*, 18 May 2005.

For the first two weeks of May, though, both main parties made an impact (65% of respondents could recall the Labour Party's 48- and 96-sheet poster adverts and 64% those of the Conservative Party) indicating that the two main parties loaded most of their poster advertising into the last couple of weeks of the campaign. For that fortnight, at least, the parties were making the level of awareness that advertisers of commercial products would expect to achieve.

Figure 38: LibDem Campaign Poster

Source: The Liberal Democrats

The Conservative Party's memorable campaign slogan "Are you thinking what we're thinking?" – meant to convey among other messages sympathy with the electorate's supposedly unspoken dislike of Britain's "soft" policies on immigration and asylum – was generally denounced by most journalists[116]. Opponents found it so distasteful that the posters became a target for defacing by members of the public – occasionally witty, but more often bluntly dismissive – the crossing out of the "not" in the slogan "It's not racist to impose limits on immigration" being one of the more printable examples. (The answer to the question, perhaps, was given by Matt in his pocket cartoon in the *Daily Telegraph* on the day after the

---

[116] See Laurence Green, "Election 2005: Off message", *The Guardian*, 27 April 2005.

election, showing a poster declaring "Conservatives: That wasn't what we were thinking")[117].

The Liberal Democrats' advertising[118] on both 48-sheet and 96-sheet posters, by contrast with that of the two bigger parties, peaked in the second half of April, achieving fourth place recall of 47% (behind the Tories, but well ahead of Labour who were not in the top ten for that period, indicating recall below 29%). They concentrated on a serious attempt to promote Kennedy particularly and the party more generally as a serious opposition contender, in what marketers term a challenger positioning strategy – in other words an attempt to displace the Tories as the main competitor party. In May, however, the Lib Dem posters were not listed among the top ten campaigns, so they must have been recalled by at most 41%.[119]

Figure 39: Labour Campaign Poster (1)

Source: The Labour Party

The Labour Party's poster advertising, designed by Trevor Beattie's agency, TBWA, only registered in the Posterwatch top ten in the first two

---

[117] *Daily Telegraph*, 6 May 2005.
[118] "Posterwatch", *Marketing*, 18 May 2005.
[119] "Posterwatch", *Marketing*, 15 June 2005.

weeks of May, when it was recalled by two-thirds of the adult public (65%). Figure 39 and Figure 40 show two examples of the types of poster that were used. In Figure 39, Blair is shown looking serious and determined, against the insincere image of Howard and not coincidentally the very same image that TBWA had used in the adverts in the pre-campaign, depicting Howard waving a watch to hypnotise the electorate in the so-called "Fagin" adverts. Figure 40 shows how political parties use posters not just as advertising in themselves but as photo-opportunities, so that the media broadcast these posters into homes around the country. In this case, Tony Blair unveils the "If you value it, vote for it" poster with Gordon Brown.

Figure 40: Labour Campaign Poster (2)

Source: The Labour Party

For many years, billboards have been used by political parties more to generate press coverage than as an advertising medium in their own right with press conferences typically organised around them. An early example was the now famous success of the 1979 Saatchi and Saatchi-inspired "Labour's Not Working" poster for Thatcher's Conservative Party which generated terrific positive press and epitomised the public's view after the Winter of Discontent. Such a device – designed to encourage greater dissemination of the poster through every broadcast and press news channel in the land – is now said to have been hijacked by the Labour Party, who in the 2005 campaign organised the poster launch but refused to take journalists' questions[120].

Direct Mail

However, 2005 was the year of "customised" campaign communications, with nearly three in ten people reporting having received a letter from a party leader addressed to them, up from the previous record of 20% in 1997, the year Blair came to office in Labour's first landslide election. The Tories did score a hit with their direct mail campaign, at least in the sense that *Marketing* reported that a quarter of the public (26%) interviewed on 19-21 April remembered having seen their direct mailing "recently", in other words during the first half of the election campaign. Neither the Liberal Democrats nor the Labour Party achieved greater recall than one person in ten during this period. The most recalled direct mailing though was Capital One's credit card offer, named by two-thirds of those interviewed (66%).[121] The Conservatives' direct mail campaign, undertaken by M & C Saatchi subdivision Immediate Sales, was also the only one of the political parties' campaigns recalled in the post-election (June) survey, by around a third (34%)[122].

Only 3% of the electorate recorded receiving a video through the post this election, up from 1% in 2001; this compares with a whopping 27% in 1997 when Sir James Goldsmith's Referendum Party sent out videos, purportedly to every household in Britain, in a bid to woo the Eurosceptic vote. He won only 3% of the vote, consigning the video-as-election-

---

[120] See "The Dirty Tricks Election", *Despatches*, Channel 4, transmitted 23 May 2005 at 8 p.m. (50 minutes).
[121] "Directwatch", *Marketing*, 5 May 2005. TNS interviewed a sample of 1,000 adults aged 16-64 on 19-21 April 2005.
[122] "Directwatch", *Marketing*, 22 June 2005. TNS interviewed a sample of c. 1,000 adults aged 16-64 on 7-8 June 2005.

propaganda to the dustbin[123] (quite literally, except in the case of those voters who reportedly found the tape to be exactly the right length to record an episode of *Coronation Street!*)

No Net Effect

2005 was going to be The First Internet Election. So was 2001. And 1997.

Observers who had noticed the impact of Howard Dean's internet campaigning in the American primaries in 2004 wondered if the same might happen here. No – we don't have primaries here! More MPs have websites or blogs than in the past, and no doubt email is gradually displacing pagers, faxes or landline telephones as the chosen way to relay instructions and advice between party headquarters and their candidates. But as a campaigning medium, or even as a major channel of news and information, the net still has a long way to go. Indeed, the one respect in which it made a minor impact in 2001 – the growth of tactical voting and vote exchange websites – was probably of less relevance in 2005 as the enthusiasm for tactical voting was less.

Certainly the internet was not entirely absent. Twice as many as in 2001 visited a political party's website during the campaign, but this represented an increase only from 2% to 4%; a somewhat more significant 7% said they had used the internet to access information on parties or candidates, but only 2% admitted that the internet had influenced the way they intended to vote; by way of comparison, 14% said they had been influenced by newspapers and 12% by the party election broadcasts. Given the phenomenal spread of internet penetration over the past few years, and the advance of broadband against dial-up with consequent implications for ease of use, we might have expected more. But it is clear that the parties have yet to work out how to exploit the new medium; their uniformly dreadful websites offer few signs that they are near to a breakthrough.

Those reporting having received an email from a political party increased to 3% in 2005 from 1% in 2001, many of whom will no doubt have

---

[123] David Hass, "The Referendum Party's video mailer strategy", *Historical Journal of Film, Radio and Television*, October 1997.

received trite emails from the likes of Alastair Campbell, Alan Milburn, Michael Howard and Liam Fox among many others.

However, use of the internet, and of new technology in general, is not divided equally throughout the population, more men than women, younger, AB, C1s in general. (This, of course, has implications not only for its effectiveness as a medium of election communication, but also for its use as a polling tool.) At the moment, though, even those who are online are not being enmeshed in the net campaigns.

Word-of-Mouth

British elections have long been spectator elections as far as the electorate is concerned, with party membership levels down significantly since the beginning of the post-war period in the 1950s and 1960s. Most electors' definition of acting politically has – since the 1980s – been to vote and, er… that's it, until 2001 of course when four people in ten decided not to bother doing that either. Only 3% of the public said they had actively supported a political party in its 2005 campaign (no change), and 2% had attended a meeting addressed by a candidate (up slightly, but this is probably the measure most affected by the difference between a pre-election measure in 2001 and a post-election measure in 2005, so this is probably of no real significance).

But what the public *do* still do is talk about the election. Whilst the tools of political advertising and news management are inordinately important in politics and in political attitude change campaigns, a key element of politics which is often under-emphasised is the importance of word-of-mouth.

The old adage of "never discuss sex, politics or religion" at dinner parties is typically disregarded at election time, and the media frequently depict those that talk about politics at these and other times as the "chattering classes". When MORI asked, in a mid-campaign survey, about the extent to which people are prepared to advocate or discourage voting for the three main parties, we found that 6% of voters would encourage others to vote for the Labour Party unprompted. The highest number (roughly one in six, 17%) would discourage people from voting Conservative, although this figure was not so much higher than those discouraging people to vote Labour (at 14%). The low figures on encouraging and discouraging of voting for the Liberal Democrats indicates that they are probably much less discussed than their two main counterparts; something that they will need to address if they are to obtain a greater share of the vote at the next election.

Figure 41: Political Word-of-Mouth by Party

Q Thinking about the ... Party, please pick one statement from this card according to which best reflects your behaviour and opinions with respect to the ... Party.

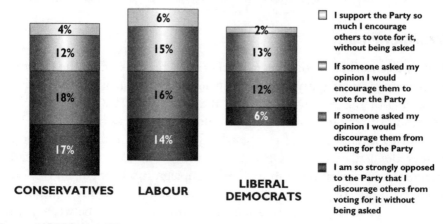

Source: MORI/Financial Times
Base: 1,106 GB residents aged 18+, 21-25 April 2005

Impact of the Campaign on Opinions and Perceptions

For all the effort, few of the campaigning methods were admitted to be effective by many voters – perhaps what we would expect to find given that most voters are not floating voters (though many who are not really floating voters, in the sense that they will almost always end up voting for the same party nevertheless believe they keep an open mind and go through the proud democratic ritual of considering the merits of all the parties and their campaign offerings before coming to their inevitable conclusion).

There is no particular difference in the hierarchy between supporters of the various parties, but Liberal Democrats were more likely to admit being influenced in every case – simple testimony to the high numbers who finally decide to vote LibDem during the campaign.

The most influential factor was the leaders' debate – much more so than Table 69 alone indicates, since the 18% who said it mattered to them represent not much short of half of those who watched it at all. Liberal Democrat voters were noticeably more likely to state that the debate affected their vote choice; not surprising since Kennedy fared best in the debate, if anyone could be declared the winner[124].

Table 69: Campaign Influences, 2001 and 2005

Q Which of these items, if any, have influenced the way you intended to vote?

	24-30 May 2001				5-10 May 2005			
	All	Con	Lab	LD	All	Con	Lab	LD
	%	%	%	%	%	%	%	%
Internet	I	I	I	2	2	3	2	4
Newspapers	15	20	15	18	14	15	14	17
Opinion polls	4	2	5	3	3	2	4	5
Party election broadcasts	14	16	18	12	12	11	13	17
Political leaflets through your letterbox	6	7	6	8	8	7	6	14
Posters on billboards	2	3	2	2	3	3	4	4
Telephone calls from political parties	I	0	I	I	*	*	*	*
The TV debate between the party leaders	21	18	24	24	18	17	20	26
The views of your local candidates	13	12	16	16	12	11	11	22
Video received from political party	0	0	0	0	*	*	*	*
Other	4	3	4	5	7	6	7	8
None of these	50	54	44	46	52	54	51	35
Don't know	2	0	2	I	I	I	*	I

Source: MORI
Base: 2,058 GB residents aged 18+, 5-10 May 2005

The Party Election Broadcasts were much the most effective of the parties' own efforts. Although the 2005 election has been typified the direct mail election[125], leaflets through the door influenced only about one

---

[124] See Joe Joseph, "We must have done something bad to deserve this", *The Times,* 29 April 2005.
[125] Dominic Mills, "Election spending went on direct mail", *Daily Telegraph*, 10 May 2005.

in twelve people in 2005, though they were twice as likely to sway people towards the LibDems as to Labour or Conservative. This may indicate that the Liberal Democrats' reliance on their own canvassing networks to deliver electoral material, rather than "junk-mail"-type deliveries by the postal system, were better received by the voters.

Both party election broadcasts and leaflets had more effect on LibDems than in 2001, as did the views of their local candidates – suggesting perhaps that many who changed their votes in protest over Iraq might have taken their local MP's stance into account, and that those Labour candidates who made a point of distancing themselves from government policy were not engaged in an entirely futile exercise, but also implying the continued effectiveness of the Liberal Democrat concentration on local campaigning. But intriguingly, despite their reputation for highly localised and effective "community politics", in terms of their campaign on the ground the Liberal Democrats were the least "local" party: research published by the New Politics Network found that in 2005 both Labour and the Conservatives had more localised content in their literature.[126]

Conservative voters were significantly less likely in 2005 than they had been in 2001 to admit to the influence of newspapers or PEBs; the PEBs also fell in importance for Labour voters.

The proportion of the public who said they were influenced by opinion polls was, as in 2001, small, with just 3% stating that it affected how they would vote.

---

[126] Justin Fisher, *General Election 2005 - A Voter's Eye View* (London: New Politics Network, 2005).

How the Public Saw It

Every year, commentators express how dull and tiresome this election is[127], or how dull other pundits and commentators are saying it is. It seems that every election, news editors send out some hapless journo to stir up apathy, and prove once again that this is the most boring election since the year dot. In fact, they're wrong, and audience after audience has been astounded when the empirical evidence is put before them, that there has been no statistical change whatsoever in the interest people have in politics at election times, going back over thirty years.

Figure 42: Interest in Politics

Q How interested would you say you are in politics?

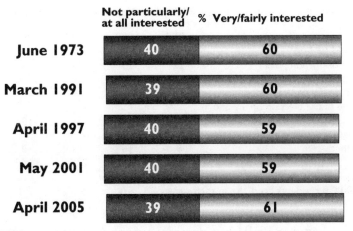

	Not particularly/ at all interested	% Very/fairly interested
June 1973	40	60
March 1991	39	60
April 1997	40	59
May 2001	40	59
April 2005	39	61

Source: MORI
Base: c. 1,000-2,000 GB/UK residents aged 18+ in each survey

Indeed, interest in the campaign was slightly up: in 2001, 30% agreed after the election that it had been an interesting campaign; in 2005, a week before polling day, 33% agreed.[128]

---

[127] See Dominic Mills, "Election spending went on direct mail", *Daily Telegraph*, 10 May 2005; Alan Travis, "Campaign blamed for low poll", *Guardian*, 4 July 2001; Paul McCann, "TV chief blames law for 'boring' poll", *Independent*, 20 May 1997.
[128] Fieldwork 28-29 April for the *Observer* and *Sunday Mirror*, see Appendix 2, survey 41 for details.

But the public are more interested in politics than you might think. If politics really is so boring, shouldn't we ban poll reportage, coverage of elections in newspapers and on TV, and especially those "incredibly dull" party election broadcasts? Apparently not. Only one in seven (15%) would ban opinion polls, a figure which has declined since 1983 – so we should be safe – and a similar number would ban party election broadcasts (14%) in 2005. Fewer of the public would ban news coverage of the election, in either newspapers or on TV and radio – in fact only one in ten in 2005, figures which are more or less level with those figures recorded in 1983 but below the high figures of 1987, when Margaret Thatcher was returned to office for the third time.

Table 70: Banning Polls and Other Election Coverage

Q   During an election campaign, do you think there should or should not be a ban on...?

% "yes, should be ban"	1983 %	1987 %	1992 %	1997 %	2005 %
...publication of opinion polls	22	25	24	16	15
...party election broadcasts of the election on TV and radio	14	25	24	20	14
...all coverage of the election on TV and radio	13	24	21	15	11
...all coverage of the election in newspapers	9	16	13	10	10
Average	14.5	22.5	20.5	15.25	12.5

Source: MORI
Base: c. 1,000 GB residents aged 18+ in each survey

Support for banning PEBs has decreased since its height in 1987, when one in four people (25%) believed that they should be banned. This is perhaps the more surprising result given that party election broadcasts are hampered by the editorial guidelines (*viz.* straitjacket) in the programme codes of the BBC and the ITC, the latter now part of media regulator, Ofcom. As one veteran advertiser put it succinctly in an interview with one of the authors:

"I mean, how would Heinz like it, if they were only allowed to advertise in a programmette which is preceded by a statement saying that 'There now follows a statement from the Heinz company', and that was scheduled in your newspaper so that you were warned not to watch it?"[129].

Indeed! Politicians and party executives don't like it much either, which is why they try to splice their PEBs up into a series of short 30-second ad breaks.

The falling desire to ban PEBs, though, does not reflect any increasing interest in them. The number reporting they are not particularly, or at all, interested in the broadcasts has been steady at two-thirds of the public over the course of the last four elections, with a higher proportion of people reporting that they were not at all interested (38%) in 2005 than ever before. There was virtually no variation in interest by age, and more tellingly only a slight difference by likelihood of voting.

Table 71: Interest in Party Election Broadcasts

Q   How interested would you say you are in party election broadcasts?

	20-24 Mar 1992 %	25-28 Apr 1997 %	29 May 2001 %	29 Apr-1 May 2005 %
Very interested	8	5	5	8
Fairly interested	28	27	30	26
Not particularly interested	31	31	32	28
Not at all interested	32	36	32	38
Don't know	1	1	1	1

Source: MORI
Base: c. 1,000 GB residents aged 18+ in each survey

But the PEBs made perhaps less impact, and were less talked about in 2005 than in any recent general election – where were the talking points to match "Kinnock: The Movie", or Jennifer's Ear, or even the Geri Halliwell cameo appearance that enlivened 2001? Perhaps the parties are losing interest, too.

But then the public profess to be not very interested in politicians' speeches either, with 55% of the public stating they are not particularly, or

---

[129] Interview between Chris Powell, Chairman BMP DDB Needham, and Paul Baines, April 1999.

211

at all interested, again a figure which has changed little in the last four
elections. There is a substantial divide here by class, though: 50% of
ABC1s but only 38% of C2DEs are interested in politicians' speeches.

Table 72: Interest in Politicians' Speeches

Q How interested would you say you are in politicians' speeches?

	20-24 Mar 1992 %	25-28 Apr 1997 %	29 May 2001 %	29 Apr- I May 2005 %
Very interested	9	7	7	10
Fairly interested	34	33	39	34
Not particularly interested	28	30	29	26
Not at all interested	28	30	25	29
Don't know	1	*	*	*

Source: MORI
Base: c. 1,000 GB residents aged 18+ in each survey

Two-fifths of the public (39%) are fairly or very interested in what the
opinion polls have to say during elections, a figure in line with reported
findings in 1992 and 2001, although around six in ten state that they are
not particularly, or at all, interested in what the polls have to say.
Nevertheless, this may be at least partly because political editors use polls
to report the "horserace", rather than to discuss how the public feel about
key political issues.

Table 73: Interest in Opinion Polls

Q How interested would you say you are in what the opinion polls say about the
election?

	20-24 Mar 1992 %	25-28 Apr 1997 %	29 May 2001 %	29 Apr- I May 2005 %
Very interested	8	7	5	8
Fairly interested	32	26	30	31
Not particularly interested	33	38	34	29
Not at all interested	25	28	30	30
Don't know	2	1	1	2

Source: MORI
Base: c. 1,000 GB residents aged 18+ in each survey

Interest in the polls was lowest in 1997, when they were suffering from a bad press as a result of their perceived failure in 1992, but 2005 restored interest to those 1992 levels. Of course, this may also reflect that 1992 and 2005 were much closer elections, and were seen as such, than those of 1997 or 2001 so the progress of the "horserace" was always likely to be of slightly more interest.

Interest in the polls was higher among intending LibDem voters (52%) than Labour (46%) or Conservative (39%), but not so high (41%) among those who said they had voted LibDem in 2001 – suggesting that attention to the polls might be a factor in switching to the LibDems (tactical voting, perhaps), as also suggested by the post-election poll measuring the influence of polls. (Table 69).

In the 2005 election, we asked the public how much they felt that the result mattered to them and their family. A majority, only just, felt that the result mattered a "fair amount" or "a great deal" but one in three (33%) were relatively indifferent and one in eight (12%) were completely indifferent to the election. It is likely that the great majority of those who were relatively or completely indifferent to the result comprise those who didn't vote. In other words, those that didn't vote most likely felt the election didn't sufficiently affect their lives, or that the parties differed little in what they offered and so it didn't make any difference who they voted for.

Table 74: Impact of the Election Result

Q How much would you say who wins this election will affect you and your family?

	All %	18-34 %	35-54 %	55+ %	Con %	Lab %	LD %
A great deal	20	16	24	19	23	21	15
A fair amount	31	34	34	26	34	32	39
Not very much	33	36	27	37	33	33	35
Not at all	12	9	12	13	8	10	8
Don't know	4	4	3	5	2	4	2
Great deal/fair amount	51	50	58	45	57	53	54
Not very much/at all	45	45	39	50	41	43	43

Source: MORI/*Financial Times*
Base: 1,009 GB residents aged 18+, 29 April-1 May 2005

There seems to be a definite distinction, though, between feeling that the result of the election will affect oneself or one's family and caring about the outcome. Not only did considerably more of the public say it was important personally to them who won than said they would be affected by the result, but the pattern was different too. This is particularly obvious when we look at age – the 55-and-overs, the "grey power" generation who are more likely than anybody else to register their vote, are in fact less likely than the rest of the public to feel the outcome will directly affect them. Nevertheless, they are most likely, and the young are least likely, to think the result is important – especially clear if we consider only those who thought it "very important".

Table 75: Perceived Importance of the Election Result

Q   How important is it to you personally who wins the General Election?

	All	18-34	35-54	55+	Con	Lab	LD
	%	%	%	%	%	%	%
Very important	45	33	40	60	51	55	41
Fairly important	35	40	40	24	39	32	40
Not very important	11	15	11	8	7	9	13
Not at all important	6	8	6	5	3	2	3
No opinion	3	4	2	3	*	2	3
Important	80	73	80	84	90	87	81
Not important	17	23	17	13	10	11	16

Source: MORI/*Evening Standard*
Base: c. 1,628 GB residents aged 18+, 3-4 May 2005

There is a lesson, too, in the analysis by voting intention. Those who intended to vote Liberal Democrat were significantly less likely to feel the result was important than Conservative or Labour voters. But they were also less likely to feel the result would make "a great deal" of difference to them. It may be that voters find it harder to vote for the LibDems unless they don't really mind which of the two major parties wins – reasonable enough, since unless the LibDems ever become serious challengers for power a vote for them (unless it is a tactical vote where one of the major parties cannot win) is opting out of that important decision. But if this is restricting LibDem support unduly in those parts of the public to whom the result of the election matters directly, then there is a real obstacle to

214

their ever breaking out of their current third place – not comforting news for Charles Kennedy.

4. The results

Who Voted Which Way

Table 76 presents the main breakdowns from MORI's final Election Aggregate analysis, our best estimate of the voting behaviour and turnout of the British public in the 2005 general election.

Table 76: How Britain Voted, 2005

| | Vote 2005 | | | | | Change since '01 | | | |
	Con %	Lab %	LD %	Oth %	Lab Lead %	Con	Lab	LD	Swing
All	33	36	23	8	3	0	-6	+4	3.0
Men	34	34	22	10	*	+2	-8	+4	5.0
Women	32	38	23	7	6	-1	-4	+4	1.5
Age									
18-24	28	38	26	8	10	+1	-3	+2	2.0
25-34	25	38	27	10	13	+1	-13	+8	7.0
35-44	27	41	23	9	14	-1	-4	+4	1.5
45-54	31	35	25	9	4	-1	-6	+5	2.5
55-64	39	31	22	8	-8	0	-6	+5	3.0
65+	41	35	18	6	-6	+1	-4	+1	2.5
Social class									
AB	37	28	29	6	-9	-2	-2	+4	0.0
C1	37	32	23	8	-5	+1	-6	+3	3.5
C2	33	40	19	8	7	+4	-9	+4	6.5
DE	25	48	18	9	23	+1	-7	+5	4.0
Tenure									
Owned	44	29	20	7	-15	+1	-3	+1	2.0
Mortgaged	31	36	25	8	5	0	-6	+5	3.0
Social rent	16	55	19	10	39	-2	-5	+5	1.5
Private rent	27	36	28	9	9	-1	-4	+3	1.5
Voting method									
Postal	34	38	22	6	4		n/a		
*2001 Vote (reported)**									
Con	90	2	6	2	-88	-10	+2	+6	-6.0
Lab	8	72	15	5	64	+8	-28	+15	18.0
LibDem	12	6	78	4	-6	+12	+6	-22	3.0

Source: MORI Final Election Aggregate Analysis
Base: 10,986 GB residents 18+ and "absolutely certain to vote"
Change figures assume report of 2001 vote is accurate

It is based on the aggregate of all MORI's voting intention polls conducted between the announcement of the election on 5 April and polling day on 5 May, involving interviews with 17,959 British adults aged 18+. Of these, 7,655 were interviewed by telephone; the remaining 10,304 were interviewed face-to-face, in home. The data are weighted to the demographic profile of the population, and also at regional level to the final result and turnout of the election (taking the 10,986 respondents, 61% of the total, who said they were "absolutely certain to vote" as having voted in line with their voting intentions, and the remainder as having not voted).

Comparisons are with MORI's Final Election Aggregate for 2001, which was compiled on a similar basis. Of course, these are net changes. The more interesting question of the gross changes – how many actually swung from and to each party, whether there was a straight swing, or a bigger movement partly cancelled out, or a circling of votes between the parties – are less easily answered. Those who follow the methodological controversies between opinion pollsters will know that MORI sets little store by the accuracy of the answers received when we ask the public how they voted at some election in the past, especially one several years ago. The most accurate means in theory of measuring the switching of voting between one election and the next would be a "panel", where voters who had been asked at the time how they had voted in one election were re-interviewed at a subsequent election. Panels however have their own problems, quite apart from generally being expensive for newspaper polling if conducted with due rigour as we did over many elections, first for the *Sunday Times* and then for the *Independent on Sunday*.

Nevertheless, with these caveats in place, and taking our respondents' reported 2001 votes at face value, we can attempt to measure the flow of the votes over four years.

The biggest aggregate change in 2005 was the 5.8% fall in the Labour share of the vote. Allowing for the changes in turnout, however, the fall in Labour support in actual votes was very close to the rise in Liberal Democrat support, just under 1.2 million. How much of this was in fact a straight switch from one party to the other?

Not a great deal, it would seem, judging by our respondents' reports of their past voting behaviour. Just over one in ten (11%) of those who said they voted Labour in 2001 switched to the Liberal Democrats in 2005; but almost half as many (5%) switched to the Tories, and three times as many (29%) didn't vote at all in 2005. However, barely half of those who said they voted Labour in 2001, 51%, did the same in 2005 – a powerful indictment of the party's performance. Yet the LibDems did not do a great deal better, retaining 58% of their 2001 supporters (though the bulk of the rest were non-voters as we project only 75% turnout of 2001 LibDems). The Tories did more respectably, 72% of their 2001 support voting for them again, 20% abstaining and only 8% switching to other parties; their problem was not leaking votes, but that they were not picking up enough new ones.

Looked at from the other angle, the Liberal Democrats were the biggest gainers: only half their support in 2005 came from those who said they had also supported the party in 2001. More than a quarter came from professed ex-Labour voters, though most of the rest was from those who didn't vote in 2001 (including those who were too young to do so, a significant factor on this occasion); only 6% had switched from the Tories. For Labour, by contrast, 86% of their supporters this time had also backed the party in 2001, with most of their new support being from those who hadn't voted at all last time – only 1% said they had previously been Conservative and 2% Liberal Democrat. Tory support consisted of 72% repeat voters, 10% who said they backed Blair in 2001 and 5% who had backed Kennedy.

But these broad-brush measures can give us only a superficial impression of the election even if they are accurate. More enlightening is to examine the patterns of change within different groups of the electorate. In particular, we can look at the way the traditional pattern of behaviour by class and gender, which has characterised British elections for as long as polling evidence has been available to measure them, is beginning to break down.

Class

Nearly forty years ago, the political scientist Peter Pulzer wrote "Class is the basis of British politics; all else is embellishment and detail"[130], a proposition which has been inflicted on undergraduate politics students as an essay topic ever since. It is no longer as obviously true as it still was when Pulzer was writing, but it certainly still has more than a grain of truth in it.

Of course, the context is very different now. Manual jobs have shrunk as Britain's heavy industry has died out: from 1970 to 1979, two-thirds of the public were in what market researchers and pollsters identify as C2DE or "working class" households; now fewer than half are.

But many of the public hold opinions about their class in defiance of conventional market research classifications. When we asked the public during the election to classify themselves as middle class or working class, 57% of them said they were working class and only 40% middle class. Indeed, back in 2002 we found that 68% of the public agreed with the statement "At the end of the day, I'm working class and proud of it", as indeed did 55% of those who we would normally in our surveys call "middle class", the ABC1s.[131]

Table 77: Self-Assessed Social Class

Q Most people say they belong either to the middle class or to the working class. If you had to make a choice, would you call yourself middle class or working class?

	1986 %	1989 %	1996 %	2000 %	2005 %
Middle class	28	30	32	35	40
Working class	66	67	61	58	57
Neither/don't know	5	4	7	7	3

Source: MORI
Base: c. 600-1,000 GB residents aged 18+

Market researchers measure something different by "middle-class and working class" from the way it is subjectively understood by the people we

---

[130] Peter Pulzer, *Political Representation and Elections in Britain* (London: George Allen & Unwin, 1967).
[131] Fieldwork 18-24 July 2002; see Appendix 2, survey 17, for details.

are polling. There are various ways of making an objective classification of "social class", but most of those that are widely used depend on occupation. The definitions used by the government statisticians seem to change fairly frequently; however, almost all market research and opinion polls in Britain, and most other countries, use the classification called "social grade", originally developed by the advertising industry's trade body, the Institute of Advertising Practitioners (IPA).

Social grade classifies people "objectively" on the basis of the chief income earner in their household, into one of six categories, A, B, C1, C2, D or E. (Until comparatively recently, objective social class was defined by the occupation of the "head of household", which meant that a wife was classified by her husband's occupation even if she was the higher earner; but classification by the "chief income earner" is now established throughout the industry.)

Table 78: Self-Assessed Social Class Compared to Social Grade

Q Most people say they belong either to the middle class or to the working class. If you had to make a choice, would you call yourself middle class or working class?

	All	ABC1	C2DE	AB	C1	C2	DE
	%	%	%	%	%	%	%
Middle class	40	56	22	68	46	27	18
Working class	57	41	75	30	51	70	78
Neither/don't know	3	3	3	2	4	3	3

Source: MORI/*Observer*/*Sunday Mirror*
Base: 1,004 GB residents aged 18+, 7-9 April 2005

There is a detailed manual classifying every possible occupation into one of these categories, but broadly the groups are divided as follows:

Grade	
A	Professionals, chief executives and senior managers to whom a considerable number of people are responsible.
B	More junior professionals and middle management in business.
C1	All others doing clerical or non-manual jobs.
C2	Skilled manual workers.
D	Semi-skilled and unskilled manual workers.
E	Those on lowest levels of subsistence including pensioners and others relying on benefits, casual workers, and others with minimum levels of income.

We usually group the first three of these, the ABC1s, under the heading "middle class" and the remainder, C2DEs, as "working class."

Market researchers in most countries use some variable, such as income or educational level, to grade their respondents into different social levels, but Britain is unusual in tying that classification specifically to "class". We do it that way, of course, because it works – over the years we have found the social grade classification to be a better discriminator for market research purposes than income or education, or than the other available class schemas, being well related both to social attitudes and consumer behaviour.

But in a sense calling it a "social class" grading is a bit of a red herring. It is not based on the sort of class distinctions that Hollywood loves to believe divide English society; it has nothing (directly, at least) to do with birth or snobbishness; nor is it related to the Marxist distinction between capitalists and workers. When we call the ABC1 group "middle class" and the C2DEs "working class" we are using somewhat arbitrary labels which are perhaps not especially well fitted, and there is no reason why we should be surprised if the public prefer to use the terms in a somewhat different way.

What does this mean in voting terms? People's own perception of their class is related strongly to their political opinions, more closely than is their objective social grade. Butler and Stokes found the same in their seminal report of the first British Election Survey, *Political Change in Britain*, back in the sixties (though they were using a different class grading)[132]. That is to say that people with "middle class occupations" who regarded themselves as working class were much more likely to vote Labour than those who did not, while the reverse was the case with voters in "working class occupations" who regarded themselves as middle class. It was almost inevitable that that would be true in the 1960s, when so much of the political debate and rhetoric were couched in class terms. But it is still true today.

Why should we care, though, except as a curiosity or to justify some mind-numbing regression equation in the next British Election Study? Because, as Professor Pulzer noted all those years ago, class used to be the basic

---

[132] David Butler and Donald Stokes, *Political Change in Britain: Forces Shaping Electoral Change* (London: Pelican, 1971), pp 103-8.

driving force behind a British election. It is far less potent now: "middle class" voters are more prepared to vote Labour, "working class" more likely (comparatively, at any rate!) to vote Conservative, which means that the parties have to frame their appeal to the voters in different terms.

Table 79: Voting Intention by Self-Assessed Social Class and Market Research Social Grade

		ABCI		C2DE	
	All	**"Middle class"**	**"Working class"**	**"Middle class"**	**"Working class"**
	%	**%**	**%**	**%**	**%**
Conservative	30	34	28	46	22
Labour	41	34	40	31	51
Liberal Democrat	21	27	22	17	15
Other	8	9	10	6	12
Undecided	*14*	*11*	*17*	*17*	*16*
Would not vote	*9*	*6*	*9*	*7*	*12*
Refused	*5*	*5*	*4*	*7*	*4*

Source: MORI/*Observer/Sunday Mirror*
Base: 1,004 GB residents aged 18+, 7-9 April 2005

The Labour government has shied away from the traditional working class issues that the party used to espouse, and is now quarrelling with the trade unions. The theory, of course, is that a modern Labour government needs some middle-class support to survive, and that is obviously true if one thinks in terms of the rise of the ABC1s to comprise half the population. But it does rather assume that these new middle classes think and act as middle classes. To some extent, certainly, they do, which is why social grade is still a useful classification for market researchers; but only to some extent.

While there is a measurable difference in the voting of ABC1s dependent on their class self-image, the difference among C2DEs is huge. Those C2DEs who feel middle class are more than twice as likely to support the Tories as those who feel working class, and there is a corresponding 20-point fall-off in Labour strength. This tendency of the "aspirational" working class to vote Tory was of course one of the factors to which to the successes of Margaret Thatcher in the 1970s and 1980s were attributed, combined with policies that fostered it such as the sale of council houses to their tenants. The trouble for the Tories now is that there are not very many "middle class" C2DEs, while there are a lot of "working class" ABC1s – in fact half of all C1s feel working class rather than middle class. Although Labour's comparative advantage here is slimmer, it adds up to a considerable number of votes; the Tories have failed to gain the benefit they should have done from the growth in the middle class.

The development of this position is, of course, an important reason why the class element in British voting seems to have weakened over the years. What has really weakened is the relationship between respondents' self-assessed social class and their class as measured on the pollsters' occupational scale.

This has crucial implications for election strategy. If the class factor that affects voting were an objective economic phenomenon, possibly vulnerable to the effects of long-term government policy but beyond the scope of short-term electoral campaigning, then come the election the parties would just have to make the best of it; but if, as seems to be the case, the relevant factor is primarily a subjective one, then like all other perceptions feeding into a voter's electoral choice it might be manipulated by party campaigners. Voters' self-image, as much as the image of the parties, might matter. In short, if Labour benefits when more people think of themselves as "working class", it may be able to find a way to play up to this and encourage them to do so. And, of course, the converse would hold true for the Tories.

Yet the Tories, or many of them, just don't get it. John Redwood, writing two months after the election, based his entire argument in a discussion of inequality in society on the assertion that "Today most people in the country would either regard themselves as middle class or classless."[133] Wrong, Mr Redwood, and it's one reason why your party is losing.

---

[133] John Redwood, "We are becoming a more unequal society", *Independent*, 13 July 2005

The Gender Gap

One of the best-known pieces of received wisdom about British voting patterns is that the women's vote is traditionally biased to the Conservatives. When Worcester first became involved in political polling in the early 1970s, he discovered that about half of the advantage the Tories enjoyed from the women's vote came from women living longer, and the well-known tendency of older people to favour the Tories.

Fairly consistently since women first won the vote in 1918, it has been believed that Tory support has been higher among women than among men, and in more recent years when opinion poll data has been available to test the hypothesis it has confirmed the popular wisdom. MORI's data shows that in the three elections of October 1974, 1979 and 1983, Labour's share of the vote was substantially higher among men than women, while the Tories and to a lesser extent the Liberals/Alliance did better among women. Indeed, the British Election Study shows[134] a similar pattern in Conservative and Labour support back to 1963 (though the Liberal vote seems have switched from being slightly higher among men to slightly higher among women at the 1970 election).

However, these shibboleths are now clearly out of date. For some seven elections, with a curious blip in the 1987 general election when the difference briefly disappeared altogether, there has been a steady decline in the benefit that the women's vote gives to the Conservatives.

This is something to which we devoted some analysis in *Explaining Labour's Landslide*[135] and *Explaining Labour's Second Landslide*[136]. The levelling of the difference between men's and women's support for Labour was considered a triumph for New Labour by Tony Blair's supporters, but left unanswered the question of whether a permanent change had been achieved or whether it arose from the specifics of the campaigns, so that women might revert to Toryism when Tony Blair's lustre began to dim. A possibility that seems to have been little considered is that the pendulum

---

[134] See Ivor Crewe, Neil Day and Anthony Fox, *The British Electorate 1963-1987: A Compendium of Data from the British Election Studies* (Cambridge: Cambridge University Press, 1991), p 6.
[135] Robert Worcester and Roger Mortimore, *Explaining Labour's Landslide* (London: Politico's Publishing, 1999)
[136] Robert Worcester and Roger Mortimore, *Explaining Labour's Second Landslide* (London: Politico's Publishing, 2001).

might swing further in the same direction, but during the 2001-5 Parliament came an intriguing new development: women were suddenly *less* likely than men to support the Conservatives, an unprecedented finding which persisted through 2004 and right up to the election itself.

These findings were entirely contrary not only to past experience and received wisdom, but to the widespread assumptions both of many commentators in the media[137] and even to some strategists and campaigners taken seriously by the political parties. It was widely believed in the national press that there was a crisis in the relationship between the Labour Party and women[138], caused principally by Blair's policy on Iraq, and this was also an impression that some pressure groups apparently felt a vested interest in sustaining. On two occasions in the run-up to the election, MORI was asked to provide a representative to appear on TV to discuss this phenomenon, and on both occasions she was "stood down" as soon as it became clear that instead of supporting the thesis she was going to offer empirical evidence to refute it.

It is perfectly true that, as already noted, women were consistently more hostile to the War in Iraq, and more generally to Tony Blair's handling of the international situation, than were men. But this did not translate into wider dissatisfaction with the government or a swing in voting intention. MORI's other attitudinal data consistently backed the message of our voting intention polls that women were no more hostile to the government than men, and it was certainly little surprise to us when the final analysis of our election aggregate voting data showed that in 2005 the gender gap had reversed.

Why were women not moved disproportionately against the government if they were disproportionately against its war in Iraq? Again the answer may be in the way that Iraq acted as an "image issue" rather than an "issue issue". Iraq's main impact on Tony Blair's standing seems to have been by damaging the public's trust in him, probably because he was seen to have deliberately misled the Commons and the public. But this was not the element that was at the root of the difference in opinions on Iraq between

---

[137] For example. Mary Ann Sieghart, "War and the women's vote", *The Times*, 7 May 2004; Jackie Ashley, "Why all sorts of women fell out of love with New Labour", *Guardian,* 6 May 2004.
[138] See for example Zoe Williams, "Sorry Tony, you're just not on our wavelength", *Evening Standard,* 1 April 2005.

men and women, which seems to have been (initially at least) that men tended to believe the war would achieve its aims while women didn't. On the issue of trustworthiness, by contrast, there was little distinction between men and women: in June 2003, 35% of men and 37% of women judged Blair trustworthy, and the week before the election the figures were 31% and 32% respectively.

Figure 43: Gender Gap in General Election Voting 1974-2005

Difference between Conservative lead over Labour among women and Conservative lead over Labour among men

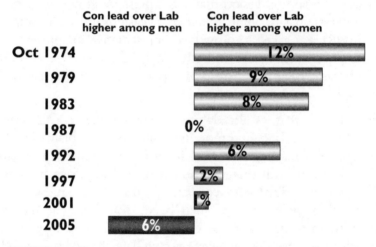

Source: MORI Election Aggregates 1974-2005 (weighted to final outcome)

Although these figures could be read as showing that Labour has steadily improved its performance among women since Tony Blair became leader, yet the data could equally be interpreted as New Labour having underperformed among men. Certainly in 2005 Blair cannot be realistically seen as having performed well among women; Labour did badly among women, but even worse among men.

However, it is more of a moot point whether Michael Howard should be seen as having done unusually badly among female voters; it could equally well be argued that the one-point fall in share that the Conservatives achieved among women was all they were entitled to expect overall, but somehow they overperformed slightly among men. Normally this sort of logic-chopping would be pointless, since there is obviously no right answer, but in the case of Tories – wondering yet again which straw to clutch at – it is potentially important in interpreting their whole election. Should they consider they made slight progress, and therefore one more heave (or two, or three) will do the trick? Or are they no further forward than ever? Therefore the question of whether men's votes are the true indicator and women's a temporary blip or vice-versa has some meaning. In this case we believe it is the women's votes that tell the truer story, and that the Tories achieved no worthwhile progress in 2005.

Table 80: Voting by Gender, Age and Class, 2005

	Vote 2005					Change since 2001			
	Con	Lab	LD	Oth	Lab Lead	Con	Lab	LD	Swing to Con
	%	%	%	%	%				
All	33	36	23	8	+3	*0*	*-6*	*+4*	**+3.0**
Men	34	34	22	10	*	+2	-8	+4	**+5.0**
Women	32	38	23	7	+6	-1	-4	+4	+1.5
Men by Age									
18-24	33	34	25	8	+1	+4	-4	-1	+4.0
25-34	29	33	27	11	+4	+5	-19	+8	**+12.0**
35-54	31	36	22	11	+5	+2	-7	+3	+4.5
55+	40	33	20	7	-7	+1	*-6*	+4	+3.5
Women by Age									
18-24	22	43	26	9	+21	-2	-2	+3	0.0
25-34	21	43	28	8	+22	-4	-6	+9	+1.0
35-54	27	40	25	8	+13	-4	-3	+5	-0.5
55+	41	34	20	5	-7	+1	-4	+2	+2.5
Men by Class									
AB	37	27	28	8	-10	-1	-4	+3	+1.5
C1	39	29	22	10	-10	+3	-9	+8	+6.0
C2	32	39	18	11	+7	+4	-10	+5	+7.0
DE	24	47	17	12	+23	+1	-8	+3	+4.5
Women by Class									
AB	36	29	29	6	-7	-5	+1	+3	-3.0
C1	34	35	23	8	+1	-3	-2	+3	-0.5
C2	34	40	20	6	+6	+4	-8	+3	+6.0
DE	25	49	18	8	+24	0	-7	+5	+3.5

Source: MORI Final Election Aggregate Analysis
Base: 10,986 GB residents aged 18+ and "absolutely certain to vote"

But in any case, as we have already suggested in our discussion of segmentation and targeting voters, it is simplistic to think in terms of "women's votes". There are big differences among the age groups and also some class distinctions. At the last few general elections, young women have been more strongly Labour than young men, while older women have been more Conservative than older men. It was because these effects cancelled each other out that the overall "gender gap" almost disappeared, and because they have now moved yet further apart that Labour now has the overall advantage.

Figure 44: The General Election Gender Gap by Age 1983-2005

Difference between Conservative lead over Labour among women and Conservative lead over Labour among men within each age group

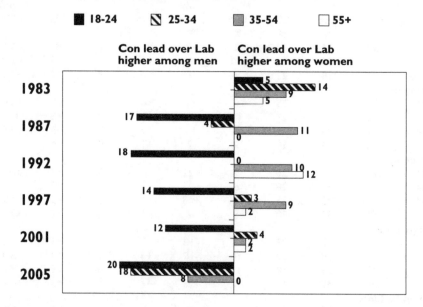

Source: MORI Election Aggregates 1983-2005 (weighted to final outcome)

As Figure 44 shows, at each of the four elections from 1987 to 2001, young (18-24 year old) women stood out as being much more Labour than men of the same age, while other age groups tilted the other way or voted much as the men did. In fact the shifts in the overall gender gap over these four elections can be clearly seen to be not a single phenomenon but a concatenation of separate effects operating among different age groups. In 1987 the "gender gap disappeared", simply because the pro-Labour tendencies of the 18-24 year old women cancelled out the pro-Tory tendencies of the 35-54 year old women. In fact the gender gap didn't disappear; its net effect was zero, an entirely different statement.

In 2005, much the biggest fall in Labour support was among men aged 25-34; the party now does better among women than among men in all but the oldest third of the electorate (those aged 55+). In fact there is no age group where the gender gap favours the Tories; back in 1983 – the last time the opposition made an election issue of a war the government had waged, though that is probably coincidental – the gender gap favoured the Tories in all four age groups.

Over the years, there seems to be a degree of congruence between the attitude changes of men and of women within each age group, whereas the patterns of the different age groups are markedly different, suggesting that it makes more sense to treat age as being the primary factor and to consider the gender gap within each age group separately, rather than the converse.

There has also emerged a dramatic interaction between gender and class. In 2001, when men and women overall voted almost equally for the parties, there was also no significant gender difference in voting within any social class – in each of the four class bands, no party's share of the men's and women's vote differed by more than 3% with the sole exception that the LibDems were significantly stronger among C1 and C2 women than among men in the same classes; this meant that the LibDems were much stronger among AB men (25%) than any other class (13% to 14%), but among women their support decreased with lower class on a much gentler gradient.

In 2005, C2 men and women behaved broadly similarly, as did DE men and women; C2s swung from Labour with the increase going equally to the Tories and LibDems, while DEs also swung but the Tories gained nothing significant.

But among ABC1s there was a clear difference between men and women, and it is this that has defined the new "gender gap": male ABC1s swung from Labour to the Tories, female ABC1s from Tories to Labour.

Of course, swing is a simplification. Among male ABs it meant only that Tories were less likely to abandon their party for the LibDems or other parties than were AB Labour-voting men; male C1s actually increased the Tory voting tendency, though the LibDems got the lion's share of the benefit from a nine-point collapse in the Labour vote. But now look at the corresponding women: the Tory vote fell among both ABs and C1s. Labour actually benefited a little among ABs, and fell less than the Tories among C1s.

How did the Tories' so fail among middle-class women? A glance at the issues they pick as the most important facing the country tells its own story. Over the course of 2004, two issues apart from the ubiquitous Iraq were of particular interest to this group – the NHS and education.[139] Not much short of half, 46%, of ABC1 women picked the NHS as one of the most important issues facing the country, compared with 33% of ABC1 men, 34% of C2DE women and 29% of C2DE men. Similarly, education was picked by 39% of ABC1 women, 28% of ABC1 men, 23% of C2DE women and 18% of C2DE men. It may well be that it was failure to appeal on these two classic "Labour issues" that lost the Tories support among the quarter of the electorate that is traditionally their strongest.

On the other hand it turns out that by the time of the election Labour's lead over the Conservatives as the party with the best policies on health care and education was much smaller among ABC1 women than among other groups. Possibly, though, the Tories' failure to campaign strongly on these issues convinced these voters that their commitment to these policies was half-hearted and therefore not a reason for voting for them. As we mentioned earlier, a party not only needs the most popular policies on an issue but must convince supporters it will pursue them once in power; if not, the very importance of the issues and the popularity of a party's policies could become a disadvantage, creating an image of a party with the wrong priorities and unfit to be entrusted with power.

---

[139] Aggregate of twelve monthly MORI Political Monitor polls: MORI interviewed a representative quota sample of 12,287 GB residents aged 18+. Interviews were conducted face-to-face, in home, in January-December 2004. Data were weighted to match the profile of the population.

18-24 year olds

We can learn more about the age-gender dimension in 2005 by tracking voting intention during the Parliament. A single poll includes far too few respondents to split it up by age and sex, but aggregating a year's worth of MORI's fortnightly polls gives us c. 24,000 likely voters to analyse.

In the youngest group, 18-24 year olds, there was a gender gap at the 2001 election but it was one that was almost identical to that in 1997, both genders having swung similarly during Blair's first term. Labour support was seven points higher among young women than among young men, while Conservative support was five points lower and LibDem support three points lower. By 2005, the gap had widened substantially, support for the Tories now being 11 points lower among young women and Labour voting 9 points higher.

Figure 45: Voting Intentions, 18-24 year olds, 1997-2005

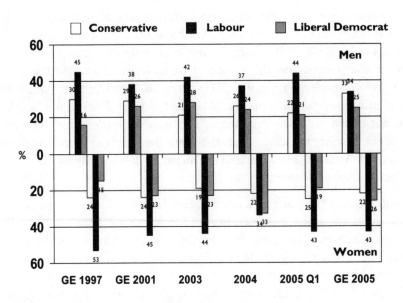

Source: MORI Election Aggregates; MORI Omnibus Aggregates
Base: c. 11,000 voters in each election aggregate; c. 24,000 adults 18+ and certain to vote each annual aggregate

To understand how this came about, though, we must stop thinking in terms of the gap (which presupposes some sort of norm, and can easily mislead us), and concentrate in changes in the vote share among young people of each gender. We can also consider the intermediate shifts in party support during the Parliament, which will indicate when shifts took place and may thereby give some clues to the reasons for them.

Young male voters were significantly more likely, 33%, to be Tory in 2005 than they were in 2001, when only 29% were Tory. By contrast, Tory share among young women fell slightly, from 24% to 22%. When we look at Labour, however, we find a fall in support among both sexes, though bigger among men (38% to 34%) than women (45% to 43%). Young women's support for the Liberal Democrats, however, was up a little (at 26%, from 23%), while the party slipped a single point among young men. Overall, then, young men swung by 4% from Labour to Conservative, while young women swung by 2% against both main parties, mostly in favour of the Liberal Democrats.

But this pattern was not the result of a steady progression in the same direction in each case. Unfortunately, we have no comparable figures for party support in 2002[140]. By 2003, young men had swung *to* Labour and away from the Tories; but the direction of movement reversed in 2004, and the swing accelerated at the 2005 election, so that the Tories had almost as much support as Labour. (The first quarter 2005 figures are out of step, but based on a smaller sample and may be misleading.) The bulk of the 2003 interviews were after the invasion of Iraq but before the succession of Michael Howard as Conservative leader. Might these two events be explanatory factors?

For young women the pattern was different. In 2003, Labour support had held almost steady since the election, but Conservative support had fallen sharply, though with minor parties (*not* the Liberal Democrats) being the temporary beneficiaries. In 2004, the Tories recovered most of their lost ground, and the minor parties fell back, but there was also a 10% swing from Labour to Liberal Democrat. But by the election, Labour support revived and the LibDems slipped back, though still retaining a three-point boost on their 2001 position.

---

[140] Because MORI was not measuring certainty of voting in its regular polls at that period.

So the critical period appears to be 2003 for young men, and 2004 for young women, in each case producing a substantial shift in party support which was subsequently reversed.

25-34 year olds

It is by no means clear why 25-34 year old men should have behaved so aberrantly. There are some slight differences in their assessment of the most important election issues, but nothing remotely big enough to explain their voting behaviour. (For example, they were more likely to say that education would be important in deciding how they would vote than were men of other ages, but still less so than women; they were much more likely than average, 56%, to pick taxation as important, but so were 35-44 year old men who did not vote in the same way).

Figure 46: Voting Intentions, 25-34 year olds, 1997-2005

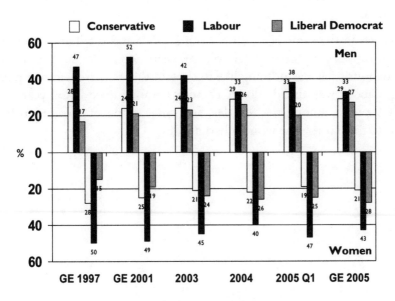

Source: MORI Election Aggregates; MORI Omnibus Aggregates
Base: c. 11,000 voters in each election aggregate; c. 24,000 adults 18+ and certain to vote each annual aggregate

They do not differ significantly from the rest of the population in their selection of the parties with the best policies on any of the key issues, except that in a couple of cases they are less likely than average to pick the Tories – which clearly would not explain a higher than average swing *to* the Tories and away from Labour. Nor do their personal assessments of Tony Blair and Michael Howard differ much from everybody else's.

One significant difference that may have a bearing is that 25-34 year old men were more likely than the rest of the electorate to believe that "The Conservative party want to cut public spending by £35 billion" – 42% of this group agreed, compared to 32% of the rest of the public. But even assuming they took this belief as a reason to vote for rather than against the Tories, it would explain only the lesser part of their move, the 5-point increase in the Tory share, and not the remaining 14-point movement from Labour to the Liberal Democrats and minor parties. In any case, it is plain from the trend graph that their switch in loyalties developed early the Parliament, rather than being a sudden reaction to anything in the election itself: indeed their voting intentions for 2004 were almost identical to their vote in 2005.

With women in the same age group, both Labour and the Tories seem to have lost support in the first couple of years after the 2001 election, though Labour's fall was nothing like the extent that occurred among men. In 2004, Labour was already down 19-points among male 25-34 year olds but only 9-points among the females; and while some of those men had switched to the Tories, the women had not.

The Gender Gap among Middle-Aged and Older Voters

The most striking point to be drawn from the trends for 35-54 year olds and the 55-and-overs is how consistently the lack of a gender gap in each age group was maintained through the Parliament.

Among those aged 35-54, the gender gap suddenly re-emerged at the election, with men and women making modest moves in opposite directions, after having previously been hardly perceptible except in support for the Liberal Democrats, which was higher among women from 2003 onwards.

Figure 47: Voting Intentions, 35-54 year olds, 1997-2005

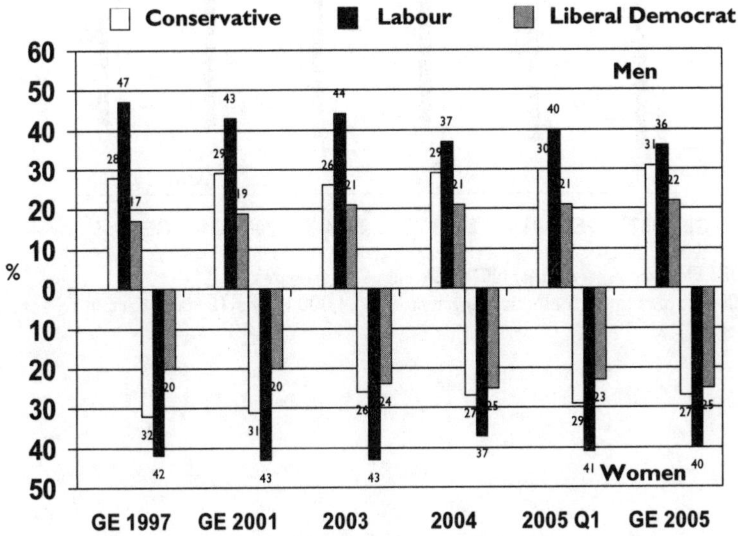

Source: MORI Election Aggregates; MORI Omnibus Aggregates
Base: c. 11,000 voters in each election aggregate; c. 24,000 adults 18+ and certain to vote each annual aggregate

The four-point difference in share of support for both Conservative and Labour was double the biggest difference at any point in the Parliament. This, we might therefore surmise, could indicate a specific effect of the election campaign, though again no obvious explanation seems to emerge. In the oldest third of the electorate the divergence was briefly as high as three points on the Tory and Labour shares in 2003, and there was a four-

235

point gap in LibDem support in 2004, but by the start of election year they had fallen back into line.

Figure 48: Voting Intentions, aged 55+, 1997-2005

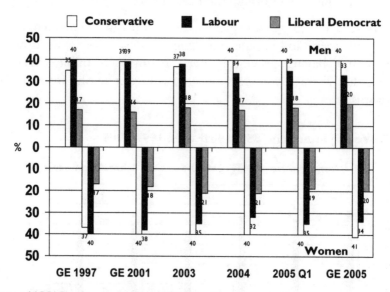

Source: MORI Election Aggregates; MORI Omnibus Aggregates
Base: c. 11,000 voters in each election aggregate; c. 24,000 adults 18+ and certain to vote each annual aggregate

Age

Age is a far more effective predictor of vote and likely influence on change of vote than gender, and is also highly correlated with turnout.

Table 81: Voting by Age, 1974-2005

	Oct 1974 %	1979 %	1983 %	1987 %	1992 %	1997 %	2001 %	2005 %
All								
Conservative	37	45	44	43	43	31	33	33
Labour	40	38	28	32	35	44	42	36
Lib/Alliance/LD	19	14	26	23	18	17	19	23
Con lead	-3	+7	+16	+11	+8	-13	-9	-3
18-24								
Conservative	24	42	42	37	35	27	27	28
Labour	42	41	33	39	38	49	41	38
Lib/Alliance/LD	27	12	23	22	19	16	24	26
Con lead	-18	+1	+9	-2	-3	-22	-14	-10
25-34								
Conservative	33	43	40	39	40	28	24	25
Labour	38	38	29	33	37	49	51	38
Lib/Alliance/LD	24	15	29	26	18	16	19	27
Con lead	-5	+5	+11	+6	+3	-21	-27	-13
35-54								
Conservative	34	46	44	45	43	30	30	29
Labour	42	35	27	29	34	45	43	38
Lib/Alliance/LD	20	16	27	24	19	19	20	24
Con lead	-8	+11	+17	+16	+9	-15	-13	-9
55+								
Conservative	42	47	47	46	46	36	39	40
Labour	40	38	27	31	34	40	38	34
Lib/Alliance/LD	14	13	24	21	17	17	17	20
Con lead	+2	+9	+20	+15	+12	-4	+1	+6

Source: MORI Election Aggregates 1974-2005 (weighted to final outcome)

In 2005, age seems to have made a dramatic difference to voting behaviour in one respect – Labour support plummeted among 25-34 year olds, falling 13 points, whereas in every other age group the fall in support was only 3-6 points. Nevertheless we have already seen that this unusual collapse in support was entirely confined to the 25-34 year old *men*; among women the swing was in line with everybody else. But there are two other purely age-related factors we must consider, if only because they were the targets of specific election campaigning – the "grey vote", and the youth vote, or more specifically students.

The Liberal Democrats will doubtless feel their capture of seats with high concentrations of students, such as Cambridge and Cardiff Central, vindicates their concentration on that section of the electorate, but this has rather obscured the fact that overall they performed rather poorly among the young – their share of the 18-24 year old vote rose only 2%, compared to their 4% gain across all age groups, despite their concentration on Iraq, supposedly a potent vote-winning issue with youth. With the turnout of the young also down again, to 37%, they will look even more of an irrelevance to strategists at the next election – another potential nail in the coffin of democratic representation.

"Grey power", by contrast, lived up to its reputation. Three-quarters, 75%, of those aged 65-and-over voted, double the turnout of 18-24 year olds, and meaning that they made up more than a quarter of the voters while 18-24 year olds made up only 7%. Bring in those aged 55-64 as well, and you have 43% of the vote – and more than half of the Tory vote. Yet the Tories were unable to exploit the falling popularity of the Blair government with the old, it being the LibDems who most profited by the 4-point fall in Labour's share.

The Ethnic Minority and Muslim vote

The prominence of Iraq in particular and more generally Tony Blair's adherence to US foreign policy and President Bush's "War on Terror" made the voting behaviour of Muslims a question of particular interest in the 2005 general election. The Liberal Democrats had won two by-elections with huge swings in constituencies with high Muslim populations by concentrating on this issue, and narrowly missed a third, and made no secret of their intent to repeat the strategy at the general election.

This naturally leads us on to considering ethnic minority voting in general, both because British Muslims are of course predominantly from ethnic minority communities, and because it also raises the interesting question of how ethnic minority voters of other (or of no) faith will be affected. Further, 9/11 and its aftermath may have damaged race relations in Britain, especially between Asians and other groups but possibly also between different Asian groups, and certainly gave impetus to the rise in prominence of asylum and immigration as one of the most salient issues; it would be unsurprising to see the Conservative concentration on this issue, but also the responses of the other parties to their lead, impacting on the voting decisions of Black and minority ethnic (BME) citizens.

In this book we are able only to present some findings which offer preliminary indications of the answers. Results from a much more detailed survey of British BME voters, conducted by MORI on behalf of the Electoral Commission and designed to amplify the findings of the academic British Election Study, will be published later in the year.

MORI examined the attitudes of British Asians to issues during the election in a survey for the BBC Asian Network.[141] Asked which issues would be most important in deciding their vote, and using much the same prompted list as in MORI's national election surveys, the leading issues are similar to those selected by the whole British adult population, with healthcare, education and law and order topping the list – there was no distinctive Asian election agenda.[142]

---

[141] Fieldwork 8-24 April 2005 for BBC Asian Network.; see Appendix 2, survey 37, for details.

[142] Although the list used did not isolate Iraq as a separate issue, it is worth noting that Iraq did not feature on the Asians' unprompted and unconstrained list of the most important issues facing the country.

Table 82: Most Important Election Issues for Asians

Q   Looking ahead to the General Election on May 5th, which, if any, of these issues do you think will be very important to you in helping you decide which party to vote for?

	British Asians %	All GB public %
Health care	50	67
Education	45	61
Law and order	34	56
Unemployment	33	25
Asylum	22	37
Race relations	21	n/a
Housing	21	27
Taxation	18	42
Pensions	15	49
Public transport	12	26
Managing the economy	10	35
Defence	6	12
Protecting the natural environment	6	20
Trade Unions	3	9
Europe	3	22
Animal welfare	1	10
Constitution/devolution	1	7
Other	3	2
Don't know	5	2

Source: MORI/BBC Asian Network/*Evening Standard*
Base: 325 British Asians aged 18+, 8-24 April 2005; 957 GB residents aged 18+, 7-11 April 2005.
Note: Showcards differed slightly between the two surveys (notably by inclusion of "Race relations" in the Asian survey, so results are not directly comparable.

Rather counter-intuitively, Asians as a whole proved more likely than the general public to describe Tony Blair as "trustworthy", but this statistic would be misleading as it was only those of Indian origin (least likely, of course, to be Muslim) who were disproportionately likely to say this: 46% of Indians but 31% of Bangladeshis and 24% of Pakistanis said Blair was trustworthy; by comparison, 32% of Britons of all races said the same in a separate survey a week after the survey of Asians was completed. It makes an important point, however, about the dangers of treating the Asian vote as a single monolithic block.

Perhaps more relevantly, though, Michael Howard was much less likely to be described as trustworthy by Asians than by the general public, though this reflected a much higher proportion of "don't knows" rather than a wider belief that he was untrustworthy. Just 15% of Asians considered Howard trustworthy (compared to 36% of all British adults), ranging from 20% of Indians to just 7% of Pakistanis; but the 47% declaring him "not trustworthy" was fractionally lower than the 52% of all adults who said the same, and did not vary significantly between the three national groups.

Charles Kennedy fared a little better, but again his image was far less favourable among Asians than among the public as a whole: only 30% of Asians thought him trustworthy (the figure for the general public a week later was 61%). The 33% feeling he was not trustworthy was not much higher than the national average 25%, but 37% of Asians (41% of both Pakistanis and Bangladeshis) had no opinion on the question whereas all but 14% of the general public could come down on one side or the other. For a leader basing much of his appeal on opposition to the War in Iraq and hoping to benefit from a Muslim swing against Labour, this was plainly extremely disappointing.

Table 83: Influences on Asian Voters

Q   Which one or two of the following, if any, do you think have an influence on the way you vote?

	%
Family member(s)	34
Friends	18
The Asian Community I come from	16
The people living in my area	10
Neighbours	4
The ethnic background of the candidates standing in my constituency	4
The religious background of the candidates standing in my constituency	4
Someone at work	3
None of these	37

Base: 325 British Asians aged 18+, 8-24 April 2005
Source: MORI/BBC Asian Network

One in three Asians (34%) said that family members have an influence on the way they vote; by contrast the ethnic or religious background of the candidate in the constituency has little influence (4% in each case), though one must of course remember that only a comparatively small number will have been offered a choice in the past between candidates one or more of whom is of their own ethnic or religious background, and one in six (18%)

say they would be more likely to vote for a political party if it had an Asian candidate standing in their constituency.

Opposition to the War in Iraq among Asians is even stronger than among the rest of the public, only 15% saying Tony Blair was right to take Britain to war.

How the Ethnic Minorities Voted

Ethnic minority voters, as has always been the case, voted strongly for Labour in 2005; however, MORI's Aggregate Analysis indicates that, taken as a whole, they swung against the government to a significantly greater extent than white voters – Labour's share fell by six points among whites and nine among BMEs. But the Liberal Democrats took only 14% of the ethnic minority vote nationally, barely gaining among this group in contrast to the four-point increase in share among whites: most of the move in support was to minor parties, who increased their support among BMEs from 2% to 8% (3% for the Greens and even 2% for UKIP).

Table 84: Voting by Ethnic Group, 2005

	Vote 2005					Change since '01			
	Con %	Lab %	LD %	Oth %	Lab Lead %	Con	Lab	LD	Turn-out
All	33	36	23	8	3	0	-6	+4	61%
White	34	35	23	8	1	+1	-6	+4	62%
All BME	14	64	14	8	50	+2	-9	+1	47%
Black	12	74	10	4	62	n/a	n/a	n/a	49%
Asian	19	57	14	10	38	n/a	n/a	n/a	47%

Source: MORI Final Election Aggregate Analysis
Base: 6,138 GB residents aged 18+ and "absolutely certain to vote"

These figures must be taken with a little caution, though, as the sample size is relatively small (only 323 BME adults[143] who were "absolutely certain to vote", the criterion we use to distinguish between voters and non-voters), and of course the subgroups within that are smaller still.

---

[143] Ethnic group was not recorded for respondents on all of MORI's election surveys.

There seems to have been a distinction between Black and Asian voters, which we could reasonably attribute to an Iraq effect (Labour's vote held up among Blacks, at 74%, but they could secure the support of only 57% of those Asians who turned out), but beyond the fact that the difference is statistically significant, and therefore probably real, we cannot be very sure of its size. Nor, in the absence of reliable figures for 2001, can we tell whether there was a higher defection from Labour among Asians than among Black voters, as perhaps we might suspect.

Turnout, at just 47%, was low among ethnic minority voters, but this is nothing new and reflects a greater degree of political disengagement, which is certainly not wholly related to race. (Ethnic minority adults are particularly concentrated in the most deprived parts of the country, where participation among all ethnic groups is low.)

An alternative approach is to examine voting patterns at constituency level, and this may give a more useful measure of the success of the parties' appeals, since many voters may have felt it pointless to switch to the Liberal Democrats in constituencies they could not win, and the Liberal Democrat campaign was of course focussed accordingly. Similarly, Respect stood in only a handful of constituencies and the Greens by no means everywhere, making the findings of a national survey potentially ambiguous.

As Table 85 makes clear, the Liberal Democrats performed better than average and Labour worse than average in constituencies with a high ethnic minority vote – in the 9 BME-majority constituencies they averaged a 9% increase in vote share while Labour lost almost 13%, and in the band of 30%-to-50% minority seats they averaged a gain between 5% and 6%, and Labour lost around 9%. Minor parties also did exceptionally well in the constituencies where members of non-white groups made up more than 40% of the population, though this reflects a few exceptional results rather than an increase spread across all such constituencies[144].

---

[144] In the 9 BME-majority constituencies, Respect stood in 3 and took 19% or better in each case, but no minor candidates saved their deposits in the remaining 6; in fact the average "other" increase here would be much higher but for Ealing Southall, where the "other share" had been 24% in 2001, including an Independent taking 12%. Similarly the 40%-50% BME band included the Respect victory at Bethnal Green & Bow and a 17% share at Poplar & Canning Town, but the "other" share rose by 4% or less in 8 of the remaining 11, and fell marginally in the other 3.

The correlation with the proportion of the constituency population that is Muslim is even stronger, implying that this was indeed a factor, though again the averages are a little misleading as they conceal considerable constituency variation and the effect of Respect candidacies, which were of course intentionally targeted in precisely those constituencies. But the strong performance of the Liberal Democrats in the 22 most Muslim seats is clear, and only slightly inflated by the inclusion of 2 by-election seats in the 15%-20% band. But we cannot, of course, tell how much this performance owed to the votes of BMEs or Muslims, and how much to LibDem campaigning targeted in these constituencies and affecting all voters.

Table 85: Vote Share Changes by Constituency Ethnic Profile, 2001-5

Constituency type	Number	Change in Con vote % share	Change in Lab vote % share	Change in LD vote % share	Change in Oth vote % share
Overall national change*	620	+0.5	-5.8	+3.8	+1.5
Population 70%+ white	580	+0.3	-5.5	+3.7	+1.5
Population 60%-70% white	18	+1.2	-8.7	+5.6	+1.9
Population 50%-60% white	13	-1.3	-9.5	+5.8	+5.0
Population less than 50% white	9	-0.1	-12.8	+9.0	+3.9
Population 15%-20% Muslim	13	-1.1	-9.9	+9.8	+1.2
Population 20%+ Muslim	9	-4.4	-15.6	+8.1	+11.8

Source: Calculated from constituency results collected by the BBC (news.bbc.co.uk)
Constituency ethnic and religious profile calculated from 2001 Census (n.b. Religion question in census was optional, and 7.5% of the population did not answer it.)
Omits Glasgow North-East and constituencies with by-elections 2001-5

Voting and Ethnic Minority Candidates

A separate aspect to the question of ethnic minorities is whether or not the nomination of an ethnic minority candidate affects voting behaviour. As we have already seen, few British Asians admit their vote would be affected by the ethnicity of the candidates; on the other hand, it has always been suspected that a significant proportion of white voters may be reluctant to vote for a Black or Asian candidate, and such prejudice was certainly assumed to be a factor in the defeat of John Taylor as the

Conservative candidate for Cheltenham, previously considered a fairly safe Conservative seat, in 1992.

Ethnic minority candidates are now much more numerous than they were in the past. Operation Black Vote's website[145] lists a total of 108 ethnic minority candidates who stood for the three major parties.

A MORI analysis comparing the constituency results at the 1997 and 2001 general elections found some statistical evidence that ethnic minority candidates did, indeed, do less well than white candidates, though the effect could only be demonstrated in the case of Labour and Liberal Democrat candidates. We have repeated the analysis using the 2001 and 2005 results, and again have found statistically significant evidence that ethnic minority candidates – of all three major parties, this time – are disadvantaged.

The difficulty with using constituency results is one of interpretation. We do not know *who* has voted in what way, nor *why* the voters vote in a certain way, except by inference – we can find differences in the character of constituencies, and associate them with differences in their voting behaviour, but it may still be unclear whether, or in what way, one causes the other.

It is no good simply working out the average number of votes that white candidates and that Black and Asian candidates received in a particular general election, because there are factors which affect how many votes a candidate receives far more powerfully than the identity of the candidate. Most significant of these, of course, is which party a candidate represents and the political character of the constituency in which he or she is standing: a Labour candidate will always get more votes in Hackney or Wigan than in Kingston-on-Thames or the Isle of Wight. And finally, of course, there are any number of specific local or personal factors that may affect a candidate's vote regardless of race.

To find out what effect a candidate's ethnic origin has on the vote, we need to compare similar cases, where the only relevant difference between the two is the candidate's ethnicity. We can never be sure of the interpretation in a single case – because a candidate of different ethnicity is by definition a different candidate, and any one of many factors may be

---

[145] www.obv.org.uk/elec2005/blackcandidates.html, accessed 13 July 2005

affecting his or her performance; but if we can look at enough different cases, and find that there is a systematic difference in the performance of candidates who have nothing in common apart from their ethnic group, then we may feel more confident that this is indeed the underlying reason. If the difference is consistent enough to be statistically significant, then we can conclude that it is probably true that a candidate's race is an important factor.

The best way to do this is to examine the votes received by candidates of the same party in the same constituency in two successive elections. The change in a party's constituency vote share tends to vary comparatively little across constituencies. Therefore, if we look at the constituencies where a party had an ethnic minority candidate in one of the last two elections but not in the other, and compare them with the constituencies where the candidate was the same ethnicity at both elections (as a "control" group), the comparison will give us an estimate of the effect – if any – of the candidate's ethnic origin on his or her vote share.

What do we find? We are forced to exclude Scotland because of the boundary changes between the two elections, and we also exclude Wyre Forest (with an independent MP and no Liberal Democrat candidate) and Bethnal Green and Bow (where George Galloway's intervention makes it plainly unsafe to generalise from the result there to draw conclusions about other constituencies). This leaves 566 constituencies, and sufficient cases for each of the three parties both where there was an ethnic minority candidate in 2001 but not 2005, and vice versa.

Table 86: Change in Vote Share for Ethnic Minority Candidates, 2005

Average change in party share of the vote (number of cases in brackets) in constituencies where:

	Candidate was BME in 2001, white in 2005	Candidate ethnicity was the same in 2001 and 2005	Candidate was white in 2001, BME in 2001
Conservative	-0.3	+0.5	-3.1
	(10)	(520)	(36)
Labour	-2.8	-6.1	-6.9
	(8)	(542)	(16)
Liberal Democrat	+7.9	+3.6	+4.5
	(19)	(519)	(28)

(England and Wales only. Excludes Bethnal Green & Bow and Wyre Forest.)

On the face of it, there is no obvious effect. Conservative candidates did worse than average both in constituencies where an ethnic minority candidate had replaced a white candidate and vice versa; Liberal Democrats conversely did better in both such cases. For Labour, it is true, new ethnic minority candidates had the worst results and new white candidates slightly better than average, but the number of cases is small.

However, we can test for significance using linear regression. Again we treat each party's candidates separately.

Table 87: Effect of Ethnic Minority Candidates, 2005

	Co-efficient of regression	Significance
Conservative	-2.54	0.000
Labour	-1.65	0.045
Liberal Democrat	-1.26	0.049

(England and Wales only. Excludes Bethnal Green & Bow and Wyre Forest.)

The results are shown in Table 87. The analysis has detected a statistically significant effect in all three cases – ethnic minority candidates of all three parties performed worse than white candidates.

The co-efficient of regression in each case, which measures the slope of the line of best fit, is the measure of how much each party's vote seems to have been affected. Selecting an ethnic minority candidate cost Labour about 1.6% of the vote, the LibDems about 1.3% of the vote and the Conservatives a very substantial 2.5%.

All these figures are statistically significant. This is what is measured in the significance column, which in effect measures the probability that the pattern might arise simply by chance. For Labour and the Liberal Democrats, the significance is 0.045 and 0.049 respectively, which means there is a little less than five chances in a hundred that the figures could have arisen by pure chance, good enough for us to rely on. As is customary in opinion polling, we use the 95% threshold for significance – any significance figure up to 0.05, or five chances in a hundred of being a coincidence, is taken as being sufficiently reliable for our purposes; but these are borderline cases, only just clear enough to trust. In the case of the Conservatives, the pattern is much clearer – there is less than one chance in a thousand that these figures could have arisen by chance.

So ethnic minority candidates seem to be significantly disadvantaged at general elections, though this is only a general conclusion, and may not apply in every case or for every candidate. But, more encouragingly, the effect is comparatively limited, 2.5% in the worst case (Conservative candidates), which is lower than the corresponding effect that seemed to be present in 2001 (when the Labour vote share was apparently depressed by 3.6 percentage points when a BME candidate was selected), and could matter in terms of the result only in the few most marginal constituencies. In 2005, there seems only one case where a bias of this size might have caused the defeat of an ethnic minority candidate – Ali Miraj, third for the Conservatives in a tight three-way contest at Watford. But it must be emphasised in any event that the analysis works only on averages, and cannot be localised to make any reliable statement about a specific case.

Clearly the most obvious and indeed overwhelmingly likely explanation is that a small minority of voters are prejudiced against black or Asian candidates, and refuse to vote for them when they would otherwise vote for the party. Nevertheless, we have to bear in mind that we have not proved this, only that there is a consistent pattern to the results in the constituencies where such candidates are chosen. Other explanations are possible. For example, it is conceivable that rather than voters being prejudiced these poor results arise from party workers campaigning less hard for ethnic minority candidates.

It is also possible that ethnic minority candidates are more likely to be selected in constituencies where their party is likely to do uncharacteristically badly than elsewhere. This is perhaps less implausible in 2005 than would be the case at most past elections. As we have seen, because of the Iraq War there was a significant correlation between the parties' performances and the ethnic make-up of constituency electorates. Both Labour and the Tories did significantly worse where there were high numbers of ethnic minority voters, regardless of the ethnicity of the candidates; but, naturally, a constituency's ethnic composition will also affect a party's likelihood of selecting an ethnic minority candidate to fight it. A high proportion of the new Conservative ethnic minority candidates were standing in inner city seats in the North and Midlands, where the party performed badly regardless of the candidate chosen.

Catholics and Protestants

Religion – in the sense of tension between the different Christian denominations – was once a highly significant factor in British elections; but it is rarely much considered today.

Its decline in significance cannot simply be dismissed as a social change – superficially, at least, Britain is not much less Christian that it used to be. In fact, nominal church membership has not fallen precipitately: in 1921 the estimated baptised membership of the Church of England was 622 for every 1,000 in the population; by 1996, it was still 511[146]. (Nevertheless, almost all of what change there has been occurred in the last few years of the century – membership was still 581 per thousand in 1980, and 557 in 1990.) In the 2001 census (the first to include a question on religion), 72% identified themselves as Christians, and two-thirds of adults said the same in those of our election surveys where we asked about respondents' religious persuasions; one in twelve belong to other religions and a quarter to none. More women are religious than men (20% of women but 29% of men told us they have no religion), and the old much more than the young (only 11% of those aged 65-and-over are agnostic or atheists, compared to 36% of 18-34 year olds).

There are considerable regional variations, of course, Catholics being most widespread in London, Scotland and particularly the North-West (where one in five are Catholic), sparsest in Wales and the South West. In London Anglicans outnumber Catholics only by two-to-one (32% and 16% of adults respectively), but there are also 18% belonging to non-Christian religions, reflecting the capital's high ethnic minority population. Interestingly, though, there is very little regional variation in the numbers repudiating all faiths.

However, many of these self-identified Christians can be only nominal adherents, since (when we asked in a 2000 survey) only 62% of the adult public said they believed in God. Churchgoing is much lower than theoretical adherence to a religion, of course, but that's not new either: in 1957, only 14% of adults said they had been to church on the previous

---

[146] David Butler & Gareth Butler, *Twentieth Century British Political Facts* (Basingstoke: Macmillan, 2000), p 558.

(February) Sunday[147]. By 1993, attendance had fallen to the extent that only 18% said that they *ever* went to church on a Sunday, but it was clearly a minority activity even half a century ago.

But what has certainly changed is that there is more acceptance of "new age" spiritualism, and other supernatural phenomena, as well as scepticism about organised religion. A 1999 MORI Social Values question gets at this trend quite neatly: 65% of the public agree that "Personal spiritual experience is more important to me than belonging to a church". This leads to what some would describe as a more credulous society. In January 1950, only 10% of the public told Gallup they believed in ghosts, and just 2% thought they had seen one[148]. By 1998 we found that 40% were saying they believed in ghosts, and 15% that they had had "personal experience" of ghosts. Similarly, in 1951 only 7% of the public said they believed in foretelling the future by cards, and 6% by stars; in 1998, 18% of the public said they believed in fortune telling or tarot, and 38% in astrology.

So perhaps, therefore, we should not be surprised to find that the old divisions between Catholics and Protestants no longer drive voting intentions. (Just as well that they don't, perhaps, with one of the major party leaders Catholic, one married to a Catholic and one Jewish.)

But for once religion intruded into the 2005 campaign, though it probably had little impact. All three party leaders were interviewed for the issue of *Cosmopolitan* published at the start of the campaign, and were asked about their stance on abortion. Michael Howard's answer that he would, personally, favour a 20-week legal limit rather than the existing 24-week limit was apparently interpreted by Cardinal Cormac Murphy-O'Connor, head of the Catholic Church in England, as a commitment to a tougher line if the Tories were elected, and praised as such. But Mr Howard disclaimed any such commitment or any intention to raise religion as an election issue, stressing "I did not make my comments in an interview with the *Catholic Herald*, I made them in an interview with *Cosmopolitan*. I was asked a straight question and I gave a straight answer."[149] Though the

---

[147] George H Gallup, *The Gallup International Public Opinion Polls: Great Britain 1937-1975* (New York: Random House, 1976), Volume I, p 404.
[148] George H Gallup, *The Gallup International Public Opinion Polls: Great Britain 1937-1975* (New York: Random House, 1976), Volume I, p 219.
[149] Michael White & Stephen Bates, "Leaders join forces to cool abortion row", *Guardian*, 16 March 2005.

Cardinal seemed keen that religious considerations should become more prominent in political debate, both Howard and Tony Blair seemed anxious to avoid any risk that this might occur.

Certainly the Tories gained no perceptible advantage among Catholics from Mr Howard's stance on abortion. As a group, in fact, Catholics were among Labour's strongest supporters. MORI surveys conducted for *The Tablet*[150] throughout the election campaign show that it was the support of Roman Catholic voters that gave Labour the edge in terms of votes cast: had no Catholics voted, the Tories would have secured a knife-edge 35% to 34% lead in the popular vote. Had only Catholics voted, the third Labour landslide would have been of monumental proportions, with Labour gaining more than half of all the votes cast and a majority measured in hundreds of seats rather than tens, while the Liberal Democrats would have almost overtaken the Tories in votes, if not in seats.

Table 88: Voting by Religion, 2005

	Con %	Lab %	LD %	Oth %	Lab Lead %	Turnout
All	33	36	23	8	+3	61%
All Christian	38	35	22	5	-3	64%
Catholic	23	53	22	2	+30	61%
Other Christian	41	31	21	6	-10	65%
Other religions	24	43	23	10	19	56%
None	21	38	27	14	17	55%

Source: MORI Final Election Aggregate Analysis
Base: 2,876 GB residents aged 18+ and "absolutely certain to vote"

The Protestant vote, however, was very different: the Conservatives had a ten-point lead over Labour among non-Catholic Christians, and if nobody but they had voted, Michael Howard would have been choosing his Cabinet on the Friday morning following the election. Tories are particularly strong in the Church of England which, while not quite living up to its old stereotype as "the Conservative Party at prayer", voted 44% Conservative to 31% Labour and 20% Liberal Democrat, a 13-point lead.

---

[150] Robert Worcester and Roger Mortimore, "Catholics Secured Blair's Third Term", *The Tablet,* 21 May 2005.

Labour support among Catholics, at 53%, stands if anything higher than in 1997 when Tony Blair was first elected: MORI surveys before that election also put Labour's share just over 50%. Catholic loyalty to Labour is in distinct contrast to the attitudes of the rest of the public. It may not be loyalty to Tony Blair, though: while fewer than a quarter (22%) of the public generally describes themselves as "Old Labour", over a third (34%) of Catholics say that best describes their political view.

Contrary to some stereotypes, the greater adherence of Catholics to the Labour Party cannot be explained in terms of social class. There is little difference between Catholic and Anglican churches in the class composition of their respective flocks, and indeed what difference there is points in the other direction – 55% of our Catholic respondents, but only 51% of those from the Church of England, were ABC1s.

Age is however a significant factor: while there are more professed Catholics in the youngest age groups (14% of 18-24 year olds) than the oldest (9% of those aged 65+), the Church of England by contrast has almost double the proportion of adherents in the oldest age group as in the youngest; the old, of course, tend towards the Conservatives while the young – when they vote – are more likely to support Labour.

Catholics were a little more likely than the rest of the public to say that, at the time we interviewed them, they might still change their mind about how to vote – a fifth of all adults but a quarter of Catholics admitted they were still wavering. In the end, though, they made up their minds in Tony Blair's direction.

Marginal Seats

Conventional wisdom accepts that the electoral system is massively biased in Labour's favour, and assuming uniform national swing this is true: Labour can trail in votes while still keeping an overall majority of seats.

But the assumption of uniform swing is falsified at each election. Of course, nobody should ever suppose that there would be a literal uniform swing, with the percentage changes in vote shares the same to the decimal point in every constituency. The essential idea of uniform swing is that the variations which will occur should not be systematic – that the swing will not be bigger in the marginals, or in particular regions or where there are large concentrations of Muslim voters.

Remember that even in this sense a uniform swing is neither normal nor expected. In most recent elections, for example, the marginals have swung differently from the rest of the country. But it is a useful and indeed arguably essential concept for political analysis – it can be used as a norm. Then, when we see, for example, that in 2005 the Muslim constituencies swung abnormally to the Liberal Democrats, we can take it that there is something to explain; without the assumption that all other things being equal all constituencies would behave in the same way, we would have no grounding to our analysis.

But when used to predict the number of seats that will be won for a given share of the national votes – for example, in interpreting the results of an opinion poll – uniform swing is admittedly crude. Nevertheless, it will often be the best tool available, since there will usually not be more detailed data available to show how the swing will deviate from uniformity; but it should still only be used with the greatest of caution and full understanding of its limitations. It is not – our journalistic friends and clients *please* note – something that the headline writers should be let loose on. We are a little weary of being blamed for the inaccuracy of our polls when the inaccuracy is in fact in the translation of the data into a seats forecast for which they are not intended and unsuitable.

The solution to this problem, of course, is to conduct more detailed polls, either across marginals or, of particular value to the individual voter, constituency polls, yet the number being commissioned seems to be steadily falling. (We know of only five constituency polls conducted in

2005 – see Table 114 on p 327). Therefore uniform swing is the best approximation we have.

Table 89: Vote Share Changes by Constituency Type, 2001-5

Constituency type	Change in Con vote % share	Change in Lab vote % share	Change in LD vote % share	Change in Oth vote % share	Change in Con vote % share
Overall national change	623*	+0.5	-5.8	+3.8	+1.5
Conservative v Labour 2001					
Marginal (margin 0-10%)					
Con-Lab	26	+1.4	-8.2	+3.7	+3.1
Lab-Con	51	+1.4	-5.4	+3.0	+1.0
Semi-marginal (margin 10-20%)					
Con-Lab	58	+1.0	-5.8	+3.1	+1.7
Lab-Con	77	+0.8	-6.5	+4.0	+1.7
Safe (margin 20%+)					
Con-Lab	21	+1.5	-4.3	+1.7	+1.1
Lab-Con	177	-0.8	-7.6	+5.2	+3.2
Conservative v LDem 2001					
Marginal (margin 0-10%)					
Con-LibDem	15	+2.2	-2.6	-0.5	+0.9
LibDem-Con	18	+0.3	-2.5	+1.7	+0.5
Semi-marginal (margin 10-20%)					
Con-LibDem	19	+1.3	-3.1	+0.9	+0.9
LibDem-Con	15	+1.2	-0.6	-2.1	+1.5
Safe (margin 20%+)					
Con-LibDem	24	+0.9	-2.6	+0.7	+1.0
LibDem-Con	11	+0.4	+0.5	-2.3	+1.4
Labour v LibDem 2001					
Marginal (margin 0-10%)					
Lab-LibDem	7	-2.9	-3.1	+8.8	-2.8
LibDem-Lab	1	+0.0	-1.6	-0.5	+2.1
Semi-marginal (margin 10-20%)					
Lab-LibDem	2	-0.8	-7.6	+6.6	+1.8
LibDem-Lab	3	-2.2	-4.1	+9.8	-3.5
Safe (margin 20%+)					
Lab-LibDem	44	-1.0	-7.6	+7.5	+1.1
LibDem-Lab	3	-0.2	-4.2	+4.9	+0.5

Source: Calculated from constituency results collected by the BBC (news.bbc.co.uk)
*Omits Birmingham Hodge Hill, Brent East, Glasgow North-East, Leicester South and Staffordshire South

Uniform swing fails as a predictor when some or all of the marginal seats behave differently. The occasional political earthquake in a "safe" seat, while possible, is rare enough to be only a minor distraction. It is overwhelmingly the swing in the marginals, uniform or not, that matters in determining the outcome of the election.

In both 1997 and 2001, Labour far outperformed its national result in the marginals, winning more seats than uniform swing would have delivered for a given vote share. In 2005, the boot was on the other foot, though you would hardly know it from many of the downbeat analyses of the Tory performance. For instance, Lord Ashcroft in his scathing attack noted that "Our share of the vote rose by just half of one per cent and in the Labour-held seats which, by definition, the Conservative Party must win if it is to form a government again, our vote share fell". [151] True, but a little misleading: Tory share rose across the Labour-held marginals and semi-marginals where the Tories were second; it fell only in the safest seats and the seats where the Tories were third or worse placed to start with. Consequently the bias was eased a little: uniform swing would have predicted that on the vote shares the parties achieved the Tories would have won only 184 seats; in fact they won 198.

Admittedly, this is still not a rosy picture: a 1.4 point rise in the most marginal target seats is simply not good enough, and even winning all 128 of the Labour-held marginal and semi-marginal seats (which would require a 10% swing) would only just have given the Tories a single-figure overall majority. To form a government to last out a five-year term they will have to start getting back some of these "safe" seats as well. But, as we shall see, it may be more useful to think of this task in regional rather than national uniform swing terms; there is a pattern to the Tories' failures.

More pertinently, though, they should be noting that the Conservative share rose in all the categories of Conservative-Labour marginals, but by much less than the Labour share fell – in fact the Labour defectors seem to have split by more than two-to-one in favour of the Liberal Democrats rather than the Conservatives. In other words, half or less of the "swing" in these seats can be considered movement to the Conservatives, the

---

[151] Michael A Ashcroft, *Smell the coffee: a wake-up call for the Conservative Party* (London: CGI Europe, 2005).

remainder presumably being "tactical unwind" – Liberal Democrats who had previously voted tactically for Labour declining to continue to do so.

They may be more relaxed about losing votes in the Labour-Liberal Democrat seats where they could not win and where their vote was clearly squeezed. The Liberal Democrats should perhaps view the pattern with a little more apprehension. They underperformed across all the categories of seats where they and the Conservatives were the main contenders, and although the Labour vote fell in most of these seats the LibDems did not squeeze it very effectively. Only in the most marginal seats that they themselves held against the Tories did the LibDems succeed in increasing their vote share by even half the fall in the Labour share. In all other five categories, the overall swing was to the Tories. Have the LibDems hit a plateau at last in their attempt to move into the Tory heartland?

Hunting the Rural Vote

Many Labour MPs, especially those in partly rural seats, seem to have been a little nervous about the impact on their support of the passage of the bill banning fox-hunting. Perhaps this and the government's repeated delays in implementing a measure promised in their first manifesto are evidence that in politics if you want your voice to be heard it helps to shout loudly. Supporters of hunting were always a minority of the population, even in rural areas, and their electoral impact would always be negligible for the simple reason that they were virtually all Conservatives already, so could not swing any further. But they were well-organised, vocal, and got an impressive number of protestors on the streets for the Countryside March, though its size was subsequently eclipsed by the Iraq protest. (That didn't change the government's mind, either.)

At the turn of the year we examined the voting intentions (extracted from our national polls) of the public in the 180 constituencies held by members of the Rural Group of Labour MPs, which are mostly rural or semi-rural. We found no significance difference between the swing against the government in these seats and across the rest of the country, which may have reassured some Labour MPs in such constituencies that their seats had not been put abnormally at risk by the hunting controversy. The election when it came not only confirmed this conclusion, but it actually transpired that Labour MPs did better defending their vote in rural than in urban constituencies. (The table is confined to England and Wales as the boundary changes in Scotland make direct comparison impossible.)

Table 90: Results in Labour's Rural Seats in England and Wales

Average change in party percentage vote share 2001-5

	Con	Lab	LD
Labour's rural seats (142)	+0.1	-5.8	+3.5
Other Labour seats (215)	+0.5	-8.1	+6.0

Source: Calculated from constituency results collected by the BBC (news.bbc.co.uk)
"Labour's rural seats" as defined by the Rural Group of Labour MPs.

That is not to say that the hunting issue had no effect on the election, however. Pro-hunt groups set up the organisation VoteOK, which apparently sent volunteer canvassers to target constituencies which were held by anti-hunting politicians (mostly Labour but some Liberal Democrat). They claimed after the election that they had "contributed to the ousting of 29 anti-hunting former MPs. 3.4 million leaflets were delivered, 2.1 million envelopes hand-addressed 55,000 posters erected and 170,000 campaigning man hours provided in a nationally co-ordinated initiative." They claimed credit for assisting the defeat of Peter Bradley, Stephen Twigg, David Rendel, Helen Clark, Huw Edwards, Melanie Smallman and Melanie Johnson among others.[152]

As VoteOK did not publish any list of the constituencies it targeted, it is impossible to make any objective test of their claims. However, campaigning assistance on the scale they mentioned could certainly be expected to have an impact. Note, though, that the impact had nothing to do with the spread of opposition to the hunting ban, and their campaigning made no mention of it – they simply worked to elect their preferred candidate. Any other lobby able to command the same number of active workers, whatever its wider support, could have done the same.

Shout loudly to make yourself heard, that's the trick.

---

[152] Charles Clover, "Anti-hunting MPs are run to ground", *Daily Telegraph*, 7 May 2005 (accessed at www.telegraph.co.uk on 30 June 2005).

Region and Nation

With the exception of some comment on the Tories' better than average performances in London and the South-East, not a great deal has been said about regional patterns in voting in the 2005 election.

Table 91: Voting by region, 2005

| | Vote 2005 | | | | | Change since '01 | | | |
	Con	Lab	LD	Oth	Lab Lead	Con	Lab	LD	Swing
	%	%	%	%	%				
All	33	36	23	8	3	0	-6	+4	3.0
E Midlands	37	39	18	6	2	0	-6	+3	3.0
Eastern	43	30	22	5	-13	+1	-7	+5	4.0
London	32	39	22	7	7	+2	-8	+5	5.0
North East	20	53	23	4	33	-1	-6	+6	2.5
North West	29	45	21	5	16	0	-6	+4	3.0
Scotland	16	40	23	21	24	0	-4	+7	2.0
South East	45	24	25	6	-21	+2	-5	+1	3.5
South West	39	23	33	5	-16	0	-3	+2	1.5
Wales	21	43	18	18	22	0	-6	+4	3.0
W Midlands	35	39	19	7	4	0	-6	+4	3.0
Yorks & H	29	44	21	6	15	-1	-5	+4	2.0

Source: Calculated from constituency results collected by the BBC (news.bbc.co.uk)

This may be because analysis by standard region obscures rather than reveals the pattern. If, however, we look at the change in vote shares since 2001 on a county level, the fact that there is indeed a pattern becomes clear. The Tories' best results were in a band across the South of England and Wales, above all Essex, but not the extreme South-West; in most of the rest of the country their support fell.

The Liberal Democrats had their strongest performances in the North and North Wales. There is less of a clear geographical pattern to Labour's losses, but it will be seen that as well as London they suffered sharp losses on Tyneside, Teesside and in the West Midlands.

Figure 49: Conservative Change in Share by County

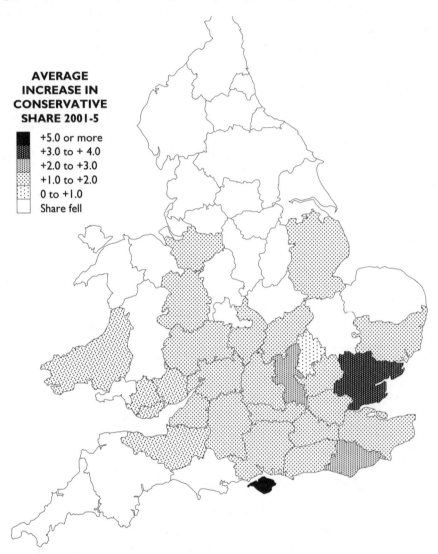

AVERAGE
INCREASE IN
CONSERVATIVE
SHARE 2001-5

+5.0 or more
+3.0 to + 4.0
+2.0 to +3.0
+1.0 to +2.0
0 to +1.0
Share fell

These regional patterns are probably most relevant in interpreting the Conservative performance. The continuing further decline of Tory strength in the North, even in an election when both their national vote share and number of seats rose, must throw real doubt on any claims that

260

they have achieved a success that they can build on in a future push for government – the "one more heave" thesis.

Figure 50: Liberal Democrat Share Change by County

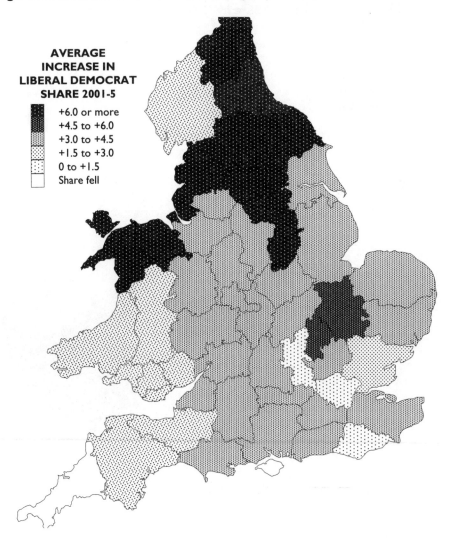

AVERAGE
INCREASE IN
LIBERAL DEMOCRAT
SHARE 2001-5

+6.0 or more
+4.5 to +6.0
+3.0 to +4.5
+1.5 to +3.0
0 to +1.5
Share fell

The English and Welsh counties where the Tory average share of the vote rose encompass just 291 seats between them: this is not adequate as a power base around which to build a Parliamentary majority, even allowing for a little help from the Boundary Commissioners and the seats they currently hold against the tide in parts of the country where their support is still falling.

Figure 51: Labour Change in Share by County

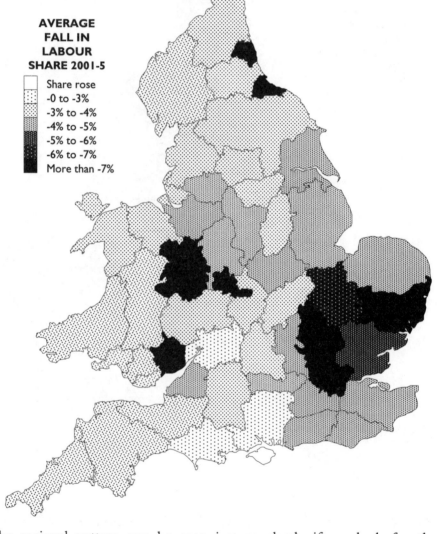

The regional pattern can be seen just as clearly if we look for the outstanding constituency results. Of the 168 constituencies across the country where the Conservative share increased by 2% or more, 46 were in London, 52 in the South East, and a further 22 were in that part of the "East of England" that used to be counted as the South East (Bedfordshire, Hertfordshire and Essex); only 48 were in the rest of the country.

It is instructive to compare this distribution of strength with past Tory victories – even those in the 1980s when Scotland, Wales and the urban centres were already slipping away. In 2005, the Tories took less than 13,000 votes across the five Liverpool seats; in 1983, despite not winning any of the constituencies there, they won more than 13,000 votes in each of three of them. In 2005, they gathered less than 13,000 Tory votes in total in the four core Manchester seats; in both 1983 and 1987 they won more than 18,000 in Withington alone, and won the seat in 1983 – it is now a LibDem gain from Labour.

London, where Conservative share rose from 30% to 32%, proved an exception to the Tories' otherwise disappointing performances in the metropolitan areas, but was less encouraging than might at first appear. Because London has a high concentration of long-term marginals, the types of seats where the Tories did especially badly in 1997 and 2001 and recovered some ground in 2005, what we see was probably not a regional effect as such. At any rate, taking 1992 rather than 2001 as the baseline, the Tories are still doing worse in London than nationally, down 13 percentage points in the capital on their share at the time of John Major's victory, whereas overall they have pulled back to within ten points of that position. They still have a weary way to go.

"Decapitation"

Probably the most highly-publicised strategy of the election – one would suppose to the fury of its devisers – was the Liberal Democrats' policy of "decapitation", targeting efforts especially at defeating prominent Conservatives who were defending marginal seats. But they took only one scalp.

The Liberal Democrats do not seem to have issued a definitive list of their decapitation targets, or indeed to have formally admitted that they were pursuing such a strategy. However, Table 92 lists the eight conceivable targets in order of marginality in 2001, including two which would have been exceptionally ambitious (Wokingham required nearly a 7% swing and Mid Sussex a 7.5% swing); Sir Michael Spicer, chairman of the 1922 Committee and as such leader of the backbench Conservatives, might not have been included in any case.

Table 92: The "Decapitation" Strategy – Constituency Results

Constituency	2005 result				Change 2001-5			
	Con %	Lab %	LD %	Oth %	Con %	Lab %	LD %	Oth %
Overall GB result	**33.2**	**36.2**	**22.6**	**9.0**	**+0.5**	**-5.9**	**+3.8**	**+1.6**
Dorset West (Oliver Letwin)	46.5	7.7	41.9	3.8	+1.9	-5.8	+0.1	+3.8
Haltemprice & Howden (David Davis)	47.4	12.7	36.8	3.0	+4.2	-3.0	-2.1	+0.9
Westmorland & Lonsdale (Tim Collins)	44.9	7.6	45.5	2.0	-2.0	-3.3	+5.1	+0.2
Maidenhead (Theresa May)	50.8	9.0	37.2	2.9	+5.8	-6.1	-0.2	+0.5
Worcestershire West (Sir Michael Spicer)	44.5	10.5	39.3	5.7	-1.5	-3.5	+5.3	-0.3
Folkestone & Hythe (Michael Howard)	53.9	12.5	29.9	3.7	+8.9	-7.7	-2.3	+1.1
Wokingham (John Redwood)	48.1	15.2	32.4	4.3	+2.0	-2.2	-0.0	+0.2
Mid Sussex (Nicholas Soames)	48.0	12.7	36.1	3.2	+1.9	-6.3	+5.0	-0.6

Source: Constituency results collected by the BBC (news.bbc.co.uk)

But it can be seen that the inclusion or omission of these three borderline cases makes little real difference to the story. All six of the high profile Shadow Ministers increased their own vote share, while (except in the barely-winnable Mid Sussex) Liberal Democrat share was steady or fell. The Liberal Democrats achieved a net swing in their favour only there and in Westmorland & Lonsdale and Worcestershire West, where the defending Conservative was less prominent and voters very likely did not consider the local election in terms of a national decapitation strategy.

Table 93: Liberal Democrat Decapitation Strategy

Average change in party percentage vote share 2001-5

	Con %	Lab %	LD %	Oth %	Gains (seats)
Possible decapitation targets (8)	+2.7	-4.7	+1.4	+1.1	1
Other Con-held, majority less than 15% (18)	+1.8	-1.4	-1.5	+0.7	1

Source: Calculated from constituency results collected by the BBC (news.bbc.co.uk)

Some commentators have assumed post-election that the decapitation strategy was not simply a failure but actively counter-productive. Nevertheless, as the comparison in Table 93 shows, Liberal Democrats did not do worse in the potential decapitation seats than in their other Conservative-held target seats. In only two of the eight on the decapitation list did the party's vote share fall by as much as the 1.5-point average fall in the remaining targets. The Liberal Democrats simply failed across the board in their bid to make substantial further gains from the Conservatives.

5. Engagement and Turnout

Falling Turnout: Introduction

One of the most disturbing features of the 2001 election was its turnout – at 59.4% the lowest proportion of the electorate to have voted since 1918, before universal adult suffrage had been established. This prompted both a great deal of research attempting to explain how turnout could have fallen so far and so suddenly, and experimentation with a number of expedients intended to alleviate the situation.

However, neither approach produced solutions which could be applied to significantly increasing turnout at the 2005 general election. The Electoral Commission had drawn some lessons from its research in planning its public information campaigns, but the principal lesson it was taught was that the problems were more deep-seated and were unlikely to be cured quickly by such necessarily short-term measures, though they might be ameliorated. The experimental methods of voting had ended in a furore at the 2004 European and local elections which raised questions over whether the cure was worse than the disease – none were authorised for use in general elections (although "postal voting on demand", already available in 2001, was continued).

Figure 52: UK General Election Turnouts, 1945-2005

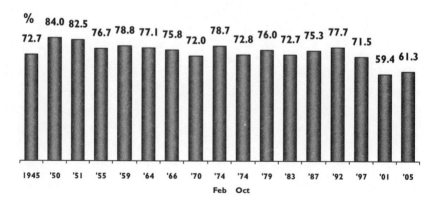

However, one comforting possibility remained, that the low turnout in 2001 depended solely on short-term political factors related to that election alone, and was unlikely to be repeated. Many fewer voters than usual felt that there was a significant distinction between the two major parties (the British Election Study found just 16% saying there was a great difference between the Conservative and Labour parties, half the previous lowest in a time series going back to 1966 and having fallen from a peak of 84% as recently as the 1987 election[153]), and there had been a fall in the number who said it was important to them who won. Arguably, therefore, the low turnout may have simply reflected unusually low concern about the outcome rather than any more endemic change.

Table 94: Importance of the Election Result

Q   How important is it to you personally who wins the General Election?

	1987	1992	1997	2001	2005
	%	%	%	%	%
Very important	55	55	36	32	45
Fairly important	30	31	33	34	35
Not very important	9	10	18	25	11
Not at all important	3	3	10	8	6
No opinion	2	1	3	2	3
Important	85	86	69	66	80
Not important	12	13	28	33	17

Source: MORI
Base: c. 1,000-2,000 GB residents aged 18+ in each survey

This now seems clearly to have been a false hope. In MORI's final poll in 2005, 45% of the public said it was "very important" to them personally who won the election, and 80% that it was at least "fairly important", considerably more than said so in 1997 or 2001. Yet turnout in 2005 was not significantly better than in 2001 – lower by 10% of the electorate than at any general election between the Great War and the end of the 20th century.

---

[153] Catherine Bromley and John Curtice, 'Where Have All the Voters Gone?', in A Park *et al* (eds) *British Social Attitudes: The 19th Report* (London: Sage, 2002), p 144.

It seems clear, then, that low turnouts are likely to be a permanent phenomenon unless we can find a solution.

The practical solutions devised and used on an experimental basis in subsidiary elections over the 2001-5 period took two approaches to the problem – making it easier to vote by tinkering with the voting process, and combining more than one election at the same time so as to encourage those electors prepared to take the trouble to vote in one of these that they might as well also vote in the others while they were at it. Both make the unspoken assumption that the abstainers would be prepared to vote if only it involved less commitment on their part, and imply that what matters is that enough people should vote, not *why* they vote.

The Government has experimented with several methods of making voting easier, notably and most controversially the use of all-postal ballots, first in a limited number of local pilot schemes and then across the whole of the North of England in the European Parliament and local government elections in 2004. Some of these experiments seemed to have had at least limited success in getting more people to vote, though at the expense of considerable controversy over whether these methods were making electoral fraud easier.

But in any case simply making voting easier does not address the root cause of falling turnout, a lower determination on the part of electors to participate. A number of bodies, notably The Electoral Commission and The Hansard Society, have commissioned research over the last four years exploring this more fundamental problem of why people vote or don't vote, and what can be done to make more of them *want* to vote, rather than simply finding a way of papering over the cracks and making the figures look respectable; much of this research has been conducted by MORI.

The research has included investigation of whether the problem is simply a matter of inconvenience, so that otherwise eager citizens are prevented from voting by unnecessarily restrictive details of the system. (It isn't). But more importantly it has begun to explore attitudes to voting, to the political system and other aspects of citizenship and community involvement, and how they are related to each other. It is here, almost certainly, that the real answer lies and although very few conclusions are yet available from research specifically concerning the 2005 election, the indications from the 2001 general election and from the European, local and devolved elections during the Parliament will almost certainly be valid in this case as well.

Turnout is lowest among the young, and it is perhaps natural to look at their opinions and values first. In 2001, just 39% of 18-24 year old electors voted, and in 2005 it was two points down, at 37%. Politicians and media alike at first blamed "apathy" among young people (and everybody but themselves for causing it). Soon, however, the work that MORI did for the Electoral Commission both using qualitative research (focus groups) and surveys showed that there was no decline in "interest" in politics (over the past thirty years), in news about the election, or the issues that faced the country, but that few young people thought the election interesting, they saw little difference between the parties and little likelihood of significant change whoever won; most who did not vote made up their mind not to vote before the campaign even began, and it was clear that it was not "apathy", but **disengagement**: disengagement from party politics, and disengagement from the politicians, who were not trusted, not transparent, and not thought by young people to be listening to young people, not even those young people who bothered to try to communicate their concerns.

Yet it is not only the young who are disengaged or staying away from the polls; these same dismissive attitudes can be found on a much wider basis. The standing of politicians is low, and the public primarily associates negative connotations with the concept of "politics". This, though, arises partly from their failure to connect the issues that concern them with the political process – a failure which leads naturally to disengagement (and which the Electoral Commission has attempted to address directly with its "I don't do politics" advertising campaigns).

Probably this alone would not cause turnout to fall significantly, since politics has never been the most highly respected of professions. But another contributory factor is suggested by the finding that a significant section of the public does not agree with the statement that "It is my duty to vote".

The importance in principle of voting is still generally accepted: in 2001, only 10% of the public agreed that "I don't think voting is very important". Nevertheless, two very distinct attitudes to voting exist in Britain. Some people, still the majority, regard it as their duty to vote, one

269

of the responsibilities of being a citizen. Others, though, feel that while it is their *right* to vote, they are under no obligation to do so if they are indifferent to the outcome. Indeed, they may perhaps feel that in such circumstances they *should not* vote, leaving the decision to be taken instead by those who have strong feelings one way or the other.

Table 95: Duty To Vote?

Q   To what extent do you agree or disagree with the following statements?
"It is my duty to vote"

	All %	18-24 %	25-34 %	35-44 %	45-54 %	55-64 %	65+ %
Agree	74	58	61	74	79	83	86
Disagree	15	24	20	15	14	12	7
Neither/don't know	11	18	19	11	7	5	7

Source: MORI survey for *An Audit of Political Engagement* (London: Electoral Commission/ Hansard Society, 2004)
Base: 1,976 UK residents aged 18+, 11-17 December 2003

Figure 53: Correlation Between Turnout and "Duty To Vote" by Age

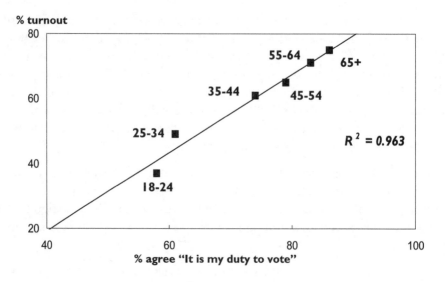

Source: MORI survey for *An Audit of Political Engagement* (London: Electoral Commission/ Hansard Society, 2004) and MORI Final Election Aggregate 2005

Base: 1,976 UK residents aged 18+, 11-17 December 2003; 17,959 GB residents aged 18+, 5 April-5 May 2005

Admittedly, there is still a high level of belief that it is one's duty to vote: three-quarters say they believe this, and only 15% disagree. However, younger people are much less likely to agree that it is their duty to vote than the middle-aged or old.

Since duty and force of habit ("I always vote") are much the most frequently-cited explanations when voters are asked to explain why they vote, any weakening in the public perception that there is a duty to vote could be expected to depress turnout. We can see a very clear correlation, too, between the proportion of each age group who say they believe in a duty to vote and the percentage turnout of that age group at the 2005 election. Figure 53 graphs the two figures against each other, showing how close all six age groups sit to the "line of best fit". In fact the R^2 statistic, which measures how much of the variation in one factor can be statistically explained by the other, is over 0.96, extraordinarily high for a relationship between two measures based on different surveys.

We cannot be certain that belief in a "duty to vote" is in decline, since we have no survey evidence from past years with which we can make comparison. But it seems a likely explanation, and if the public will not vote out of duty or habit, the need to give them a positive reason to vote becomes acute. If values are changing, this injects an age aspect into the turnout problem which may permanently affect the voting behaviour of entire generations, a cohort (or "tree-ring") effect. But that still begs the question of why turnout should have fallen so precipitately – if belief in a duty to vote has fallen, this is surely an evolution that has taken a number of years.

In 2004, MORI investigated the relationship between various aspects of voting, civic participation and social values as measured in the survey published as *An Audit of Political Engagement* by The Electoral Commission and the Hansard Society in March 2004; MORI's further analysis of the data using multivariate statistical techniques was reported to the Electoral Commission as *Rules of Engagement?* in August 2004. We found that the factors that most closely relate to propensity to vote are a belief that involvement in politics works ("efficacy") which is much the most

271

powerful influence, and a feeling of knowledge about, and interest in, the political institutions.

Efficacy is defined by belief that getting involved in politics can change how the country is run, feeling a sense of satisfaction when one votes and wanting to have a say in how the country is run, and believing that being active in politics is not a waste of time, as well as that people have a duty to vote.

The second dimension about **knowledge and participation** is not surprising. Much past research has shown that the more people know about an institution, the more favourably disposed they are towards it, and generally the more likely they are to connect with it – a principle encapsulated in the maxim "Familiarity breeds favourability, not contempt". In politics, those who claim to know more about politics say they are more likely to vote. Of course, it works both ways: those who are involved through voting, or even contacting their MP, are more likely to have, and to seek, greater knowledge about politics and political institutions than those who do not. This leads to a cycle of success; the converse cycle of failure is perhaps a closer model of the present situation.

Another important finding was that falling turnout is *not* simply a symptom of wider decline in civil responsibility. Many of those who do not vote nevertheless feel strongly about issues that others would feel come within the political sphere; many of those who do not engage in any "political" activity are active and enthusiastic in communal activities they see as "non-political". In particular, what we called "good causes activism" – being prepared to help organise charity events, for example, or playing an active part in non-political organisations – is not related to propensity to vote. These activities, which would normally be considered aspects of "good citizenship" and helpful in building up "social capital" do not, apparently, lead their participants to turn out at the ballot box.

Demographic factors (even newspaper readership) also contribute little to understanding likelihood of voting independent of other aspects of political engagement. Commitment to the various political parties, by contrast, is a highly significant factor – propensity to vote is closely related to knowing which party one intends to vote for. While this is not remotely surprising, it emphasises how important to turnout is the success of the parties in appealing to the public, and voters' ability to discriminate between them.

This has particular implications for the interpretation (and encouragement) of electoral turnout. Most theorists, and most politicians, take it as read that voting is a facet of good citizenship. The public – especially the young – do not necessarily agree: they may be good citizens in other ways, yet not feel that voting is an important part of that. The problem is that not everybody sees a connection between the two – and that not everybody sees that as a "problem".

Turnout in 2005

Overall, turnout in Great Britain in 2005 was 2.2% higher than in 2001. The increase varied regionally from no change in Wales to a 3% increase in London and the West Midlands; turnout was lowest in the North-East and North-West (57% – scant evidence of long-term beneficial effects from the all-postal voting experiment in 2004), highest in the South-West (67%).

The disappointment of the election turnout was in the 2% decline in the voting of the young, 18-24s, from the woeful 39% last time to just 37% in this election. Despite all the efforts of the political parties and civic groups, the Electoral Commission and the media, to capture the attention and involvement of young people, they continued to be disengaged.

Table 96: Turnout by Types of Voters

	Profile of		Turnout			Profile of		Turnout	
	Elec-torate	Voters	2005	Chg		Elec-torate	Voters	2005	Chg
All	100%	100%	61%	+2	Men by Age				
Men	48%	48%	62%	+1	18-24	6%	4%	39%	-4
Women	52%	52%	61%	+3	25-34	9%	7%	49%	+2
Age					35-54	18%	18%	64%	0
18-24	11%	7%	37%	-2	55+	16%	19%	74%	+1
25-34	17%	14%	49%	+3	Women by Age				
35-44	20%	19%	61%	+2	18-24	6%	3%	35%	-1
45-54	16%	17%	65%	0	25-34	9%	7%	48%	+2
55-64	15%	17%	71%	+2	35-54	18%	18%	61%	+1
65+	21%	26%	75%	+5	55+	19%	23%	73%	+6
Social class					Men by Class				
AB	24%	27%	71%	+3	AB	12%	14%	70%	+2
C1	29%	30%	62%	+2	C1	14%	15%	63%	+1
C2	21%	20%	58%	+2	C2	11%	10%	57%	+1
DE	25%	23%	54%	+1	DE	11%	9%	55%	-1
Tenure					Women by Class				
Owned	32%	37%	71%	+3	AB	12%	14%	71%	+3
Mortgage	40%	40%	60%	+1	C1	15%	15%	61%	+2
Social rent	18%	15%	51%	-1	C2	10%	10%	58%	+2
Private	9%	7%	51%	+5	DE	15%	13%	54%	+4

Source: MORI Final Election Aggregate Analysis
Base: 17,959 GB residents aged 18+, 5 April-5 May 2005

Although turnout has probably always been lowest among the young, the degree to which the gap has widened in the last thirteen years is dramatic. In 1992, MORI estimates that 63% of 18-24 year olds voted, 15 points lower than the overall turnout or, expressed another way, the young were about four-fifths as likely as the average adult to get to the polls. In 2005, that ratio had fallen to three-fifths, and the gap widened to 24 percentage points.

Table 97: Percentage Turnout by Age (Estimates from MORI Data)

	1992 %	1997 %	2001 %	2005 %
All	78	71	59	61
18-24	63	51	39	37
25-34	76	64	46	48
35-44	} 80	73	59	61
45-54		79	65	64
55-64	82	80	69	71
65+	83	79	70	75

Source: MORI

It is important to distinguish "rational" abstention – a greater tendency not to vote where one's vote is less likely to affect the outcome – from more general disengagement that assumes that voting is unnecessary in all cases. Whether or not supporters of proportional representation are right in believing that a change in the electoral system would increase turnout by reducing the number of "wasted votes" and therefore increasing the rational incentive to turn out, it is certainly true that turnout is – as it was in the past – higher in marginal seats. But this may be a result of the parties' greater concentration of their campaigning efforts in those seats, rather than solely of the voters' recognition of the tactical situation.

Turnout rose from 2001 in all types of constituency, but generally by more in marginal seats than in safe ones, widening the existing gap. As the degree of targeting in party campaigns has also increased, this would be at least consistent with the difference being a campaigning effect rather than a "rational voter" effect. When the analysis is broken down to show the different patterns of party competition, it is evident that turnout rose most in constituencies where the Liberal Democrats were the challengers, and least in those seats already held by the Liberal Democrats, regardless of which party was best placed to defeat them.

Table 98: Turnout by Constituency Type, 2001-5

Constituency type (By 2001 result)	Average Turnout 2001 %	Average Turnout 2005 %	Change in Turnout %
Overall national turnout	59.1	61.3	+2.2
Marginal (margin 0-10%)	63.3	65.8	+2.5
Semi-marginal (margin 10-20%)	62.1	64.5	+2.4
Safe (margin 20%+)	55.6	57.5	+1.9
Major party safe seats			
Conservative	62.6	64.7	+2.1
Labour	53.9	55.8	+1.9
Major party marginals			
Con-Lab (0-10% margin)	62.2	63.9	+1.7
Lab-Con (0-10% margin)	62.9	65.7	+2.8
Lab-Con (10-20% margin)	61.3	63.2	+1.9
LibDem v Conservative			
Con-LD (0-10% margin)	65.3	68.6	+3.3
Con-LD (10-20% margin)	64.8	69.5	+4.7
LD-Con (0-10% margin)	66.0	68.6	+2.6
LD-Con (10-20% margin)	63.6	65.3	+1.7
LD-Con safer	63.7	65.5	+1.8
LibDem v Labour			
Lab-LD (0-20% margin)	60.4	63.4	+3.0
LD-Lab	58.1	59.4	+1.3
Other	60.9	62.7	+1.8

Source: Calculated from constituency results collected by the BBC (news.bbc.co.uk)

The Reputation of Politicians and Politics

The standing of politics is low. It affects public attitudes to politicians, political institutions, policies, and probably to parts of the public sector that would not strictly be considered "political" at all. To all intents and purposes, "political" has become a pejorative term in modern Britain.

We have already seen how trust in the government and in Tony Blair has slipped during the current Parliament. But distrust of politicians generally goes beyond any short-term factors such as these. Indeed, the existing climate of willingness to believe the worst of politicians probably contributed to Blair's travails, ensuring that scepticism about his motives and honesty in his handling of the international situation from 9/11 onwards were always uppermost in the public mind – even though he probably started from a higher base of trust than would most modern Prime Ministers.

Table 99: MORI Veracity Index

Q Now I will read out a list of different types of people. For each, would you tell me whether you generally trust them to tell the truth or not?

% trusted to tell the truth

	'83	'93	'97	'99	'00	'01	'02	'03	'04	'05
	%	%	%	%	%	%	%	%	%	%
Doctors	82	84	86	91	87	89	91	91	92	91
Teachers	79	84	83	89	85	86	85	87	89	88
Professors	n/a	70	70	79	76	78	77	74	80	77
Judges	77	68	72	77	77	78	77	72	75	76
Clergyman/Priests	85	80	71	80	78	78	80	71	75	73
Scientists	n/a	n/a	63	63	63	65	64	65	69	70
Television news readers	63	72	74	74	73	75	71	66	70	63
The Police	61	63	61	61	60	63	59	64	63	58
The ordinary man/woman in the street	57	64	56	60	52	52	54	53	55	56
Pollsters	n/a	52	55	49	46	46	47	46	49	50
Civil Servants	25	37	36	47	47	43	45	46	51	44
Trade Union officials	18	32	27	39	38	39	37	33	39	37
Business Leaders	25	32	29	28	28	27	25	28	30	24
Government Ministers	**16**	**11**	**12**	**23**	**21**	**20**	**20**	**20**	**23**	**20**
Politicians generally	**18**	**14**	**15**	**23**	**20**	**17**	**19**	**18**	**22**	**20**
Journalists	**19**	**10**	**15**	**15**	**15**	**18**	**13**	**18**	**20**	**16**

Source: MORI/BMA/*The Times*
Base: c. 2,000 GB residents aged 15+/18+ in each survey (c. 1,000 in 1997)

277

Politicians are generally distrusted. This can perhaps be most easily tracked through MORI's regular "veracity" poll; only journalists have ever scored below "politicians generally" and government ministers in this measure of public trust.

Table 100: Perceptions of MPs' Motives in the 1990s

Q In general, whose interests do you think MPs put first – their own, their constituents', their party's or their country's?

	1994	1996
	%	%
Own	52	56
Party's	26	27
Constituents'	11	7
Country's	5	5
Other	1	1
No opinion	5	4

Source: MORI

More than half the public in two MORI surveys during the 1990s said they felt that MPs put their own interests before any others, and another quarter thought they put their party's interests first.[154]

Table 101: Perceptions of MPs' Motives in the 1940s

Q Do you think British politicians are out merely for themselves, for their party, or to do their best for their country?

	1944
	%
Themselves	35
Party	22
Country	36
Don't know	7

Source: Gallup. Reported in George H Gallup (1976), *The Gallup International Public Opinion Polls: Great Britain 1937-1975* (Random House, New York), volume I, p 96.

In fact, low public opinion of politicians' motives goes back long before the accusation of sleaze was common. It is perhaps startling to discover that even more than half a century ago, at the height of World War Two,

---

[154] MORI interviewed 820 GB residents aged 18+ by telephone on 10-11 January 1994, in a survey for *The Sun*, and 1,620 GB residents aged 18+ face-to-face, in home, on 23-26 May 1996.

the majority of the public distrusted their political masters, as a Gallup poll in 1944 demonstrated.

One immediate reaction of politicians when faced with the public's distrust is to blame the tone and content of media coverage of politics. It is true that politicians in general and parties in particular get a "bad press", their imperfections being held up for all to see. But there is more to it than that. Not only are the politicians themselves often complicit in this, exaggerating the significance of their opponents' faults for short-term partisan advantage, but the impact seems to be much more than for other professions.

Unlike, for example, doctors or the police, the public refuse to give politicians the benefit of the doubt. Surveys demonstrated that trust in the police was undented by controversies such as the Stephen Lawrence case, just as doctors in general seem untarnished by hospital scandals or even the murderous revelations about Harold Shipman.

Table 102: Public Confidence in "Most Doctors"

Q As you may have heard or read, doctors have been reported in the press or on TV recently in an unfavourable light, e.g. the Bristol surgeon inquiry and stories about Alder Hey and other hospitals retaining body parts. Thinking about those stories and taking your answer from this showcard, how well or badly would you say that most doctors do their job nowadays?

	2001 %	2002 %
Very well	26	24
Fairly well	58	63
Neither well nor badly	10	8
Fairly badly	3	3
Very badly	1	1
Don't know/no opinion	2	1
Well	84	87
Badly	4	4
Net well	80	83

Source: MORI/BMA
Base: c. 2,000 GB residents aged 15+ in each survey

Such is the public's trust in doctors that they are prepared to treat even high-profile scandals as isolated incidents. In MORI surveys for the BMA in 2001 and 2002, we explicitly reminded respondents of the stories in the press and on TV, with a question apparently strongly loaded against doctors; yet in two successive years' surveys the public refused to take the bait, and only 4% would say that "most doctors" do their job badly nowadays.

The police offer perhaps a closer comparison than doctors, for here much of the bad press in recent years has concerned the integrity of individual officers, and accusations of either corruption or racism. Yet confidence in police officers has survived untarnished. In a survey in 1999 at the height of coverage of criticism of the police in the Stephen Lawrence case[155], only 21% would agree "Most police officers are prejudiced against Black and Asian people" – a low figure in itself and unmoved since figures of 22% and 23% respectively in previous surveys in 1989 and 1994.

By contrast, questions about "most politicians" elicit very negative opinions. In October 1994, for example, a Gallup poll found that 64% of the public agreed that "most members of Parliament make a lot of money by using public office improperly"[156]. It is the preparedness of the public to believe the worst about politicians which makes them, and the image of the whole political system, so vulnerable.

Role of Political Parties

But within the political system we can make distinctions. It is the political party which is its most execrated feature.

Public regard for political parties is low. Indeed, they are the least trusted of political institutions as measured by the regular Eurobarometer surveys (although this distrust is not confined to Britain). In the latest survey available, conducted in October-November 2004, just 15% of British adults said they tended to trust political parties; 78% said they "tend not to trust" them. The government in Britain is twice as trusted as the parties (32%), though still hardly scoring well, and Parliament fares a little better still (37%).[157]

---

[155] MORI interviewed 802 residents aged 16+ by telephone on 19-21 February 1999 for *The Sun*.
[156] Gallup *Political and Economic Index*, Report 410 (October 1994).
[157] European Commission Standard Eurobarometer 62, Autumn 2004. British fieldwork was conducted by TNS UK, who interviewed 1,310 UK adults face-to-face, in home, on 5 October-8 November 2004. Details at http://europa.eu.int/comm/public_opinion/index_en.htm

In recent years, disregard for parties has seen practical expression in the election of independent candidates where, in the past, party nominees would have triumphed; and, plainly, refusal to vote altogether is another symptom.

It seems clear that the public does not really understand the function of parties or why they are necessary to a modern representative democracy. They are seen as corrupt cartels whose only purpose is to debase the independence and integrity of elected representatives. Hostility to the political parties seemingly acts as a deterrent to involvement. People seem to see "politics" as more of an obstruction to proper governance of the country, rather than a means of engagement, and "party politics" in particular.

In fact our research finds in other fields, not merely the political, that "independence" is a criterion for trust – "independent" groups and scientists are trusted more across a range of issues (for example, pollution or BSE) than those working for business or government. There is support for "independent" organisations to audit public agencies, so long as they have the power to hold the agency to account and bring about organisational change. But what this amounts to is distrust of government, big business, the establishment and their institutions. It is rare for the public to demand that an environmental scientist be "independent" of Greenpeace. In the political sphere, it is the parties that are seen as the epitome of all the public thinks is wrong with the system.

The public's negative attitude towards parties does not exist in a vacuum – the pretext offered by elections to express opinions, not only in the privacy of the polling booth but publicly as well, may be creating a vicious circle. We are able to track one aspect of this, using a measurement developed from the MORI Excellence Model, used by a number of major corporations to test their corporate image. It measures the extent of positive or negative "advocacy" – how many of the public are prepared to recommend voting for, or not voting for, a particular party to somebody else, especially without being asked to do so. This gives an indication of the strength of both the positive and negative "word of mouth" atmosphere surrounding the major parties.

The comparison between the parties and the light it throws on the 2005 result is discussed elsewhere (pp 205-6). But in the context of

281

understanding low turnouts, note the level of negativity towards all the parties.

Table 103: MORI Excellence Model – "Word-of-Mouth"

Q Thinking of the ... Party, please pick one statement from each section on this card according to which best reflects your behaviour and opinions with respect to the .... Party.

	Con			Lab			LibDem		
	'97	'01	'05	'97	'01	'05	'97	'01	'05
	%	%	%	%	%	%	%	%	%
I support the Party so much I encourage others to vote for it, without being asked	3	2	6	10	6	4	2	1	2
If someone asked my opinion I would encourage them to vote for the Party	11	10	15	21	17	12	9	7	13
If someone asked my opinion I would be neutral about voting for the Party	42	57	42	45	57	40	60	68	56
If someone asked my opinion I would discourage them from voting for the Party	22	16	16	11	11	18	11	11	12
I am so strongly opposed to the Party that I discourage others from voting for it without being asked	12	10	14	3	4	17	4	5	6
Don't know/no opinion	10	5	7	9	4	9	14	8	11
Net support	-20	-14	-9	+17	+8	-19	-4	-8	-3
Net "strong" support	-9	-8	-8	+7	+2	-13	-2	-4	-4

Source: MORI/*Financial Times*
Base: c. 1,000 GB residents aged 18+ in each survey

At the last three elections, negative advocacy of political parties has been more common than positive advocacy. Taken overall, adding the "pro" and "anti" advocates for the three parties[158], in 1997, 15% of the public were voluntarily encouraging others to vote for a party while 19% were urging them not to do so. By 2001, the totals were 9% and 20%, a two-to-one negative ratio. In 2005, it was 12% to 37%, three-to-one negative (despite a significant rise in positive advocacy of the Tories). And if ordinary members of the public were really going around telling each other not to vote, it is hardly surprising that many did not. Thus, mistrust of the political parties feeds on itself.

Finding a way to promote understanding of the positive contribution of parties to the polity is likely to be a step towards restoring public respect for the political system.

Role of Individual MPs

At the other end of the scale, trust in particular individuals can sometimes transcend distrust in the political sphere as a whole. Indeed, there is little doubt that Tony Blair once benefited considerably from this, and even now more than half the public say they trust Gordon Brown.[159] In a MORI survey for the British Medical Association[160] in 2004, only 28% of the public were satisfied with the way "politicians generally" were doing their job, and 27% with "government ministers". However, in a separate survey, 42% were satisfied with the way their own MP was doing his job. Furthermore, it is clear that there is a link between satisfaction with MPs and turnout: while 42% of all electors said they were satisfied with their MP, 49% of those "certain to vote" were satisfied[161].

Efficacy

Tied in with all of this is the question of efficacy – what does voting achieve, and what difference does it make which politician or party wins?

---

[158] This involves an element of double-counting in that some respondents will be arguing against voting for more than one party, but is a fair measure of the total prevalence of negativity in the political atmosphere.
[159] Fieldwork on 28-29 April for the *Observer* and the *Sunday Mirror*; see Appendix 2, survey 41, for details.
[160] Fieldwork on 26 February-2 March 2004 for the BMA; see Appendix 2, survey 28, for details.
[161] Fieldwork December 2003 for the Electoral Commission and the Hansard Society; see Appendix 2, survey 27, for details.

283

Again, because "politics" is a dirty word it colours many of the assumptions that the public make. A majority of the public (55%) disagree that being active in politics is a waste of time, although 22% agree. On the other hand, only just over a third (36%) think that "when people like me get involved in politics, they really can change the way the UK is run"[162].

And, so long as they can directly see the point of voting, the public are quite prepared to vote. Voting in referendums on transfer of council housing stock to housing associations, where the outcome is of direct relevance and importance to everybody who can vote, has averaged a 78% turnout[163].

Naturally, this feeling of relevance will tend to come with greater knowledge and understanding of the people and institutions involved. Few of the public are familiar with their MP or local councillor, or feel they know much about the doings of elected bodies. In May 2001, only two in five, 41%, of the public could accurately recall the name of their Member of Parliament[164]; in December 2003 it was 42%.[165] (Surprisingly, a General Election campaign in full swing in 2001 apparently gave no boost to the figures, perhaps a measure of the true disconnection of the less interested part of the public from electoral politics.) This is a sharp fall from a previously steady level of knowledge: in March 1991, 52% could give a correct answer to the same question[166]; this was not a significant change from 1973 when, in the "State of the Nation" survey for Granada TV, 53% could do so, or even from the 51% that Butler and Stokes found[167] able to name their MP in 1963. In this respect, the public seems less politically aware than a few years ago.

---

[162] Fieldwork December 2004 for the Electoral Commission and the Hansard Society; see Appendix 2, survey 31, for details.

[163] David Hencke, "Blair suffers defeat in battle of the Almo", *Guardian*, 21 July 2005.

[164] Fieldwork on 15 May 2001, for *The Times*; see Appendix 2, survey 3, for details.

[165] Fieldwork December 2003 for the Electoral Commission and the Hansard Society; see Appendix 2, survey 27, for details.

[166] MORI interviewed 1,547 GB residents aged 18+ on 7-25 March 1991 for the Joseph Rowntree Reform Trust.

[167] David Butler and Donald Stokes, *Political Change in Britain: Forces Shaping Electoral Change* (London: Pelican, 1971), p 509. Recall was higher (55%) among those respondents who remained in the panel, giving a slightly misleading aspect to the table of results as recorded in the second edition (*Political Change in Britain: The Evolution of Electoral Choice*, London: Macmillan, 1974, p 475).

It is clear that many of the public these days have little "feel" for the workings of the political system. We found it significant and interesting that when asked the name of their parliamentary constituency, respondents were considerably more likely to name their constituency correctly if its name was the same as that of the local authority, and that many of the wrong answers our interviewers collected were correct local authority or local ward names. Understanding of the distinction between parliament and council, and their functions and duties, may be low – a problem familiar to many MPs and councillors who are consistently contacted with complaints about matters outside their aegis.

When faced with an objective test of knowledge, they score pretty poorly, too[168]. In the political "quiz" we set as part of the December 2003 survey for the first Electoral Commission/Hansard Society *Audit of Political Engagement*, two-thirds accepted as fact the false statement that "There must be a general election every four years". (Just as well perhaps that Tony Blair decided to ask for a renewed mandate after four years anyway – if he had decided to see out his full term, how many more would have failed to vote because they got the year wrong?)

Since we know that the public is more interested in outcomes than processes, we might dismiss this lack of knowledge of political structures and personnel as not fundamental. But the public can be just as ignorant of vital details of policy proposals or achievement, their views often inaccurate and coloured by prejudice. A striking example where ignorance can be demonstrated by comparison with objective fact was the public's understanding of privatisation in the early 1990s. MORI research for British Gas in June 1993 found that only 4% of the public thought that the average price that they were charged in real terms for telephone services had gone down since privatisation, while 60% thought it had gone up. In fact prices had fallen by more than a third. Similarly, only 6% thought gas prices had fallen and 46% that they had risen; in reality they had fallen by 20%. The present government would feel that the same problem is hampering acceptance of their success in improving public services.

Public familiarity with politics and politicians is low, and familiarity with politicians at least is falling. Since it seems clearly established that greater

---

[168] Fieldwork December 2003 for the Electoral Commission and the Hansard Society; see Appendix 2, survey 27 for details.

familiarity is linked to greater favourability, this trend points to possible further worsening of the standing of politics in the future if conditions remain unchanged. Communication by parties and by other institutions with the public is generally poor, and there are signs that the public may be becoming less receptive to material such as election leaflets. The poor standing of politics, again, is probably acting as an inhibiting factor in this process, the same vicious circle — what is ultimately necessary is to find a way to break through the public's refusal to give politicians due credit for their achievements, in which case more voters may begin to see the point of voting for them.

How and When Children Form Political Opinions

How has the youngest generation of adults come by its ideas? MORI research for the *Nestlé Family Monitor* between March and May 2003 investigated the political opinions of secondary school children in England and Wales, and found some disturbing patterns.[169] Coming just after the invasion of Iraq, and in the wake of considerable involvement of young people in the protests against it, the survey was perhaps taken at a point when we might expect pupils to have been especially politically alert, though maybe also angry with, and cynical about, the government.

Several themes emerge from the findings. As one would expect, the views of pupils in the 11-18 age bracket broadly resemble the views of 18-24 year olds, but in a less-finished form.

Both the actual and perceived knowledge of politics, and interest in political issues, increase as pupils grow older. However, negative or cynical attitudes to politicians and to political parties seem to grow at the same time. On the other hand, many young people also hold positive attitudes to the electoral process in general, their cynicism being directed more at short-term specifics (the next General Election rather than elections in general, and distrusting current politicians and political parties while caring about political issues and in many cases having active involvement in protests and signing petitions). Yet although most profess ignorance and their willingness to learn, many do not accept that they will have a "duty to vote" when old enough.

Unsurprisingly, given their age, many of the pupils expressed a lack of interest in politics and elections. Around half of 11-18 year olds said it was not important to them personally who won the next General Election (i.e. the one held in 2005), but its perceived importance was higher among older pupils.

Asked why they might not vote, nearly half (47%) of those not certain they would vote if they were old enough said the reason was that they were

---

[169] See Appendix 2, survey 22, for survey methodology details. The full survey is reported and discussed in the *Nestlé Family Monitor No 16: Young People's Attitudes Towards Politics* (London, 2003), and the findings were further analysed in Roger Mortimore and Claire Tyrrell, "Children's acquisition of political opinions", *Journal of Public Affairs*, Vol 4 no 3 (2004), 279-298.

"just not interested in politics". Similarly, one in five (21%) gave as a reason that they had better things to do with their time.

But negative attitudes to elections and politics among young people are not simply "apathy". Most young people care about the world in which they live and are prepared to devote energy to doing something about it – or, at the very least, will join in when their friends do. When asked which community and school activities they had participated in within the past year, just 14% admitted to having done none of the 13 activities on our list.[170]

Charity fundraising and school events were the most frequent activities, but a significant percentage of young people were also participating in the more political forms of activity. A quarter said they had signed a petition, one in eight had got other people to sign a petition, and one in ten said they had been on a protest. All these types of political involvement, though, are essentially single-issue activities; very few young people – just 2% – said they had helped with a political party, and only 10% that they would be interested in doing so in the future.

Asked to select which of a list of issues (based mainly on those issues that are most frequently named as important by adults) were among the most important facing the country, they gave answers broadly similar to those we would expect from adults, with differences of emphasis but no signs that they have an entirely distinct political agenda of their own.

One notable divergence, though, was in the low salience that pupils gave to Europe as an important issue, ranked by some way last of the 18 items on the list. It may be that the economic and constitutional issues such as the Euro and the EU are rather more technical in nature than most of the other issues on the list, and would therefore naturally be less accessible to the young. On the other hand, of all the issues on the list it is the most

---

[170] The full list of activities was: "Helped with fundraising/collected money for charity" (which 50% said they had done), "Helped with a school event" (44%), "Taken part in a sponsored event" (40%), "Signed a petition" (25%), "Helped organise a charity event" (17%), "Got other people to sign a petition" (13%), "Been on a protest" (11%), "Been elected officer of a school club/student union" (10%), "Helped with disabled people" (9%), "Campaigned on behalf of a group/charity" (9%), "Helped with a religious group" (8%), "Helped with a political party" (2%) and "Worked in a charity shop" (2%).

"political" in the sense that the issue is explicitly one of process rather than of concrete outcomes.

Encouragingly, the youngsters tended to be positive about the principles of voting. As Table 104 shows, only a few felt that voting is not important, and the majority believed that the way people vote makes a difference to the way the country is run. Both beliefs were more frequent among older pupils.

Table 104: Pupils' Attitudes to Voting and Elections

Q Below are some things that young people have said about voting. How strongly do you agree or disagree with each? Please tick one box only on each line.

		Agree	Disagree	Neither/ don't know/not stated
I feel it will be my duty to vote when I am old enough	%	46	21	33
The way people vote makes a difference to the way the country is run	%	62	11	27
None of the political parties have policies/ideas I like	%	22	26	52
I don't think voting is very important	%	19	44	37

Source: MORI/Nestlé Family Monitor
Base: 914 pupils aged 11-18 in England & Wales, March-May 2003

On the other hand, only 46% agreed that "I feel it will be my duty to vote when I'm old enough", although again agreement was significantly higher, 57%, among those who would be old enough to vote in May 2005 than among those who would not, 43% (and, indeed, higher among this group than among 18-24 year olds, though the exclusion from the sample of those leaving school at 16 would be expected to give some bias in favour of higher engagement).

Knowledge of political parties and of politicians among pupils is low. Shown pictures of Tony Blair, Iain Duncan Smith (still the Conservative leader at the time of the survey) and Charles Kennedy, and asked to name each, nine in ten correctly identified Mr Blair, but only a quarter recognised IDS and 18% Kennedy.

Later in the questionnaire, young people were shown a list of politicians and asked which, if any, they had heard of. Around nine in ten said they

289

had heard of Tony Blair and, with the war in Iraq dominating the news at the time of the survey, almost as many had heard of George W Bush. The names of other senior cabinet ministers such as Jack Straw, Gordon Brown, and David Blunkett were recognised by just over half. But Vladimir Putin's name rang a bell with only 21%, and the travails of Northern Ireland seem to have made little impact: only 29% had heard of David Trimble, 25% of Gerry Adams and 20% of Ian Paisley.

The most dramatic finding, though, was one that contradicts our general principle of "familiarity breeds favourability" (as do some people who achieve notoriety, and some corporations either because of what they produce and market or because of their corporate behaviour, such as Enron).

Table 105: Children's Trust in Politicians and Journalists

Q For each of the different types of people listed below, would you trust them to tell you the truth or not?

		All		Younger (born after 1/5/87)		Older (born before 1/5/87)	
		Would trust them to tell the truth	Would not trust them to tell the truth	Would trust them to tell the truth	Would not trust them to tell the truth	Would trust them to tell the truth	Would not trust them to tell the truth
Government Ministers	%	27	40	28	36	22	53
Politicians Generally	%	18	42	19	37	15	56
Journalists	%	13	64	15	62	9	71

Source: MORI/*Nestlé Family Monitor*
Base: 914 pupils aged 11-18 in England & Wales, March-May 2003

Knowledge of political parties and figures is higher among older pupils. We would therefore expect, all other things being equal, to find that older pupils' attitudes to parties, politicians and politics in general should be more positive than their younger counterparts'. In fact, the opposite turns out to be the case. Increased knowledge of politicians seems to equate with increased acceptance of negative attitudes towards them: those who know more, or feel they know more, and those who are older, are more likely to distrust politicians and more likely to apply negative descriptions to the political parties. The process of political learning, far from dispelling myths and negative preconceptions as one might have hoped, seems to be one of absorbing and accepting these preconceptions and prejudices. Indeed, it looks almost as if these prejudices are precisely what the increase of "knowledge" comprises.

Table 106: Parental Transmission of Voting Behaviour

Percentage who would vote Conservative/Labour/Liberal Democrat when they believe that...

	Conservative	Labour	LibDem
...both parents vote for the party	67%	62%	44%
	n=110	n=174	n=45
...only mother votes for the party	27%	26%	42%
	n=51	n=47	n=36
...only father votes for the party	28%	44%	18%
	n=44	n=55	n=20
...neither parent votes for the party	4%	5%	4%
	n=668	n=597	n=772

Source: MORI/*Nestlé Family Monitor*
Base: 873 young people living with two parents/step parents

It is clear, too, that family influence is of immense importance. Voting intentions are still largely inherited from parents, forty years after Butler and Stokes first proved it was so[171]. Two-thirds of those with two Conservative parents would vote Conservative, and almost as many with two Labour parents would vote Labour[172]. Liberal Democrats seem to be much less effective at transmitting their political beliefs to their children. There are also differences between the parties when only one of two parents vote, but the sub-sample sizes are very much smaller here, and not too much weight should be put on the conclusions. Perhaps more telling, though, is how very few young people would vote for a party supported by neither of their parents: just one in twenty or fewer in the case of each of the three major parties.

---

[171] David Butler and Donald Stokes, *Political Change in Britain: Forces Shaping Electoral Change* (London: Pelican, 1971, especially pp 66-78.
[172] By way of comparison, Butler and Stokes, *op. cit*, p 69, found that in the 1960s 75% of those with two Conservative parents were Conservative voters, and 81% with two Labour parents were Labour voters. But that was a survey of voting adults.

Even stronger than the inheritance of voting behaviour, though, is the inheritance of non-voting behaviour, a new and corrosive development since the 1960s: 75% of those who say they think that neither of their parents would vote also say they themselves would not vote, and another 10% of these do not know how they would vote. In terms of voting, the best predictor of children's intending not to vote is that they believe their parents do not vote either. Other negative attitudes are presumably similarly propagated. Breaking this vicious cycle will require other influences on young people to be more effective in overcoming family influences

The findings raise the question of how effectively "citizenship" is being learned in schools, and how far the introduction of citizenship lessons in the National Curriculum will change this. Our survey was conducted before the first year of National Curriculum lessons in Citizenship had been completed. The main influences on pupils at present seem to be their parents and – though they profess to distrust journalists – the media. (Only 35% said they got "information on issues facing Britain" from teachers.) Citizenship education, of course, ends at 16, and many leave school at that age. "Catch them young" ought to be the watchword.

Encouraging Turnout With New Voting Methods

One of the first reactions to falling turnout was to blame the inconvenience of current voting arrangements, even before the shock of the record low in 2001 – if only voting could be made easier, it was argued, by moving polling day to weekends, or putting polling stations in places such as supermarkets, or using postal voting or new technology to let the public vote from home, the problem would melt away.

It was in pursuit of such theories that much of the Electoral Commission's energy in its first few years of existence was directed to overseeing trials of variants of the voting method, mostly in local government elections. A condition of local authorities being permitted to run such pilot schemes has been that public reactions to the experiments should be properly measured to gauge its success, and wider research outside the pilot areas has also been commissioned, so we have a wealth of data on the voters' own opinions of these experiments and of the principles behind them.

We suspect, though, that the main premise is a fallacy, and therefore the whole programme is misconceived. Few are failing to vote because they find it genuinely impossible – if, instead, they had been faced with the need to get to the bedside of a dying loved one at some time on polling day they would have managed it. It is not a question of impossibility but of priorities – voting is simply not important enough to most Britons for them to be prepared to arrange the rest of their lives to make it possible, or to miss out on whatever other activity they would normally be engaged in on a Thursday. Consequently, while making voting easier may help slightly at the margins (and is probably justifiable provided it can be achieved without compromising the whole basis of the franchise), it does not go a step towards solving the central problem of the democratic deficit, which is not that people don't vote, but that they don't *want* to vote.

E-voting, Text Voting, Moving Polling Stations...

Over the last five years the number of variant voting methods used on an experimental basis has been considerable: electronic voting methods, altering or extending the hours of polling, various versions of all-postal voting, and other innovations. Each of these pilot schemes was proposed

293

by a local authority and authorised by the Office of the Deputy Prime Minister (ODPM). In 2003, when the focus was on e-voting, the experiments included methods as diverse as electronic voting machines in the traditional polling stations, voting by telephone, voting by text message, voting by digital TV and internet voting. What all these experiments with the exception of all-postal voting had in common, however, was that none of them consistently produced an increase in turnout.

In fact in general we have found no strong demand for change from the traditional method of voting in a polling station; in 2003, three-quarters of the public said they were satisfied with the current process of voting in elections in the UK. [173] (This was true even though half were unaware of the already implemented change in the law to allow postal voting on demand). The traditional method seems to have very positive associations, a perception of being "tried and tested", as well as strong "romantic" connotations for some people.

But at this stage there was little resistance to the innovations in principle – even those who would not choose to use a particular method felt it should be available for others to take advantage of.

A commonly-held myth is that the young would be far more likely to vote if the available methods included expedients such as voting by phone or on the internet, as used to register votes in reality TV shows and other audience-participation events popular with that age group. Cited in support was the frequently-repeated canard that more young people vote to determine the winner of the TV series *Big Brother* than vote in general elections (or even as it has sometimes been asserted, that more people in total vote in *Big Brother* than in general elections.) This is nonsense. As Brian Wheeler noted in an analysis for the BBC News website after the election[174], there were just under 6.4 million votes cast during the 2004 live final of *Big Brother 5,* which presumably includes some at least from an older age group. Our turnout projections suggest about 5.5 million voters under 35 got to the polls on 5 May. But this ignores multiple voting, perfectly permissible in *Big Brother.* Wheeler cites research by Janet Jones of

[173] MORI research for the Electoral Commission. See Appendix 2, survey 23, for methodological details.
[174] http://news.bbc.co.uk/go/em/fr/-/1/hi/uk_politics/4586995.stm

Aberystwyth University, which found that 54% of viewers will vote once a week during a nine-week run of *Big Brother*, but 10.5% voted between two and five times a week and 3% said they voted more than five times a week.

But even were it true that more young people voted in *Big Brother* than in the general election, what is it supposed to prove beyond the fact that general election turnout is lamentable? Willingness to vote in a TV show in which one is interested is no indication of whether one would vote in a general election in which one is not interested, even were it to be made as simple to do. The fact remains that the e-voting methods that have been tried in practice at local elections seem not to have increased turnout (even in Windsor & Maidenhead in 2003, where they also experimented with extended voting hours and voting at more convenient locations such as supermarkets and stations). Why should general elections be different?

It is true that surveys before the experiments were conducted found more of the public saying that various innovations would increase their likelihood of voting than said they would reduce it, or (like those by MORI for the Electoral Commission, discussed in *Explaining Labour's Second Landslide*)[175] found most people at least prepared to pick one or two that were "most likely to encourage you personally to vote at the next General Election". But it is always best to be wary of reading too much into such results – one can be more likely to vote than one was, and still unlikely to do so.

Our research for the Electoral Commission after the 2003 pilots suggested that the convenience factor works only among those who, during the campaign, already intend to vote, but don't always make it to the polling station on the day. There is a substantial segment of the population who make a decision not to vote for reasons of political disconnection (expressing opinions such as "politicians break their promises", "we never see our elected representative" or "they don't talk about issues important to me"). In other words, they don't vote because they don't want to, not because they can't. In fact, 61% of non-voters in the postal pilots and the 63% in the e-voting pilots said that the new arrangements made no difference to their decision not to vote. Similarly, those who did vote, even if they agreed that the new methods were a spur to vote, claimed that they

---

175 Robert Worcester and Roger Mortimore, *Explaining Labour's Second Landslide* (London: Politico's Publishing, 2001), p 191-3.

would have voted anyway. Of course, it could be argued that as the public accepts better the importance of general elections, such expedients would have more effect at a general than at a local election. But you wouldn't want to bet on it.

Understanding of the position is not helped by publication of "research" which entirely misses the point. After the election, towards the end of July, a YouGov poll was published by Cisco Systems which it was said led to the conclusion that "Some 66 per cent of people who did not vote in the last general election would be more likely to vote next time if online voting was available".[176] This, of course, being a YouGov survey, was based on the responses of an online panel, people who have already volunteered to take part in online surveys on political topics.

All-Postal Voting

The methodological innovation for which most was hoped was all-postal voting, which unlike the other methods experimented with seems to have produced convincing increases in turnout. In all-postal elections, postal voting entirely replaces traditional methods – there are no polling stations, and every registered elector is sent a ballot paper to be returned by mail or left at a council drop-off point. This was piloted at a number of local elections from 2000 to 2003, then disastrously on a much wider scale in 2004, applying to both European Elections and local elections across the four northernmost regions of England.

This increase in turnout was achieved despite the fact that far from there being a public demand for it, the majority of the public was opposed to the idea before it was introduced: a poll in May 2002 found only 34% of the public would support abolishing voting in polling stations, so that all voting was by post, while 53% would oppose it.[177] As already mentioned, the main reaction from the public to the proposal of more diverse voting methods was to support the availability of choice, and the demand for choice cuts both ways: one of the criticisms from the all-postal pilots (even among those who found it a simple and convenient way to vote) was that there should have been the choice to vote in a polling station.

---

[176] James Brown, "Concept of online voting 'very popular'", *Computing*, 22 July 2005.
[177] Fieldwork 10-12 May 2002; see Appendix 2, survey 15, for details.

And this was before the conduct of the 2004 elections began to raise widespread fears about the security of ballot paper delivery, potential abuse of the loss of secrecy of the ballot involved in voting by post, and the involvement of the political parties in collecting completed ballot papers from voters.

Of course, it is impossible to escape the suspicion that one purpose of the large-scale use of the all-postal method in 2004 was cynical political gain, since it was apparently widely believed that it would cause a higher turnout in the regions where it was used and that this would benefit the Labour Party; the decision was taken in direct defiance of the Electoral Commission's advice that the scheme should be limited to two regions, and was pushed through both houses of Parliament against both Conservative and Liberal Democrat opposition – the second European election in a row in which Labour has defied the convention that electoral reforms are pursued only either with all-party support or with the direct mandate of a manifesto pledge approved by the voters at a general election.

Far from benefiting from the all-postal method, Labour got a bloody nose at the European elections, as they did again in the North-East referendum on regional government, which was conducted under similar rules. In the former case, at least, this was probably because they misunderstood the mechanism by which all-postal voting tends to drive up turnout. The convenience and immediacy of having a ballot paper delivered through the letter-box is one factor, and may remind border-line enthusiasts to vote. But probably just as important, especially in local elections, is the certainty of receiving any literature through the door at all, reminding the voters not only of the existence of the election but of the choices that they can make; with falling levels of canvassing and leafleting in modern elections, this may be the only direct contact an elector has with the electoral process. But if so, then it is the fringe parties, who would never have the manpower to campaign across whole regions, who would expect to benefit even more than the established parties from a guarantee of a mail-drop in elections where the Post Office free mailout does not apply. Given the known strength of the BNP in the North West, added to the more unexpected surge for UKIP in the East Midlands once Robert Kilroy-Silk declared his candidature, the increase in turnout was never likely to be as beneficial as

Labour headquarters clearly expected. (We could have told them so, had they wanted to listen.)

Nevertheless, in its declared aim the experiment succeeded. Turnout in the 2004 European Parliament elections was declared as 38.2% in Great Britain, compared with 23.1% in 1999 – while it is not entirely clear how much of this rise can be attributed to the use of postal voting as opposed to combining these elections with those for local authorities, where applicable, some at least of the increase was clearly attributable to the all-postal method.

But at what cost to the credibility of British elections? The leader in the next day's *Times* was scathing: "…a profoundly unsatisfactory process… the confusion, uncertainty and sheer incompetence endured over the past few weeks are completely unacceptable… chaos… a kamikaze exercise… a worthless bargain (increased turnout) if… some electors being disenfranchised …shambles… legitimacy of the democratic ritual has been devalued…"[178].

It clearly caused administrative problems so severe as to throw the reliability of some results into doubt. Worse, there were numerous allegations in the press suggesting either direct fraud or at best unethical practices by some parties and campaigners, and ICM's post-election survey for the Electoral Commission found a quarter of the public saying they thought electoral fraud or abuse had been a very big or fairly big problem in the 10 June elections[179].

The Electoral Commission, previously a cautious supporter of the all-postal method, was unequivocal in its reaction, recommending "all-postal voting should not be pursued for use at UK statutory elections".[180]

The problems of security are not necessarily just with all-postal voting methods, although their introduction has highlighted the problem and perhaps spurred the criminals into action. The cases heard in the election court in 2005, when the judge described a local election of the previous year as showing "evidence of electoral fraud that would disgrace a banana

---

[178] "Pantomime Politics", *The Times*, 11 June 2004.
[179] *The June 2004 Elections – The Public's Perspective* (ICM report to the Electoral Commission available at www.electoralcommission.org.uk).
[180] Electoral Commission, *Delivering Democracy – the future of postal voting* (August 2004), available at www.electoralcommission.org.uk.

republic" and declared the result void, involved postal voting in a conventionally conducted election.

While it seems clear that the introduction of postal voting on demand has offered a facility which many voters find convenient and sensible, it has also raised fears about its abuse and the scope for "vote stealing". Nor does a 61% turnout in 2005 suggest it has done much to encourage more people to vote – it is overwhelmingly a method used by those who would vote in any case. That is not an argument against it, but it certainly weakens the case in favour if it must be balanced against a threat to the integrity of the electoral system. The introduction of individual registration as recommended by the Electoral Commission, which might offer local Returning Officers the means to collect a signature from every voter against which both applications for postal votes and the statutory declarations returned with postal ballots could be checked, might tighten up some of the loopholes – though almost certainly not within the existing timescale of allowing applications for postal votes to be made within six days of the poll, surely unworkable. In any case, it now appears this reform is also unlikely to be pursued.

Compulsory Voting

Reports in the press since the election[181] suggest that at least one government minister, Geoff Hoon, is now backing compulsory voting as the latest Elastoplast for the turnout problem. A MORI survey in 2002 found[182] just under half the public, 45%, saying they would support the policy, but 50% opposing it, the week before the publication of a private member's bill in an earlier attempt to introduce it. What support there is does not seem to be particularly driven by the recent low turnouts – before the record-low turnout at the 2001 election, an earlier poll had found 47% in favour, and in 1991 (when turnouts were much higher), 49% said they supported the policy and 42% that they opposed it[183].

---

[181] Patrick Wintour, "Hoon calls for compulsory voting", *Guardian*, 4 July 2005; Tom Baldwin, "We should force people to the polls, says Hoon", *The Times*, 4 July 2005.

[182] Fieldwork on 10-12 May 2002; see Appendix 2, survey 15, for details.

[183] MORI interviewed 1,547 GB residents aged 18+ on 7-25 March 1991 for the Joseph Rowntree Reform Trust.

Support for compulsory voting is a little higher among older voters, but even among 16-24 year olds two in five (more than turn out at the moment) think it would be good idea. The policy is also supported a little more strongly by Labour supporters (54%) than by those who back the Conservatives (48%) or Liberal Democrats (46%), though it is probably too cynical to link this to the likelihood that it would be Labour that had most to gain from increased turnout.

It seems arguable that all-postal voting increases turnout somewhat, while none of the other alternatives that have been tried have been proven to do so. Compulsory voting would also do so, albeit in a different way. But this treats the symptom rather than the cause of disengagement; furthermore, the damage that all-postal voting does to the integrity of the electoral system in the process – both by genuinely increasing the scope for fraud and in raising public doubt about the honesty of the results – seem to us overwhelming arguments against pursuing this or any similar expedient further.

As it is, few of the public trust politicians in general or the present government in particular. After the divergence of the exit polls from the final result of the 2004 US Presidential elections, millions of distrustful Americans were convinced (and many still are) that it was the exit polls that were right and the election had been fixed. A government that persistently weakens the safeguards built into the electoral system, that makes a series of administrative changes that reduce rather than increase transparency, and which when fraud is detected at local government level is seen to be the party that would have benefited from it, risks building similar distrust here. Would you buy a used ballot box from this man?

Achieving a higher turnout is a worthy aim, but it means little in itself, and it should certainly not be pursued at the expense of public confidence in the integrity of the electoral system (let alone so recklessly as to genuinely put that integrity into doubt). For a healthy democracy, we need to maximise the number of people who care enough about who is elected to want to vote, and to minimise the obstacles put in their way so that they are able to do so. Anything else is missing the point – and the same applies to compulsory voting.

Why Worry About Turnout?

If there is a distinction between "good citizenship" and voting then it is no longer possible to avoid addressing the question of what we hope to achieve by encouraging turnout in the first place.

Do we believe that the act of voting is good in itself for the voter? That is potentially a strong argument, but one that is rarely made, and which would certainly be harder to establish if there is a complete disconnect between civic and electoral virtue.

Or do we argue that high turnout is necessary to the credibility of the political system and to the legitimacy of governmental power that claims to rest on a democratic mandate? This argument seems a specious one if the mandate is no more than a Potemkin village, maintaining a façade of public acceptance regardless of the real level of informed consent. Expedients which inflate the turnout figures without increasing the number who cast a valid vote, or which promote voting at the expense of weakening its connection with voters' engagement, fail to tackle the underlying problems.

If we believe that it really strengthens the functioning of a democracy to maximise real turnout by motivated and discriminating voters who will feel they have a responsibility for the outcome and a stake in the wider governmental structure, solutions that address symptoms rather than causes are inadequate. It is not enough to make people vote, what is necessary is to make them *want* to vote. If the aim of encouraging higher turnouts is understood on this more specific basis, then it is increasing engagement on a wider front which must be aimed at, and turnout viewed only as an important indicative symptom rather than the primary indicator of health.

Voting clearly cannot be divorced from "politics". "Politics" as the public prefers to understand that term is a minority activity, and is verging on being a minority interest. Worse, "politics" is that activity pursued by that widely-reviled creature "the politician". Hostility to the concept of politics presumably acts as a deterrent to involvement. Many of the public seem to see politics as an obstruction to, rather than the means of, proper government of the country.

It seems probable that a general improvement in the standing of politics and politicians, if it could be brought about, might change those relationships. It might even in this way be possible to re-establish a connection between voting, political engagement and other aspects of "good citizenship".

6. What Next?

The Next Four Years

So, the election is over – Tony Blair has "got away with it", and has a sufficient majority for the next four years. What next?

The first question, naturally, is whether Mr Blair will – or should – last out his four or five year term. He has already pledged that this term will be his last, and newspaper reports suggest that he is also intending to retire from his seat in the Commons, but such pledges are not necessarily binding. (If unsubstantiated rumour is correct, he may already have gone back on a private promise to Gordon Brown to step down in the last Parliament.) On the other hand, it can now be argued that as the public voted in the knowledge of his commitment not to serve in Number 10 beyond the present Parliament, his re-election should be considered conditional on it.

Table 107: Should Blair Go?

Q Regardless of how you are personally going to vote, if Tony Blair is re-elected Prime Minister later this week, do you think he should step down within two years or should he remain Prime Minister for longer than two years?

	All	Con	Lab	LDem
	%	%	%	%
Step down within two years	53	72	35	66
Remain PM for longer than two years	34	21	51	24
Don't know	13	7	14	10

Source: MORI/*Evening Standard*
Base: 1,628 GB residents aged 18+, 3-4 May 2005

At any rate, most of the public at that point seemed content with the notion that he would step down. In our immediate pre-election poll, more than half the public said they thought he should step down within two years, and while this was (naturally) a more widespread feeling among supporters of the Opposition than of the Government, even among Labour voters a third felt he should go within the first half of the Parliament.

A similar question posed a couple of days earlier, but offering respondents a wider choice of options found more than a third of adults thinking he

303

should step down straight away, and more than half named a time before the end of 2006.

Figure 54: When Should Tony Blair Step Down?

Q If Labour wins the coming General Election, when do you think Tony Blair should step down as Prime Minister?

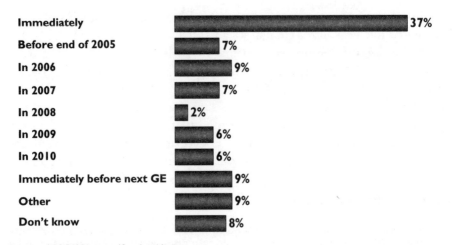

Immediately	37%
Before end of 2005	7%
In 2006	9%
In 2007	7%
In 2008	2%
In 2009	6%
In 2010	6%
Immediately before next GE	9%
Other	9%
Don't know	8%

Source: MORI/*Observer/Sunday Mirror*
Base: 1,007 GB residents aged 18+, 28-29 April 2005

If Blair does retire, it will presumably be Gordon Brown who replaces him, though it would perhaps be unwise to take even that for granted. But the timing of the handover has a number of implications. Will it be before or after November 2008, when President Bush's successor is elected? If another Republican is elected it might mean no more than continuity in the White House and in American foreign policy, but if a Democrat were to win (Hillary, conceivable but unlikely) how will the "Special Relationship" develop, and how will the identity of the man in Downing Street at that moment affect matters?

Then we might wonder what sort of a Prime Minister Gordon Brown will be, and indeed how Tony Blair's tenure has affected the very nature of the office. Many of his critics have accused him of paying less attention to Parliament than any of his predecessors, and indeed at times of riding roughshod over his Cabinet colleagues as well. Has the premiership become more "presidential" in the last eight years, or will that continue to depend on the personality of the incumbent? Will the fact of having pursued a policy as unpopular as the Iraq War and yet secured re-election embolden future PMs – or, for that matter, Blair himself – to future defiance of public opinion? (And if so, some will call it "being out of touch" and others "conviction politics".)

One clear hurdle to be cleared is the future of the European Union, which we consider in detail below; and, of course, there will be the usual challenge of maintaining economic prosperity, to say nothing of finally convincing the public that Labour has delivered on its promises of public services improvement.

Then we must consider any further operation of the Law of Unseen Consequences. One of this government's persistent failings has been to make constitutional changes in blithe disregard for the political implications. They implemented devolution in Scotland and Wales, and seemed startled that devolving power seemed to weaken the central party's grip over its politicians there. They started to reform the House of Lords, saying they would give it more relevance and democratic legitimacy suitable to its existence in the modern age, then were shocked when the half-reformed House took this as its cue to stand up to the Commons. They passed the Human Rights Act, giving the courts the duty of commenting on the legitimacy of (though no power to disregard or veto) new legislation, without appreciating that this would inevitably create tension between ministers and judges, as has duly occurred over the government's response to the threat of terrorism, especially after the London bombings of 7 July 2005.

We should therefore not be much surprised to find the government making other difficulties for itself over the next four years. One, not directly of its own making, will come with the introduction of proportional representation for council elections in Scotland from 2007. This will reduce Labour's councillor base north of the border, and perhaps increase tension between local government and the Scottish executive. If, as many campaigners would like, the same change were to be introduced in England and Wales, the effects might be more far-reaching. While not on the agenda at the moment, it is a possible future concession if ever the government needs to buy Liberal Democrat support for any reason – but if so, its possible impact should not be under-estimated.

305

The Opposition

Tory Leadership and Future Prospects

Another year, another new Tory leader. As we write, the Conservative Party leadership election contest is only beginning to warm up, and we cannot tell whether the party will opt for David Davis or David Cameron (currently the two front-runners, it seems) or for somebody else. Whoever they choose, unless it is the veteran Kenneth Clarke, it will be somebody virtually unknown to the wider public, who will effectively start with a clean slate.

Figure 55: The next Conservative leader?

Q If the Conservatives lose the General Election and Michael Howard steps down as party leader, which one of the following politicians I am going to read out, if any, would you like to see lead the Conservative Party?

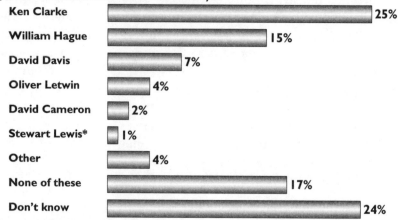

Ken Clarke	25%
William Hague	15%
David Davis	7%
Oliver Letwin	4%
David Cameron	2%
Stewart Lewis*	1%
Other	4%
None of these	17%
Don't know	24%

Source: MORI/*Observer*/*Sunday Mirror*
Base: 1,007 GB residents aged 18+, 28-29 April 2005
*= Dummy name

When we asked the public just before the election to name their favourite choice for the next Conservative leader, Ken won easily, but nobody apart from the political anoraks knew anything about the other candidates. William Hague, who certainly will not be entering the lists, came second, and more than two-fifths wouldn't pick any of the names even at random. Not that these figures disqualify any of the potential candidates from being a successful leader – in 1992, when we asked the public who should replace Neil Kinnock, John Smith won easily with 53% of the vote, but trailing far behind on just 1% was an obscure young frontbencher none of the public had ever heard of, name of Tony Blair. Wonder what happened to him?[184]

Whoever the new leader is, he (or she) will achieve nothing worthwhile without recognising that nothing worthwhile has been achieved already. "One more heave" will not do it – all the Tories have done with their previous heaves is to rock the wardrobe a little so it has settled back resting on their foot! The Tory share fell between 1992 and 1997 from 42% to 31%. The rise from 31% to 33% between 1997 and 2001 can be entirely attributed to their vote holding up a little better in the face of a fall in turnout, and not to any recapture of support. From 2001 to 2005 it effectively flat-lined: the "swing" was almost entirely an effect of internal dissension among the left, with Labour supporters shifting to the LibDems but not considering the Tories. Although the Tories gained some seats as a result, it was because of a private argument over which they can have little influence, and they may be entirely powerless to prevent the left patching up their differences and taking those seats back again in 2009. More of the same means more flat-lining.

Some Tories still seem to be determined to believe they had a reasonably successful election. What planet are they living on? Others think the problem is that the Conservatives failed to appeal to "uncommitted voters". What "uncommitted voters"? Most of those that existed were wavering between Labour, the LibDems or staying at home, not even considering the Tories to reject them. Before you can start winning new voters they have to take you seriously as an option.

While it is true that the Labour vote is soft, it is soft in the direction of the LibDems rather than the Tories, which halves its usefulness at best. (At worst, they will vote tactically and not defect at all when there is a risk of Tory gains.) In our final pre-election poll, 28% of Labour voters said they might still change their minds, but of them half said that if they did they would vote LibDem instead, and only one in seven that their second choice was the Conservatives. The Conservative Party has been reduced to

---

[184] MORI interviewed 934 GB residents aged 18+ on 10 April 1992 for the *Sunday Times*.

an irrelevance for the majority of British voters, and until that can be changed they will never form another government.

Those Tories who worry about the image or "brand" of the party are nearer the mark. Voters' prejudices and preconceptions about the party colour their reception of everything they hear or read about it, the credibility of its policies and the respect they will give to its leader. (Note the research during the election, discussed on p 163, that found policies were less popular when identified as being a Conservative policy than if simply put to respondents on their merits, out of context.)

That means whoever becomes leader is going to have a problem, because the leadership election can't be put off until after the party has been repositioned. (Indeed, it needs the new leader to achieve that.) There is a danger that he or she will suffer the same fate as Neil Kinnock, successfully transforming the party's image yet being left behind and identified by the public with the old rather than the new party. The Conservatives might settle for that, even; but if they are only about to elect their Neil Kinnock, are they still 14 years from getting back into government?

Liberal Democrats

And where next for the Liberal Democrats?

In 2005, they made no real progress in their Conservative-held targets, the type of constituency that has made up the bulk of their gains in the last few elections, though they did consolidate their grip on most of the ones they had already captured. That is not necessarily to imply that they have reached the end of the road in terms of swaying the loyalties of former Conservative voters, however: seven of the party's twelve gains from Labour were in seats held by the Conservatives in the 1980s – Manchester Withington, Leeds North-West, Cambridge, Birmingham Yardley, Bristol West, Cardiff Central and Falmouth & Camborne. The new Dunbartonshire East, also, is substantially based on the old Strathkelvin & Bearsden, again a Tory seat in the 1980s. It may be that similar seats will be their most fruitful territory for expansion in the future.

On the other hand, it may be trickier this time than in the past simply to hang on to the gains they have already made. Because several of their gains were made with unusually large swings, they have not won the seats that are most naturally their territory. In many cases, they were clearly dependent on the student vote, motivated by two specific issues (Iraq and student fees) which may not apply next time, and because of the transient nature of students most of the individual voters will have moved away and their replacements will have to be won over again from scratch. Add to that the boundary changes, which will disrupt the usual LibDem tactic of digging in locally to secure an incumbency advantage, and it might look a little awkward.

If as seems likely much of the increase in the Liberal Democrat share in 2005 was a combination of "tactical unwind" (getting back votes that would normally go to Labour in seats the Liberal Democrats cannot win anyway, irrelevant to the real task) and Labour protest against Tony Blair and New Labour or Iraq rather than rejection of Labour as such (votes which may go back home once Blair has been replaced as leader), the first question must surely be not whether the Liberal Democrats can make further progress but whether they can hold what they already have. If so, they really can talk about having broken the mould of British politics.

The European Constitution

The French referendum vote against the proposed EU constitution, three weeks after the British general election, made Tony Blair's 2004 promise of a British referendum on the issue redundant. This left Blair with a tricky problem in foreign policy and diplomacy, patching up the EU and finding a new *modus vivendi* with the British presidency of the Union looming, but averted a potentially very awkward crisis in domestic politics.

While the French "non" vote was generally expected by the time the moment came, it seemed almost inconceivable in April 2004 when Mr Blair promised a British referendum vote. Barring some supernatural premonition of the French decision, the promise of a British referendum was surely a mistake, since it was highly unlikely that the government could have secured the "yes" vote for which it was compelled to argue; defeat in a referendum would have left the government both exposed internationally and damaged politically at home. Even the apparent short-term partisan advantage, depriving the Tories of a *casus belli* with which they were arguably damaging the government, didn't stand up to scrutiny: though some commentators described the referendum promise as having "shot the Tories' fox", in reality it simply removed from the agenda the issue that had wasted Tory time and divided Conservative from Conservative more than any other at the two elections Blair had won.

Europe is the dog that didn't bark in the 2005 election. The Conservatives have for many years now seemingly been unable to discuss Europe without being seen to be divided or being perceived as obsessed by an issue of secondary importance to most voters. Michael Howard deserves credit for running a tight ship during the election campaign and keeping his party on board, in contrast to the 2001 General Election where William Hague's last election pitch was to "save the pound", but Blair's referendum promise made Howard's task easier.

If the Prime Minister doubted the hostility of the public to the European ideal as shown in the opinion polls, UKIP's 16% share of the vote at the 2004 European elections made it plain that not all the public takes continued British membership of the EU for granted. And he should have noted the experience of the North-East referendum on regional devolution in October 2004: opinion moved against the government as the campaign progressed so that a vote in which approval of the government's proposals was originally assumed to be a foregone conclusion ended in humiliating rejection. The government can no longer rely on its ability to manipulate the public will.

The election past, the referendum became a live issue and the next electoral challenge for the government. Had the French (and Dutch) voted in favour, and the British government kept to their commitment of a UK referendum next Spring, Tony Blair would have had a much more difficult task in carrying the public on this issue. MORI's research during the election[185] found that almost two thirds of the public were opposed to British adoption of the constitution – including 36% who said they were strongly opposed, which was up from 25% in January 2005. With political debate and the merits of politicians in people's minds, the task of winning the referendum looked even more impossible than it had a few months earlier.

Table 108: Trends on Attitudes to the European Constitution

Q Which of the following best describes your own view of whether Britain should adopt the new European constitution?*

	22-27 July 2004 %	28 Oct- 3 Nov 2004 %	10-15 Feb 2005 %	28-29 April 2005 %
Strongly support	8	8	10	9
Generally in favour but might change mind	23	22	21	20
Generally against but might change mind	23	28	27	27
Strongly against	27	27	25	36
In favour	31	30	31	29
Against	50	55	52	63
Net in favour	-19	-25	-21	-34
"Waverers"	46	50	48	47
Don't know	19	15	17	8

Source: MORI
Base: c. 1,000/c. 2,000 adults 16+/18+ in each survey
Asked as "... view of Britain adopting..." before April 2005

---

[185] Fieldwork conducted 28-29 April for the *Observer* and *Sunday Mirror;* see Appendix 2, survey 41, for details.

The British public's negativity towards the EU seems to arise both from perceptions of the practical effects of EU membership and lack of sympathy with the "European ideal". The latest *Eurobarometer* survey, for example, finds that only four in ten (40%) think that the UK has benefited from membership of the EU – this is easily the most negative attitude of any of the 15 established member states (the average for the whole EU is 55%).[186] In 2003, only 19% of Britons said they "tend to trust" the European Union; in Autumn 2004, though, the figure had risen to 35%.[187]

Generally negative attitudes about the EU may also rest on the belief that Britain is distinct from Europe. Most Britons do not think of themselves as European – in the same Eurobarometer survey, 55% considered themselves "British not European" rather than partly or totally European (and the figure was 62% in 2003). Similarly, 90% of Britons declared themselves "very proud to be British", but only 50% said they were "proud to be European", while 42% were not.

It is worth comparing opposition to the EU constitution with attitudes to two other related questions, joining the Euro and retaining British membership of the European Union. In July 2004, MORI posed similar questions on all three issues to the same sample[188]. At the aggregate level, we found that support for adopting the constitution was the lowest of the three issues – overall 31% were either strongly or generally in favour of the constitution, compared with 36% for the single currency and 50% for membership of the European Union.

While opinions are fairly similar on adopting the constitution and joining the Euro, the majority opposing both, rather fewer would want Britain to leave the EU altogether, the majority in this case being on the other side. Furthermore, those who oppose joining the Euro or signing the constitution are firmer in their views (more than half holding their views strongly and not feeling liable to change their mind) than are those against

---

[186] European Commission Standard Eurobarometer 63, Spring 2005. British fieldwork was conducted by TNS UK, who interviewed 1,347 UK adults face-to-face, in home, on 11 May-12 June 2005. Details at http://europa.eu.int/comm/public_opinion/index_en.htm.

[187] European Commission Standard Eurobarometer 62, Autumn 2004. British fieldwork was conducted by TNS UK, who interviewed 1,310 UK adults face-to-face, in home, on 5 October-8 November 2004. Details at http://europa.eu.int/comm/public_opinion/index_en.htm.

[188] Fieldwork on 22-27 July 2004 for the Foreign Policy Centre; see Appendix 2, survey 30, for details.

EU membership; at the other end of the scale a slightly higher proportion of supporters hold strong views on retaining EU membership than on the Euro or the constitution.

Britain's generally sceptical attitude towards the European Union sheds little direct light on the more specific question of opposition to the EU constitution. Hostility to the EU does not necessarily imply opposition to a constitution which will in some ways restrict its operations. Indeed (according to Eurobarometer[189]), Britain is in favour of "a constitution for the European Union" by 49% to 29%. But there seems to be much less enthusiasm for the specific constitution now being proposed – or, at least, for that constitution as it is perceived, filtered through the reporting of the British media and interpreted by its political supporters and opponents.

So what were the prospects of winning over the voters to support of the constitution? Or, indeed, what are the prospects, assuming some renegotiated treaty must eventually be put on the table? Again the July 2004 survey gives some clues, though it fails to reflect the full level of hostility to the constitution revealed in the most recent poll.

Table 109: Attitudes to the Euro and EU by Attitudes to the Constitution

		British adoption of the European constitution	
		Strongly support %	Strongly oppose %
British participation in the single currency	Strongly support	58	4
	Wavering	33	21
	Strongly oppose	7	74
	Don't know	2	1
British membership of the EU	Strongly support	89	2
	Wavering	8	33
	Strongly oppose	3	62
	Don't know	0	3

Source: MORI/Foreign Policy Centre
Base: 1,063 GB adults 18+, 22-27 July 2004

---

[189] European Commission Standard Eurobarometer 62, Autumn 2004..

Among those who were strongly against the constitution, three-quarters had also decided against the Euro, with only 4% in favour and one in five wavering. Somewhat fewer, but still 62%, were strongly against British membership of the EU. This finding is one with profound implications: the majority of those most committed against the constitution are not opposed to it on some matter of detail, thinking that there is some alternative arrangement which would make the EU run better, nor is their problem with the idea of a constitution for the EU as such. They are opposed to the very principle of British membership of the EU as well as to adopting this constitution, and the two views are presumably closely linked. It implies that it is pointless to refuse to take this group at their word and believe that they can be won over to the merits of the constitution, because the whole point of introducing the constitution is to achieve an aim to which they are implacably opposed. It suggests that there is solid principle behind their opposition to the constitution and every likelihood that they will, therefore, turn out to vote it down, forcing the government to look elsewhere for votes with which they can be countered.

Probably the expanded number who are "strongly opposed" found in the April 2005 poll are not so fully committed to the same extent. But it is reasonable to assume, at any rate, that they will not be easily swayed.

Of much more direct interest to the outcome of a referendum are those who are wavering on the constitution, since their eventual voting behaviour is still in doubt. As they feel prepared to change their minds, it is they who in theory are most likely to be swung if they find their views on the single currency or membership of the EU conflict with their views on the constitution. It is no surprise that the vast majority of constitution waverers are also wavering on both whether Britain should remain a member of the EU (82%) and on British participation in the single currency (72%). Those who are not are twice as likely to be "strongly opposed" to as "strongly in favour" of the Euro (17% to 8%). In contrast, they are almost five times as likely to be "strongly in favour" of as "strongly opposed" to membership of the EU (14% to 3%). Very few waverers are committed opponents of the Union.

Crucially, this means that there is a qualitative difference between the majority of strong opposers of the constitution and those who are "generally opposed" but might change their minds – they differ not just in

314

strength of views on a single scale but in the whole foundation of those views: two-thirds of committed opponents are anti-EU in principle, while the same is true of only a handful of waverers. The latter are a different species of voter altogether.

A more detailed analysis of the likely behaviour in a referendum of different groups of voters is set out in our pamphlet published by the Foreign Policy Centre in the summer of 2004[190].

Exercising Political Leadership

The possible impact of any future referendum campaign on public opinion and on turnout will depend substantially on how susceptible to influence the public's views are – although the majority say they might change their minds if they were persuaded that the arguments pointed in the other direction, that is an empty promise unless there is somebody or something they trust sufficiently for it to be potentially persuasive.

Unlike the 1975 referendum, the main party leaderships in the expected, but not delivered, constitution referendum – at least in its original form – would have been pulling the wavering voters in opposite directions. This may also be the case among leading businessmen. Back in 1998, almost 80% of Britain's Captains of Industry said they supported the principle of Britain participating in a single European currency. By 2003, opinion among this group was evenly divided – 47% in favour, 48% against – and not significantly better in 2004 (53% to 47% in favour).

Many people believed that politicians would be the key to influencing voters who were unsure about the impact of the constitution. If this is the case, then the influence of politicians would have been through not only the arguments they deploy, but the general trust and confidence that the public have in them for taking decisions in Britain's interests. Indeed, the image of the politicians could well be of even greater importance in any future referendum about an institution that people know little about, and feel no connection with.

---

[190] Mark Gill, Simon Atkinson and Roger Mortimore, *The Referendum Battle* (London: Foreign Policy Centre, September 2004).

In 1975, what did the trick was a united appeal by politicians that the public trusted, and by the media. Today, few voters trust the government sufficiently on Europe, or on anything else, to be sold an unpopular policy. This time, too, most of the press will almost certainly be on the other side, as will the Conservative leadership. Tony Blair has no easy answers.

In short, we no longer believe that Tony Blair, or for that matter Gordon Brown, could win a referendum on the European Constitution within the lifetime of the 2005 Parliament. Of course, the promise of a referendum given by Tony Blair in 2004 applied only to the original constitution and has now lapsed – but how much political capital and credibility would have to be sacrificed to refuse a vote on the new proposals, whatever they are? Tony Blair still has a problem, albeit not quite the same one he seemed to have six months ago.

Redistribution of Seats

Before the next general election, the Boundary Commissions are likely to have completed their work. New boundaries across England and Wales will mean that the post-2005 arrangement of marginals and safe seats will be swept away. The swings needed to take constituencies at the next election will be different from the pattern at the moment, and the Tories are confident it will work to their advantage.

Nevertheless, the Tories should not expect too much. The equalisation of constituency electorates in England will help them, but it will certainly not dispel the whole or even a significant part of the "bias" in the electoral system, as some seem to think. As the boundaries currently stand, Labour has a 111-seat advantage over the Tories atequal shares of the vote. Past boundary reviews have been worth at most 20 to 30 seats to the Conservatives. No rearrangement of boundaries that the Boundary Commissioners would or could recommend will alter the fact that assuming uniform swing Labour will get more seats for a given share of the vote.

A month after the election, leading Conservatives were quoted in the press as calling on the Boundary Commission to ensure that constituency electorates were equal. Those who equate the bias with the difference in electorate size of Labour and Conservative seats are missing the point – only a tiny part of the pro-Labour bias arises from the difference in electorate sizes within England. If they believe that equalising constituency electorates (which, within the restrictive limits of the rules that Parliament has laid down for them by statute, the Boundary Commissions will do) will level the electoral playing field, they will have a nasty shock come the next election.

Oliver Heald, shadow constitutional affairs secretary, got a little nearer the heart of the problem: "The average number of votes cast for the winning party was 18,833 in Labour seats, compared with 22,763 in Conservative seats. There is something seriously wrong with the electoral system when 90,000 more people in England vote Conservative and Labour get 90 or so more seats."[191] But the difference in the number of winning votes is a

---

[191] Jill Sherman, "Boundary system is unfair to us, claim Tories", *The Times*, 13 June 2005.

political, not a geographical phenomenon, and such inequalities are inherent in the first-past-the-post system.

There are a number of reasons for the bias. Firstly, not all constituencies are the same size: those in Wales have systematically lower populations than those in England (as did those in Scotland before the 2005 election). As Labour is much the strongest party in Scotland, Wales, and those parts of the country losing population (inner cities and the North), it tends to pick up its seats "cheaper". Although constituencies within each country will be redrawn, the inequality in favour of the Welsh will remain. Secondly, the LibDems are generally stronger in the Tories' strong areas than in Labour's, so the Tories use up many votes winning seats against the LibDems while most of Labour's votes are being used directly to fight for seats against the Tories. Thirdly, most of the seats the LibDems win would be Tory if the LibDems did not exist; again, many Tory votes are "wasted" fighting but not winning these seats, while far fewer Labour votes go the same way. Finally, Labour's votes are distributed more effectively: they "waste" fewer of their votes piling up big majorities or losing in safe seats and have a higher proportion concentrated where they will do most good, in the marginals.

There is an argument, incidentally, that the bias towards Labour is not really as big as it looks. Labour's safe seats are the constituencies with the lowest turnouts and where the turnout has fallen fastest at recent elections. It is probable that the majority of these non-voters would vote Labour if they voted at all, and it seems likely that many of them fail to vote only because they know that their vote is not needed, since Labour is sure to win their constituency. Similarly, probably more Labour supporters are voting tactically than Conservative supporters, simply because there are more seats marginal between Conservative and Liberal Democrat than between Labour and Liberal Democrat. If so, then it can be argued that the "real" Labour support is higher than the share they secure at the polls and that some of the "extra" seats they win for a given share of the vote merely reflects this.

The system is not always biased to Labour – in the 1950s and 1960s the tilt was very much the other way. (In 1951, for example, Labour won most votes and yet the Tories got an overall majority in the House of Commons.) And it is possible it could disappear at any moment – our calculations of how many seats would be won at the next election for any given share of the votes are based on "uniform swing", i.e. assuming that everywhere in the country shifts its votes by the same amount. In fact, Labour's lead in seats in 2005 was a little less imposing than many had believed would result from a three-point lead in votes, because the swing was *not* uniform and for once the deviation worked against Labour rather than in the party's favour.

Whenever the Tories do better in marginal seats than in the rest of the country, Labour's disadvantage would diminish. In 2005, they *did* do a little better, easing the bias a little, though not nearly enough to reverse the advantage Labour built up by over-performing in the marginals in 1997 and 2001. Indeed, this was always predictable. In both 1997 and 2001 Labour benefited from two advantages – low Tory morale contrasting with effective Labour organisation ensured that the latter campaigned far more effectively on the ground (a difference which bites most in the marginals, where both parties' efforts are most concentrated), and most LibDems preferred Labour to the Conservatives, allowing a squeeze and switch of tactical votes. Consequently, at both elections Labour won more seats than uniform swing would have predicted given its vote share. Neither was the case in 2005, although the apocalyptic "tactical unwind" feared by some Labour supporters did not fully materialise.

But this also points an important lesson for the future. While it is true that the electoral system is currently "biased" to Labour in terms of the translation of votes into seats, much of this bias is political rather than systemic, and could melt away if political circumstances change. Labour gained disproportionately in marginal seats in 1997 and 2001; but was this a permanent shift in the distribution of votes, or was it simply factors specific to those two elections? The evidence of 2005 is inconclusive, matters moving in the Tories' direction but only slightly so. If the latter, then the "bias in the electoral system" may really be no more than a temporary and unnatural Labour advantage in the marginals, an ever-more-tightly wound spring that might be released to drive voting patterns in the opposite direction at any moment. But it is no good relying on the Boundary Commissions to help.

Labour's Fourth Landslide?

In *Explaining Labour's Second Landslide*, we made one firm prediction: that the general election would be held on 5 May 2005.[192]

Why were we able to forecast the election timing with such certainty and accuracy so long ago? The Parliamentary mandate ran out after five years, i.e., June 2006. No Prime Minister wants to chance "events, dear boy, events" in the final year of his or her mandate. Local government elections are held on the first Thursday in May. Governments usually do badly in local elections. Prime Ministers do not like to hold General Elections in the wake of bad election results. Or in the dark. Or in holiday times. Or when Parliament isn't sitting on the day he or she wishes to go to the Palace to ask for a dissolution.

Therefore, we tend to have elections in the spring, and how better to get turnout up, to run the least risk of disruption, and to maximise the chance of re-election? On Local Election Day in May of the fourth year of your term. That's why 5 May 2005 has been our forecast of the date of the next election since 2001.

Prime Ministers with poor poll ratings and their backs to the wall, as Jim Callaghan had in 1978 and John Major in 1997, tend to ignore this. Because, they suspect (Callaghan) or know (Major) that they are going to lose, they hang onto power and perks to the last minute, hoping that a miracle will save them. It didn't, either of them. They also tend to prefer longer campaigns. In theory, Gordon Brown might be in the same position next time around, assuming Tony Blair has kept his pledge to hand over power before the end of the Parliament, but we doubt it. The next election, we believe, will be held in 2009. Not, though, on the first Thursday in May: 2009 is a European Parliamentary election year, and as in 2004 the English local government elections will almost certainly be moved to the same date; holding the general election then, too, will maximise turnout in all three, to Labour's probable advantage, and avoid the potentially disastrous position of asking the British people to vote twice in a month and put up with eight weeks of continuous election campaigning.

---

[192] Robert Worcester and Roger Mortimore, *Explaining Labour's Second Landslide* (London: Politico's Publishing, 2001), p 321.

320

So – always assuming that we haven't so fallen out with the rest of the EU by then as to have withdrawn from the Union altogether – expect a general election on 4 June 2009. We will, Methuen willing, be here to tell you what the public thought about it, and why it happened the way it did, a few months later. And a fourth Labour term? Don't bet against it.

Appendix 1: Polls and Polling

The Polls in 2005

For once, the clear winners of the election were the opinion polls. Every one of the final predictions was comfortably within the margins of error; indeed, no single poll was out by more than two points for any party, a performance not matched since 1959.

NOP would have been spot on, only the second time any poll has been accurate to the decimal point (first time ever was MORI in 1983), if their figures hadn't added up to 101%. Maybe they accounted for some of the extra postal ballots cast?

The clustering of the polls sets to rest the claim by some that the internet polls are intrinsically more accurate than conventional polls properly done. Both rely on adjustments for turnout and replication of the demographic profile of the electorate, and the fact that they are a snapshot at the time they were taken, not (like the exit poll) of voters as they left the polling stations. It also represents a recovery of face for the internet polls from the gross errors in this country in June 2004 and in the American presidential election in November when the two internet polls were further out by some margin than the least accurate of the 15 telephone polls reported on the final two days of the election.

National Voting Intention Polls

There were 55 separate polls published during the 2005 campaign, more than at any of the last three elections, and despite some carping about "volatility" there were no more than the statistically inevitable number of outliers or "rogue polls".

Until polling day, there was a small but consistent difference between the internet-based polls on the one hand and the "conventional" (telephone or face-to-face) polls on the other. The conventional polls averaged Conservative 32%, Labour 39% and Liberal Democrat 21%: every one of the 32 had Labour and the Liberal Democrats at these figures ± 3, and all but one had the Conservatives within the same margin of the average.

(The exception was the final Populus tracker poll, which may have been affected by fieldwork over the Bank Holiday weekend.) The internet polls averaged Conservative 34%, Labour 36% and Liberal Democrats 22%; all 24 were within ± 3 points of these averages for all three parties, and 22 of the 24 were within ± 2 points.

Table 110: The Polls Published 8 April-22 April

Company	Client	Fieldwork (Published)	Sample	Con %	Lab %	LD %	Oth %
YouGov	DTel	5-6 Apr (8 Apr)	5,108	35	36	21	8
MORI	Obs/SMi	7-9 Apr (10 Apr)	1,004	33	40	19	8
ICM	STel	7-8 Apr (10 Apr)	1,012	34	38	20	8
ICM	DMi/GMTV	9 Apr (11 Apr)	1,009	33	38	22	7
BPIX	MoS	?-9 Apr (10 Apr)	1,615	37	37	20	6
YouGov	STimes	7-9 Apr (10 Apr)	1,552	35	37	21	7
YouGov	DTel	8-10 Apr (11 Apr)	1,514	36	36	20	8
NOP	Indy	8-10 Apr (12 Apr)	956	32	38	21	9
MORI	EveStd	7-11 Apr (13 Apr)	1,156	35	39	21	5
ICM	Guard	10-12 Apr (14 Apr)	1,524	33	39	21	7
BES	ESRC	11-16 Apr (17 Apr)	1,350	37	35	21	7
YouGov	STel	12-14 Apr (15 Apr)	2,240	33	38	22	7
BPIX	MoS	?-15 Apr (17 Apr)	1,403	36	35	20	9
ICM	STel	13-15 Apr (17 Apr)	1,521	30	40	22	8
Comm	IoS	11-15 Apr (17 Apr)	1,000	34	40	20	6
YouGov	STimes	14-16 Apr (17 Apr)	1,482	35	36	23	6
ICM	DMi/GMTV	16-Apr (18 Apr)	1,000	33	41	20	6
YouGov	DTel	15-17 Apr (18 Apr)	2,011	32	36	23	9
NOP	Indy	15-17 Apr (19 Apr)	958	32	37	21	10
Populus	Times	14-17 Apr (19 Apr)	1,000	31	40	21	8
MORI	FT	15-18 Apr (19 Apr)	1,005	32	40	21	7
ICM	Guard	17-19 Apr (21 Apr)	1,513	33	39	22	6
Populus	Times*	17-20 Apr (22 Apr)	1,420	34	39	20	7
BES	ESRC*	17-22 Apr (23 Apr)	1,201	34	37	22	7
MORI	Sun	18-19 Apr (22 Apr)	1,001	32	39	22	7
YouGov	DTel	19-21 Apr (22 Apr)	1,474	34	37	22	7

Source: MORI Polltrack (www.mori.com/polltrack)

*="Rolling poll" (figures published daily from a sample replaced gradually over several days): to avoid double-counting of the same respondents, the table includes only the final poll in each series and each earlier poll not overlapping in fieldwork dates with later polls in the table.

For key to abbreviations, see next table

Table 111: The Polls Published 24 April-5 May

Company	Client	Fieldwork (Published)	Sample	Con %	Lab %	LD %	Oth %
ICM	STel	20-22 Apr (24 Apr)	1,524	33	39	21	7
Comm	IoS	19-22 Apr (24 Apr)	1,003	35	40	18	7
BPIX	MoS	?-22 Apr (24 Apr)	?	34	36	22	8
YouGov	STimes	21-23 Apr (24 Apr)	1,490	33	37	23	7
ICM	DMi/GMTV	23 Apr (25 Apr)	1,015	33	39	20	8
Populus	Times*	21-24 Apr (26 Apr)	1,425	32	41	20	7
BES	ESRC*	23-28 Apr (29 Apr)	1,184	33	38	20	9
YouGov	DTel	22-24 Apr (25 Apr)	1,831	33	37	24	6
NOP	Indy	22-24 Apr (26 Apr)	959	30	40	21	9
MORI	FT	21-25 Apr (27 Apr)	2,256	34	36	23	7
ICM	Guard	24-26 Apr (28 Apr)	1,547	33	40	20	7
YouGov	DTel	26-28 Apr (29 Apr)	2,070	32	36	24	8
BES	ESRC*	23-28 Apr (29 Apr)	1,184	33	38	20	9
Comm	IoS	23-28 Apr (1 May)	1,091	31	39	23	7
Populus	Times*	25-28 Apr (30 Apr)	1,428	31	40	22	7
ICM	STel	27-29 Apr (1 May)	1,532	31	39	22	8
MORI	Obs/SMi	28-29 Apr (1 May)	1,007	33	36	22	9
YouGov	STimes	28-30 Apr (1 May)	1,400	33	36	23	8
BPIX	MoS	?-29 Apr (1 May)		33	37	21	9
YouGov	DTel	29 Apr-1 May (2 May)	1,309	33	36	24	7
MORI	FT	29 Apr-1 May (3 May)	1,009	29	39	22	10
YouGov	Sky	2-3 May (4 May)	2,368	32	36	25	7
Populus	Times*	29 Apr-2 May (4 May)	1,420	27	41	23	9
NOP	Indy	1-3 May (5 May)	1,000	33	36	23	8
ICM	Guard	1-3 May (5 May)	1,532	32	38	22	8
Populus	Times	2-3 May (5 May)	2,042	32	38	21	9
BES	ESRC*	29 Apr-4 May (5 May)	1,380	33	35	24	8
YouGov	DTel	3-4 May (5 May)	3,962	32	37	24	7
Harris Int		1-4 May (5 May)	4,116	33	38	22	7
MORI	EveStd	3-4 May (5 May)	1,628	33	38	23	6
AVERAGE (from 5 April)				33	38	22	8
AVERAGE (FINAL POLLS ONLY)				33	37	23	8
RESULT (GB)		5 May		33	36	23	8

Source: MORI Polltrack (www.mori.com/polltrack)
KEY: BES=British Election Study; BPIX=British Polling Index; Comm=CommunicateResearch; Harris Int=Harris Interactive; DMi=*Daily Mirror*; DTel=*Daily Telegraph*; EveStd=(London) *Evening Standard*; FT=*Financial Times*; Guard=*Guardian*; Indy=*Independent*; IoS=*Independent on Sunday*; MoS=*Mail on Sunday*; Obs=*Observer*; SMi=*Sunday Mirror*; STel=*Sunday Telegraph*; STimes=*Sunday Times*.
Full details of sample size and fieldwork dates for the British Polling Index polls were not always published by the Mail on Sunday.

324

Since both sets of polls reached the right final result it is futile to attempt to prove which of these two slightly different pictures of the campaign was most nearly accurate; both methods have proved that they can work, within their limits, in the only objective test of their accuracy that is available. For the record, Tables 110 and 111 give the full list of all those polls of which we are aware.

Non-National Polls

In contrast to the burgeoning number of national polls, there were fewer non-national polls published during the 2005 election than we can ever previously remember.

Only two of the national pollsters (ICM and YouGov) found a client to poll Scottish voters during the campaign, and in each case only for a single measure shortly before polling day; they were joined as in previous elections by Scottish Opinion. None of these three polls were conducted quite late enough to qualify as "prediction polls"; nevertheless, ICM's was as close to the final result as was their final national poll, though those by YouGov and Scottish Opinion were not. Neither TNS System Three, who polled at the very start of the campaign, nor MORI Scotland who published one voting intention survey earlier in the year, produced anything based on fieldwork in the final month.

Table 112: Scottish Polls in the 2005 Election

		Con	Lab	LD	SNP	Oth
Scottish Opinion/*D Record* (26-28 Apr)	%	16	40	17	21	6
YouGov/*Scottish D Telegraph* (26-29 Apr)*	%	19	35	22	20	4
ICM/*Scotsman* (30 Apr-1 May)	%	15	39	22	20	4
RESULT (5 May)	%	**16**	**40**	**23**	**18**	**4**

Nor, as far as we can tell, were there any polls in Wales (where there have usually been one or two in the past), or in any of the English regions. This, presumably, must reflect a reluctance of media clients to commission such polls, since the national pollsters would be delighted to conduct them, quite apart from the reputable and competent local agencies such as Beaufort Research in Cardiff.

ICM conducted two pairs of polls in marginal seats, one for Channel 4 and the other for the *News of the World*, in each case one poll in the 93 most marginal Labour-held constituencies where the Conservatives came second in 2001, and the other in the 33 most marginal seats where Conservatives and Liberal Democrats held first and second place in either order. The polling was relatively accurate (the apparent over-estimate of Labour in the Conservative-Liberal Democrat marginals probably indicating simply that decisions to vote tactically were made late, and matching the similar pattern we reported around the same time from the analysis of those interviews from MORI's national polls which had been conducted in marginal seats).

Table 113: ICM Polls in Marginal Seats

		Con	Lab	Lib	Oth
LABOUR-CONSERVATIVE MARGINALS					
7-10 April (Channel 4)	%	37	40	17	6
12-14 April (*News of the World*)	%	36	42	17	4
Result (5 May)	**%**	**38**	**40**	**16**	**5**
CONSERVATIVE-LIBERAL DEMOCRAT MARGINALS					
7-10 April (Channel 4)	%	40	20	35	5
12-14 April (*News of the World*)	%	40	19	37	4
Result (5 May)	**%**	**43**	**13**	**40**	**4**

Source: ICM Research

However, because of the considerable divergence of constituency results, broad-brush marginal polls such as these could not have yielded a very accurate seat projection. If editors are interested in accurately predicting numbers of seats rather than votes won (and since any further Labour decline or Tory recovery at the next election will push us towards hung Parliament territory, where such predictions will become much more important), they will have to consider commissioning more polls of smaller groups of marginals, carefully psephologically designed to yield the necessary information. The successful exit polls show it can be done – not only in 2005, when the NOP/BBC and MORI/ITV teams and their respective academic consultants came together, but also in 1997 and 2001, when both the Curtice & Fisher design for the BBC/NOP polls and the Rallings & Waller designs for the MORI/ITV polls produced accurate projections.

Just five constituency polls reached the attention of the national media, although it is possible that others of which we are not aware were reported locally. Constituency polls have a special relevance in British elections since they can, if accurate, supply essential information for prospective tactical voters, who must at best be making an educated guess at the current situation in their own constituency if they have to rely on national polls (even national polls of marginals) and assumptions of uniform swing. In a sense this sets them apart from all other published polls in their relationship with the voter and role in the electoral system – they act not merely as part of the election news reporting, satisfying the public's curiosity and supplying strategic information about the course of the campaign, but have the potential to give the voters direct information that they need to know on how best to use their votes.

Table 114: Constituency Polls in the 2005 Election

		Con	Lab	LD	PC	Oth
CARDIFF NORTH						
NOP poll (published 27 Apr)	%	35	40	19	5	1
Result	%	37	39	19	4	1
Difference		+2	-1	0	-1	0
FINCHLEY & GOLDERS GREEN						
ICM/*Guardian* poll (25-29 Apr)	%	39	39	18	-	5
Result	%	39	40	17	-	4
Difference		0	+1	-1		-1
HALTEMPRICE & HOWDEN						
ICM/*Guardian* poll (25-29 Apr)	%	45	12	38	-	5
Result	%	47	13	37	-	3
Difference		+2	+1	-1		-2
SHIPLEY						
ICM/*Guardian* poll (25-29 Apr)	%	37	41	15	-	7
Result	%	39	38	15	-	8
Difference		+2	-3	0		+1
YNYS MÔN						
NOP poll (published 24 Apr)	%	21	29	10	33	7
Result	%	11	35	7	31	16
Difference		-10	+6	-3	-2	+9

Of course, constituency polls are only likely at best to be possible in a tiny minority of constituencies, but they can certainly be justified in a great deal more than five – not only for that democratic information function, but as adding more to the breadth of information available to the news media reporting the election than yet another national voting intention poll.

Judging the accuracy of constituency polls is difficult, since to be useful they need to be conducted days before the election rather than as an eve-of-poll prediction, and since if successful they may influence votes and contribute to their own divergence from the result. But the success of the 2005 polls is clear – four of the five within a three-point margin of error for every party[193], and even in the case of NOP's poll in Ynys Môn, which attracted some criticism, correctly identifying that it was a close contest between Labour and Plaid Cymru, the only practical information needed by a tactical voter.

Perhaps one other poll worth mentioning, if only for the vituperative condemnation it received in one internet blog[194], was by Scottish Opinion for the *Aberdeen Press & Journal*. It appeared under what its internet critic called the "amazingly dishonest headline" LABOUR SET TO HOLD KEY MARGINALS, and reported that "Strong challenges posed by the Liberal Democrats in Aberdeen South and by the SNP in Ochil and South Perthshire are set to fail" on the basis of extrapolation from a regional poll, presumably by uniform swing. That, of course, though a beloved tactic of journalists, can be decidedly risky. Our blogger certainly thought so, dismissing the journalists as "scumbags" and Scottish Opinion as not "competent", and concluding "Whichever way you look at it, Vicki Harris [Liberal Democrat] will be the new MP for Aberdeen South, and Annabelle Ewing [SNP] will return to Westminster as the MP for the new Ochil & South Perthshire constituency". Labour, you may remember, held both seats – pollsters, and journalists, not guilty. Again.

---

[193] A stricter criterion than it would be fair to apply had they not met it, since pollsters would claim only a "margin of error" of ±4% given the sample sizes used in these polls.
[194] The pro-SNP blog scottish-independence.blogspot.com, normally a reasonably measured if not necessarily impartial commentator on polls.

MORI Methodology Explained

MORI's final poll of the 2005 election campaign, published in the London *Evening Standard* on election day, predicted the Conservative and Liberal Democrat shares of the vote spot-on, and missed Labour by two percentage points – well within the normally accepted margins of error. Though not complacent, and vividly aware that every new election throws up new challenges, we regard this performance as satisfactory.

This is vindication of our belief that it is still perfectly possible to achieve a representative sample of the British public through well-executed quota sampling methods, with no need for radical weighting. This note sets out the detail of the methodology used, both in the campaign polls (which do not differ in essentials from our regular monthly polls between elections) and the final prediction poll which, as always, took into account some extra considerations necessary to a prediction which we do not consider appropriate for the regular "snapshot" measurements.

What Does MORI Do?

MORI's chief principle in the way we publish our political polling data is transparency. As far as possible we aim to report directly the questions that we put to the public and the proportions of our sample that have given us each possible answer in reply. Where it is necessary to explain the implications of the data or to further manipulate it so that its meaning is clear, we try to explain at every step what we have done and why, but also to ensure that the raw data remains available so that anybody who doubts our analysis can see for themselves and know what the answer would have been if different assumptions were made. We use no "black box" methods or trade secrets.

Exact question wording and "topline results" are normally published in full for all our published surveys on our website. We are always happy to supply free on request for any individual published survey the detailed computer tables, which show weighted and unweighted case counts. For our election polls, these are freely available on our website at www.mori.com.

Being based on quota sampling, "margins of error" are, strictly speaking, incalculable. However, empirical experience over many years has shown that in Britain polls conducted by weighted quota sample have a variance broadly similar to a pure probability (random) sample of the same size, and it is therefore customary to quote confidence limits as if a random sample had been used. The "margin of error" due to sampling variance is therefore considered to be ±3% on a sample of 1,000 respondents.

Our voting intention polls have three simple elements – sampling, demographic weighting and filtering.

Sampling: MORI's voting intention polls are conducted either by telephone or face-to-face in respondents' homes. The exact details of how we select the people we invite to take part in our polls differs somewhat between the two interviewing methods, but the principle in both cases is "quota sampling".

Our surveys aim at drawing a representative quota sample of the adult population in Great Britain (not including Northern Ireland). The election polls, including the final prediction poll, were mostly conducted by telephone, using random digit dialling but selecting respondents with the help of quotas rather than using a strict probability-sampling approach.

Quotas are set by age, sex, social class (occupation) and work status, and interviewers may interview anybody within the household who falls within their quota and is willing to be interviewed at that time or within the fieldwork period. (Note that since the method is not intended to be a probability sample, we make no attempt to randomly select household members or to make a set minimum number of call-backs if no answer is received; in this we differ from most of the other telephone pollsters.)

For our face-to-face Omnibus surveys, interviewers are sent to 210 ward-sized sampling points around the country, carefully selected so that their inhabitants comprise a microcosm of the whole population, where they knock on doors to find respondents who fit their quota (which is different for each sampling point). The quota includes housing tenure rather than social class, but the procedure is otherwise similar to the telephone surveys.

Each poll uses a fresh sample of c. 1,000 or c. 2,000 respondents, and these are chosen to ensure that they broadly match the adult population in their distribution of the sexes, of age, of social class or housing tenure, and of working status (that is whether the respondent works full-time, part time or not at all), as well as geographical spread. The responses we receive from these respondents form our unweighted or raw data.

Demographic weighting: Because the quotas will never achieve a quite perfect distribution of our sample between the different demographic groups, and because we prefer to ensure that the sample is representative in more different respects than it is practical to include in the quota system, we then weight the data[195]. In fact the effect of demographic weighting is normally very small, since our sampling method ensures that each sample rarely diverges much from the ideal, and it is really more a fine-tuning process than anything. (In fact, there was not a single MORI voting intention poll published between the start of 2005 and election day in which the weighting made a difference of more than a single percentage point for any of the three major parties' overall unfiltered voting intention share.) Unweighted figures from any published MORI poll are always available on request, and for the election polls can be downloaded from our website.

The standard weighting variables that we use are for region, sex, age, social class (occupation), housing tenure and working status, though the design might sometimes be altered if it seemed advisable for a particular survey. In particular, an extra weight may be added if it seems that the existing weighting design has failed to correct a sample imbalance. Weights are set at national or regional level, and combined by rim-weighting. Data for both weights and quotas are derived from the Census, from the Registrar-General's population estimates (the official annual updates of the census figures), the Labour Force Survey and the National Readership Survey, as well as from other MORI surveys where appropriate.

Filtering: The final voting intention figures are subject to one further process, since our "headline" or "topline" percentages do not include the whole sample. First we exclude those who are undecided how they would

---

[195] Weighting means, quite simply, that in adding up the figures we treat each different group as if we had the number of responses that we would have if the sample was perfectly representative. For example, if we found that 55% of our sample were women, since we know in fact that women make up only 52% of the adult population, in adding up the figures we would count each woman as 52/55 of a response, and vice versa for the men, assuring that in the final results women account for their correct 52% share of influence.

vote, those who say they would not vote at all and those (usually only a small number) who won't say. This leaves us with those who have named one of the parties, and voting intention percentages are always presented on this basis, since it is directly comparable with the way in which election results are normally published. The numbers undecided, saying they would not vote and refusing to answer are always given in the full report of the results of a poll on our website at www.mori.com, and normally also in the technical note that accompanies the reports of MORI's polls in our client newspapers.

In recent years we have adopted a second filter, to cope with the problem of low election turnouts. In the past, when the vast majority of British adults could be relied upon to vote, at least in general elections, we could be reasonably confident that a poll that accurately measured the voting intentions of the electorate would also accurately predict how an election held at that moment would pan out. (As recently as 1992, remember, 78% of the electorate voted.) These days, however, many of the public are less sure that they will vote, and supporters of the Labour Party are considerably less likely to say they are certain they will vote than are Conservatives; consequently, there is generally a substantial difference between the party vote shares if you consider the responses of everyone who names a party for which they would vote and if you consider only the people who say they are certain to vote. Our "headline" voting intention figure, which we consider to be the most useful indicator of the political climate, has since 2002 been calculated by excluding all those who are not "absolutely certain to vote". We measure this by asking our respondents to rate their certainty to vote on a scale from 1 to 10, where "1" means absolutely certain not to vote and "10" means absolutely certain to vote, and only those rating their likelihood of voting at "10" are included.

This filtering, though stricter than that used by most of the other companies, was probably not strict enough, as it meant the final projection effectively assumed a turnout of 70% against the eventual figure of 61%, and is an issue we must explore further in future.

The rationale for this is not that we necessarily think that these are exactly the respondents who will vote, that no 10s will fail to vote and that no 8s or 9s will get to the polls, but that this is likely to give us the best approximation of the political profile of those who do vote. In other words, we think that the 8s and 9s who vote will be more like 10s than they will be like the rest of the 8s and 9s. Weighting to this scale, as ICM and Populus do, instead of using it as a filter, would be likely to underestimate the extent of differential turnout, and the experience of the 2001 election – when we over-estimated Labour share and under-estimated abstention – convinced us that we should use the most stringent turnout filter available.

The Final "Prediction" Poll

For the final poll, two extra adjustments were added[196]. We began, as usual, with demographic weighting, using the same variables and targets as for our other telephone polls throughout the election; and the voting intention table was filtered based on 10/10 "absolutely certain to vote" plus "already voted by post". Except for including those who said they had already voted, this was again exactly as on the previous polls.

Then a voting intention was imputed for those who said they were certain to vote or had already voted but refused to say how. We did not do this in the previous campaign polls, but did so in the final poll in 2001 (and signalled in *Explaining Labour's Landslide* that we would do so[197], as it would have improved our final poll in 1997). Generally, we consider that such an adjustment is not necessary except in the final poll, as the number of refusals in the "peacetime" face-to-face polls is small, usually 1% to 2%, but it is clearly justified and necessary when refusals reach 9% of those certain to vote. Those who said they would not vote or did not know how they would vote were, however, excluded as usual from the percentages.

The past vote imputation was calculated on the basis of newspaper readership, i.e. refusers were assumed to split their votes in the same proportions as non-refusers who read the same newspapers, this being the most complete relevant data available. In the event the imputed votes split almost evenly between Tories and Labour, and the adjustment moved the overall voting intentions by only one percentage point.

---

[196] Separate tables showing the data after each stage are included in the final set of computer tables, which can be downloaded from MORI's website.
[197] Robert Worcester and Roger Mortimore, *Explaining Labour's Landslide* (London: Politico's Publishing, 1999), p 172.

A final additional adjustment was made for differential turnout. Because the projected turnout from the final poll seemed unrealistically high (70%), and because this increase had partly arisen from the closing of the projected turnout gap between the parties since the start of the election campaign, we judged that the predicted turnout was likely to include a degree of exaggeration, and that this exaggeration was likely to be greatest among the groups whose claimed certainty of voting had increased most sharply (i.e. Labour and LibDem voters). The adjustment therefore aimed at reducing the extent to which the turnout gap between the parties had been closed since the start of the campaign. The data from the final poll was compared with that from the March MORI Political Monitor (the last before the election campaign), and the proportional increase in projected turnout for each of the three main parties measured: for Labour and the Liberal Democrats a new turnout figure was calculated by reducing the *excess* proportional increase in turnout (i.e. over and above that found among Tories) by a third. The final voting intention figures were then down-weighted on this basis. Again the effect was very modest: in round figures projected turnout for Labour was reduced from 76% to 73% and for the LibDems from 75% to 73%. In retrospect a bigger adjustment on this basis might have been justified. (Discounting the whole narrowing of the turnout gap instead of one-third of it would have given us final figures of 34:36:22.)

We had made allowance for one further adjustment by conducting a call-back on the Wednesday of some respondents we had spoken to on the Tuesday, to guard against the possibility of last-minute swing. In the event, though, no adjustment was necessary on the basis of the call-back data, it seeming clear that no significant last-minute movement was taking place.

The Exit Poll

We should take a brief diversion to mention the exit poll, although none of the data discussed in this book is derived from it. Unlike the exit polls in many countries such as the USA, the British exit polls are no longer designed as "analysis polls", to measure who voted which way and why – the broadcasters have decided it is no longer worth the (admittedly considerable) extra cost, and content themselves with "prediction polls", which measure nothing but numbers of votes, in such a way as to feed into a psephological model that predicts the result in seats.

In 2005, for the first time, BBC and ITV combined to commission a single exit poll, which was conducted jointly by MORI and NOP. It predicted the Labour majority in seats *exactly* (a British and conceivably a world first), and the shares of the vote within one percentage point. Full credit must be given to the academic team (John Curtice, Steve Fisher and Colin Rallings) responsible for the statistical model used to convert the polling data into a prediction. The poll was conducted in 120 polling stations across the country, all but a handful ones where the MORI or NOP exit poll also operated in 2001, so that a straight comparison could be made between the findings.

Table 115: The Record of the British Exit Polls, 1997-2005

Projections of Labour seats

	MORI for ITV	NOP for BBC	MORI/NOP for BBC & ITV	Election Result
1997	410	429*		419
2001	417	408		413
2005			356	356

*In 1997 the precise NOP projection was not published, but was broadcast as indicating an overall majority of "about 200".

In Britain, unlike most countries, election results are not published at polling station level. Given the huge variation in political character between polling stations, and the tiny fraction of the roughly 40,000 that can be practicably included in a poll, a purely random selection would produce findings with a margin of error far too wide to be useful, and the only alternative to using polling data from a previous election is to judge

335

the political character of a polling station by psephological inference; but the ability to measure change in votes, which varies much less than the absolute strength of the parties, allows a reliable ridge-regression model to be constructed that predicts the probabilities of each party winning each seat. These probabilities were then summed to produce the overall prediction, and to surpass the already impressive record of accuracy of the British exit polls in recent elections. This was despite the complications caused by the huge increase in the number of postal votes, which naturally cannot be included in the exit poll and must be measured indirectly to calculate a compensating factor.

Pundits and Predictions

Reuters, as in past recent elections, put together a poll of 18 "experts" to predict the outcome at the start of the campaign, publishing their predictions on 8 April 2005. Unfortunately they did not, as they have sometimes in the past, identify the individual predictions of their panel, who were the usual mix of pollsters and academics[198], and there was not in any case a great deal of scope for panellists to embarrass themselves. Their predictions of Labour's majority were published only in 40-seat bands, but the most frequently selected band was a correct prediction of a 40-79 seat overall majority, the choice of 10 of the 18. The remaining 8 predicted a higher majority. All put Blair's chances of victory at between 70% and 100%, with 90% being the median.

In the pre-election issue of the *British Journal of Politics and International Relations,* four British academic or academic teams were lured into expounding forecasting models. All, at least, hit upon the right winner. David Sanders[199], working from a variety of polling sources of "popularity data", emphasising both that the reliability of his model was dependent on the accuracy of the assumptions built into it and that he considers forecasting more an art than a science, produced a vote share prediction of Labour 38%, Conservative 31%, Liberal Democrat 22% and others 9% – not at all bad months before the election! Paul Whiteley[200] predicted Labour to win 358 seats, the Conservatives 213 and the Liberal Democrats 47, somewhat less impressive. Belanger *et al*[201] made a forecast from economic data and the government's approval ratings, which predicted Labour to win 41.8% of the vote and 57.7% of the seats (i.e. 373 seats).

---

[198] The panel members were: Sir Robert Worcester of MORI, Colin Hay of the University of Birmingham, Andrew Russell of the University of Manchester, Steven Fielding of the University of Salford, Dominic Wring of Loughborough University, Patrick Dunleavy at LSE, Eric Shaw of the University of Stirling, Neil Carter of the University of York, Geoffrey Foote of the University of Teesside, Philip Lynch of the University of Leicester, Stephen Wilks of the University of Exeter, Sydney Elliott of Queen's University Belfast, David Denver of the University of Lancaster, Nick Moon of NOP. Four participants did not wish to be identified.

[199] David Sanders, "Popularity Function Forecasts for the 2005 UK General Election", *British Journal of Politics and International Relations*, Vol 7 (2005), 174-90.

[200] Paul F Whiteley, "Forecasting Seats from Votes in British General Elections", *British Journal of Politics and International Relations*, Vol 7 (2005), 165-73.

[201] Eric Belanger, Michael S Lewis-Beck and Richard Nadeau, "A Political Economy Forecast for the 2005 British General Election", *British Journal of Politics and International Relations*, Vol 7 (2005), 191-8.

Borisyuk *et al* used neural networks to develop a forecast based the interpretation of expert opinion. Their three experiments on different bases put Labour's likelihood of victory at 71%, 75% and 91%; they made no attempt to predict seat or vote shares.[202]

More ambitious in the prediction game were Matthew Lebo and Helmut Norpoth, professors of political science at Stony Brook University in New York[203], who built up a statistical model of British general elections which in terms of votes would have picked the winner correctly in each of the 16 contests from 1945 to 2001, while in seats it would have made one wrong pick out of 16 contests (a narrow miss in 1951), deviating from the actual results by an average of 27 seats.

The model used two key variables as the basis of its prediction, the approval rating of the Prime Minister (Tony Blair's rating 34% in January and February 2005, lower than that of any previously re-elected Prime Minister), and the cyclical element that used to be called the "electoral pendulum".

However, their prediction for 2005 was that Labour would retain their lead over the Conservatives in the House of Commons but lose the popular vote (predicting a Tory lead of 3.4%) and fail to capture enough seats to avoid a Hung Parliament, being only 32 seats ahead.

They were wrong on both counts, unfortunately. At 2 failures in 15 to predict the seat distribution, the Lebo/Norpoth model now has an equal record with Dr Roger Mortimore's Sweet FA Prediction model[204], which would have given a correct prediction of all but the 1959 and 1983 general elections and, more pertinently, has now successfully predicted two

---

[202] Roman Borisyuk, Galina Borisyuk, Colin Rallings and Michael Thrasher, "Forecasting the 2005 General Election: A Neural Network Approach", *British Journal of Politics and International Relations*, Vol 7 (2005), 199-209.

[203] Matthew Lebo and Helmut Norpoth, "Labour to Lose Commons Majority and Popular Vote, Electoral Model Predicts", *Press Release*, 24 March 2005, Stony Brook University, Stony Brook, New York.

[204] The Sweet FA Prediction Model states that if the FA Cup holders at the time of the general election normally play in predominantly blue or white shirts, a Conservative overall majority will follow; if they play in predominantly red or yellow shirts, Labour wins. A hung Parliament will result if their shirts are an equal mix of these two groups of colours, as in the case of Sunderland (red and white stripes), who held the Cup at the time of the February 1974 election. At the time of the 2005 general election, the FA Cup holders were Manchester United, who play in red. See Appendix 2 of *Explaining Labour's Second Landslide* for a more detailed exposition of the theory.

elections since it was first published. Such an exercise demonstrates how difficult it is to predict the outcomes of elections on the basis of analyses of the past.

Appendix 2: MORI Polls Cited

The following gives the full details of the surveys by MORI cited in the text. (Details of surveys by other contractors, where known, are footnoted at the point of citation.)

1. BMA survey, June 2000: MORI interviewed a representative quota sample of 2,014 GB residents aged 15+, face to face, in home, on 22-27 June 2000, as part of MORI's regular CAPI Omnibus survey. Data are weighted to match the profile of the adult population. The survey was conducted for the British Medical Association.

2. *Mail on Sunday* Mandelson Resignation Poll: MORI interviewed a representative quota sample of 1,001 GB residents aged 16+ by telephone on 25-26 January 2001, as part of the regular MORI Telephone Omnibus. Data are weighted to match the profile of the population. The survey was conducted for the *Mail on Sunday*.

3. *Times* Campaign Poll (2001), Week 2: MORI interviewed a representative quota sample of 1,019 GB residents aged 18+ face-to-face, in home, on 15 May 2001. Data are weighted to match the profile of the population. The survey was conducted for *The Times*.

4. Electoral Commission Election Survey 1 (2001): MORI interviewed a representative quota sample of 1,801 UK residents aged 18+ by telephone on 9-15 May 2001. Data are weighted to match the profile of the population. The survey was conducted for the Electoral Commission.

5. MORI Political Monitor, August 2001: MORI interviewed a representative quota sample of 1,031 GB residents aged 18+ face-to-face, in-home on 23-28 August 2001, as part of MORI's regular CAPI Omnibus survey. Data are weighted to match the profile of the adult population. The Omnibus survey carried questions for both for *The Times* and the *Daily Mirror*.

6. *News of the World* Post 9/11 Poll 1: MORI interviewed a representative quota sample of 500 GB residents aged 18+ by telephone on 14 September 2001. Data are weighted to match the profile of the population. The survey was conducted for the *News of the World*.

7. *News of the World* Post 9/11 Poll 2: MORI interviewed a representative quota sample of 513 GB residents aged 18+ by telephone on 21 September 2001. Data are weighted to match the profile of the population. The survey was conducted for the *News of the World*.

8. ITV Post 9/11 Poll: MORI interviewed a representative quota sample of 607 GB residents aged 18+ by telephone on 9 October 2001. Data are weighted to match the profile of the adult population. The survey was conducted for ITV's *Tonight with Trevor McDonald*.

9. *Mail on Sunday* Afghanistan Poll: MORI interviewed a representative quota sample of 603 GB residents aged 18+ by telephone on 1-2 November 2001. Data are weighted to match the profile of the adult population. The survey was conducted for the *Mail on Sunday*.

10. BMA Trust in Doctors Poll, 2002: MORI interviewed a representative quota sample of 1,972 GB residents aged 15+, face-to-face, in home, on 7-13 February 2002, as part of MORI's regular CAPI Omnibus survey. Data are weighted to match the profile of the adult population. The survey was conducted for the British Medical Association.

11. MORI Political Monitor, February 2002: MORI interviewed a representative quota sample of 1,069 GB residents aged 18+, face-to-face, in home, on 21-26 February 2002, as part of MORI's

340

regular CAPI Omnibus survey. Data are weighted to match the profile of the adult population. The survey was conducted for *The Times*.

12. *Time* Poll: MORI interviewed 1,003 GB residents aged 18+ by telephone on 15-17 March 2002. Data are weighted to match the profile of the population. The survey was conducted for *Time* magazine.

13. CRE "Voice of Britain" survey: MORI interviewed a representative quota sample of 822 GB residents aged 16+ and a total of 610 further "booster" interviews with members of ethnic minorities. Interviews were conducted face to face, in home, during April 2002. Data are weighted to match the profile of the adult population. The survey was conducted for the Commission for Racial Equality.

14. Green Issues Communications Poll: MORI interviewed a representative quota sample of 1,067 GB residents aged 15+, face to face, in home, on 18-22 April 2002, as part of MORI's regular CAPI Omnibus survey. Data are weighted to match the profile of the adult population. The survey was conducted for Green Issues Communications.

15. MORI Telephone Omnibus, May 2002: MORI interviewed a representative quota sample of 1,009 GB residents aged 16+ by telephone on 10-12 May 2002, as part of the regular MORI Telephone Omnibus survey. Data are weighted to match the profile of the population.

16. Transatlantic Trends survey: MORI interviewed a representative quota sample of 1,000 GB residents aged 18+ by telephone on 5-30 June 2002. Data are weighted to match the profile of the population. The survey was conducted for the German Marshall Fund of the United States and the Chicago Council on Foreign Relations. Full details of this survey, other surveys in the series, and data from other countries included in the surveys, can be found at www.transatlantictrends.org.

17. MORI Omnibus, July 2002: MORI interviewed a representative sample of 1,875 GB residents aged 15+, face-to-face in-home on 18-24 July 2002, as part of MORI's regular CAPI Omnibus survey. Data are weighted to match the profile of the adult population.

18. MORI/UEA Risk Survey, July 2002: MORI interviewed a representative sample of 1,547 GB residents aged 15+, face-to-face in-home on 6-31 July 2002, with sub-samples of approximately 300 used for the detailed questions about each of the five risk cases. Data are weighted to match the profile of the adult population. The survey was conducted for the Centre for Environmental Risk at the University of East Anglia (UEA).

19. *FT* "One Year On" Survey, September 2002: MORI interviewed a representative sample of 506 GB residents aged 18+, by telephone on 5-8 September 2002. Data are weighted to match the profile of the adult population. The survey was conducted for the *Financial Times*.

20. Iraq "Ides of March" poll: MORI interviewed a representative quota sample of 968 GB residents aged 18+ by telephone on 14-16 March 2003. Data are weighted to match the profile of the population.

21. Iraq post-invasion poll: MORI interviewed a representative quota sample of 969 GB residents aged 18+ by telephone on 28-31 March 2003. Data are weighted to match the profile of the population.

22. *Nestlé Family Monitor* No 16: MORI conducted classroom based self-completion sessions with 914 pupils aged 11-18 in 33 schools and colleges across England and Wales on 3 March–22 May 2003. The survey was conducted on behalf of Nestlé UK, as part of a series of research studies into family life in Britain.

23. Local Election Pilot Scheme Evaluation Surveys, 2003: MORI's conducted 29 quantitative surveys in pilot areas. For each survey, MORI interviewed a quota sample of c.200 residents by telephone in that local authority pilot district on 2-12 May 2003. Samples were stratified to ensure 100 interviews with voters and 100 with non-voters in each area. In addition 10 focus groups were conducted (two in each of five local authority areas). The research was conducted for the Electoral Commission. MORI's report to the Commission, and the Commission's own report, can both be downloaded from the Electoral Commission's website, http://www.electoralcommission.gov.uk/about-us/may2003pilots.cfm.

24. *FT* "State of Britain" Survey, April 2003: MORI interviewed a representative quota sample of 2,075 GB residents aged 18+, face-to-face in-home on 10-15 April 2003, as part of MORI's regular CAPI Omnibus survey. Data are weighted to match the profile of the population. The survey was conducted for the *Financial Times*.

25. *FT* Survey, June 2003: MORI interviewed a representative quota sample of 1,002 GB residents aged 16+ by telephone on 20-22 June 2003. Data are weighted to match the profile of the population. The survey was conducted for the *Financial Times*.

26. MORI Telephone Omnibus, August 2003: MORI interviewed a representative quota sample of 971 GB residents aged 18+ by telephone on 8-17 August 2003. Data are weighted to match the profile of the population.

27. Electoral Commission/Hansard Society *Audit of Political Engagement*, Survey 1: MORI interviewed a representative quota sample of 1,976 UK residents aged 18+, face-to-face in-home on 11-17 December 2003, as part of MORI's regular CAPI Omnibus survey with additional interviews in Northern Ireland. Data are weighted to match the profile of the population. The survey was conducted for the Electoral Commission and the Hansard Society and published as *An Audit of Political Engagement*, 2004.

28. BMA Trust In Doctors Poll, 2004: MORI interviewed a representative quota sample of 2,004 GB residents aged 15+, face-to-face, in home, on 26 February-2 March, as part of MORI's regular CAPI Omnibus survey. Data are weighted to match the profile of the adult population. The survey was conducted for the British Medical Association.

29. MORI Delivery Index, March 2004: MORI interviewed a representative quota sample of 831 GB residents aged 18+ by telephone on 26 February-2 March, as part of MORI's regular Telephone Omnibus survey. Data are weighted to match the profile of the adult population.

30. Foreign Policy Centre European Constitution Poll: MORI interviewed a representative quota sample of 1,063 GB residents aged 18+, face-to-face, in home on 22-27 July 2004, as part of MORI's regular CAPI Omnibus survey. Data are weighted to match the profile of the adult population. The survey was conducted for the Foreign Policy Centre.

31. Electoral Commission/Hansard Society *Audit of Political Engagement*, Survey 2: MORI interviewed a representative quota sample of 2,065 UK residents aged 18+, face-to-face in-home on 2-21 December 2004, as part of MORI's regular CAPI Omnibus survey with additional interviews in Northern Ireland. Data are weighted to match the profile of the population. The survey was conducted for the Electoral Commission and the Hansard Society and published as *An Audit of Political Engagement 2*, 2005.

32. MORI Delivery Index, February 2005: MORI interviewed a representative quota sample of 963 GB residents aged 18+ by telephone on 25-28 February 2005, as part of MORI's regular Telephone Omnibus survey. Data are weighted to match the profile of the adult population.

33. MORI Political Monitor, March 2005: MORI interviewed a representative quota sample of 1,795 GB residents aged 18+ for voting intention and of 935 GB residents aged 18+ for other questions, face to face in-home, on 17-22 March 2005, as part of MORI's regular CAPI Omnibus survey. Data are weighted to match the profile of the population.

34. *FT* Election Poll 1: MORI interviewed a representative quota sample of 1,001 GB residents aged 18+ by telephone on 1-3 April 2005. Data are weighted to match the profile of the population. The survey was conducted for the *Financial Times*.

35. *Observer/Sunday Mirror* Election Poll 1: MORI interviewed a representative quota sample of 1,004 GB residents aged 18+ by telephone on 7-9 April 2005. Data are weighted to match the profile of the population. The survey was conducted for the *Observer* and the *Sunday Mirror*.

36. MORI Omnibus Wave 13/2005: MORI interviewed a representative quota sample of 1,973 GB residents aged 18+, face to face in-home, on 7-11 April 2005, as part of MORI's regular CAPI Omnibus survey. Data are weighted to match the profile of the population. The Omnibus survey carried questions for both for the *Evening Standard* (ES Election Poll 1) and the *Financial Times* (FT Election Poll 2).

37. BBC Asian Network poll: MORI interviewed a sample of 325 British Asians, structured to ensure an adequate sub-sample size within each of the three national-origin groups (110 Indians, 105 Pakistani and 110 Bangladeshis). Interviews were conducted face to face in home and in street on 8-24 April 2005, in wards with an Asian population of greater than 10%. 14% of the interviews were conducted in mother tongue languages other than English. Data are weighted to the known population profile of GB Asian adults. The survey was conducted for BBC Asian Network.

38. *FT* Election Poll 3: MORI interviewed a representative quota sample of 1,005 GB residents aged 18+ by telephone on 15-18 April 2005. Data are weighted to match the profile of the population. The survey was conducted for the *Financial Times*.

39. *Sun* Election Poll: MORI interviewed a representative quota sample of 1,001 GB residents aged 18+ by telephone on 18-19 April 2005. Data are weighted to reflect the national population profile. The survey was conducted for the *Sun*.

40. MORI Omnibus Wave 15/2005 (FT Election Poll 4): MORI interviewed a representative quota sample of 2,256 GB residents aged 18+ by face-to-face, in-home on 21-25 April 2005, as part of MORI's regular CAPI Omnibus survey. Data are weighted to match the profile of the adult population. The survey was conducted for the *Financial Times*.

41. *Observer/Sunday Mirror* Election Poll 2: MORI interviewed a representative quota sample of 1,007 GB residents aged 18+ by telephone on 28-29 April 2005. Data are weighted to match the profile of the population. The survey was conducted for the *Observer* and the *Sunday Mirror*.

42. *FT* Election Poll 5: MORI interviewed a representative quota sample of 1,009 GB residents aged 18+ by telephone on 29 April-1 May 2005. Data are weighted to match the profile of the population. The survey was conducted for the *Financial Times*.

43. Eve of Poll survey (*Evening Standard* Election Poll 2): MORI interviewed a representative quota sample of 1,628 GB residents aged 18+ by telephone on 3-4 May 2005. Data are weighted to match the profile of the population. The survey was conducted for the *Evening Standard*.

44. Post-election survey: MORI interviewed a representative quota sample of 2,058 GB residents aged 18+, in-home, face to face, on 5-10 May 2005, as part of MORI's regular CAPI Omnibus survey. Data are weighted to match the profile of the population.

45. Deloitte/MORI Delivery Index survey, May 2005: MORI interviewed a representative quota sample of 975 GB residents aged 18+ by telephone on 13-15 May 2005. Data are weighted to match the profile of the population. The survey was conducted for Deloitte.

Appendix 3: Are The Polls Fixed?

We reproduce an exchange of emails during the 2005 election:

Sent: 19 April 2005

To: MORI

Subject: your election polls

I am most concerned at the political bias of your polling methods. Are your clients the left wing press, like the *Financial Times*, *The Guardian* etc.?

The question that you ask seems to me to be less than straight forward, like which party will you vote for in the general election. You appear to prepare the question in such a way that it becomes almost an interview.

Your results are quite a way away from the more direct question type polls conducted by the internet using companies.

I have the impression that MORI is in the pockets of the Government and its media supporters, like "Tony's Cronies", hoping for a knighthood or a peerage. I know this sounds cynical but as an ordinary voter it is most depressing to see the media manipulating – what appears to be – an apathetic electorate.

Yours sincerely

Dear …

You must be joking. Years ago, when we were doing the Labour Party's private polling (for the best of all capitalist reasons), our fieldwork supervisor in Scotland afterwards said she'd figured out who our client was…the Scottish Nationalists! She was wrong; so are you. Do you really think that the *Financial Times* is a left wing newspaper? And we don't work for the *Guardian*. Thursday we're in the *Sun*. Last week the *Evening Standard* (they are part of the *Daily Mail* Group).

You must be the only person in the country that thinks our questions are anything other than completely objective and systematic. As to the "straightforward" questions up on the telly, radio and newspapers and magazines, most of them are biased.

Cheers

Sir Robert Worcester, KBE (I've already got my knighthood)

Founder and Chairman, MORI.

PS Your letter and my reply will feature in our next book, if that's OK with you. Should give everyone a laugh!

Appendix 4: The Election "Grid"

	Profile of		Vote 2005				Lab Lead	Change since '01				Turnout	
	Elec-torate	Voters	Con	Lab	LD	Oth		Con	Lab	LD	Swing	2005	Chg
	%	%	%	%	%	%	%					%	'05-'01
All:	100	100	33	36	23	8	3	0	-6	+4	3.0	61%	+2
Gender:													
Men	48	48	34	34	22	10	*	+2	-8	+4	5.0	62%	+1
Women	52	52	32	38	23	7	6	-1	-4	+4	1.5	61%	+3
Gender gap (M/F)			+2	-4	-1	+3	-6	-1	0	-1	-1.0		
Age:													
18-24	11	7	28	38	26	8	10	+1	-3	+2	2.0	37%	-2
25-34	17	14	25	38	27	10	13	+1	-13	+8	7.0	49%	+3
35-44	20	19	27	41	23	9	14	-1	-4	+4	1.5	61%	+2
45-54	16	17	31	35	25	9	4	-1	-6	+5	2.5	65%	-0
55-64	15	17	39	31	22	8	-8	0	-6	+5	3.0	71%	+2
65+	21	26	41	35	18	6	-6	+1	-4	+1	2.5	75%	+5
Age gap(65+/18-25)	100	100	-13	-3	+8	-2	-16	-13	+2	+7	-11.0		
Social class:													
AB	24	27	37	28	29	6	-9	-2	-2	+4	0.0	71%	+3
C1	29	30	37	32	23	8	-5	+1	-6	+3	3.5	62%	+2
C2	21	20	33	40	19	8	7	+4	-9	+4	6.5	58%	+2
DE	25	23	25	48	18	9	23	+1	-7	+5	4.0	54%	+1
Class gap (AB/DE)	100	100	+12	-20	+11	-3	32	+13	-25	-1	-12.0		
Housing tenure:													
Owned	32	37	44	29	20	7	-15	+1	-3	+1	2.0	71%	+3
Mortgaged	40	40	31	36	25	8	5	0	-6	+5	3.0	60%	+1
Social renter	18	15	16	55	19	10	39	-2	-5	+5	1.5	51%	-1
Private renter	9	7	27	36	28	9	9	-1	-4	+3	1.5	51%	+5
Postal voters			34	38	22	6	4		n/a			73%	n/a
2001 Vote (reported):													
Con	20	25	90	2	6	2	-88	-10	+2	+6	-6.0	80%	-20
Lab	37	42	8	72	15	5	64	+8	-28	+15	18.0	71%	-29
Lib Dem	12	14	12	6	78	4	-6	+12	+6	-22	3.0	75%	-25
Region:													
East Midlands	7	8	37	39	18	6	2	0	-6	+3	3.0	63%	+2
Eastern	9	10	43	30	22	5	-13	+1	-7	+5	4.0	64%	+2
Greater London	13	11	32	39	22	7	7	+2	-8	+5	5.0	58%	+3
North East	4	4	20	53	23	4	33	-1	-6	+6	2.5	57%	+1
North West	12	11	29	45	21	5	16	0	-6	+4	3.0	57%	+1
Scotland	9	9	16	40	23	21	24	0	-4	+7	2.0	61%	+3
South East	14	15	45	24	25	6	-21	+2	-5	+1	3.5	64%	+2
South West	9	10	39	23	33	5	-16	0	-3	+2	1.5	67%	+2
Wales	5	5	21	43	18	18	22	0	-6	+4	3.0	62%	0
West Midlands	9	9	35	39	19	7	4	0	-6	+4	3.0	61%	+3
Yorks & Humberside	9	8	29	44	21	6	15	-1	-5	+4	2.0	59%	+2
Men by Age:													
18-24	6	4	33	34	25	8	1	+4	-4	-1	1.5	39%	-4
25-34	9	7	29	33	27	11	4	+5	-19	+8	12.0	49%	+2
35-54	18	18	31	36	22	11	5	+2	-7	+3	4.5	64%	-0
55+	16	19	40	33	20	7	-7	+1	-6	+4	3.5	74%	+1
Women by Age:													
18-24	6	3	22	43	26	9	21	-2	-2	+3	0.0	35%	-1
25-34	9	7	21	43	28	8	22	-4	-6	+9	1.0	48%	+2
35-54	18	18	27	40	25	8	13	-4	-3	+5	-0.5	61%	+1
55+	19	23	41	34	20	5	-7	+1	-4	+2	2.5	73%	+6
Men by Class:													
AB	12	14	37	27	28	8	-10	-1	-4	+3	1.5	70%	+2
C1	14	15	39	29	22	10	-10	+3	-9	+8	6.0	63%	+1
C2	11	10	32	39	18	11	7	+4	-10	+5	7.0	57%	+1
DE	11	9	24	47	17	12	23	+1	-8	+3	4.5	55%	-1
Women by Class:													
AB	12	14	36	29	29	6	-7	-5	+1	+3	-3.0	71%	+3
C1	15	15	34	35	23	8	1	-3	-2	+3	-0.5	61%	+2
C2	10	10	34	40	20	6	6	+4	-8	+3	6.0	58%	+2
DE	15	13	25	49	18	8	24	0	-7	+5	3.5	54%	+4

Source: MORI Final Election Aggregate Analysis
Base: 17,959 GB residents aged 18+, 5 April-5 May 2005

List of Tables and Illustrations

Tables

Figures

353

Glossary

1922 Committee - Committee of Conservative backbenchers currently chaired by Sir Michael Spicer, which determines the timing and organisation of Conservative leadership contests and votes of confidence in current leaders

Agenda-setting – A term used in journalism and public relations to denote how particular issues are disseminated in the news media. The key debate is whether news organisations decide their own news agendas and to what extent they are influenced by special interest groups, including political parties

Al Qaeda – Literally meaning 'the base', this shadowy terrorist franchise – headed by Osama Bin Laden – is thought to be the mastermind behind the 9/11 attacks in America and a host of other attacks on western targets around the world since the late 1980s

Anorak – An item of clothing particularly used in harsh weather, or more colloquially a pejorative term for someone who's a bit weird and tends to have strange habits, like enjoying politics (i.e. political *anorak*)

Approval ratings – A measure of how much the public approves or disapproves of a particular politician, party or government

BBC – British Broadcasting Corporation

Black Wednesday – The day Britain was ejected from the Exchange Rate Mechanism – see below – on 16 September 1992 whilst John Major was Conservative Prime Minister

BMA – British Medical Association

BME – Black and Minority Ethnic citizens

BNP – British National Party - A far-right political party with ultranationalist pretensions

Boundary Commission – A statutory body responsible for the periodic review of constituency boundaries, with a view to ensuring that electors are equally represented around the country

354

BSE - Bovine Spongiform Encephalopathy (or "Mad Cow Disease") – A fatal disease contracted by cows as a result of them being fed contaminated bonemeal, and which eventually transferred to humans, causing the fatal Creutzfeldt-Jakob Disease (CJD). In Britain, all export of beef was banned by the EU from March 1996-August 1999 as a result of cows contracting BSE, costing the taxpayer billions of pounds in compensation payments to British farmers

CAPI – Computer Aided Personal Interviewing - A method of data collection using a hand-held personal computer designed to reduce the time required for data input and analysis

CATI – Computer Aided Telephone Interviewing - A method of data collection using a computerised telephone system, often using random digit dialling, designed to reduce the time required for data input and analysis

Class – System of classification of citizens based on their socio-economic grouping which is determined by the job position of the highest wage earner in the household providing their rank or order in society and typically broken down into working class, middle class and upper class. For a discussion of "class" as measured in opinion polls ("social grade"), see pp 228-233

Common Market – The precursor European organisation to the European Union, where member state collaboration was based principally on economic co-operation

Confidence – A measure of the degree of statistical reliability associated with an estimate of margin of error. For a sample of 1,000, typically plus or minus three per cent.

Constituencies – Geographic regions each having one representative in the House of Commons, typically comprising between 60,000-70,000 electors, though sometimes much less in some cases, e.g. in rural regions such as the Highlands of Scotland, Scottish islands, and occasionally significantly more, notably the Isle of Wight.

Delivery Index – A MORI research product that measures expectations of government policies towards the state of Britain's economy and Britain's public services

Elastoplast - The trade name for small medical dressings typically used to cover cuts and grazes to prevent infection

Electoral Volatility - The propensity for electors to vote for different parties at successive elections. There are two measures of electoral volatility. Net volatility which is the net change in voting support between two elections and overall volatility which refers to the total number of vote switchers between consecutive elections

Electorate – Those citizens who are eligible to vote in any given election, which in British general elections excludes prisoners, the insane, children (under 18 on the date of the election) and foreign (except Irish and Commonwealth) citizens, as well as those otherwise eligible whose name is not included on the electoral register.

EP – European Parliament

ERM - Exchange Rate Mechanism – A financial system set up by the European Community in 1979 to reduce exchange rate variability and secure monetary stability in preparation for the introduction of a single currency, the Euro

ESRC – Economic and Social Research Council – A British research council dedicated to the financial support of the development of social scientific research and development, principally through universities and accredited research institutions

Eurobarometer - A periodic survey commissioned by the European Commission to determine attitudes of citizens in EU member states towards the EU and other subjects

Excellence Model – A MORI research product, based on research among an organisation's stakeholders, which measures how effectively each relationship is contributing to the organisation's success. It also identifies those issues which need to be addressed to move the relationship forward

Exit Poll – A prediction survey in Britain, designed to project the number of seats in the House of Commons, as well as the share of the vote, obtained by the main parties in a General Election. The 2005 exit poll was based on exit interviews with more than 20,000 voters at 120 polling stations across the country conducted by MORI and NOP jointly for both ITV and BBC. (See pp 36-36.)

First-past-the-post – The electoral system in operation in Britain where the country is split into a set number of constituencies, currently 646, each comprising typically around 60,000-70,000 electors. In such a system, the political party which gains a majority of constituencies, rather than a majority of aggregated voters within those constituencies, wins the election and forms government

Gallup – A pioneering polling company, set up by George Gallup in the US, and the first to set up a polling operation in Britain in the late Thirties. No longer in the opinion polling business in Britain.

Gender Gap – As used here, the difference in party support between men and women.

Green Book – Extensive reports written after every general election between 1974 and 1992 by MORI analysing the published polls during the election period. See **Red Book**

Grey Power – The idea that the roughly a third of the adult population 55 years and over should be important targets for the political strategist because there are about twice as many of them, and they are twice as likely to vote, as their 18-34 year old counterparts, also a third of the adult populations, making their vote 'worth' four times as much

Hutton Report – The report produced by Lord Hutton based on the government enquiry into the death of Dr David Kelly, the government weapons inspector

ICM – A public opinion poll and market research company in the UK, mainly polling for the *Guardian* Newspaper.

IDS – Iain Duncan Smith, the short-serving Tory leader

Issue Salience – The level of importance of an issue

ITN – Independent Television News

Keystone Kops – A series of silent American film comedies about incompetent policemen

LBC – London Broadcasting – A radio station which opened on the 8th of October 1973 at 6am from studios in Gough Square, just off Fleet

Street, and was the first licenced commercial radio station on the UK mainland. Worcester was its first political analyst, beginning in November 1973.

Majority – Strictly, one over half. In this context, typically refers to the difference between the number of seats the government party has, less the seats of all the other parties in the House of Commons (overall majority). The notion of majority is important because it determines how easily it will be for a government to pass legislation in the face of opposition from other parties. It also refers to the number of excess votes a party achieves in relation to its principle opposition party within a constituency expressed in units of electors, or as a percentage of the electorate

Marginal Seats – Any seat, or constituency, where the first placed party has a majority over the second placed party, as a proportion of the votes cast within the constituency at the last election, of technically 10% and below, although the media often refer to any key seats being targeted by the opposition parties as marginal

Floating Voters – A voter with either no specific allegiance to a political party or whose allegiance changes between elections and whose unpredictable decisions can determine the outcome of those elections

MEP – Member of the European Parliament

Modus Vivendi – Means literally mode of living

MORI – Market & Opinion Research International – A UK market research company, founded by Sir Robert Worcester in 1969, now the 19th largest market research company in the world, majority owned by its employees.

MP – Member of Parliament

MRSA – An abbreviation for methicillin-resistant staphylococcus aureus, a bacterium, termed by the media as a hospital 'superbug', sometimes lethal particularly in those with compromised immune systems or foreign body instrumentation, caused by improper hygiene maintenance in hospitals

NHS – National Health Service – Britain's oft-derided, free-at-the-point-of-use, health service

NOP – National Opinion Polls – A UK market research organisation founded in the mid-fifties, recently acquired by the German market research company GfK.

OAPs – Old age pensioners typically defined as over 65 years old for men, and 60 years old for women, in Britain, based on the ages at which these groups of citizens receive their state pension

Omnibus surveys – A regularly scheduled survey typically comprising sets of questions on different topics or items, and purchased by numerous clients at any one time

Operation Black Vote – A campaign designed to increase turnout amongst African and Afro-Caribbean voters

Orange Book – Subtitled 'reclaiming liberalism', this is a book written by prominent Liberal politicians outlining free market solutions to societal issues, and published in time for the 2004 Liberal Democrat party conference

PEBs – Party election broadcasts – Short political programmes typically around 2 ½ to 5 minutes, given free to each main political party in proportion to the popular vote they achieved at the previous election by the network television channels to disseminate their political messages

Perceptual Map – A means of spatially representing how voters or consumers perceive a particular product, or service, or in political terms, a political party or candidate, vis-à-vis its competitors, based on common attributes shared by all the competing products, services or political entities

PFI – Private Finance Initiative – A government programme for injecting private sector funding into public investment projects

Political Triangle – A Worcester political construct which explains British voting behaviour in terms of the proportions of voters who vote for a party based on axes of party image, leader image and policies at each election, with the three axes expressed as a triangle, and when underpinned by values, as a tetrahedron

Pollsters – Public opinion poll companies and practitioners, involved in the systematic collection of data on public opinions, attitudes and values, typically for the news media, political parties, and business

Porkies – Cockney rhyming slang, abbreviated from pork pies, meaning lies

Potemkin Village – A false or hollow construct, abstract or real, particularly used in the political context after a Russian Minister of the same surname who is, some say falsely, said to have constructed false villages in the Crimea to impress Empress Catherine II of his conquests

Private Eye – A satirical fortnightly political magazine, in the past 'so close to the bone' that its editor has frequently wound up in court in libel actions

Probability sample – A sampling method where everyone eligible has an equal opportunity of selection, also, in which the probability of a respondent's, or other sample unit's, inclusion is known beforehand and is greater than zero

Public Opinion – The aggregated opinions of the general public, typically towards issues of political or societal importance, affected by marketing communications, propaganda, and the news media, and measured systematically using survey methods, see Views

PwC – PricewaterhouseCoopers - The global accountancy and audit firm

Quota sample – A alternative to probability sampling, which includes a minimum number of respondents from specified sub-groups (strata) in the population, designed to ensure the sample is representative of the population on key parameters (e.g. age, sex, working status)

Red Book – The extensive analysis of Labour Party private polling carried out by MORI published after every election between 1974 and 1987; all lodged at ESRC Data Archives.

Referendum (or **plebiscite**) – This is a direct vote in which the whole electorate of a country is asked either to accept or to reject a specifically worded proposal, typically of national importance or which has implications for national sovereignty

Respect – A political party set up by dissident, breakaway, Labour MP, George Galloway

Social grade – see **class**

Spin – A pejorative term used to denote the way in which political parties, and businesses, manage their press relations to ensure that they present themselves on a particular issue in the best way possible and sometimes with limited allusion to the reality

Tactical Voting – This occurs when electors vote for a party most likely to win in a particular election, even if it is not their most preferred option, in order to keep another less favoured party from winning

TBWA – The advertising agency which worked for Labour in 2005

Topline results – Comprises a technical statement on how a survey was conducted and when, together with frequency distributions for key questions asked in a particular survey, effectively constituting a summary for market researchers of a particular quantitative research project

Turnout – The proportion of the electorate, often expressed as a percentage, who vote in any given election

UKIP – United Kingdom Independence Party

UN – United Nations – The multi-national inter-governmental body dedicated to the development of world peace and co-operation

Veracity Index – A MORI research construct which determines the extent to which the public trust people in different occupational groupings

View – The *opinion*, *attitude* or *value* measurement of people's beliefs.

Voter segmentation – The division of target markets, or groups of consumers/voters, into smaller more manageable groups based on specific customer/voter characteristics or voting/consumer behaviour patterns to more effectively target resources at them in order to secure their business/vote

Voter Vault - Software bought from the American Republican Party by the British Conservative Party to help them target their direct marketing campaigns more effectively

Weighting – See p 331

WMD – Weapons of Mass Destruction – Such weapons can be either chemical, nuclear or biological

YouGov – An internet-based public opinion polling organisation

Zero-sum game – This construct describes a situation in which a participant's gain is matched exactly by the losses of another participant(s). It derives from economics and specifically the sub-branch, game theory

Index